POPULATION CONTROL

Population Control

Theorizing Institutional Violence

EDITED BY
JEN RINALDI AND KATE ROSSITER

McGill-Queen's University Press
Montreal & Kingston • London • Chicago

ISBN 978-0-2280-1907-7 (cloth)
ISBN 978-0-2280-1930-5 (paper)
ISBN 978-0-2280-1981-7 (ePDF)
ISBN 978-0-2280-1982-4 (ePUB)

Legal deposit fourth quarter 2023
Bibliothèque nationale du Québec

Printed in Canada on acid-free paper that is 100% ancient forest free (100% post-consumer recycled), processed chlorine free

This book has been published with the help of a grant from the Canadian Federation for the Humanities and Social Sciences, through the Awards to Scholarly Publications Program, using funds provided by the Social Sciences and Humanities Research Council of Canada.

Financé par le gouvernement du Canada | Funded by the Government of Canada | Canada | Conseil des arts du Canada | Canada Council for the Arts

We acknowledge the support of the Canada Council for the Arts.

Nous remercions le Conseil des arts du Canada de son soutien.

McGill-Queen's University Press in Montreal is on land which long served as a site of meeting and exchange amongst Indigenous Peoples, including the Haudenosaunee and Anishinabeg nations. In Kingston it is situated on the territory of the Haudenosaunee and Anishinaabek. We acknowledge and thank the diverse Indigenous Peoples whose footsteps have marked these territories on which peoples of the world now gather.

Library and Archives Canada Cataloguing in Publication

Title: Population control : theorizing institutional violence / edited by Jen Rinaldi and Kate Rossiter.

Other titles: Population control (Montréal, Québec)

Names: Rinaldi, Jen, 1983- editor. | Rossiter, Kate, editor.

Description: Includes bibliographical references and index.

Identifiers: Canadiana (print) 2023045559X | Canadiana (ebook) 2023045562X | ISBN 9780228019305 (paper) | ISBN 9780228019077 (cloth) | ISBN 9780228019817 (ePDF) | ISBN 9780228019824 (ePUB)

Subjects: LCSH: People with disabilities—Violence against—Canada. | LCSH: People with disabilities—Abuse of—Canada. | LCSH: People with disabilities—Institutional care—Canada. | LCSH: Inmates of institutions—Violence against—Canada. | LCSH: Inmates of institutions—Abuse of—Canada. | LCSH: Inmates of institutions—Institutional care—Canada.

Classification: LCC HV1568 .P67 2023 | DDC 362.4/04850971—dc23

This book was typeset by Marquis Interscript in 10.5/13 Sabon.

Contents

Introduction 3
Jen Rinaldi and Kate Rossiter

SECTION ONE ROOTS OF TOTAL INSTITUTIONAL VIOLENCE

1 Making Sense of Institutional Violence through Social Theory: An Autoethnography of Adolescent Trauma and Survival 27
Claudia Malacrida

2 "Spectacles of Humiliation": Symbolic Violence and the Regulation of Good Shepherd Inmates 47
Rie Croll

3 Manufacturing Structural Vulnerability and Institutional Violence: The Language of Childhood and Disability 68
Katharine Viscardis

4 The Societal Underpinnings of Institutionalizing Othered Bodies: A Typology of Institutional Violence at the Huronia Regional Centre and the Mohawk Institute 92
Annalise Clarkson

SECTION TWO LOATHING IN THE TRANSINSTITUTIONAL ERA

5 Invisible Institutions: Institutionalization of People Labelled with Intellectual/Developmental Disabilities 115
Megan Q. Linton

6 The Violence of Work: Sheltered Workshops in Ontario, Canada 137
Siobhán Saravanamuttu

7 Institutionalizing Unfree Labour in Ontario's Seasonal Agricultural Worker Program Farmsteads 159
Shanti Fernando and Jen Rinaldi

8 Danger, Safety, and the Rhetoric of Urban Crisis: Institutional Logics and Windsor's Downtown Core 179
Jijian Voronka, Adrian Guta, Tina (Jordan) Nguyen, Grace Shaw, and Aman Ahluwalia Cameron

SECTION THREE CARE QUA VIOLENCE

9 Gendered and Disability Violence, Uninterrupted: Law's Formulation of and Complicity in Violence against Women Labelled with Intellectual Disability in Community-Based Institutional Settings 201
Tess Sheldon

10 The List as Deterrent for "Others" 238
Alex Tigchelaar

11 We Want You to Listen: The Shelter Video Project Collective on Colonial/Capitalist Violence 268
The Shelter Video Project Collective: Kim Jackson, Shirley Berry, Sandie Guignard, Asil Lavoie, Lisa LaBlanc, Minutet Nima, Opal Sparks, Marlene Bluebird Stickings

12 Kaleidoscope: Hope in Action beyond Institution 293
Mo Korchinski, Lynn Fels, and Ruth Elwood Martin

Index 319

Our collection is possible thanks to the support of a Social Science and Humanities Research Council Connection Grant. This funding enabled the editors and authors to meet regularly to work out the themes that cut across chapters, and to engage in collective theorizing. We the editors are also grateful to authors for their thoughtful contributions, and to our publisher for supporting this project.

We have spent the last ten years working alongside survivors of the Huronia Regional Centre – learning from them and taking to heart their calls to action. This collection is dedicated to these remarkable people, and to populations that have had to endure institutional violence.

Introduction

JEN RINALDI AND KATE ROSSITER

The stories are burned into our memories: of name-calling and fight clubs and cinder blocks and forced feedings and sedative injections. This collection's editors, Jen Rinaldi and Kate Rossiter, have worked with institutional survivors since 2013 to document histories of the Huronia Regional Centre – Canada's largest, oldest, and longest-standing facility to house children and youth with intellectual disability diagnoses. Violence was an inescapable through-line across the stories that survivors told us. The instances that survivors described were brutal, but also quotidian: deeply and inextricably embedded in Huronia's culture, as ordinary as eating a meal or dressing for the day. In another project we theorized the institutional conditions that made possible and normalized Huronia's violence (Rossiter and Rinaldi 2019). But the history we sought to make sense of felt larger than Huronia itself.

Patterns of violence manifest in other sites of confinement in the Canadian context, including residential schools (Monchalin 2014; TRC 2015), internment camps (Oikawa 2012), correctional facilities (Martin et al. 2014), psychiatric facilities (Daley, Costa, and Beresford 2019; Dyck and Deighton 2017; Reaume 2000), hospital schools (Burghardt 2018; Malacrida 2015), laundries for "fallen women" (Andrews 2018; Croll 2019), and emergency shelters (Ranasinghe 2017), among myriad other examples. Scholarly analysis of these social spaces reports physical, emotional, and sexual abuse, as well as active and passive forms of neglect and maltreatment, across different kinds of facilities, times in history, regional locations, government and staff turnovers, and types of population.

While varied forms of institutional life bear striking resemblances – for example, the use of isolation, physical restraint, compromised privacy, and humiliation to control institutionalized populations – institutional violence has yet to be studied as a unique and predictable social phenomenon reliant on an underlying set of assumptions regarding the need to at once care for, and constrain, sub-populations. Such an approach is needed because forms of violence are neither aberrations nor the by-product of a few bad staff members or a few poorly run facilities. Rather, violence is endemic to the logics of institutionalization, whether this happens within classic institutional spaces or in the kinds of spaces and practices common to the contemporary landscape of care and containment.

Understanding the patterns and nuances of institutional violence as a social problem and affective economy is not only important for advancing scholarly knowledge; it is also critical to supporting those who have endured institutional life, and can provide evidentiary grounds to argue against present and future institutional projects. Understanding the organizational and environmental dynamics that have caused violence is imperative to preventing violence from reoccurring. Comprehensive historical and contemporary analysis of the structural conditions that cut across forms of institutional violence can therefore inform opposition to institutionalization as a social response to vulnerability. This kind of scholarship is especially urgent as the totalizing institutional model breaks down but the logic of institutionalization remains – reproducing itself in more insidious forms that still have the power to generate violence.

THE COLLECTION'S PURPOSE

The authors in this collection contend with the affective impulses that drive institutional violence: care and loathing. These impulses have historically operated as deeply entwined reactions to unruly populations. They drive the structural framing of populations as abject or misfit, and motivate the necessity of state-sanctioned forms of care provision. State and social actors have developed versions of total institutionalization in order to solve the putative social problems that unruly populations are presumed to pose. Violence frequently runs rampant within institutional spaces, for violence functions as the unbridled enactment of care and loathing. However, what renders this collection distinct is that the authors argue that institutional violence is not dependent on brick-and-mortar spaces, but rather emerges from the twinned impulses of *care* and *loathing*. As such, institutional violence is related less to spatial relations and more to the circulation of specific affective economies related to care, vulnerability, and social devaluation. Logics of institutional violence, then, are the structural and organizational by-products of larger affective forces.

Care is a key organizing principle in total institutional orders, their ostensible driving force. A rubric of care sanitizes institutional violence, makes this violence possible and palatable, because care opens up access to institutionalized bodies. Being separated off from the wider community positions institutional residents in relationships of structural dependency and strips them of the ability to manage their own well-being. The caregivers in these relations have the authority to come into contact with, and hold control over, their charges. But care in and of itself does not motivate the violence of institutional encounters. Simmering beneath the surface of reactions to vulnerable populations is aversion. This loathing signals a devaluation of the institutionalized, and is also often the *raison d'être* for their incarceration or surveillance in the first place. Loathing therefore indicates both larger social discourses that devalue particular groups and populations (often those that are vulnerable or that require social support beyond what is deemed normal or acceptable) and the dehumanizing practices to which devalued populations are continually exposed.

This edited collection works to unpack the Gordian knot of care and loathing that we argue lies at the crux of institutional violence. The movement toward deinstitutionalization was supposed to sever this knot through practices of normalization and community integration. However, this affective entanglement, and the violence it begets, remains inextricable. While large-scale total institutions are less prevalent, the *logic* of institutional violence – the structured, organized provision of care to loathed populations – remains intact. In this collection, contributors present forms of violence that exemplify this dynamic. First, in the section *Roots of Total Institutional Violence*, they look at historical portraits of institutionalization where this Gordian knot was deeply entwined. Then, chapters in a section titled *Loathing in the Trans-institutional Era* explore expressions of loathing that leave certain populations vulnerable to state intervention under the guise of care. The concluding section, *Care Qua Violence*, contains chapters that consider moments of social care that are always undermined by the presence of a social loathing that is central to the mechanics of managing vulnerable populations.

This edited collection is intended primarily for scholars. Scholarly analysis of the history and importance of institutional violence is relevant to social scientists, and chapters that focus on structural conditions are particularly relevant to the disciplines of sociology, history, anthropology, and public health; chapters that engage with legal and political frameworks are relevant to health care policy and administration and legal studies; and the collection's commitment to theorizing forms of violence that target minority groups is of value in youth and children's studies, disability studies, women's and gender studies, and critical race studies. The driving argument should be of interest to scholars whose work engages with issues of disability, health law and policy, violence, incarceration, organizational behaviour, and critical theory. Further, we intend this collection to provide health care and social service providers and policy makers with a clear argument against institutionalization and custodial models still prevalent across the world, on the grounds that violence is an inextricable condition of institutionalization.

Our specific focus on historical and contemporary Canadian examples ensures the edited collection constitutes a rigorous contribution to Canadian scholarship. The majority of the case studies in this collection are based in Ontario. The over-representation of Ontario reflects a few dynamics: first, Ontario is Canada's most populous province and thus simply offers more opportunities to study techniques of population management. Second, Ontario has historically acted as a model for institutional care across Canada. Huronia, for example, provided a model for how to design and run similar institutions in the Canadian context, and acted as a bridge between institutions in other countries to Canadian institutions. These two dynamics mean that Ontario is a locus for scholarship on institutionalization, and this is reflected in the collection's contents. However, institutionalization has shaped the social fabric across Canada and thus this collection also includes entries and authors from the east and west coasts as well as the prairies.

Despite our focus on the Canadian context, a mixed-methods approach and cross-disciplinary theory of violence broadens the work's appeal to international scholars. Indeed, the range of examples in the text shows that organizational logics cut across regions regardless of geography; and Canada is not the only country in the world to construct prisons, institutions, and detention centres.

DEFINING OUR TERMS

The Total Institutional Model

As we have described elsewhere (Rinaldi 2021), the term institution found in sociological scholarship can broadly refer to social organizations. Examples include systems of law and government, religion, schools, and families. These types of institutions are objects of sociological study for their internal rules of functioning, the social roles and meanings they ascribe to individual actors, and the ways they shape human behaviour. A *total* institution is a kind of institution that is much more closed off from wider social spaces. Canadian sociologist Erving Goffman is credited with popularizing the term *total institution*, which he adapted from his professor Everett C. Hughes (Becker 2003; Vienne 2010). Hughes was interested in studying concentration camps as an emblematic example of nucleated institutions, or what he called "totally organized communities" (Vienne 2010, 10). Goffman (1961) went on to study total institutions in the context of psychiatric asylums. He defined the total institution as "a place of residence and work where a large number of like-situated individuals, cut off from the wider society for an appreciable length of time, together lead an enclosed, formally administered round of life" (11). He identified the "handling of many human needs by the bureaucratic organization of whole blocks of people" (6) as the total institution's defining fact. Those needs could include sleep, food, health, hygiene, education, and play.

There are many iterations of total institutions, including long-term care homes and orphanages, asylums and quarantine centres, prisons and detention centres. For Goffman (1961), total institutions share four features in common. First, "all aspects of life are conducted in the same place" (6) and under a centralized singular authority. Second, people who share similar defining characteristics carry out every part of their day altogether. Third, "all phases of the day's activities are tightly scheduled," and that schedule is "imposed from above" (6). Fourth and finally, the institution has an official mission that the imposed activities are meant to fulfil: for instance, rehabilitation, work, cure, or care.

Goffman's concept of the total institution has been widely influential in sociological theory, but it has also been hotly contested especially by theorists who developed sophisticated analysis of social space.

Dominique Moran (2013, 2014) critiques the idea of the total institution for having clearly delineated boundaries that separate institutional living from wider societies. She prefers readings of those boundary lines as porous (Baer and Ravnesberg 2008), like a permeable membrane (Farrington 1992). The collection of "structures, mechanisms and policies" that establish this membrane "maintain, at most, a selective and imperfect degree of separation between what exists inside of and what lies beyond prison walls" (Moran 2013, 340). Anna K. Schliehe (2016) argues that scholars should read Goffman more generously given he himself wrote about the dynamic relationship between total institutions and wider society. It would be reductive, then, to take the term *total* too literally, for these types of institutions are not entirely closed systems, not walled off from larger societies but instead integral components of wider social ordering work. What is important is that these types of institutions are closed enough to espouse their own internal rules and systems of meaning, and closed enough to ensure that those subjected to the rules are denied recourse or escape (Goffman 1961, 1963). The total institution may best be defined not by its surrounding walls, but by its tightly organized relations that serve wider social, economic, and political purposes.

Goffman (1961) wrote about total institutions so he could call attention to their deplorable conditions. A key feature to the total institution is the "staff-inmate split" (9): a rigid binary arrangement between the many residents, and the fewer staff members tasked with supervision. According to the terms of this arrangement, staff only spend their workday in the institution, and are otherwise integrated in the outside world. The boundary lines are so firm that social mobility between the two groupings is restrictive, social distance between them is wide, and communication reflects a paternalistic power imbalance. Staff are vested with power, and use that power to impose social control over their charges. They do so through techniques of defacement: stripping an institutionalized subject "of his usual appearance and of the equipment and services by which he maintains it" (20), such as clothes and toiletries. The institutional arrangement also empowers staff to enact techniques of disfigurement, or "mortification of the [resident's] self by way of the body" (21). Examples include beatings and shock therapy. In a closed social system, defacement and disfigurement come to be normalized, such that they reflect "the legitimated objectives of the institution" (85). In her contribution to this collection, Claudia Malacrida identifies how these techniques are cemented in the service of the institution's overarching purpose: "as Goffman explains, a key purpose of total institutions is to break down the previous identity of the inmate to permit the rebuilding of a new person" (42).

Goffman's analysis catalyzed a movement that challenged the legitimacy of institutional authority across twentieth-century North American and Western European countries (Crossley 2006; Gambino 2013). In the years since Goffman wrote, social arrangements have shifted – but rather than dismantlement, these arrangements diffused in a process that has been called transinstitutionalization. An "unwieldy and contested term" (1), Tobin LeBlanc Haley and Chelsea Temple Jones (2020) characterize transinstitutionalization as "the numerous ways in which institutionalization and institutionalizing conditions are sustained ... hidden in plain sight" (1), often in the guise of multiple connected social services that espouse to provide support, but which often reiterate older forms of violence. Along these same lines, Siobhán Saravanamuttu writes for this collection: "although deinstitutionalization meant closing the door on the physical total institution, much of its disciplinary and surveillance tactics became dispersed or transferred to spaces occupied by disabled people in the community" (161). This arrangement extends beyond the management of disability and includes the organization of other populations deemed unruly and in need of care.

Following deinstitutionalization movements of the 1960s, the wholesale state-based warehousing of particular populations has abated, and in its place has emerged a much more fractured landscape of practices for the management of populations deemed vulnerable or threatening to the larger social order. Liat Ben-Moshe (2020) refers to this landscape as a "carceral matrix": a network of carceral locales, or "enclosures, especially prisons, jails, psychiatric hospitals, and residential institutions [as well as] *particular logics and discourses*" (1–2, emphasis ours). Her term draws from Michel Foucault's (1977) concept of the carceral archipelago. Foucault first invoked this image – the scattered cluster of islands that connect beneath the water's surface – to refer to a transmission of disciplinary mechanisms across a social space. The total institution is not wholly closed off but is instead compact and concentrated; and with the closing of large-scale institutions, their techniques unspool, reaching into community space. This collection rests on this very premise that, while the process and structure of institutionalization has shifted, the logics and driving forces of institutionalization persist.

Violence and Its Institutional Form

This edited collection traces the lines of institutional logics because institutionalization in all its forms generates violence. Particularly striking political theories of violence developed as a way of framing the Holocaust, a historical event that tied genocidal violence to the spatial conditions of the concentration camp (Agamben 2005; Felman and Laub 1992; Pitzer 2017). Walter Benjamin, a Jewish intellectual who experienced imprisonment and exile under Nazi occupation and died by suicide when trying unsuccessfully to escape, penned a foundational critique of violence (Derrida 1990; Felman 2002). For Benjamin (2019), violence of the human world functions as either 1) a tool of governance, a means for making or preserving law; or 2) the redemptive, revolutionary acts that destroy law to create a better world. Hannah Arendt (1970), herself a Jewish scholar subjected to imprisonment and exile during the Nazi era (Felman 2002), developed this analysis, careful to frame violence and power as distinct, but connected. She described violence as one way of directing the distribution and transference of power. People who already have easy access to power may use violence to reinforce their relationships; while people without power may use violence to claim it, to disrupt the terms of their political relations. These theories posit that violence is relationally and politically grounded, and could be coercive or liberatory depending on its direction.

This political relationship between the sovereign and citizen opens up key implications: first, relationships can be complex, and can extend beyond the interpersonal; and second, power has a role to play. Sociologist Johan Galtung (1969), famous for founding peace and conflict studies, offered a more expansive reading of the relationships that manifest violence. He defined violence as "that which increases the distance between the potential and the actual" (168). For example, violence does not factor into unavoidable cancer diagnoses, but violence becomes an influential element in cancer diagnosis when the patient is a citizen of Ontario's Chemical Valley or Alberta's Tar Sands. In these instances, something unnatural got in the way of a citizenry's potential to live their lives cancer free, and put that reality out of reach. The actors responsible for this violence are not easy to land on: political actors at various levels of government across several election cycles; corporate actors who profit from the industry; on-site management who do not enact proper safety protocols. Galtung introduced a new type of violence to encompass these complexities: violence can be structural when it lacks an explicitly personal subject-object relationship. Violence is structural, then, when it is attributable to practices and policies that shape daily living. Put another way: "structural formulations of violence embed interpersonal violence in unjust social, political, and economic systems of inequality and associated social relations (e.g., sexist, racist, classist, and ableist) that permeate all social institutions" (Daley, Costa, and Beresford 2019, 12). This framing of violence accounts for the press of settler colonialism, white supremacy, eugenics, and cis-heteropatriarchy, which can be incredibly violent systems in ways that extend beyond the interpersonal sphere.

Institutionalization as structural violence has been an object of study particularly in disability studies scholarship – a field that incorporates both sociology and political theory. Liat Ben-Moshe, Chris Chapman, and Allison C. Carey's *Disability Incarcerated: Imprisonment and Disability in the United States and Canada* (2014) explores multiple sites of incarceration disabled people experience, including prisons, psychiatric facilities, total care institutions, and group homes. Andrea Daley, Lucy Costa, and Peter Beresford's *Madness, Violence, and Power: A Critical Collection* (2019) conceptualizes relations of power and inequality, to show how they produce violence against disabled persons. Chapters focus on Canadian examples of facilities that hold persons with intellectual and psychiatric disabilities, and show the ways violence against vulnerable populations spills out into community space, operates slowly, and is magnified in neoliberal contexts. Claire Spivakovsky, Linda Steele, and Penelope Weller's transnational text *The Legacies of Institutionalisation: Disability, Law and Policy in the "Deinstitutionalised" Community* (2020) examines law's role in processes of institutionalization, and how law is implicated in institutional histories. The contributors grapple with institutions that housed disabled populations at the nexus of other interlocking oppressions, including colonialism, sexism, and racism.

Unruliness

In the institutional setting, assertions of individual autonomy and personhood are deeply at odds with the institutional imperative, and a site upon which both structural and interpersonal violence occurs. Autonomy qua acts of resistance tend to be read as acts of violence that call for intervention or management – although we actively resist categorizing acts of resistance alongside other types of oppressive or punitive violence that permeate the institutional sphere. This narrow cataloguing does work to mark and sustain institutionalized populations as *unruly* – outside the bounds of control, in need for intervention. While unruliness might take a variety of forms – including non-compliance with treatment plans, refusal to self-monitor at the behest of a state surveillance apparatus, acts of anger or defiance against forms of authority – these acts share common ground. That is, unruliness as a category is comprised of assertions of subjective will and desire. This is particularly true when such assertions contravene the will of the state or state-sanctioned organizations tasked with keeping a population contained and managed and "safe."

For example, in our own research on Huronia, we have asked survivors to reflect on how official files kept on them when they were residents differed from their own experience of captivity. Uniformly, survivors detailed the ways in which official files elided their attempts to resist totalizing institutional demands and assessments, while relieving the institution itself from the responsibility of genuine care. For example, episodes of violent punishment are rarely clearly articulated in resident files; survivors instead are constructed as behaviourally challenging and in need of intervention by ward staff, and punishments are noted by medical staff without detailing the cause of the injury. Survivors, however, remember that these punishments occurred for speaking out against cruelty, defending other residents, and defending their own sense of choice or dignity, even in ways that caused harm to self and others.

These are explosive expressions of a liberatory impulse, moving in one direction in the context of power-laden relations. Institutional recognition of these interpersonal moments as the only kind of violence misses the other side of the ledger, and the wider context altogether, effectively overlooking the structural workings of violence (Steele and Dowse 2016). The actions of the unruly, then, require a reframing as resistance in relation. Resistance is an affective response, "in the form of grief, anger, fear or endurance to an everyday negotiation with the power relations [a person or population is] is embedded in" (Karu 2021, 520). The surfacing of acts of resistance in the institutional context signal that wider structural forces are at work – that the institutionalized are reacting to the injustices of institutionalization (Alldred and Fox 2017; Zembylas 2021). The authors in this collection situate unruliness in order to unpack the broader affective relation of the institutional encounter.

Twinned Techniques of Institutional Violence: Care and Loathing

When we frame resistance as an affective response, we are here referring to affect as "visceral forces beneath, alongside, or generally other than conscious knowing … that can serve to drive us toward movement, toward thought and extension, that can likewise suspend us" (Seigworth and Gregg 2010, 1). Affect is the force that circulates and transmits between subjectivities – binding them together, mobilizing them to action, orienting them in relation to one another. Sara Ahmed (2001, 2004) describes this phenomenon as an affective economy, a marketplace where affect moves like currency that can be distributed and invested. The affective economy can operate and even flourish in a closed system like the total institutional setting, but can just as well expand across wider networks like the carceral archipelago that trans institutionalization gives way to.

In this economy, the circulation of affect can be concentrated around particular meanings. To this end Ahmed (2010) describes affect as ontologically sticky, which she explains accordingly: "Affect is what sticks, or what sustains or preserves the connection between ideas, values, and objects" (29). This quality of stickiness means that there are populations that bear the burden of their associations. She uses hatred as an example of this kind of affective work. Hatred is a constellation of negative orientations that firms up subject categories, setting "clear boundaries which distinguish *us* from *them*" (Zembylas 2007, 179). Rendering the *them* distinct from the *us*, ugly ideas stick and cling to the object of hatred, positioning populations in a relation of "against-ness." Worse still, hatred carries a particularly egregious affective force given it mobilizes the hater in the direction of annihilating or exterminating the hated (Ahmed 2017; Opotow and McClelland 2007). In this collection we posit that a particular subset of negative orientations – a specific kind of hatred – ripples through the institutional relation. We're not addressing every kind of hatred, but rather feelings more like *loathing*, which can encompass revulsion and disgust, as well as resentment and disdain.

Loathing motivates antagonistic violence against the institutionalized. In the transinstitutional era, populations that have previously been targets for total institutionalization continue to face state-based and collective loathing. In their contribution to this collection, for example, Jijian Voronka and colleagues describe the metanarratives that stick to homeless populations: "marginalized bodies become what is hindering capitalism rather than the debilitation that results from it" (213). Business owners in Windsor's downtown core are motivated by these associations to call for security measures to clean up public space. In effect they mobilize police violence against the people they loathe.

But loathing is not the only affective force driving institutional violence. It would be impossible to understand institutional violence without also referencing care. Care is a different kind of binding agent, an entirely different set of orientations in the affective economy, given it orients toward "with-ness" rather than "against-ness." Found in feminist theorizing, care can carry an affirmative affective charge, connecting people in affectionate relationships. The labour that care motivates can encompass decisions and practices that value the cared-for. Care, then, can operate as an ethically sound reaction to populations that experience vulnerabilities – which can be inevitable, tied to embodiment, or due to historical, structural disadvantage.

However, "oppressive legacies and coercive potentials" (Kelly 2011, 562) are folded into the DNA of care. Independent Living movements that catalyzed deinstitutionalization rooted their activisms in critiques of care provisioning (Hughes et al. 2005; Watson et al. 2004). Specifically, they called out the institutional practices of confinement, constraint, and sanitation as violence under the guise of care. An affective reading of care would hold it is not only a guise, not a smokescreen, but is actually the connective tissue between staff and resident that makes violence possible. For care grants access to the bodies of vulnerable and vulnerabilized populations. It is an affect that facilitates intimate, potentially invasive contact. For example in this collection, Tess Sheldon writes on how institutional violence persists in group homes, materializing as reproductive control – including menstrual tracking and barriers to parenting. She writes that these protective measures are premised on eugenics-based "stereotypes … about the capacity to parent" (243) that stick to intellectually disabled women.

Institutionalized populations sit at the nexus of this push and pull dynamic, trapped in relationships with authorities that both loathe and care for them. Institutionalization, then, has functioned as a way of managing personal and collective emotional reactions to the unruly – unruly for their resistance, but also ontologically unruly for existing in ways that transgress social ordering. These impulses of care and loathing drive someone with power to degrade the bodies of those they hold power over. It is precisely this relation that exposes the institutionalized to violence – to a closing off from the potential to be safe, to feel loved, to make choices, to have control. These affective dimensions to the institutional relation may oscillate, varying in intensity depending on the conditions on the ground, the population in question, and their needs in the moment; yet these forces are co-constitutive in an equation that generates institutional violence.

LOOKING FORWARD

It is our hope that attention to the affective forces that motivate institutional violence will help facilitate a collective recognition and eradication of persistent institutional logics. Ben-Moshe (2020) is herself preoccupied with how to enact true de-institutionalization, which she defines as threefold: first, "the process of closing down carceral locales" (39); second, movement into community, because "deinstitutionalization is not only about space but about people" (39); third, "and perhaps most importantly, I conceptualize deinstitutionalization … as a social movement, an ideology opposing carceral logics" (39). Deinstitutionalization that avoids the trap of transinstitutionalization must do more than close down the brick-and-mortar buildings; it must put institutional logics and their organizing forces out of circulation.

Deinstitutionalization, then, shares resonances with the prison and police abolitionist movement (Ben-Moshe 2014; 2020; Fritsch, Monaghan, and van der Meulen 2022). Abolitionism has its own history, rooted in ending the peculiar institution of slavery and its re-materialization as forms of anti-Black racial captivity (Coyle and Nagel 2022; Kaba 2021; Purnell 2021). The deinstitutionalization movement can learn from abolitionists to imagine otherwise, to the extent that "abolition is a horizon, a desire for the future, but it is also a series of actions in the present [that ask] what are some of the tangible ways people keep each other safe" (Pasternak, Walby and Stadnyk 2022, 6).

Deinstitutionalization can draw from the prison abolition movement precisely because the total institutional model, its manifestation in varied sites of confinement, and its attendant strategies of containment (including eugenics and criminalization), have deep roots in white supremacist and settler colonial aims (Ben-Moshe 2020; Fritsch, Monaghan, and van der Meulen 2022). The originating, underlying function of total institutional logics was racial captivity, in response to the perceived threat of non-white populations (O'Leary and Ben-Moshe

2019; Rodriguez 2006). Other and intersecting marginalized populations have been caught up in the dragnet of population management projects – management of what Goffman termed "spoiled identities" (Ben-Moshe 2020, 93) – that at their core are unintelligible without referencing racial hierarchy.

Practically speaking, abolition speaks to the desire to end practices of institutionalization, while we can also envision the growth of new logics that escape the affective entanglement of care and loathing. Such novel logics might re-envision the scope of how we constitute the category of "human," work to centre those who have been historically denied a place in this category, and undertake the labour of challenging the notion of unruliness not as a call to dominate or control but to support as radical expressions of selfhood. This work might occur through the creation of new spaces that invite different kinds of interactions, or from practices that actively refute affective economies of care rooted in loathing. Examples of how such re-envisioned logics might look in practice can be found in Mo Korchinski and colleagues' chapter, which departs from other chapters in this collection by describing a prison project in which prisoners' sense of personhood was deeply supported.

CHAPTER OUTLINE

This edited collection brings together experts on institutional violence from across Canada. The authors included in this collection hail from regions across the country, represent a wide array of disciplines, take vastly different methodological approaches, and span a range of career stages – from emerging doctoral student scholars to established experts. The editors' original intention was to organize a writing workshop, and to that end we were successful in applying for funding from the Social Science and Humanities Research Council Connection Grant program. When the novel coronavirus pandemic and its resultant economic shutdowns and travel restrictions thwarted plans for an in-person social gathering, the editors arranged a series of virtual meetings across the duration of a year. Authors met all together and in smaller groups to discuss the development of their respective chapters and the connective intellectual tissue between chapters. The organization of the text into three sections was born of these ongoing conversations and marks an attempt to break the Gordian knot of institutional violence into its component parts: care and loathing in state sanctioned settings.

Section One: Roots of Total Institutional Violence

Our first section presents historical moments where the total institutional model carried traces of both care and loathing, gathering up the tangles of these affects. The chapters in this section focus on the experiences of youth populations whose age, gender, disability diagnosis, Indigenous status, or combinations thereof trapped them in relationships of created dependency. And yet they were not entitled to the innocence of youth, given they encountered caregivers' judgment and investments in their reform – either to save young women from disrepute or to mold children into model (white) citizens.

Our first chapter in this set is "Making Sense of Institutional Violence through Social Theory: An Autoethnography of Adolescent Trauma and Survival," written by renowned sociology scholar Claudia Malacrida from the University of Lethbridge. This chapter is a deeply personal autoethnographic account that describes how young Malacrida's caregivers enacted symbolic violence by treating her trauma as a personal failing. She traces her lack of sexual and reproductive agency through her time living on the street and in carceral settings.

Cultural sociologist Rie Croll of Memorial University of Newfoundland penned the next chapter, "Spectacles of Humiliation: Symbolic Violence and the Regulation of Good Shepherd Inmates." In it, Croll presents findings from a ten-year ethnographic study of laundries and reformatories for girls and women that were in operation in Canada and around the world 1835–1996. Echoing Malacrida's experience, the women of Croll's study unpack the kinds of soft or symbolic violence they encountered while incarcerated in the name of rescue and reform.

Our third chapter, titled "Manufacturing Structural Vulnerability and Institutional Violence: The Language of Childhood and Disability," was written by Trent University Canadian and Indigenous studies graduate Katharine Viscardis. Viscardis uses interview and archival data to showcase intellectually disabled survivors' experiences of institutionalization at the Huronia Regional Centre (in operation in Ontario 1876–2009). She shows how the systematic dehumanization of disabled children rendered them vulnerable to a range of abuses.

Last in this section, critical disability studies scholar Annalise Clarkson contributed "The Societal Underpinnings of Institutionalizing Othered Bodies: A Typology of Institutional Violence at the Huronia Regional Centre and the Mohawk Institute." Clarkson's archival analysis compares the kinds of abuse and abandonment children experienced at Huronia and the Mohawk Institute (an Ontario-based residential school for Indigenous children in operation 1834–1969). Seen also in Croll, the author here argues institutional logics serve as a tool of the colonial state designed to generate a settler citizenry and to excise misfits from wider community.

Section Two: Loathing in the Transinstitutional Era

This second section shows how loathing carries through across the fragmentation of institutional logics. The collection of chapters here holds in common a focus on labour and poverty, where loathing is attached to socio-economic worth. These chapters are also bound by articulations of social loathing, as expressed through particular kinds of practices within the community, that leave unruly populations subject to forms of humiliation, socio-economic deprivation, and totalizing forms of community surveillance. Following the disintegration of brick-and-mortar institutions and the concomitant turn toward privatization on the one hand and ill-funded "community care" on the other, these chapters collectively argue that neoliberalism drives the diffusion of institutional logics. Here forms of community care are linked to expectations and measurements of productivity, and provisions are stripped so bare that abandonment becomes the key kind of violence the affected populations experience. Also key to understanding the theorizing in this section, contributors frame the project of making a productive workforce and abandoning lost causes as rooted in problematic histories of race and racialization.

Carleton University student Megan Q. Linton (who is originally from Winnipeg) wrote the first chapter in this section, titled "Invisible Institutions: Institutionalization of People Labelled with Intellectual/Developmental Disabilities." In it she systematically describes current Canadian institutions that house and provide wrap-around services to intellectually disabled populations. This typology shows the operations of transinstitutionalization – and particularly how institutionalization is not just a space but also a way of thinking.

York University political science student Siobhán Saravanamuttu penned "The Violence of Work: Sheltered Workshops in Ontario, Canada." This chapter studies the historical and ongoing policy framework for Ontario-based non-competitive settings that employ intellectually disabled workers. Saravanamuttu argues that sheltered employment extends the total institutional mandate to rehabilitate and normalize citizens found wanting – which devalues their labour in the meantime and justifies wage inequity.

Next is "Institutionalizing Unfree Labour in Ontario's Seasonal Agricultural Worker Program Farmsteads," by political scientist Shanti Fernando and legal studies scholar Jen Rinaldi from Ontario Tech University. In an analysis of pandemic reporting in major Canadian media outlets, the authors describe the living and working conditions temporary foreign workers experience on seasonal agricultural worker program farms. Fernando and Rinaldi connect economic abuse and abandonment to historical experiences of unfree labour, in a version of institutional violence that serviced white supremacy.

University of Windsor School of Social Work scholars Jijian Voronka, Adrian Guta, Tina (Jordan) Nguyen, Grace Shaw, and Aman Ahluwalia Cameron wrote "Danger, Safety, and the Rhetoric of Urban Institutional Logics and Windsor's Downtown Core" as the final contribution to this section. Citing Malacrida, the authors argue that moral and racial panics about an urban crisis sustain institutional logics as forms of community care to manage unhoused populations in downtown Windsor. Voronka and colleagues frame preventable deaths as state-based violence enacted on a psychiatrically disabled, racialized, and impoverished population.

Section Three: Care Qua Violence

The edited collection's final section turns from articulations of loathing toward practices ostensibly designed to provide care, and explores how loathing permeates these practices in such a way as to engender (further) violence. The chapters that constitute this section share a focus on women's experiences, particularly disabled, Indigenous, and impoverished women. The chapters also share community-grounded perspectives on how the legal system acts as a conduit that moves unruly populations from the general community into ostensible caregiving spaces, and marks them as loathed in the process. Not only do legal systems and their appointed caretakers fail to protect marginalized populations, but also the settings designed offer care risk committing their charges to a carceral pipeline – exposing marginalized populations to the violences of disciplinary strategies, policing, and imprisonment. Thus, these chapters seek to undermine existing discourses that reassure the public that care is being provided for those deemed most in need of intervention.

Legal scholar Tess Sheldon from the University of Windsor contributed the first chapter for this section, titled, "Gendered and Disability Violence, Uninterrupted: Law's Formulation of and Complicity in Violence against Women Labelled with Intellectual Disability in Community-Based Institutional Settings." Sheldon engages in socio-legal analysis to unpack how group homes extend the legacy of total institutions by enacting violence against intellectually disabled women. Specifically, group homes do not robustly respond to the continued prevalence of sexual abuse, engage in menstrual suppression as a hygienic measure, and present barriers to parenting supports.

The second chapter in this set is "The List as Deterrent for Others," by Concordia University humanities student Alex Tigchelaar. Like Sheldon, Tigchelaar anchors her argument in legal analysis (as well as ethnography) and takes up the nuances to misogynistic violence (in this case against sex workers). She charts how institutional violence has adapted to become *sites*-specific in its work to organize an historically over-criminalized population. Since the decriminalization of sex work in a Supreme Court decision, socio-legal machinery has shifted in its management of sex workers now driven by a narrative of community care. But the rhetorical shifts only shield police violence, which has remained unchanged.

Postdoctoral fellow Kim Jackson at Wilfrid Laurier University, as well as community members Shirley Berry, Sandie Guignard, Asil Lavoie, Lisa LaBlanc, Minutet Nima, Opal Sparks, and Marlene Bluebird Stickings authored "We Want You to Listen: The Shelter Video Project Collective on Colonial/Capitalist Violence." In this chapter, unhoused people describe their experiences of institutional violence in a Toronto-based shelter, focusing on living conditions and disciplinary protocols. The authors demonstrate that systems of capitalism and colonialism shape the shelter space in ways that engender these violences.

Our final installment is called "Kaleidoscope: Hope In Action beyond Institution," by Mo Korchinski of the Collaborating Centre for Prison Health and Education, education scholar Lynn Fels from Simon Fraser University, and population and public health scholar Ruth Elwood Martin from the University of British Columbia. This chapter charts the reform programs developed at the Alouette Correction Centre for Women in British Columbia to centre Indigenous knowledge and improve women's health and well-being. The authors critically assess whether these programs mark Alouette as an exemplar, in a context where violence is embedded in the carceral model.

REFERENCES

Agamben, Giorgio. 2005. *State of Exception*. Translated by K. Attell. Chicago: University of Chicago Press.

Ahmed, Sara. 2001. "The Organization of Hate." *Law and Critique* 12: 345–65.

– 2004. *The Cultural Politics of Emotion*. New York: Routledge.

– 2017. *Living a Feminist Life*. Durham: Duke University Press.

Alldred, Pam, and Nick J. Fox. 2017. "Young Bodies, Power and Resistance: A New Materialist Perspective." *Journal of Youth Studies* 20, no. 9: 1161–75.

Andrews, Valerie J. 2018. *White Unwed Mother: The Adoption Mandate in Postwar Canada*. Toronto: Demeter Press.

Arendt, Hannah. 1970. *On Violence*. New York: Harcourt.

Baer, Leonard D., and Bodil Ravnesberg. 2008. "The Outside and Inside in Norwegian and English Prisons." *Geografiska Annaler: Series B. Human Geography* 90, no. 2: 205–16.

Becker, Howard S. 2003. "The Politics of Presentation: Goffman and Total Institutions." *Symbolic Interaction* 26, no. 4: 659–69.

Ben-Moshe, Liat. 2014. "Alternatives to (Disability) Incarceration." In *Disability Incarcerated: Imprisonment and Disability in the United States and Canada*, edited by Liat Ben-Moshe, Chris Chapman, and Allison C. Carey, 255–72. New York: Palgrave Macmillan.

– 2020. *Decarcerating Disability: Deinstitutionalization and Prison Abolition*. Minneapolis: University of Minnesota Press.

Ben-Moshe, Liat, Chris Chapman, and Allison C. Carey, eds. 2014. *Disability Incarcerated: Imprisonment and Disability in the United States and Canada*. New York: Palgrave Macmillan.

Benjamin, Walter. 2019. *Reflections: Essays, Aphorisms, Autobiographical Writings*, edited by Peter Demetz. Boston: Mariner Books.

Burghardt, Madeline C. 2018. *Broken: Institutions, Families, and the Construction of Intellectual Disability*. Montreal and Kingston: McGill-Queen's University Press.

Coyle, Michael J., and Mechtchild Nagel, eds. 2022. *Contesting Carceral Logic: Towards Abolitionist Futures*. New York: Routledge.

Croll, Rie. 2019. *Shaped by Silence: Stories from Inmates of the Good Shepherd Laundries and Reformatories*. St John's: Iser Books.

Crossley, N. 2006. *Contesting Psychiatry: Social Movements in Mental Health*. Abingdon: Routledge.

Daley, Andrea, Lucia Costa, and Peter Beresford, eds. 2019. *Madness, Violence, and Power: A Critical Collection*. Toronto: University of Toronto Press.

Derrida, Jacques. 1990. "Force of Law: The 'Mystical Foundation of Authority.'" Translated by M. Quaintance. *Cardozo Law Review* 11: 920–1045.

Dyck, Erick, and Alex Deighton. 2017. *Managing Madness: Weyburn Mental Hospital and the Transformation of Psychiatric Care in Canada*. Winnipeg: University of Manitoba Press.

Farrington, Keith. 1992. "The Modern Prison as Total Institution? Public Perception Versus Objective Reality." *Crime and Delinquency* 38, no. 6: 6–26.

Felman, Shoshana. 2002. *The Juridical Unconscious: Trials and Traumas in the Twentieth Century*. Cambridge: Harvard University Press.

Felman, Shoshana, and Dori Laub, eds. 1992. *Testimony: Crises of Witnessing in Literature, Psychoanalysis, and History*. New York: Routledge.

Foucault, Michel. 1977. *Discipline and Punish: The Birth of the Prison*. New York: Pantheon Books.

Fritsch, Kelly, Jeffrey Monaghan, and Emily van der Meulen. 2022. "Resisting the Criminalization of Disability: Cripping Disability Injustice toward Accessible Decarceral Futures." In *Disability Injustice: Confronting Criminalization in Canada*, edited by Kelly Fritsch, Jeffrey Monaghan, and Emily van der Meulen, 1–46. Vancouver: UBC Press.

Galtung, Johan. 1969. "Violence, Peace, and Peace Research." *Journal of Peace Research* 6, no. 3: 167–91.

Gambino, Matthew. 2013. "Erving Goffman's Asylums and Institutional Culture in the Mid-Twentieth-Century United States." *Harvard Review of Psychiatry* 21, no. 1: 52–7.

Goffman, Erving. 1961. *Asylums: Essays on the Social Situation of Mental Patients and Other Inmates*. New York: Anchor Books.

– 1963. *Stigma: Notes on the Management of Soiled Identity*. New York: Simon and Schuster.

Hughes, Bill, Linda McKie, Debra Hopkins, and Nick Watson. 2005. "Love's Labours Lost? Feminism, the Disabled People's Movement and an Ethic of Care." *Sociology* 39, no. 2: 259–75.

Kaba, Mariame. 2021. *We Do This 'Til We Free Us: Abolitionist Organizing and Transforming Justice*. Chicago: Haymarket Books.

Karu, Bhavneet. 2021. "Politics of Emotion": Everyday Affective Circulation of Women's Resistance and Grief in Kashmir." *Ethnography* 22, no. 4: 515–33.

Kelly, Christine. 2011. "Making 'Care' Accessible: Personal Assistance for Disabled People and the Politics of Language." *Critical Social Policy* 31, no. 4: 562–82.

Leblanc Haley, Tobin, and Chelsea Temple Jones. 2020. Sites and Shapes of Transinstitutionalization. *Canadian Journal of Disability Studies* 9, no. 3: 1–15.

Malacrida, Claudia. 2015. *A Special Hell: Institutional Life in Alberta's Eugenic Years*. Toronto: University of Toronto Press.

Martin, Ruth, Mo Korchinksi, Lynn Fels, and Carl Leggo, eds. 2014. *Arresting Hope: Women Taking Action in Prison Health Inside Out*. Toronto: Inanna Publications and Education.

Monchalin, Lisa. 2014. *The Colonial Problem: An Indigenous Perspective on Crime and Injustice in Canada*. Toronto: University of Toronto Press.

Moran, Dominique. 2013. "Between Outside and Inside? Prison Visiting Rooms as Liminal Carceral Spaces." *GeoJournal* 78: 339–51.

– 2014. "Leaving Behind the 'Total Institution'? Teeth, Transcarceral Spaces and (Re)Inscription of the Formerly Incarcerated Body." *Gender, Place and Culture* 21, no.1: 35–51.

Oikawa, Mona. 2012. *Cartographies of Violence: Japanese Canadian Women, Memory, and the Subjects of Internment*. Toronto: University of Toronto.

O'Leary, Meghann, and Liat Ben-Moshe. 2019. "The Politics of 'Treatment' and 'Choice' in Neo-Liberal Times." In *Madness, Violence, and Power: A Critical Collection,* edited by Andrea Daley, Lucia Costa, and Peter Beresford, 115–35. Toronto: University of Toronto Press.

Opotow, S., and S.I. McClelland. 2007. "The Intensification of Hating: A Theory." *Social Justice Research* 20, no. 1: 69–84.

Pasternak, Shiri, Kevin Walby, and Abby Stadnyk. 2022. "Introduction." In *Disarm, Defund, Dismantle: Police Abolition in Canada*, edited by Shiri Pasternak, Kevin Walby, and Abby Stanyk, 1–11. Toronto: Between the Lines.

Pitzer, Andrea. 2017. *One Long Night: A Global History of Concentration Camps*. New York: Back Bay Books.

Purnell, Derecka. 2021. *Becoming Abolitionists: Police, Protests, and the Pursuit of Freedom*. New York: Astra House.

Ranasinghe, Prashan. 2017. *Helter-Shelter: Security, Legality, and an Ethic of Care in an Emergency Shelter*. Toronto: University of Toronto Press.
Reaume, Geoffrey. 2000. *Remembrance of Patients Past: Patient Life at the Toronto Hospital for the Insane, 1870–1940*. Toronto: University of Toronto Press.
Rinaldi, Jen. 2021. "What Survivors See: Creative Condemnations of Total Institutionalization." *Emotion, Space and Society* 40: 1–8.
Rodriguez, Dylan. 2006. "(Non)Scenes of Captivity: The Common Sense of Punishment and Death." *Radical History Review* 96: 9–32.
Rossiter, Kate, and Jen Rinaldi. 2019. *Institutional Violence and Disability: Punishing Conditions*. London: Routledge.
Schliehe, Anna K. 2016. "Re-Discovering Goffman: Contemporary Carceral Geography, the 'Total' Institution and Notes on Heterotopia." *Human Geography* 98, no. 1: 19–35.
Seigworth, Gregory J., and Melissa Gregg. 2010. "An Inventory of Shimmers." In *The Affect Theory Reader*, edited by Melissa Gregg and Gregory J. Seigworth, 1–25. Durham: Duke University Press.
Spivakovsky, Claire, Linda Steele, and Penelope Weller, eds. 2020. *The Legacies of Institutionalization: Disability, Law and Policy in the "Deinstitutionalized" Community*. London: Bloomsbury Publishing.
Steele, Linda, and Leanne Dowse. 2016. "Gender, Disability Rights and Violence against Medical Bodies." *Australian Feminist Studies* 31, no. 88: 187–202.
TRC (Truth and Reconciliation Commission of Canada). 2015. *A Knock at the Door: The Essential History of Residential Schools*. Winnipeg: University of Manitoba Press.
Vienne, Philippe. 2010. "The Enigma of the Total Institution. Rethinking the Hughes-Goffman Intellectual Relationship." *Sociologica* 2: 1–31.
Watson, Nick, Linda McKie, Bill Hughes, Debra Hopkins, and Sue Gregory. 2004. "(Inter)Dependence, Needs and Care: The Potential for Disability and Feminist Theorists to Develop an Emancipatory Model." *Sociology* 38, no. 2: 331–50.
Zembylas, Michalino. 2007. "The Affective Politics of Hatred: Implications for Education. *Intercultural Education* 18, no. 3: 177–92.
– 2021. "The Affective Dimension of Everyday Resistance: Implications for Critical Pedagogy in Engaging with Neoliberalism's Educational Impact." *Critical Studies in Education* 62, no. 2: 211–26.

SECTION ONE

Roots of Total Institutional Violence

I

Making Sense of Institutional Violence through Social Theory

An Autoethnography of Adolescent Trauma and Survival

CLAUDIA MALACRIDA

I have always found it difficult to declare myself as a specific "type" of scholar: my work spans classical feminist topics such as childbirth, pregnancy loss, the medicalization of women's bodies, and motherhood. It also sits squarely within disability scholarship through my oral histories on the institutionalization of people identified as intellectual or psychologically "inferior," or my research on the challenges disabled people face in accessing housing, money, love, reproductive and sexual justice, parenthood, or respectful and inclusive dealings with helping professionals.

In neither of these scholarly fields do I feel completely at home. My work as a feminist scholar sits on the edge because I have been firmly poststructuralist in my approach to understanding gendered inequalities, and because I have understood gender to, at times, be the least of some people's problems. As a disability studies scholar, my interests in disabled and nondisabled mothers and the policing of normative motherhood (which often simultaneously excludes disabled women as mothers) have posed challenges to tidy alignments. Additionally, my own embodiment as temporarily abled stands against the frequently argued idea that a disabled identity or embodiment is foundational or necessary to good disability scholarship. I have often felt challenged in making sense of these competing understandings, subject positions, and approaches in my work.

Thinking about institutional violence has given me an opportunity to reflect upon, and surprisingly, to reconcile these apparent fissures. In preparation for this book, the members of this collective joined online to discuss commonalities, challenges, and how to write about institutional violence despite the isolation, anxiety, and fragmentation of the COVID pandemic. In that meeting, we were asked what led us as researchers to be interested in the concept of institutional violence. The question was in fact more pointed, asking what the concept of institutional violence *meant* to each of us. For the first time, amongst a group of professional colleagues, I mastered my shame and decided to answer without representing myself as distanced and intellectual in my pursuits, but instead to honestly connect the personal to the political, the embodied to the academic. In turn, these generous and compassionate colleagues encouraged me to use those experiences as the basis for this writing. In this chapter, I offer an autoethnography of institutional violence through a critical self-reflection and narrative analysis that seeks to do more than simply "tell a good story," but instead works to connect personal experiences to broader social, cultural, and historical systems (Ellis, Adams, and Bochner 2011). In examining my adolescent experiences of unwanted pregnancy and incarceration in the juvenile justice system, I hope to illuminate how routinized and seemingly beneficent institutional violence can be, how it penetrates the most intimate aspects of life, and how it operates to constrain the individual while simultaneously upholding normative orders about who can and should control the body. I then turn to an examination of how these experiences of institutional violence have informed my teaching, research, and writing.

ABUSE AND ITS LEGACY

From the age of seven or eight, I was sexually abused by a relative I trusted and loved. I only came much later to understand it as abuse, and I'll admit that this history clouded my judgement quite a bit as I grew up, leading me to understand love and acceptance as necessarily mediated through sex. From late childhood through to early adulthood I was perceived as needy, or promiscuous, or simply "oversexed," depending on who applied the label.

Throughout my late childhood and adolescence, my mother embarked on an aggressive quest to determine what was wrong with me. Why was I so unhappy, so oppositional, so "wild"? I remember my first home visit by a social worker at about eight or nine years of age. I was told that a nice lady would come to talk with me and try to help me. But as the interview proceeded, it became clear she was there to figure out why I was such a problem child; why was I so difficult? I had no idea how to explain myself because I really didn't understand why I couldn't just get things right; it was only decades later that I understood that the secret I carried and the shame I felt about it left me unmoored, on a dark and lonely sea.[1] But for that visit, I must have covered well enough, because when the report came back, I was described – to my mother's outrage – as a pleasant and cooperative child who seemed to be just fine.

But (and to give my mother some credit) I wasn't fine. I was a misfit hungry for acceptance, an unruly child longing for approval, someone who never got the boundaries just right. I always seemed to be the kid who got caught, who went too far, who was defiant, who never lived up to her potential. I never knew how to be liked, or how to trust appropriately, or how to be happy, and I was never sure how to fix that, despite my fervent desire to be good and "normal."

The biggest issue was that I seemed to always make my mother angry or disappointed.[2] It knew that my failure was not only worrying but shameful to her, a reflection of her failure as a mother. My relationship with my mother came to be mediated over the ensuing seven or eight years by encounters with educators, psychologists, psychiatrists, social workers, and ultimately the family justice system, who were variously recruited and discarded as they tried to sort out "what was wrong with Claudia" despite that Claudia had an obviously caring, respectable, and highly engaged mother.

Shortly after the social worker was dispatched, a family psychiatrist was brought on board to assess "what was wrong with Claudia." After the first couple of visits, he suggested family therapy, and so we endured a couple of excruciating sessions in which my mother cried and accused, my father swore and shut down, and ultimately, they both refused to continue. My abuser was not part of those sessions, but I doubt I'd have had the temerity or perhaps even the awareness to expose him if he had been. For two more years, I continued alone with the therapy sessions, despite that it didn't seem to really "improve" me.

With adolescence, although the sexual abuse eventually ended, outside the home things really spiralled. I was smart but struggling in school. I had teachers who sometimes were kind, and I wanted to be good, but I was constantly in the principal's office and often suspended from school for bad behaviour. I came from a "good family," but I was sexually precocious. I was bright, but I consistently underperformed academically. This was in the early 1960s. Nobody thought to ask whether I was being sexually abused at home. Even I didn't think I was being abused, to be honest. I assumed this was just as much my fault as his, and it was only many years later that I connected the abuse to my inability as a child to comply with gendered childhood norms, or to my constant "acting out," as the many adults in my life called it. I was as mystified as all those concerned adults as to why I couldn't just settle down, live up to my potential, and make my distraught mother (and by extension, everybody else) happy.

Unsurprisingly, at barely fifteen I became pregnant. And in the context of a home in which I had been consistently psychiatrized, scapegoated for family problems, and blamed for causing my mother's significant emotional and psychological distress, I felt I had only one option. I ran away to a city several miles away.

It wasn't a great success. I panhandled a bit, stayed with some older friends, slept under a bridge, and lied about my age so I could stay in the room of a shelter worker. To be honest, when my father showed up with a couple of police officers less than a week later, I felt almost relieved. I was a nice, middle-class girl – I had no idea how to survive on the streets, and even I could sense that my resources had been pretty much exhausted.

In the shelter while I gathered up my backpack, my father, who did not smoke, handed out candies and cigarettes to people with whom he would ordinarily never interact.[3] The police officers who had arrived with him left us, and my father and I boarded a bus to head back home. As we arrived in my hometown, he told me that because I'd run away and the police had been involved, I was going to have to spend the night in a facility for "kids with problems." It seemed fair to me – or at the very least it didn't surprise me. I had been in the system in an attenuated way for while by then, so I wasn't particularly unused to interacting with helping professionals. Maybe I'd finally get some help, and besides, it offered me a one-night stay of execution prior to having to go home and tell my mother why I'd run.

That night, I arrived at the downtown Child and Youth Services Remand Centre, a non-descript, windowless building of squat cinder block walls topped with in-leaning barbed wire. I'd passed it hundreds of times on my way through town and never noticed it before. It's still there all these decades later.

My father dropped me at the door and handed me to a stern middle-aged woman who made me remove my clothing, books, backpack, and jewelry, and take a good long shower in front of her. She checked me over thoroughly (open your mouth, bend over, raise your arms, lift your hair, spread your legs), and handed me the navy-blue cotton jumpsuit and laceless sneakers that would be my uniform (except for court days) for what turned out to be almost three months. The remand centre consisted of about fifty cells, separated between boys and girls by a shared kitchen with separate eating facilities. The cells, each with two metal bed frames hanging off the walls, were lit with natural light via a high, narrow strip of glass block. Bathrooms (toilets and showers) were shared and doorless. The girls' common room faced onto an unused basketball court surrounded by nine-foot cinder block walls topped with barbed wire. During my time there, I never saw a blade of grass, except during the weekly cleaning we provided in the superintendent's house attached to the facility. His residence had the only out-facing windows in the building so that, even though I knew it was probably exploitive that inmates should do his housekeeping, I was happy to have the opportunity to be somewhere that allowed me to see a bit of nature in the outside world.

The first days were terrifying. No adult in the prison or in my family was able or willing to tell me what to expect, how long I would be there, or most importantly, what I needed to do to get out. After getting up the first morning, making my bed, toileting collectively – and publicly – with my new roommates, and then gathering in the dining area, I began to get some sense of what to expect in the child court system. My fellow inmates – all of them young, most of them incarcerated for similar failings to my own – included some repeat "offenders" who were happy to explain the system I now found myself in. I was told it could be weeks or months before a decision would be made about what was to be done with me, and that I might as well hunker down and get used to it.

During my time inside, I had two visits with my parents – awkward visits punctuated by my mother's sobs, and long silences. It took a couple of weeks for my first court date, which was followed by several hearings over the ensuing weeks. These involved social workers, witness statements from teachers and school counsellors, and considerable testimony from my mother, all of it inventorying my poor attitude, my promiscuity, my pathological behaviours, my inability to live up to my potential, outlining the heroic efforts and compromises made on my behalf, and my failure to appreciate the concern of the adults around me. I was never asked to really explain myself, nor did I meet with any of these expert witnesses while incarcerated but for one, a court-appointed psychiatrist. In fairness, I am not sure that my insights would have been much help, given how uncomprehending I was about my own life at the time.

One thing I did know, and said when asked by the judge, was that I did not want to return home. This created quite a scene in the courtroom, with my mother breaking down piteously and my father leaving the court visibly shaken. I was hopeful when I heard the judge say he would take this information under consideration, but he simultaneously remanded me for a further three weeks to consider the particulars of my case. That was probably when I did myself in, muttering audibly, "Fuck that. Maybe you should spend three weeks in there instead!" While this may now read like a moment of plucky resistance, I assure you that it did not help my case, and it probably did gain some sympathy for the adults in the room who had to deal with me.

In the meanwhile, I did not miscarry my pregnancy, which – even more than wanting to get out of jail and not live with my parents – was my fervent desire. Instead, I experienced morning sickness, ate horrible food, outgrew my navy cotton jumpsuit, and became ostracized by the women who worked as guards in the facility. I found it ironic and even a little hurtful that, although the place was peopled with runaways, shoplifters, and writers of bad cheques, becoming pregnant somehow marked me as more tainted than the others.

The question of my pregnancy did figure in the court assessment, although I was not directly asked what I wanted to do about it. Rather, as noted above, I had a meeting with a court-appointed psychiatrist assigned to evaluate my situation. We met very briefly, and in one of the two visits I had with my mother during my incarceration, she informed me that she and the psychiatrist had also met to discuss my case, determining that it was important that I be held responsible for my poor life choices. I would have that baby.[4] I was told that it was a good opportunity for me to take time to reflect upon my behaviours.

In the end, and unsurprisingly, my encounter with the child justice system got me nothing that I really wanted and many things that I did not. I was deemed incorrigible, a status crime[5] designation frequently imposed on defiant or sexually misbehaving girls under the Juvenile Delinquents Bill. This bill operated in Canada from its inception in 1908 until its 1984 repeal, although the social norms of the late 1960s and the availability of birth control reduced its usage from the 1970s forward – just a little too late for me.[6]

I was placed on probation and made a ward of the courts under my parents' supervision until I reached my eighteenth birthday. The terms of my probation included completing grade ten by correspondence, adhering to the rules laid down by my parents, seeing a probation officer on a weekly basis, and attending monthly sessions with the same court-appointment psychiatrist who felt that denying me an abortion was a good first step in our therapeutic relationship. In principle, this meant that if I did not comply, I would find myself back in jail. In practice, it meant that my parents owned me in a way that was officially sanctioned and absolutely iron clad.

TOTAL INSTITUTIONS

Erving Goffman, in his classic treatise, outlined several types of populations held and the manifest purposes served by what he termed total institutions. Some are meant to provide care for those children and adults considered dependent or incapable; some provide quarantine to those with physical illness, mental illness, and/or disabilities; some are prisons to protect the community from danger; some institutions foster "improvement" through industry or education, such as boarding schools or work camps; and others, like convents, offer residents a retreat from the world (Goffman 1961). However, the manifest purposes served by these institutions only tell a partial story; as Goffman explains, a key purpose of total institutions is to break down the previous identity of the inmate to permit the rebuilding of a new person.

For Goffman, this new person is often the inmate, or the monk, or the patient, who is only brought to this new identity and its attending compliance through the erasure of their former self (Goffman 1961). Thus, entering the institution is marked by removing civilian clothing, and separating the individual from their worldly identity through ritual washing and checking of bodily cavities and crevices, and providing a new embodiment, primarily through imposing a uniform. These are the first steps towards deconstruction of the former self. And of course, this erasure is a form of violence, directed brutally and relentlessly at one's sense of self, working to destroy one's personal autonomy.

My induction to jail was clearly meant to separate me from my worldly self and to break down my personal boundaries. The shower, the body search, the doorless toilets, and the silent gaze of the matron were objectifying, invasive, and shameful, and they conveyed to me that my body was no longer my own. But beyond that, the shapeless, scratchy, ugly uniform, and the confiscation of my clothing, shoes, toiletries, hair clips, and cosmetics were a clear message that at least in that place, I was not the person who walked through that door. It may seem trivial, but it was also particularly galling to me, as a gendered teenaged being whose identity had very much centred on being seen and thought of as attractive and fashionable, to have that part of myself disappeared.

While these efforts at erasure work to produce compliance amongst inmates of total institutions, there are also longer-term goals at play, so that the individual who enters and experiences this violence is not only destroyed and rebuilt for life within the institution, but they are also refashioned for a fitting life upon leaving it. The goal of rehabilitation or reconstruction is central to the broad network of total institutions that sprang up from the eighteenth through to the mid-twentieth century across Canada. Scholars have noted that this network of institutions provided a way to contain individuals deemed to be lacking or different or troublesome, but they were also the means of producing a well-behaved, compliant, and productive citizenry and work force through stern rehabilitation (Dowbiggin 1995; Malacrida 2015; Trent 1994). This network included many kinds of carceral but not necessarily criminal institutions that only recently have come to be understood by historians, activists, and academics as brutal, unjust, and shameful. First and foremost among these were residential schools for Indigenous children, but also included are orphanages for children whose parents were either deceased or unable to care for them, "homes" for pregnant and unmarried girls and women, long-term care and training facilities for deaf, blind, and disabled children, psychiatric facilities, and juvenile detention "homes" for children who broke the law or who were charged with status offences such as truancy, vagrancy, or sexual impropriety.

Total institutions, set behind walls, tucked into otherwise unremarkable city streets, or isolated in pastoral settings on the edges of towns across the nation, were often understood as dark but open secrets by Canadians. As children, we grew up knowing about reform schools and orphanages, and that we could be sent to them if we were bad or if we had the misfortune of having parents who were dead, unable, or unwilling to provide for us; Indigenous children knew well the threat of removal in the form of residential schools and, later, child welfare and social workers. In the world of intellectual difference, not only survivors, but former workers and community residents have spoken about "training schools" for intellectually disabled children and adults as a spectral and pervasive threat for children who did not fit in at school or whose families were deemed unfit (TRC 2016; Malacrida 2015; Sangster 2002). This threat is in fact a key function of total institutions; not only do such places do the work of destroying and reforming inmates' attitudes and behaviours or – as in the case of Indigenous residential schools, their culture and identity – but they exercise their power beyond institutional walls by warning community members about the price of noncompliance. Thus, the reach of institutional violence extends beyond the institutions themselves, permeating consciousness and controlling the behaviours of the wider community.

INSTITUTIONAL NETWORKS OF POWER

Total institutions were not the sole governors of our behaviours, thoughts, and emotions as young people. Michel Foucault has given us a more diffuse model of power than the top-down model traditionally offered through structural sociological lenses. To him, power is not only (or even primarily) exercised through institutions such as the total institutions described above. Nor is power centred in the law or the government, but instead he saw social control working through a dense, multi-nodal network of operations. These operations include discourse, or how we speak, know, and enact what is normative within a society, and practice or how these knowledges are distributed and deployed through and upon human subjects. In a Foucauldian model, the threat of the total institution was just one set of operations, working within a broad and cohesive network of discourses, practices, and institutions to together engender modernity's newly pressing needs for social conformity. The networks of total institutions that arose with modernity were only the manifest outcropping of what he has referred to as the great confinement that accompanied modernity (Foucault 1988).

Foucault identified sexuality as a particularly "dense transfer point of power relations" within these networks of discourse, practice, and nodal institutions (Foucault 1990). I would add that childhood – with its imagined innocence, its lack of stability, its dangerous and simultaneously vulnerable character, and its need to result in a docile, educated, and productive citizenry – is another profoundly dense transfer point in modern power relations.

The concept of connected, circulating institutional discourses and practices as networks of power and social control permits us to understand the normative coherence they evidence. In addition to the institutions of the legal system, the education system, the child welfare system, and the medical/public health systems, community groups like Girl Guides and Brownies, and religious groups are also institutional nodes in this network of power relations, all of them working together to (re)produce "good" children from "good" families. As well, what Nikolas Rose has called the "psy sector" – a system of helping professionals including child welfare workers, social workers, school counsellors, psychologists, and psychiatrists that burgeoned alongside the growth of total institutions in the West – also contributes to this critical task (Rose 1990). Thus, the school counselor's reports, the report cards, the child psychiatrists' reports, the testimonies from my former CGIT[7] leaders, and the lengthy litany of woes my mother presented as a mother, worked together in the courtroom to produce me not only as a girl like any other who required careful guidance in order to remain morally, emotionally, and psychological right, but also as an intractable challenge to that work.

Of course, the family was the key institutional node in this network. Parents are both subject to and (re)producers of normative ideas about parental care and responsibility, and they are empowered by and held liable for their work in governing childhood. My mother, as the family voice in that courtroom, was both informed by and drawing upon the accepted discursive practices of the institution of the proper middle classed family during her performance. Thus, she was keen to be seen as a good parent in control of her child, a woman firmly located in the middle class and sharing its values, which, as noted earlier, informed not only the Juvenile Delinquents Bill of the early twentieth century, but that also animated the entire network of institutions that arose during those years to resolve the problem of troubled youth. She vigorously defended her performance of mothering, setting herself up as the victim of an ungrateful and unruly child, the partner of a man who both undermined her maternal authority by his affection for me and his refusal to actively join in the project of my reform, and a woman who had worked tirelessly with other members of the network to get to the bottom of my seemingly intractable troubles. With her teary testimony and her performative deployment of maternal care and nurturance, her discursive claims about unmarried sexuality as dangerous, childhood as a risky element in the social order, and ours as a heteronormative two-parent family in which "mother knew best," she was speaking the only language the court was fully prepared to hear and value. I remember watching this masterful performance and seeing it as manipulative and frustrating, and although I was enraged, I felt perfectly helpless to combat it. There was never a question of whether or how my story was going to be heard and understood in that courtroom, because her language and practice aligned seamlessly with the discursive practices of all the institutions involved.

WHAT IS VIOLENCE?

Just as the institutions involved in my situation expanded beyond what we often stereotype as an "institution" to include a wide assortment of seemingly benign and loosely affiliated entities, the role of violence in this history is complex. I was never beaten, starved, or threatened with physical violence while in jail. But as we have learned from survivor narratives from many quarters, violence takes on multiple forms and these are often as traumatizing and effective in exerting control and inflicting trauma as is physical violence. Thus, violence has come to be understood as including physical, psychological, emotional, and sexual violence as well as neglect, all of which damage the safety and well-being of its victims. It includes forced bodily compliance, forced behavioural compliance, and forced psychological compliance through destroying its victims' freedom of motion and action, freedom of thought and feelings, and their bodily autonomy. Above all, violence seeks to disempower.

For me, one of the most lasting forms of violence has been the experience of sexual, and more specifically, reproductive violence. To be forced to continue with an unwanted pregnancy was not only a blow to my bodily autonomy, but grief over having given that child up has been a lifelong punishment. My daughter was born in 1969, the year that the lobbying efforts of doctors, women's advocacy groups, community organizations, and church leaders finally convinced the Canadian government to decriminalize the sale of birth control (Canadian Public Health Association 2021). However, this decriminalization had no benefit for me, as I remained unable to access birth control or abortion without parental permission until I turned eighteen, almost three years later.

Although the claim is often made by anti-choice activists that abortion is traumatic, Nancy Greene Foster's comprehensive study of women who were unable to obtain abortions because their pregnancies were too advanced, found women experienced a wide range of negative outcomes for being denied abortion, including negative mental health outcomes. In retrospect, I believe that I struggled with my mental health, although my recollection of this time in my life is not one of high emotion or obvious mental instability. Rather, I recall being listless and numbed for the six or so months remaining of my pregnancy, and for the childbirth itself. I believe I was in a sort of walking semi-consciousness for most of that time. I never really cried about it until much later when I finally got out of my childhood home and began to reflect on things, and then the pain and sense of loss caused me deep distress for decades.

My continued pregnancy was coerced, and it also forced me into a relationship of submission. Greene Foster's (2020) study did not include minors whose grounds for abortion denial may have echoed my situation, but she did find that one of the key reasons women sought abortions – second only to financial or family size concerns – was so they would not be tied to the man with whom they had become pregnant. In my case, it was not so much a matter of being tied to the baby's father that I wished to avoid, but I did not want to be bound to my mother any tighter than I already was. Being a fifteen-year-old pregnant person tied me to her in a complex and harmful relationship of dependency, shame, contrition, and martyrdom. In those years, it was often the practice to send "unwed mothers" to a special residential setting for young girls in trouble. However, in my case, the court-ordered psychiatrist and my mother both determined that the best route would be for me to do schooling at home and remain in the home until I gave birth. My mother was ecstatic, as she was able to keep tabs on me, and she also simultaneously used my condition to show others her long-suffering beneficence. But I secretly resented this display of my condition as a badge of my mother's honour, and I sharply felt the shame[8] of my condition. I rarely left the house for the next six months, nor did friends come by, given my public and stigmatized status. In a sense, this amounted to an attenuated but quite effective additional incarceration – a literal confinement.

Within the Remand Centre itself, violence manifested in subtle ways. The use of isolation and the policing of emotions was built into the daily routines and spatial design of the facility. Although there was room for sharing, each of us was given our own cell. This should not be confused with privacy; as noted earlier, toileting and showering was always done collectively in a room where neither toilets nor shower stalls had doors.

Instead, the isolation of our cells operated as a disciplinary force. The cells were separated from each other, and because each door had a viewing slot that opened only from outside, we were unable to see one another once we were in our cells. Finally, the matron's office that oversaw us from the end of our hallway, ensured we did not break the rule of silence once we were bedded down, which occurred shortly after dinner each night. This clearly made for long, lonely nights, but the use of solitude was ramped up when transgressions occurred. Twice during my incarceration, the entire population was punished with twenty-four hours of solitary confinement, both times for minor offences like laughing too much or not getting our chores done.

There was psychological violence as well. One night, a new girl was interned, and we heard her cries and crashing sounds coming from her cell throughout the night. Some of us called for the matrons to check on her, and those requests were stolidly denied. We were told to mind our own business, and that the girl was just being hysterical. In the morning when we were let into the bathroom, we met our new cellmate for the first time. Her shirt, face, and hair were covered in dried blood and she had angry abrasions all over her forehead and scalp; apparently, she had been bashing her head against her door for long stretches throughout the night. This was not told to us by the matrons, but by the girl herself later in the day. Seeing her shocked me, and it registered for me the dangerousness of being in that facility. It was terrifying to think she was harming herself and crying for help and nobody came to her aid.

My parents weren't monsters. They were emotionally manipulative and worried people who were not very insightful and faced with a situation they had no skills for, but they loved me to the best of their ability. So, when Easter came and I was still in jail, they dropped off a book and a chocolate egg. When the matron handed this to me, the foil wrapping of the egg was removed, and the hollow egg was broken in small pieces; similarly, the book looked as though it had been well-thumbed, and the spine was cracked and torn. I was told this was the result of routine searching for drugs, weapons, or other contraband. This was my parents' gift, given to a fifteen-year-old kid on the most hopeful holiday of the Christian calendar. More than the strip search, or the solitary confinement, or the bloodied girl in the cell next to mine, for some reason, that invasion of privacy – and the violence of it – disturbs me still.

The psychological violence operated outside of the Remand Centre as well, in that I remained tightly bound to the carceral system through mandated probation officer visits and forced psychiatric supervision. Honestly, the probation wasn't a hardship; the officer was a young fellow who seemed to like me and treated me with decency and kindness. Although the court had mandated weekly visits to continue through until my eighteenth birthday, by mutual agreement we soon only met monthly and eventually not at all. But the psychiatrist was another story. Although I met him bi-weekly, then monthly, for two and half years, I never saw him as someone with whom I could share personal issues in confidence, knowing that he and my mother met regularly to discuss my case, and that he had been at least complicit in the decision to deny me an abortion. We spent over two years meeting regularly, and the topic of my sexual abuse never came close to the surface, undoubtedly because of my lack of trust, but also because I never really got a sense that he liked me or cared enough to understand what drove me. After the probation officer ended our meetings, I did suggest that we do the same. He strongly disagreed, and said, "this just confirms your mother was right, you really are a selfish little bitch." This was said while looking in my face and smiling, which felt deeply disorienting. We continued for several more months until I was old enough to finally refuse further meetings.

THE EFFECTS OF INSTITUTIONAL VIOLENCE

My transition to adulthood took place at the blunt end of institutional violence, trapped within a network of subtle forms of interinstitutional power, and the effects were lasting, colouring my ways of being, perceiving, and understanding. Most obviously, as soon as I was able to get out from under the court order, I left home and never really turned back. Leaving home so young meant I did not go the expected route of going to college and then getting a job, but I instead rushed into heteronormative coupledom very early in life, marrying for the first time at just nineteen years of age. Unsurprisingly, my relationship with my parents never really healed, although we did manage to achieve some cordiality in later years.

The emotional and psychological legacy of those experiences also lingered. I have written elsewhere how institutional violence simultaneously intertwines the practices that Michel Foucault described as disciplinary, alongside the heavier-handed practices that Erving Goffman characterized as dehumanizing (Malacrida 2005). The commonality, however, rests in the outcome: docility in the short term and, in the longer term, internalized self-regulation, self-judgement and silence over what has been done because of a deeply ingrained sense of shame. Coming to terms with my past, and even more, being free to speak of it, has taken much time and effort. And for me, becoming well and learning to feel strong has come through critical social theory.

I was thirty-six years old when I finally went to university. My initial goals were to obtain well-paid and respected work that would accommodate a family, and so I took education and psychology courses, believing these to be the pathway to a better life. In the summer between my third and fourth year, however, I took two sociology classes – one on gender and the body and the other on deviance and social control – and it felt like I had finally come home. Feminist theories on the moral and social regulation of women and girls through bodily discourse and practice, and sociological theories on social control that exposed how "deviance" and "difference" are used to engender social cohesion and produce subordinated subjectivities made perfect sense to me. Indeed, they read like an operator's manual for my life.

Concepts like the sociological imagination, and feminism's foundational understanding of the body and the personal as deeply political, gave me permission as a nascent scholar to make those connections in my own work (Mills 2001; Grosz 1987; Weedon 1987). A few second-year courses turned the tide, but obtaining a doctorate in sociology did for me what years of therapy and red wine could not: it gave me a lens with which to understand my world, and a voice with which to speak about it.

In the classroom, that has meant offering students reading materials, assignments, and discussion forums that make those connections in a structured and supported way. I do this to facilitate my students' own widening sociological lenses, to help them to make the connections of the personal to the political in their own lives, and to be able to critically examine the normative and seemingly benign practices that order their values, habits, and self-concepts. On rare occasions, I have even included some of my own history as part of this pedagogy.

When I have shared parts of my story in a classroom – which has only occurred a couple of times in senior or graduate seminars – I have done so with a conscious belief that it is important for students to understand that unjust incarceration and enforced psychiatrization are not abstract concepts, but that its survivors are among us, indeed they are us.

Beyond the classroom, my research and writing has been a long series of testimonies, drawing on methods that intertwine feminist standpoint theory in which those who experience power and inequality are understood as the most reliable and powerful witnesses against systemic inequality and systemic violence. Played against those testimonies, I use post-structural theory to unpack the covert ways that those survivors' testimonies are situated within the language and practice of outwardly benign educational, social work, medical, family, and gender systems.

Substantively, this has meant examining the ways that institutions such as medicine, the workplace, the family (and I use that term to describe an institution, not individual households or relationships), public education, and psychiatry work together to minimize stillbirth and early infant loss (Malacrida 1999); to individualize maternal responsibility, "choice," and compliance in childbirth (Malacrida and Boulton 2014); to understand the psychiatric and behavioural labelling of children who learn and act differently in schools (Malacrida 2003); to discipline mothers as responsible for all of their children's successes and "failures" (Malacrida 2001); and to "protect" children from being raised by disabled mothers, who are often characterized as deficient or inappropriate to parenthood (Malacrida 2009a, 2009b).

Most importantly, I have used these tools and personal experiences to examine how networks of medical, educational, and moral systems worked to place certain "kinds" of children from certain "kinds" of families into a total institution in Canada where children identified as "defective" were incarcerated for life and often involuntarily sterilized (Malacrida 2015). Further, I have used the tools Goffman and Foucault have left us to unpack the immediate and long-term effects of that institutional violence on the lives, identities, and spirits of those who have survived it (Malacrida 2005).

In all this work, my personal early experiences emphatically do not stand in for methodological rigour, nor do they provide me with de facto legitimacy as an interlocutor of other peoples' pain. However, my experiences of invasive, controlling, and violent intra-institutional "help" as a child and adolescent have been the glue that connects my seemingly disparate sociological investigations. Further, it is my sincere hope that those early experiences, coupled with an intellectual training and knowledge that has been both enlightening and liberatory, permit me to speak against institutional violence in its multiple guises and its broad-ranging ills in important and enduring ways.

NOTES

1 In reality, the abuse was only one piece – albeit a big one – of the emotional minefield that was my family.

2 As an adult, and a feminist one, I have come to understand that assigning my mother sole responsibility for my childhood problems absolves my father of his responsibility for creating a safe space for a growing child. But my father was steadfastly absent in these struggles, leaving my mother and I to battle each other. My memories of this time remain focused on her and me, with him as an unhappy, unhelpful witness.

3 My family's middle-classed location – intact family, professional father, highly engaged mother – worked well with the police and in the child and family court system. I am not sure, for example, that my father would have been permitted to take me home to another town if we were of a different social position. In the end, I think, this reflected that my parents were seen as partners in my "correction," rather than as part of the problem.

4 After a very long and difficult delivery, I gave birth to a little girl three days before Halloween. I remember being in hospital afterward and hearing the sound of fireworks through the window. As an indication of my maturity, I recall feeling quite sad that I wasn't out trick or treating and setting off firecrackers like "normal" fifteen-year-olds. I was never to hold that baby, nor was I permitted to name her. I only later came to understand the depth of those losses; in the moment, I think I just wanted to get through that part of my life and get free.

5 Under the Juvenile Delinquents Act (JDA), it was common to charge and retain girls and women under the rubric of "status crimes" for behaviours that would be perfectly legal if the individual was an adult or a married woman (Sangster 2001).

6 The JDA also arose from a broader impetus of protecting the middle and upper-middle classes from the threat of increased urbanization and the perceived unruliness of working class and poor youth and families – as did

much of the "child-saving" movement of the early twentieth century (Hogeveen 2008). My "hypersexuality" and non-compliance in school and within my middle-classed family positioned me squarely in the crosshairs of the social anxiety that motivated the bill and the institutions that arose from it.

7 Canadian Girls in Training (CGIT) is a church-based training program for girls between eleven and seventeen. Members sport a quasi-military uniform and meet weekly to prepare for leadership in their future family, work, and community roles. Reflecting some of the core concerns raised by dangerous girls like me, the CGIT pledge asks its members to "cherish health, seek truth, know God, serve others, and thus, with His help, become the girl God would have me be." In addition, this group included sex education within its mandate, drawing on theological and psychological models of sexual self-control (McCraken 2015).

8 In her masterful book on the abuses of the Magdalen Laundries, Rie Croll unpacks the role of internalized shame in ensuring "wayward" girls' and women's obedience and silence (Croll 2019).

REFERENCES

Canadian Public Health Association. 2021. "History of Family Planning in Canada." Accessed 2 February 2021. https://www.cpha.ca/history-family-planning-canada.

Croll, Rie. 2019. *Shaped by Silence: Stories from Inmates of the Good Shepherd Laundries and Reformatories*. Saint John's, Newfoundland: ISER Press, Memorial University.

Dowbiggin, Ian. 1995. "Keeping This Young Country Sane: C.K. Clarke, Immigration Restriction, and Canadian Psychiatry, 1890–1925." *Canadian Historical Review*: 598–627.

Ellis, Carolyn, Tony E. Adams, and Arthur P. Bochner. 2011. "Autoethnography: An Overview." *Historical Social Research* 36, no. 4: 273–90.

Foucault, Michel. 1988. *Madness and Civilization: A History of Insanity in the Age of Reason*. New York: Vintage Books.

– 1990. *The History of Sexuality. Volume I: An Introduction*. New York: Vintage Books.

Goffman, Erving. 1961. *Asylums: Essays on the Social Situation of Mental Patients and Other Inmates*. Garden City, New York: Doubleday Books.

Grosz, Elizabeth. 1987. "Notes toward A Corporeal Feminism." *Australian Feminist Studies* 5 (Summer): 1–16.

Hogeveen, Bryan. 2008. "Discontinuity and/in the Early Twentieth Century Ontario Juvenile Court." *Journal of Historical Sociology* 20, no. 4: 605–21.

Malacrida, Claudia. 1999. "Complicating Mourning: The Social Economy of Perinatal Death." *Qualitative Health Research* 9, no. 4: 504–19.

– 2001. "Motherhood, Resistance and Attention Deficit Disorder." *Canadian Review of Sociology and Anthropology* 38, no. 2: 141–65.

– 2003. *Cold Comfort: Mothers, Professionals and ADD*. Toronto: University of Toronto Press.

– 2005. "Discipline and Dehumanization in a Total Institution: Institutional Survivors' Descriptions of Time-Out Rooms." *Disability and Society* 20, no. 5: 523–37.

– 2009a. "Gendered Ironies in Home Care: Surveillance, Gender Struggles and Infantilization." *International Journal of Inclusive Education*: 1–20.

– 2009b. "Performing Motherhood in a Disablist World: Dilemmas of Motherhood, Femininity and Disability." *International Journal of Qualitative Studies in Education* 23, no. 1: 99–117.

– 2015. *A Special Hell: Institutional Life in Alberta's Eugenic Years*. Toronto: University of Toronto Press.

Malacrida, Claudia, and Tiffany Boulton. 2014. "The Best Laid Plans? Women's Choices, Expectations and Experiences in Childbirth." *Health: An Interdisciplinary Journal for the Social Study of Health, Illness and Medicine* 18, no. 1: 41–59.

McCraken, Krista. 2015. "Canadian History." Accessed 9 February 2021. http://activehistory.ca/2015/12/canadian-girls-in-training-100-years-with-a-purpose.

Mills, C. Wright. 2001. "The Sociological Imagination." In *Social Theory: Continuity & Confrontation (A Reader)*, edited by Roberta Garner, 322–30. Peterborough, ON: Broadview Press.

Rose, Nikolas. 1990. *Governing the Soul: The Shaping of the Private Self*. London: Routledge.

Sangster, Joan. 2001. *Regulating Girls and Women: Sexuality, Family, and the Law In Ontario, 1920–1960*. Don Mills, ON: Oxford University Press.

– 2002. *Girl Trouble: Female Delinquency in English Canada*. Toronto: Between the Lines.

TRC (Truth and Reconciliation Committee of Canada). 2016. *A Knock on the Door: The Essential History of Residential Schools*, edited by National Centre for Truth and Reconciliation. Winnipeg: University of Manitoba Press.

Trent, James W. 1994. *Inventing the Feeble Mind: A History of Mental Retardation in the United States*. Berkeley: University of California Press.

Weedon, Chris. 1987. *Feminist Practice and Poststructuralist Theory*. Oxford: Basil Blackwell.

2

"Spectacles of Humiliation"

Symbolic Violence and the Regulation of Good Shepherd Inmates

RIE CROLL

> We need to comprehend the social world in terms of the relationship between the processes of embodiment and institutionalization … We create institutions to reduce our vulnerability and attain security, but these institutional patterns are always imperfect, inadequate, and precarious. Learning to live in society means learning how these institutions work or fail to work.
>
> (Turner 2006, 27)

Between 2009 and 2019 I conducted ethnographic interviews with women who had been child inmates of Roman Catholic Sisters of the Good Shepherd laundries and reformatories for girls and women (Croll 2019). These in-depth interviews revealed former inmates' immediate and enduring experiences of penal confinement in church and state-supported institutions. This last generation of Good Shepherd survivors were incarcerated between the 1930s and the 1960s yet the Good Shepherds, a French[1] Order, founded by Saint Mary Euphrasia Pelletier, began operating their reform mission in France in 1835.[2] From there the Good Shepherd operation proliferated throughout France, Britain, Ireland, Canada, Australia, New Zealand, the Netherlands, the United States, and elsewhere before they closed their last institution of this kind in Dublin in 1996. Across time and place these institutions were known variously as Homes of the Good

Shepherd, Good Shepherd refuges, and Magdalene laundries, among others. Their stated purpose, of supporting women and girls "who had fallen into licentiousness" (St Basius 1890, 60),[3] can be generally translated as the rescue of so-called "prostitutes," unwed mothers, and "incorrigible" girls. For the countless thousands thus characterized, this meant often unwilling confinement in a carceral system that professed to reform and care for them.

I worked for ten years with the women whose experiences are at the centre of this work. This length of time was necessary for several reasons but foremost was former inmates' reluctance to speak. Gathering their accounts involved them bringing forth stories out of the shadows that society has not wanted told. The abuse and stigmatization that these girls and women suffered had left them wary about conveying their incarceration experiences. Complicating this further still was that in their confinement they had been systematically regulated to silence and upon their release, many were told never to mention that they had been there. In *Shaped by Silence: Stories from Inmates of the Good Shepherd Laundries and Reformatories* (Croll 2019) I united former inmates' very personal narratives with a socio-historical analysis. Here, I extend that analysis to consider how violence, particularly the regularized "symbolic" or "soft" violence embedded in this form of incarceration, merged with other forms of violence to further dehumanize former inmates, and significantly alter their self-perceptions (Bourdieu 2001, 1). In this chapter's second section (*Victim Blaming: From Stigma to Stigmata*) I probe how inmates' resulting derogation, and associated negative sense of self, is an outcome of ongoing victim blaming and stigmatization – another naturalized configuration of soft violence – by church and state. This section likewise considers how social hierarchies become unwittingly internalized by inmates as did the deep contradictions of meaning and purpose inherent in the institutionalization of these girls and women. Ultimately, however, as this chapter's third section (*Countering Domination*) explores, those who relayed their stories to me were engaged in ongoing counter inscriptions, or in disrupting and sometimes even rewriting damning cultural characterizations of them through numerous acts of signification – not the least of which was eventually defying silence by making their stories public. While symbolic violence creates "the internalization of humiliations and legitimations of hierarchy that results in self-blame for misfortunes and a naturalization of the status quo" (Bornstein 2005, 111), former inmates' many acts of signification, during and post institutionalization, point to an awareness, however small or unconscious, that the power relations normalizing their humiliation and diminishing them in the name of benevolence and moral assimilation were unjust.

Soft or symbolic violence works, Bourdieu tells us, when subjective and objective structures are in accord with each other (Calhoun et al. 1993, 172) in a way that normalizes certain social injustices, cruelties, or hierarchies, and leads us to accept them as natural or inevitable. An example of this normalization, one that undergirded the Good Shepherd mission, was gender inequality.[4] Since the laundries were intended for a certain supposedly unruly and morally suspect (based on normative sex and gender roles) class of women and girls, their confinement as inmates was broadly condoned. A widespread cultural conviction that "wayward" women needed to be taken possession of and given protection helped to validate and legitimatize the Good Shepherd's specific "rescue" and "reform" approach (Sangster 2001, 199–200; Hughes 1985, 19, 25). Regardless of the actual circumstances that led to their incarceration – which for those I interviewed was rooted in their intersections with poverty, familial sexual abuse and neglect, immigrant status, and/or Indigeneity – the state and church agreed that the women and girls sent there would benefit from this form of incarceration, wherein, as their Good Shepherd "caretakers" maintained, each person would be treated "with the same care of Jesus, the Good Shepherd" (Good Shepherd Sisters n.d.). In compelling contrast, former inmates report having been persistently discredited and degraded by the nuns who told them repeatedly that they were bad, dirty, and unlovable. Likewise, the unpaid cleaning that they performed (in what are now sometimes referred to as religious sweat shops) was supposed to provide them with skills but also served as a humiliating exercise in penitence, a washing away of their sins and their disgrace as purportedly fallen women. In this way, symbolic violence functioned as an instrument of social control that protected the existing social order.

Bourdieu conceived symbolic violence as a practice of violence that delivers power without force and thrives with the consent that it is permitted in dominant systems of meaning and symbolism (Jenkins 1992, 66). The social permission that it receives thus legitimates it so that it is often misrecognized, rarely mentioned, and therefore operates mostly unseen. For example, because the control and "protection" of women's sexual morality was formalized (and so legitimized and normalized) within the Good Shepherd carceral system, as it was/is more broadly, it initially went mostly unrecognized as violence, even by the inmates.[5] The general ethos that the girls and women confined therein were there for their own good as well as for society's sake, to halt the spread of their moral contagion, further legitimized the nuns' various uses of power.[6] Given this overarching protectionist tenet, one hurtfully punctuated by family and state abandonment of girls and women to these places, many inmates assumed moral responsibility for their incarceration.

The Good Shepherd nuns' "duty," as laid out in their regulations, was to bring penitents "from the most shameful disorders to a chaste life" (Sisters 1890, 60). This duty meant re-molding their charges to fit prevailing socio-religious perceptions of virtuous womanhood (Titley 2006, 2), despite the suffering caused by the regimes and discourses underpinning their so-called reform mission. This undertaking justified the intentional breaking down of inmates' identities, which took the form of a series of personal subtractions – in addition to their silencing these included the denial of an education, infantilizing and renaming them, forced head shaving, nail cutting, and other "spectacles of humiliation,"[7] intended to control unruly bodies and re-form tainted beings.

These institutions served as colonizing tools as well as dumping grounds for society's unwanted girls and women and within the reformatories their devalued social location furthermore served to justify practices of humiliating subordination, another form of symbolic violence that, as Bornstein writes, are intended "to injure or destroy the recognition of mutual personhood" (2005, 111). Bornstein's observation was confirmed by the former inmates I interviewed, who consistently characterized their care as less than human. For instance, one former Toronto inmate, Autumn,[8] described the extraction of her teeth that took place during her incarceration as subhuman treatment. It was a common practice of the Good Shepherds to extract rather than fill inmates' teeth. From Autumn's perspective, the nuns did not deem them worthy of dentistry that would allow them a small measure of self-esteem. Autumn described it as "a cruel system that planted the doubt in you and denied you your humanity and dignity." In other words, the Good Shepherd "reform" institutions, as culture-defining and culture-replicating apparatus, did little to provide inmates with a clean start. The everyday, normalized violence of these institutions eroded their dignity and self-worth and proved powerful in shaping their life-long inequality. Their consequential diminished cultural legitimacy effected former inmates' social and economic opportunities in complex ways. In short, when they attempted to re-enter their communities, they discovered that, to borrow Garland Thompson's (2011) concept, they had been rendered misfits. And "to misfit into the public sphere," says Garland-Thompson, "is to be denied full citizenship" (601).

So effective was the nuns' symbolic structure of domination that overt, physical violence (while present) was less necessary as a strategy of control. The soft or "gentle" violence, as Bourdieu sometimes also called it, that functioned in its place altered inmates' self-concepts, almost indiscernibly. It was not that the symbolic assertions of violence went undetected by the inmates, but that rather they were so deeply embedded in "asymmetrical social relations" (Roumbanis 2019, 202) that the effect was not readily identifiable and so was only gradually realized. Former Australian inmate Janice Konstantinidis[9] said that the whole process of incarceration progressively took hold as a sense of humiliation that she still carries: "I can't be exact about where and when the humiliation came from. It was from within, I think. The 'knowledge' that I was a bad person, bad enough to be locked up. The fact that we were always expected to be submissive, either to the nuns or the dominant girls was humiliation as well. I can't recall feeling any pride." So normalized in language and structure, negative messages about the inmates thus became habitualized in powerful forms of social control that produced the silence of a disgraced population.

Silence was but one aspect of a moral/structural framework set out in the Early Good Shepherd regulations. Regulation booklets made clear the conduct and practices that both nuns and inmates were to follow – they provided an operational blueprint that served to completely standardize these reformatories. Inmates functioned within a deliberate, calculated, uniform, rational scheme, that worked similarly from country to country and across time. These guidebooks outlined times and locations for speaking, topics of conversation, and various other practices that remained strictly regulated as late as the 1950s and 1960s, and in some cases beyond. In each institution, from country to country, before sunup, inmates were jolted awake with the loud clapping of a nun's hands. This was their directive to drop to their knees at their bedsides and recite prayers. With bells signalling their waking movements, inmates operated in lock step, on command and primarily in silence; they lined up to go to the bathroom, they dressed and undressed in unison, they lined up to go to chapel, they ate with heads down in silent rows at long refectory tables, and most spent upwards of eight hours each day labouring in industrial laundries, in silence. The symbolic ritual of cleaning, the rigid gendered routine of this work, and the isolation from society, was designed to re/form inmates, under the auspices of care. Yet, ex-inmates repeatedly told me that no reform or care materialized in these places and that with a nullity of community and governmental oversight, various practices of overt and symbolic violence overlapped on their bodies and psyches in numerous forms, including corporal punishment, neglect, sexual abuse, isolation, and derogation.

Those I interviewed said that the nuns folded institutional violence into their view of them as pollutants (gender pollutants in particular) in need of enforced penance. This perception was rooted in the order's constitutions, wherein the sins of inmates are associated with disease: To "destroy one sin in a soul," say their instructions, "is a greater benefit than to cause the cessation of a general pestilence" (Sisters 1890, 142). This equation, and related views, caused residents to consider themselves "dirty," in comparison to the "pure and clean" nuns (Swain and Hillel 2010, 167) who perceived them as unalterably deviant and regularly berated them as bad and beyond redemption. These and similar violent organizational mechanisms proved to be the most difficult for inmates to overcome because they became integrated into their sense of self. Ex-inmates explained to me that the physical forms of violence they endured were more obvious to them as abuse and so, to some extent, in the aftermath of institutionalization they were able to separate their identities from it.

Fifty or more years following their releases ex-inmates continue(d) to grapple with the complicated, unresolved effects of symbolic violence. Janice, for example, described what the nuns called weekly "instruction" as one means of reinforcing inmates' amoral state. She characterized this as a regularized exercise in degradation, a normalized shaming of sorts in which inmates were reminded that they were "evil and bad." Similarly, weekly instruction for the inmates in Autumn's reformatory was a pointed weekly recap of similar messages, that, as she said, "we were worthless creatures that would amount to nothing … Hell was our destination." These standardized reminders of their failings as human beings, and their destiny, reaffirmed the other degrading messages they were berated with throughout the week, while they worked and ate.

Former inmates maintained that their forced social exile and strategic silencing permanently displaced them. Cut off from society, as they were, in what Foucault called "heterotopias of deviation"[10] (1984, 47) they were morally segregated from their communities; some characterized their displacement to these institutions as a social devaluation that remained with them. Foucault's notion, "heterotopias of deviation," reminds us that symbolic violence is not simply an ideological practice but unfolds in violent places such as the Magdalene laundries. With this notion, Foucault helps to elucidate such social spatial arrangements wherein the deviant, sick, and/or othered body is removed from the mainstream while the rational for that removal, and the separate space itself, represent central political relations of that time and place. The condoned spatial sequestration of girls and women from their families and communities (a symbolic violence in itself) justified institutional practices of soft violence, including a withdrawal of empathy for this aberrant population (Bornstein 2005, 111). In these socially marginal spaces (which often existed on the social peripheries and did not allow for public access), the Good Shepherd reformatories physically and socially isolated generations of women. Out of public sight, what the nuns called "training" and what their detainees described as enslaved labour unfolded in meticulously rationalized schedules designed to extract from the inmates the maximum degree of labour and penitence.

Hughes maintains that "the fundamental taxonomic principle" of the Good Shepherd system was conversion, which he describes as a "simple distinction between a fallen nature and a graced re-birth" (1985, 322). The socially segregated work that the inmates were forced to perform in the pursuit of their supposed "re-birth," the washing of dirty laundry and institutional cleaning, represented their "transformation from sin to salvation," and must, Hughes argues, be understood in that framework (105). Yet, while a conversion of souls was certainly the stated purpose of this mission, former inmates reported receiving contradictory messages about themselves. For example, despite being targeted for "saving" by the church and state, ex-inmates told me that they were treated as unsalvageable. Beneath the Good Shepherds' stated purpose of providing them with a safe harbour and a new beginning was a methodically organized exercise in inmate contrition that, inmates say, functioned chiefly as a reminder of the indelible stain that they were said to embody as sinful and disgraceful women.

VICTIM BLAMING: FROM STIGMA TO STIGMATA

The Good Shepherds' system of punishment conveyed an expectation that inmates would accept themselves as "deviant" upon internalizing the external rationales for their incarceration. This was part of a victim blaming discourse, structuralized by the Good Shepherds' both in the language used to define and communicate with the inmates and in the symbolism of the cleaning they were forced to perform. The perception, candidly relayed to them, was that they deserved to be locked away and that they would carry their stain indelibly. They were told that their characters were permanently soiled, that they were beyond reclamation. They could not, like the dirty laundry they incessantly scrubbed, ever be considered fully clean in the nuns' eyes. Furthermore, inmates were expected to acknowledge their fallen natures and work compliantly to overcome them. But as Autumn pointed out, redemption was unreachable because the clear message was that "hell was our destination." So, while the Good Shepherds assured the state that in their eyes the inmates were redeemable,[11] inmates maintained that the treatment they received contradicted that promise. Former Australian inmate Rachael Romero maintained, "that sense of condemnation of us [was] the most abusive thing of all."[12]

Through repeated exposure, many inmates grew to see themselves as deserving of the disparagement and punishment they received. More troubling still, stigmatizing categorization combined with repetitive victim blaming to result in what Bourdieu called "destiny effect," a perspective in which the dominated assumed "the dominant point of view on themselves" (2001, 119). This form of symbolic violence, as an internalized hierarchy, was ensured and sustained through repeated messages that underscored inmates' lack of social value as bad, dirty, morally threatening, and unworthy beings. Whereas I mentioned earlier, former inmates maintained that they could eventually separate themselves from the corporeal forms of violence, for some chronic stigmatization and degradation became embodied. "Misrecognition" of this sort is often exploited in victim-blaming discourses, where individuals and groups are assumed accountable for their suffering, masking the power relations that are responsible for domination (Thapar-Bjorkert et al. 2016, 37). Autumn located inmates' misrecognition in the treatment they received; she said they were considered a "worthless herd" whose imprisonment was endorsed by family abandonment as well as a community and state renouncement of them, as delinquents. Being abandoned by all concerned, "by those who should have protected us," she added, "only increased our worthlessness" and solidified the perception that they had only themselves to blame for their circumstances. With no one to amend the nuns' punitive portrayal of them, she said, "we soon came to see ourselves as they saw us, as things without value."

Those I interviewed felt that their bodies came to exude other's damning perceptions of them. Janice spoke of it in terms of growing to identify with the labels – "slut," "bad," "broken," that the nuns berated them with. Such chronic denigration, together with the many formally instituted subtractions and the gendered cleaning labour inmates performed, affected a breaking down of their confidence and sense of self. In this way regularized negative characterizations moved inwards and came to be borne psychically as well as physically – as "durably and deeply embedded" features (Bourdieu 2001, 39). Chaparral Bowman, a former Saint John, New Brunswick laundry inmate, described how the nuns' view of her character became instilled and then reinforced as a deeply fixed self-perception of being, "broken-up and upside down." She told me that being conceived of rape and being of Indigenous heritage rendered her among the "lowest of the low" in the nuns' estimation. This perception was conveyed to her by, among other things, repeatedly being called a "sinner" and a "bastard," which in turn seriously damaged and her sense of self.

And as a young child in a mirrorless institution Chaparral found confirmation of the nuns' judgement of her in a toilet bowl reflection. When she stared into the refracted water of the bowl, she saw that her "face was broken up and in pieces." This reflection was reinforced when, at supper, Chaparral looked at the back of her spoon and noticed that she "was upside down on the back and right side up but squished in the front … and I thought in my child's mind that … I was broken up and I was upside down. And I carried that, and I wouldn't look at anybody. That was what I thought everyone could see." Similarly, New Zealand inmate Kate Reid described instituted practices that, for her, became deeply entrenched. For one thing, she told me, "You weren't allowed to even have eye-to-eye contact." "I still can't do it," she said, "people all the time say to me, bring your head up." Maureen, a former Irish Good Shepherd inmate, likewise said, "It took me ages to hold my head up. I felt ashamed … I felt worthless."

Maureen's, Kate's, and Chaparral's embodied responses to this environment epitomize Bourdieu's understanding of destiny effect, he maintains that "what is 'learned by body,' is not something that one has ... but something that one is (Bourdieu 1990, 73). Their bodies, in other words, eventually exuded the repetitive normalized symbolic violence that shaped them. After their release, former inmates told me, they continued to operate with eyes lowered, voices silenced, and bodies, when possible, kept away from public scrutiny. For, as Rachael explained, they believed that others could read from their bodies what they felt and where they had been. Rachael thought that they could see the damage that had been done to her, that she not only carried her incarceration experience internally but that she "had signs all over [her] of defilement." As Janice put it, "our bodies wore it." Rachael likened the embodied nature of this disgrace to the religious phenomenon of stigmata, which she characterized as a kind of religious branding worn externally for all to see: "You know, like I felt tattooed," she told me.

The subtractions of self that were key to inmates' supposed redemption further debased them and contributed to this sense of being marked. Of these deletions the removal of their names was a significant blow to their stability. Former Irish inmate Maureen Sullivan[13] told me that her birth name was the last vestige of her family and identity. The nuns' erasure of it, felt like an act of "violence" that broke her down to a "nobody," yet its confiscation was justified as protection. Magdalenes were repeatedly told that their old identities were a source of shame and needed to be taken from them, for their own good. Early Good Shepherd guidebooks phrased it this way: "in respect for her feelings each [penitent] is given a different name from that which she bore in the world" (Sisters 1890, 9). For many, however, the stripping away of their names annulled them through an erasure of the last vestige of what they thought was theirs.

Former inmates also spoke about the nuns' diminishing gaze as heightening their sense of stigmatization. They characterized it as not merely panoptic or surveillant, but as penetratingly judgmental and derogatory. This ubiquitous form of derogation combined with other facets of the Good Shepherd regime to create a uniquely powerful form of levelling. Kate described the surveillance as unrelenting and the stare of the nuns as akin to psychic assault. In line with this reaction, Flam and Beauzamy discuss the human gaze as a "constituting power" that can be manipulated towards violence (Flam and Beauzamy 2008, 222). In addition to the mutually reinforcing social construction of self that Cooley called the "looking glass self,"[14] they point out that the "constituting reflection" can unfold as a harmful dynamic. It can also be turned into "an instrument of superordination, superiority and contempt, of surveillance, control and discipline" (ibid.). Indeed, under "the constituting, disciplining, subordinating and ... contemptuous gaze" (to use their excellent phrase) of the nuns, inmates were diminished and rendered powerless (ibid., 222–3). Autumn said, "My ... body ... my psyche ... did not belong to me. I was under their control ... I had no sense of being at all."

The intrusive scrutiny that Autumn and others described was, like the removal of their names, justified as an act of protection. Since a protectionist motivation confers largely unexamined authority to the dominant (Jabri 2013, 134), it creates a concerning hierarchy. Historically, As Sangster points out, it "meant the increased moral surveillance of working-class and poor girls; protection meant incarcerating 'promiscuous' girls who had not broken the law but were deemed in need of moral re-education" (Sangster 2002, 3). Thus, protection as judgemental surveillance, "slid into stigmatization, marginalization, and incarceration" (Sangster 2001, 3). Even in the language used to address the inmates, a righteous ideology of protection is present. Despite the reported age of laundry inmates as being fourteen years and older, for instance, one description from benefactors touring the Eastern Canadian Good Shepherd laundries states, "The girls are never referred to except as 'children,' and every sister is called by them 'mother'" (Benefactors 1915, 50). Calling adult inmates "children," said Janice, effectively "infantilized and disempowered" them and robbed them of their identities; "this was a way of levelling and humiliating us."

Under the auspices of care and protection inmates were forbidden to mention their former lives; their lives, like their names, were purportedly a mark of shame. Indeed they were harshly discouraged from speaking at all. While punishments for speaking without permission ranged from slapping and punching inmates to solitary confinement, the most powerful punitive effect of this silencing was the belief that they were not worthy of speech. Janice said that one effect of this and other losses of self was having "no sense of entitlement"; she did not feel worthy of even having "basic human rights and freedoms." The Good Shepherds "taught us to see ourselves this way," she maintained. With nothing to ameliorate the conviction that they were irreparably indecent, these messages took hold as truths.

COUNTERING DOMINATION

Underpinning the Good Shepherds' protectionist mission was an inculcation of inmates with the gendered "order of things,"[15] which took the form of a hyper-structured and unrelenting exercise in cleaning, humiliation, and prayer. Given that this system of moral reformation both drew from and reproduced a broadly supported meaning and symbolism, it was expected that inmates would assume their place within it. Samuel characterizes such adaptations as knowing one's place or having a "sense of placement," including an awareness of one's rank, and acting accordingly (2012, 27). For the Good Shepherd inmates this meant adjusting their thoughts, feelings, and behaviours to their subjugated positions within the prevailing classification structure.

As we've seen, inmates' bodies, minds, and spirits were bent to the nuns' pervasive and all-surveillant apparatus. Under these circumstances they did what they could to sustain themselves, often through small expressions of agency. Such acts of self-preservation affirm Flam and Beauzamy's contention that the victims of symbolic violence are often "both aware and hurt" and occasionally manage "to strike back" (2008, 222). Inmates were not, in other words, simply victims of the "order of things" – they devised strategic counter responses to being put in their place. These strategies were numerous and included skin cutting and inking, deliberate self-injury such as crushing their limbs in the laundry presses, running away, as well as communicating secretly through the exchange of holy cards. Among these, perhaps the most overt resistance to the silencing was making public their stories of institutionalization.

Some inmates reified the pain and alienation of their degraded state (and other inexpressible sufferings) by skin cutting and tattooing themselves. The intention of these forbidden acts varied but primarily they communicated their pain and loneliness and affirmed their existence. "For one thing," Rachael told me: "[The nuns] were saying that we were defiled and so forth and then we were hurting ourselves externally, as they were hurting us internally." In a sense, it was an autonomous response to being psychically defiled: with no one to confide in, in a world of enforced silence, cutting and tattooing were defiant acts of signification. Rachael described it as "a sort of individuation thing," a courageous personal expression in a place where all self-expressions had been denied.

Inmates were prohibited from mentioning their lives on the outside; nor could they write to anyone about "what was really happening" (Maureen) within the institution: conversations were monitored; outgoing and incoming mail was censored. But self-wounding and inking communicated their suffering and confirmed connections with one another and loved ones on the outside. Some inmates, for example, carved the initials of someone dear to them into their skin in defiant expressions of care. Thus, that which they were not allowed to speak about – their pasts, their loved ones, their emotional responses to the often intangible and inexpressible effects of the institutional violence – could be realized and represented in this way. Even these small gestures, Autumn felt, "helped them to cope," they were self-sustaining measures. She felt that they brought "temporary relief" and she later appreciated body carving and inking as a self-directed "resistance to losing themselves."

These forms of "symbolic homeopathy,"[16] were slight correctives to the symbolic violence being enacted upon inmates, if only as pale substitutes for understanding and care (LeBreton 2018, 37); as Autumn noted, "anyone who survived that reformatory environment found their own way to do so, they had to." LeBreton contends that carving and tattooing the skin, that "border between self and other" (LeBreton 2018, 33), helps to ease the powerlessness caused by a loss of self. This "consented-to pain" is a "kind of survival technique, a way of escaping death" (39), and the many intrusive incisions of soft violence. At least for brief periods of time, these counter inscriptions "can reorganize and stabilize the trauma victim's world, providing a 'voice on the skin' when the actual voice is forbidden" (McLane in LeBreton 2018, 46).

Inmates' exchange of holy cards was another subversion of the silencing endorsed by the Good Shepherd carceral system in that it too served as an expression of voice and community building where none was permitted. The pocket-sized, collectible cards, with a religious image such as a saint on one side and a prayer on the other, were given to inmates by the nuns on religious feast days and at Christmas and Easter, as concrete manifestations of the virtues they were meant to aspire to. Since holy card exchanges were authorized by the nuns, they were above suspicion and eluded censorship. The cards, however, were sometimes appropriated by the inmates for their own communications. Where very few exchanges were permitted between inmates, the sanctioned exchange of these cards was a way that they could circumvent the nuns' surveillance while building scraps of community. "Always watched," said Rachael, "We could not pass notes or letters unless the nuns read them first, but the holy card was ok. It carried our "voice" however coded, however muffled." The cards, she said, represented a "currency – emotional currency – in a place where expressions of contempt are the norm; where you can't trust anyone because of coercion, and it is unwise to share secrets." Rachael described inmates' holy card exchanges as "a sanctioned ... purified, way of showing loyalty and caring between people." They allowed the Magdalenes "to say what otherwise may not be said, to give each other courage." In short, they were another tiny self-procured antidote to the alienating effects of voicelessness.

In the Good Shepherd reformatories communication with and about the outside world was prohibited and the vetting of all ingoing or outgoing letters further safeguarded this censorship. As a result, once released, ex-inmates found it difficult to contact other former inmates, since they had no way to track their whereabouts. Locating one another was further complicated by the nuns' practice of renaming inmates, since they often did not even know one another's birth names. In Autumn's Toronto reformatory, however, some inmates circumvented this problem through a strategic re-gifting of their holy cards. They exchanged their cards having put their home addresses on them in code. They wrote their house number on one card and on the next one they exchanged they provided their street name. "We would never put the city," Autumn told me, "that went to memory, and in those days, postal codes were not required." In this manner, inmates could exchange addresses undetected, so that once released, contact with one another was possible. This tactic permitted Autumn and a friend she had made while incarcerated to reconnect through letters and those communications, in turn, provided crucial validation of one another's incarceration experiences. For a chronically discredited population traumatized by institutional and other violences, post-Magdalene relationships were often few and difficult to maintain.

Despite the many small acts of resistance, they employed while institutionalized, a persuasive sense of having moral responsibility for their incarceration initially silenced most former inmates about their experiences with the Good Shepherds. Even decades after their incarceration, some who I spoke with would not tell those closest to them about this part of their lives. Samuel regards shame as "deeply social," and says it is "exacerbated by its tendency to remain unarticulated" (2012, 9). But in refusing to continue to bear that shame and in choosing to make their stories public, thereby violating the rule of silence that marked their captivity, former inmates engaged in a conscious and public form of resistance. Their accounts permitted them to reclaim themselves while also providing insight into generations of Magdalenes' attempts to resist domination and sustain themselves during confinement. While the residue of symbolic violence continued(s) to grip former inmates as social and self-estrangement six decades or more after their institutionalization, the development of agency and attempts to resist domination, even under these powerful forces, emerged as common themes in their narratives.

EXILE

The structural violence that was regularized within these places of supposed reform and care served to turn stigma and victim blaming into misrecognition. Effectively, the inmates grew to identify with the labels used to justify their incarceration, thus fulfilling the nuns' original intention of silencing a disgraced people. Janice said that once she was free of institutionalization, she was never quite free. She carried the stigma of the "slag from the mag" along with an ever-present dread of re-institutionalization. To quell the anxiety that this fear created and to avoid stigma she sought to always maintain "the cleanest house." The nuns' emphasis on cleaning and cleanliness had fixed in Janice the view that bad women are dirty and must clean perpetually. From this message she came to equate cleanliness with respectability and hoped that a spotless home might camouflage her "dirty" history. She told me that she hoped that it would demonstrate to others that she was "very good." "It was a demonstration of a good person," she added. Driven by this edict, she felt compelled to strive for an image of clean while feeling "very unwell" for decades following her confinement.

Others too told me that the lingering outcome of incarceration with the Good Shepherds was self-estrangement. "That carries on into your adult life, said Chaparral, "it doesn't go away. You have to make a conscious effort not to dwell on it because if you do, it's there ... There's a feeling always of being lost." With no firm sense of self to combat the humiliations that were directed at them, soft violence took hold in the inmates I interviewed as truths, which initially prevented them from recognizing their treatment as unjust, their accompanying subordination as embedded and prevented the more overt forms of domination (including economic and physical exploitation and abuses) from being recognized as such.

Beneath the nuns' broadly naturalized project of gentle care and "doing good" lay, then, what inmates experienced as devastating judgment of their character; one that implied they could never be "good" people. An abiding cultural conviction that "wayward" women needed to be taken control of and given protection helped to validate and legitimatize the Good Shepherd's specific "rescue" and reform approach. But ironically the supposed cure for women and girls' presumed immorality did little to provide inmates with a clean start. On the contrary, the system of incarceration that was supposed to reform them, proved powerful in shaping their life-long inequality; "they damaged us, said Rachael, our sense of our own value and our potential." So, despite the Good Shepherd order being "guided by the principle that 'One person is of more value than a world'" (Good Shepherd Sisters n.d.), inmates' laundry experiences left them adversely marked and exiled from society. As we have seen, they came to wear their stigma in and on their bodies and felt that their incarceration experiences were legible to others. This made getting jobs and keeping them difficult. Kate said that she lost many jobs because of her abovementioned inability to maintain eye contact. Others told me that they preferred to work alone and in silence. Overall, the diminished cultural legitimacy that resulted for these women effected their social and economic opportunities in complex ways.

Personal experience, particularly that conveyed by historically silenced voices, contributes immeasurably to understanding the deleterious effects of the forms of violence that both endorse carceral (and related) institutions and operate within them. In the case of the Good Shepherds, the stories former inmates relayed are artefacts of a particular moral double standard – a contradiction located not only in the unequal cultural treatment of men and women but, fatefully, in the highly rationalized and widely supported mission behind women's supposed protection and rescue. Laundry survivors' insider's testimonies intimately reveal that the kinds of hidden violence that support and thrive surreptitiously within such structures are often the most deeply damaging because they are intended to become embedded in the self, in ways that reshape and dehumanize. The result of this legitimate violence for those I interviewed was a social disembeddedness that resulted in a permanent sense of their outsider status as inevitable and irreversible. In combination with this, former inmates described a sometimes-immobilizing disbelief in their own value and credibility, one that they carried for decades after their releases.

In tandem with an analysis of former inmates' incarceration experiences, Bourdieu's theory of symbolic violence sheds light on how a naturalized ideology concerning the supposed care of these morally contagious "bad" girls and women created social indifference to the suffering caused by the Good Shepherds. Furthermore, considering this symbolic violence as naturalized ideology helps us to better comprehend the slow public response to the inhumanities executed in the name of this mission. Its naturalization empowered the Good Shepherd system of reform and permitted the principles underlying it to operate unchecked, and therein ensured its success as a deeply effective tool of social othering. Because the forms of power that put inmates "in their places" were likewise initially read by many inmates as legitimate domination, in the sense that it had been constructed to appear logical, normal even, and therefore inevitable, its recognition as violence came slowly for many and not at all for some. Yet, as we have seen, those I interviewed shared a recognition that the social perceptions of them as fallen, loathsome, and irredeemable were unjust, and through small and large acts they challenged the ideologies that justified their confinement. Their various methods of resistance, including the telling of their stories, contest the necessity and efficacy of this form of hierarchical gendered control and make tangible and recognizable symbolic violence's hidden processes and its intricate consequences. In this way and others, an analysis of former inmates' various counter inscriptions refocuses our attention on both the forms and effects of symbolic violence and on the agentic capacity of those who suffered within this broadly supported system of "care."

NOTES

1 Although many Magdalene institutions used the Anglicized spelling, Magdalen, I use the French spelling Magdalene, in keeping with the Good Shepherds' origins.

2 The Congregation of the Sisters of the Good Shepherd began as a branch of the Order of Our Lady of Charity (founded in Caen, France, by Saint John Eudes). Each convent of the Order of Our Lady of Charity was independent and operated autonomously. With the Good Shepherds,

Sister Mary Euphrasia Pelletier created a new governing structure that permitted nuns and other resources to be transferred between convents as needed. The new congregation received the name Our Lady of Charity of the Good Shepherd of Angers, better known as Sisters of the Good Shepherd.

3 The Good Shepherds, originally a French order of nuns, are but one of several Catholic orders that ran Magdalene laundries – including the Sisters of Mercy and the Sisters of Charity (Luddy 2007, 77).

4 Bourdieu considers gender domination to be "the paradigmatic form of symbolic violence" (Bourdieu and Wacquant 1992, 170).

5 The word "promiscuous," for example, which Sangster maintains was "used repeatedly in legal judgements to categorize and punish women," was consistently aimed at those girls confined to Good Shepherd laundries and reformatories (Sangster 2001, 200).

6 According to Maria Luddy, these homes supposedly sheltered those sent there from social stigmatization while simultaneously rescuing them from the potential of falling into prostitution: "The exclusions enforced by these homes" promised "respectable" society "freedom from contamination" (804).

7 Janice Konstantinidis, a former Australian inmate, used this term to depict an array of diminishments levelled at Magdalene inmates.

8 Autumn is a pseudonym. All quotations attributed to Autumn are taken from a series of interviews between Autumn and Rie Croll, which took place between 2013 and 2017.

9 All quotations attributed to Janice are taken from a series of interviews between Janice and Rie Croll, which took place between 2009 and 2015.

10 The heterotopia, as developed by Foucault is "A place (or notional place) that exists as an ordinary part of a society but which is also in some way demarcated, separate, or marginal, meaning the norms of wider society (though present) can become blurred, undermined, resisted, or transformed by different modes of thought and behaviour arising within the place itself (*OED Online* March 2020). Within this broad concept, Foucault delineated various types of heterotopias, such as heterotopias of deviation, which epitomize the Good Shepherd institutions. These are spaces, such as prisons, "in which individuals whose behavior is deviant in relation to the required mean or norm are placed." In contrast to utopias, these are "real places" in that they "do exist" and that they are "formed in the very founding of society" as something akin to "counter-sites" (Foucault 1984, 46–9).

11 According to Alberta's 1912 "Annual Report: Dependent and Delinquent Children," The Good Shepherds were "held to be the most successful on the American Continent today" in the reform of wayward girls (Alberta 39).

12 All quotations attributed to Rachael Romero are taken from a series of interviews between Rachael and Rie Croll, which took place between 2009 and 2016.

13 All quotes attributed to Maureen Sullivan are taken from a series of interviews between Maureen and Rie Croll, which took place from 2009–17.

14 "A composite of how we see ourselves, how others see us and how we think others see us" the self-concept and emotional well-being are tied to a reciprocal social feedback loop (Delanty 2008, 222).

15 "Of all forms of 'hidden persuasion,'" according to Bourdieu, "the most implacable is the one exerted, quite simply, by the order of things" (Bourdieu and Wacquant 1992, 168).

16 According to LeBreton, "it is a way of taking control by hurting oneself in order to feel less pain ... it is a form of symbolic renewal through destruction" (2018, 37).

REFERENCES

Alberta. 1912. "Annual Report: Dependent and Delinquent Children." Department of Attorney General.

Bornstein, Avra. 2005. "Political Violence." In *Encyclopedia of Social Measurement*, 109–14. Elsevier: Academic Press.

Bourdieu, Pierre. 1989. "Social Space and Symbolic Power." *Sociological Theory* 7, no. 1: 14–25.

– 1990 *The Logic of Practice*. Cambridge: Polity Press.

– 2000. *Pascalian Meditations*. Oxford: Polity Press.

– 2001. *Masculine Domination*. Translated by Richard Nice. Stanford: Stanford University Press.

Bourdieu, Pierre, and Loïc J.D. Wacquant. 1992. *An Invitation to Reflexive Sociology*. Chicago: University of Chicago Press.

Calhoun, Craig, Edward LiPuma, and Moishe Postone. 1993. *Bourdieu: Critical Perspectives*. University of Chicago Press.

Croll, Rie. 2019. *Shaped by Silence: Stories from Inmates of the Good Shepherd Laundries and Reformatories*. St John's: ISER Books.

Flam, Helena, and Brigitte Beauzamy. 2008. "Symbolic Violence." In *Identity, Belonging and Migration*, edited by Gerard Delanty, Ruth Wodak, and Paul Jones, 221–40. Liverpool: Liverpool University Press.

Foucault, Michel. 1984. "Of Other Spaces, Heterotopias." *Architecture, Mouvement, Continuité* 5: 46–9.
Garland-Thomson, Rosemarie. 2011. "Misfits: A Feminist Materialist Disability Concept." *Hypatia* 26, no. 3: 591–609.
Good Shepherd Sisters. n.d. www.goodshepherdsisters.org.
Hughes, Peter E. 1985. "Cleanliness and Godliness: A Sociological Study of the Good Shepherd Convent Refuges for the Social Reformation and Christian Conversion of Prostitutes and Convicted Women in Nineteenth Century Britain." PhD diss., Brunel University.
Jabri, Vivienne. 2013. *The Postcolonial Subject*. New York: Routledge.
Jenkins, Richard. 1992. *Pierre Bourdieu*. London: Routledge.
LeBreton, David. 2018. "Understanding Skin Cutting in Adolescence: Sacrificing a Part to Save the Whole." *Body and Society* 24, nos 1–2: 33–54.
Luddy, Maria. 2001. "Moral Rescue and Unmarried Mothers in Ireland in the 1920s." *Women's Studies* 30: 797–817.
– 2007. *Prostitution and Irish Society 1800–1940*. Cambridge: Cambridge University Press.
McCarthy, Rebecca Lea. 2010. *Origins of the Magdalene Laundries: An Analytical History*. Jefferson: McFarland and Company.
[NA]. 1915. "Some Benefactors of the Different Monasteries of Our Lady of Charity of the Good Shepherd Founded by the Provincial House of Montreal."
Nicholls, Tracey. 2012. "Concerning Violence against Women: A Fanonian Analysis of Colonizing the Women and Girl's Body." *e-cadernos ces* 16. http://journals.openedition.org/eces/1047#ftn4.
Roumbanis, Lambros. 2019. "Symbolic Violence in Academic Life: A Study on How Junior Scholars Are Educated in the Art of Getting Funded." *Minerva* 57: 197–218.
Samuel, Chris. 2012. "Suffering and Justice: Symbolic Violence, Oppression, Legitimacy." PhD diss., Queen's University.
Sangster, Joan. 2001. *Regulating Girls and Women: Sexuality, Family, and the Law in Ontario, 1920–1960*. Don Mills: Oxford University Press.
– 2002. *Girl Trouble: Women and Girls Delinquency in English Canada*. Toronto: Between the Lines.
Sisters of Our Lady of Charity of the Good Shepherd. 1890. *The Rule of St Augustin and the Constitutions for the Religious of the Congregation of Our Lady of Charity of the Good Shepherd of Angers*. Toronto: St Basius Seminary.

Swain, Shurlee, and Margot Hillel. 2010. *Child, Nation, Race and Empire: Child Rescue Discourse, England, Canada, and Australia, 1850–1915*. Manchester University Press.

Thapar-Björkert, S., L. Samelius, and G.S. Sanghera. 2016. "Exploring Symbolic Violence in the Everyday: Misrecognition, Condescension, Consent and Complicity." *Feminist Review* 112, no. 1: 144–62.

Titley, Brian. 2006. "Heil Mary: Magdalene Asylums and Moral Regulation in Ireland." *History of Education* 35, no. 2: 1–15.

Turner, Bryan S. 2006. *Vulnerability and Human Rights*. University Park: Penn State University Press.

3

Manufacturing Structural Vulnerability and Institutional Violence

The Language of Childhood and Disability

KATHARINE VISCARDIS

In 2009, shortly after the Huronia Regional Centre (HRC),[1] Orillia, was closed, former residents of the institution launched a class action lawsuit against the province of Ontario, accusing the province of systemic neglect, and accusing institutional staff of physical, emotional, and sexual abuse. The lawsuit ended with a multi-million-dollar settlement in 2013. Since the HRC's closure, survivors have been sharing their experiences with the hopes that their testimonies will educate others about the significant and long-lasting harms of institutionalization. HRC survivors have shared their oral histories in art form, in academic journal articles, and through public presentations. A handful of survivors also recounted their experiences of institutional violence to me during my doctorate research about the experiences of the HRC's child residents.[2] I conducted interviews with survivors, attended public talks and events held by survivors, and I gathered testimony from news media, social media, and archival documents. After receiving approval from Trent University's Research Ethics Board, I interviewed five survivors who were residents of the HRC between 1960 and 1980. Survivors who participated in my research project provided verbal and written consent to have their experiences shared in my dissertation and future academic work. This chapter uses some of the data collected during my dissertation research and provides a small piece of a much larger project centred around developing a social history of institutionalization, uncovering the truth of institutional violence both historically and presently, and answering the following question: how can some children be treated so violently in a world that proclaims to view children as precious, important, and lovable?

In this paper, I recount specific examples of situational physical, sexual, and psycho-emotional violence taken from interview data that was gathered during my doctoral research, as well as the testimonies of former child residents found in the archival collection, RG 4-154.[3] I share these experiences to lay out the reality of institutional violence at least in the context of the HRC. Following the sharing of former resident testimony, I provide some insight to answer the overarching question noted above. I locate the roots of violence against child residents of the HRC in broader social conceptions and intersections of childhood and disability. This chapter argues that institutional violence against children in the HRC was, in many ways, an embodied effect of the broader patterns of cultural and social discrimination and ableist violence. Institutional violence against children in the HRC was an embodied effect of an historical trend of dehumanization, a trend which created significant structural vulnerability for marginalized children in Ontario.

CHILDREN'S EXPERIENCES OF INSTITUTIONAL VIOLENCE IN THE HRC, 1960–80

Violence against children was a consistent and culturally pervasive phenomenon in the Huronia Regional Centre. Children experienced various forms and degrees of violence ranging from physical and sexual abuse to emotional and psychological torment. Recognizing the systemic nature of violence is necessary for a thorough understanding of the all-encompassing nature of the violence children experienced in the HRC, but this chapter focuses on the situational experiences of violence experienced by individual children and perpetrated by members of staff.[4] The examples of institutional child abuse provided emphasise the violent nature of the HRC, a nature that stands in sharp contrast to the narrative of care and protection espoused by facility administrators and the province of Ontario over the course of the institution's tenure. For organizational purposes, I have separated the following examples of institutional violence against children into specific categories of violence, but it should be noted that the forms of violence described below frequently overlapped.

Physical Violence and Punishment

Survivor testimony reveals that "day to day discipline [and] corporeal punishment" were the modus operandi of the institution. Children were subjected to various forms of physical assault under the guise of "punishment." Henry (pseudonym),[5] admitted to the HRC's "School Cottage" in or around 1959 at the age of eleven, recalls many punishments himself and other children were subjected to:

> Now, I can't speak for the girls, but I can the boys. So, yeah, so, a lot of times, you know, we were just minding our own business doing stuff and it didn't matter what you did they would still say "you, you, you, you, you're on punishment" for god knows what ... Ok, so what they did was, they took a pair of shoes and they had the sole taken off of that shoe and left the heel on. Then they would take adhesive tape and they'd go all around it like this [he gestures that the tape would be wound around the shoe sole] and then ... You had to hold your hand out and they would hit you with it several times. When it came to me, I got it a few times. But the worst thing about it is that if you don't respond they take you to the washroom, put your hand under the cold-water tap, and then would hit you. And that would make it sting. And if they couldn't find that, you know what an old radiator brush is like – well they would pull your pants down and hit you right across the bare seat until it was red and sore.

David (pseudonym), admitted in 1964 when he was ten years old, also recalls being hit with the sole of a shoe: "They use the old sole of a shoe, you know, then they put bandage, eh, tape and wooden sticks and [J.K.] would hit you on the hand, but he never hit me."

As Henry recalls, children were sometimes forced to witness the slaughtering of animals on the institution's farm as "punishment." Henry remembers that: "For punishment, they would show us how they killed the cows. So, the first time we went they would, they would, take a potato sack, put it over the cow's head, and then they would take a sledgehammer ... And they would hit the cow over the forehead two or three times ... And we had to watch. The other way they did it was the other way around. They wouldn't do that. They would just take a gun and shoot the cow in the forehead till the cow fell to the floor. So, again, we had to watch. So, it was supposed to have been a form of punishment."

Voices from the archives offer further evidence of the corporeal punishment children experienced in the HRC. One former child resident testified to police in the 1990s that the staff would "use the bottom of a shoe to hit him" and that "he would be locked out of the ward, on a screened balcony which was not heated in the winter. He would be left there to freeze as punishment" (OPP n.d., 45). Similarly, Oliver (pseudonym), who was admitted to the HRC in 1967 at the age of ten, recalls being forced to "stand outside naked in the winter" (Oliver n.d., 5). Oliver also describes a punishment called "hobbling." Staff would smack the bottom of children's feet with the "sole of a leather shoe" until blood was drawn "[making] walking extremely painful" (5).

As noted by survivors, physical violence was often presented as punishment although the children had done nothing wrong. Yet some physical violence occurred without warning and under the pretense of discipline. For example, Oliver's first experience with physical violence occurred just moments after his admission. Oliver, a ward of the Children's Aid Society (CAS), was taken to the institution by a social worker. As he watched her drive away from a dormitory window, a staff member struck him across the head with the handle of a broomstick, causing his head to bleed. Oliver also describes witnessing other residents being abused by staff. For example, he witnessed a ten-year-old boy being beaten with a two-by-four. The violence children experienced was particularly sadistic, a sadism captured in the fact that the abuse of children was sometimes used as entertainment for staff. For instance, Oliver recalls being taught boxing by some members of staff who would then make the children fight one another. Staff members would place bets on which child would win the fight. Oliver explains that the children "became as the Roman gladiators of old, fighting for the amusement of the guards some of whom bet on us" (6). Ronald (pseudonym), admitted to the HRC at the age of five and a resident between 1960 and 1968, describes a similar game: "The staff ... made me fight against two to three older patients. They wrapped something around our hands" (Police Statement 1990). Ronald recalls other humiliating "games" designed for the entertainment of staff, some of which included the administration of sedative drugs: "I was ... transferred to the Pavilion where I stayed for nine months. I had been receiving injections by the staff there. They had gambled on how long it would take me to go under, unconscious. Other times I had been given, I think was, chloral hydrate, which tasted very bad ... I was forced by staff to gamble for them called game thirty-one. If I lost, I would get a beating" (Oliver n.d., 6). John (pseudonym) also recalls physical assault that occurred when he was a child at the HRC. "One of the staff counsellors," John explains, "throwed my head into the cement wall and that's how I had a concussion ... when we were going outside, right, I dropped right to the floor. Like, I passed out."

Sexual Violence

HRC survivors identify a pattern of sexual degradation and exploitation as well. Examples of sexual violence are pervasive in survivor narratives and in the archival records. Brian Logie was a resident of the HRC in 1962 and stayed there from age seven to thirteen. He recalls being subjected to regular sexual abuse at the hands of staff members and other residents. He explains that he used to try to avoid the staff on nightshift: "'Cause they used to come. 'Oh, you have to use the washroom.' 'No, I don't.' 'You have to use the washroom.' 'No, I don't.' And, you know, the next thing you know I'm taken to the bathroom. I remember they would bugger me." Similarly, John would sleep with a butter knife under his pillow to defend himself from nightly sexual abuse. When Brian attempted to protest sexual violence, he was subjected to significant physical pain: "They used to put my hand in the vice. And then they said 'you gotta do this, you gotta do this or I'll break your knuckles.' And I did exactly what they said to do because the pain was too much. I couldn't handle it anymore. Then if I didn't – this was all within the first year before I learned to do what they say." Brian also recalls that sexual violence often occurred during normative institutional "caring" routines, such as when the children were bathed: "Four or five of us in the shower at the same time and then he used to tell us, 'bend down,' forgive me, 'pull your, pull your [foreskin] back, bend over.' I was touched often. He says, 'well we are checking to make sure you got everything.' Yeah, right on. Yeah, right on. Alright. And then sometimes I got beat. Stood up against the wall until everybody was finished and then that's when it [sexual abuse] first started. I'm saying to myself, you know, maybe this is normal. How come an adult can take a shower with a child?" Brian explains that a staff attendant would enter the shower: "he used to make me wash his privates."

Cindy Scott, admitted to the HRC at age seven in 1971, also experienced and witnessed sexual violence. Cindy shared the following:

> I was in the institution. I was in Cottage D. Ok, they, yeah. What they done to me. One of the staffs at nightshifts, he was following me to the bathroom and he wants me to touch his penis ... So, I wasn't very comfortable. And, I also, there was about seven staff in the daytime, in the afternoon, I was naked and there was seven staff. I was sitting on the bed too. They are all looking at my body. And, also, they put the green hose at the private area where my bum is, and I was sick. I was filling ... with water. I told them to stop. They wouldn't stop. So, I was very sick. Another time I was in the playground, there's about two male staff. They raped one of the girls in the back of the bush ... One of the girls couldn't sit down, and you know, they were doing the deeds in behind.

Another former child resident described his experience of sexual violence to the police in 1990: "the staff ... put me in bed on my stomach and raped me between my legs in the evening. Doctor [J] fondled me, stuck his private parts out and led my hand. This happened in the staff office about five times" (Police Statement 1990). He recalls being raped by other residents while staff members watched: "I was put in an enclosure where the needles were being given, put on a bed and being held down by older patients and raped by another one. Staff were watching and laughing when I screamed from pain" (police statement 1990). Likewise, a child resident was forced into a sexual "relationship" with an institution staff member when he was approximately nine years old; a relationship that spanned many years and continued after his release from the HRC when he was sixteen. The same child also accused another staff member of sexually abusing him between the ages of ten and eleven (OPP n.d.).

Cases of sexual violence in the HRC highlight the complexity of the violence children experienced. Sexual violence was so common-place and almost routine in the lives of some child residents that they lived in a state of perpetual fear. Far from the popular adage of "sleeping like a baby," children like Brian and John went to bed fearful of sexual violence, deliberating about how they could avoid it and considering how they could defend themselves against it.

Psycho-Emotional Violence

The violence children experienced or witnessed in the HRC had tremendous psycho-emotional impacts. Psycho-emotional violence refers to acts of violence that threaten the psychological and emotional self (Goodley and Runswick-Cole 2013). Forcing children to watch animals being slaughtered at the institution's farm, as described by Henry, is an example of psycho-emotional violence in the HRC. Another took of psycho-emotional violence used against the children was the spectre of death. The threat of death was held over children to engender submission to institutional order. For example, HRC survivor Betty Bond recalls that the only time she was ever allowed to go outside of the institution was to be escorted to the facility cemetery. "We were shown the gravesites," Betty explains, "and told if we weren't good little girls, we'd end up in there" (cited in Beattie 2016). She was just a child at the time, confronted with the threat of death and burial in the institution's cemetery.

Many survivors of the HRC continue to struggle with the memories of institutional violence they endured as children. The psycho-emotional violence and the trauma of institutionalization is strikingly evident in how institutional violence manifests in the lives of survivors now. Speaking of a memory of seeing a young boy being killed by an HRC attendant, John describes his current struggle of dealing with the psycho-emotional fallout: "I had a dream about it, but I don't know if it's true or not. Bad ones. I even yell in my sleep. My wife hears me sometimes yelling. Is it gonna ever get any better?" John developed lifelong enuresis because of the trauma he experienced as a child institutionalized in the HRC. Likewise, Cindy describes the psycho-emotional impact of the abuse she experienced: "I going through everyday life trying not to remember. I keep getting flashbacks all the time about what I grew up to, that place in the institution at the HRC." Brian also struggles with nightmares: "But, memories still come back. She [his wife] tells me I wake up yelling. [I] wake up like my body's in a cold sweat like, I says to myself, I'm looking around saying, "oh, gee, what the hell. Did I dump water on myself?" No. It will never go away." David still struggles with the question of why he was treated so poorly in the facility and has since attempted to contact former staff members to ask them for answers. It is clear in survivors' testimonies that the emotional, psychological, and sometimes physical impact of institutional abuse has left a painful legacy in their lives. Survivors whose stories are shared above are left with an unremitting question: How could this happen to children?

In what follows, I offer some insight to answer this question by uncovering the discursive foundations of violence against institutionalized children. Understanding the historical context of ableism and its intersection with childhood can help uncover some of the discursive roots of institutional violence experienced by children in the HRC. The discussion below demonstrates that institutional violence against children in the HRC was rooted in broader patterns of care and containment. It stemmed from both the new social standard of the time to provide custodial care for children-in-need and "the disabled," and the contiguous idea that unruly bodies, such as those of disabled children, were a menace to social and genetic health, and therefore needed to be restrained.

THE LANGUAGE OF CHILDHOOD

The status "child" or the language of childhood was one foundational cause of institutional violence in the HRC. Children were increasingly idealized over the course of the twentieth century, perceived as a special sub-group of persons distinct from adults. In fact, it has been suggested that children emerged from a process of "sentimentalization" at the turn of the twentieth century (Zelizer 1985). Childhood, during this process of sentimentalization had been reconceptualized as a period of weakness and vulnerability, and children were increasingly viewed as sacred or sentimental beings. Children were, and continue to be, understood as innocent, vulnerable, passive, nonautonomous objects of adult care and intervention (Zelizer 1985). The perception of children as sacred and sentimental stands in drastic contrast to the experiences of children in the HRC as detailed above. It is difficult to understand that such a discourse of childhood could exist in tandem with institutional violence. On critical evaluation though, it can be argued that those conceptions of children as innocent, weak, passive, and nonautonomous, were major factors influencing the violent treatment of children in custodial settings like the HRC. The language of childhood, especially the discourse of innocence, has served as a legitimizing force for the institutionalization of children in Canada for decades, as will be described below.

As Meyer (2007) notes, moralizing children, seeing them as "sacred" or inherently innocent, has allowed for "a range of practices and opinions" (102) to be legitimized, such as the practice of admitting children to custodial care institutions. Institutionalization is justified "in the name of the child" (102). Children whose vulnerability was believed to be "at risk," such as those who grew up in so-called "unhealthy" or "immoral" families and environments – children of the poor and working class, children from racialized and/or immigrant families, and children identified as developmentally disabled – were more likely to be admitted to an institution to "better" protect their innocence (Rooke and Schnell 1983). The discourse of innocence, which perceives children as "immature, weak, and vulnerable" (87) has influenced children's experiences of institutional violence by providing one pathway to institutional admission.

Furthermore, the discourse of innocence, or the language of vulnerability, can impact how children experience the social world in general, and the institution in particular, because it produces real structural vulnerability (Rooke and Schnell 1983). Through the discourse of innocence, "children's needs are defined by adults and children's agency is constrained in the name of protection" (87). This creates and continues to reinforce "unequal power structures that make children structurally and socially vulnerable" (91). This structural vulnerability is especially evident in the context of child institutionalization (Australian Commission into Institutional Responses to Child Sexual Abuse 2017). The violence children experienced in the HRC is certainly reflective of the broader patterns of power that exist between children and adults and reflects the structural vulnerability of children in the facility. Children's vulnerability was bolstered by the nature of the institution itself, which required children to be completely isolated from family and friends and denied them any control over their lives. In her study of the Michener Centre in Alberta, Claudia Malacrida (2015) makes a similar observation, emphasizing that the institutional design created a pattern of vulnerability and violence. She explains that situational violence was supported by "the enormity of the power that people working there wielded over the inmates" (109). Institutional violence, she explains, "reinforced the reality that these children and adults were living in a setting in which anything could happen to them, over which they had little if any control" (109). As also highlighted by Kirk Baert, class action lawyer with Koskie Minsky, residents of the Huronia Regional Centre "[had] no way of getting in touch with their family members. They [were] subject to the complete authority and whim of those who [were] taking care of them, who decide[d] how much they [got] to eat, who decide[d] when they [were] punished" (cited in Gutnick 2011). Children were particularly vulnerable to the unequal power balance between themselves and adult staff because they were subject to the institutional design *and* because they were children, a category of persons historically denied any power agency whatsoever. The extreme vulnerability of institutionalized children to violence is captured in the definition of a dangerous institution provided by Margaret Hall (2002). An institution is particularly dangerous for children when it is "marked by an extreme power imbalance, in which the ordinary disparity of power between adult and child is accentuated by a child's particular vulnerability, as a 'delinquent,' for example, or because of race or ethnicity. Another marker of the dangerous institution is the isolation of the child within the 'total institution'... in which children are cut off from families and communities. Where family members are unable to care for the child, resulting in the residential placement, those family members may also be unable to advocate on the child's behalf" (296). Henry's understanding of the "punishments" children experienced aptly captures the absolute structural vulnerability and powerless position of children within the HRC: "if you end up on punishment but haven't done anything wrong, what does that prove? You know, to them, it proved that they were in control. That they had the power to do whatever they wanted. Our lives were not our own. Our lives belonged to the staff."

The discourse of childhood described above, which presented children as being especially likely to require institutional care, and the structural vulnerability it produced had variously embodied consequences for children admitted to the HRC. The practice of forced nakedness and communal showering, as described by Brian, for example, offers some insight to show how such structural vulnerability can be a pathway to institutional violence. Children were frequently required to be naked around their peers and staff, to shower in large groups, and to use the toilet in view of others. The practice of communal showering was likely justified by several things, such as the need for institutional efficiency, but it may also have been justified partly by the believed innocence and passivity of children combined with the denial of personal autonomy and agency. It is often assumed that children don't require privacy, that they are unaware of their own nakedness or the nakedness of others, and that they cannot provide consent, by virtue of being young (a common belief about persons with disabilities as well). These assumptions lead to the denial of children's privacy and bodily autonomy, and exacerbated their structural vulnerability. Brian's testimony certainly implies that the bodies of children within the HRC were viewed as being open to nonconsensual touching, and that it was believed that there was no need for privacy or consent.

Survivor testimony indicates that in the HRC children's bodies were perceived as being "accessible," which heightened their vulnerability to situational violence. And, for Brian, and others, this increased vulnerability led to sexual violence. As well, the real need for physical care that young children require, especially those with physical and/or developmental disabilities, as Christine Chisholm identifies in her study of "thalidomiders" in Canada, can put them at greater risk of abuse: "The way mistreatment and abuse occurred can be discussed by first considering the particular vulnerability thalidomiders experienced because they often needed to expose their bodies to the hands of others" (Chisholm 2019, 212). Speaking of one individual who experienced sexual abuse as a child, Chisholm notes that "her vulnerability made her accessible and an object of violence" (216). Brian's testimony highlights the paradoxical reality that HRC care routines made children within the institution vulnerable to violent sexual interactions. Brian's testimony also captures the confusion that children likely felt as the normative, yet violent, institutional model of care (bathing and washing) collided with situational abuse that was supported by, and likely disguised within, that model of care. Brian, as he explains, questioned the normality of an adult sharing a shower with a child and his testimony implies that he knew the ward attendants carrying out the routine physical care of children, such as checking the boys for cleanliness after showering, may have had ulterior and more sinister motives.

Furthermore, the intersection of disability and childhood confounded children's structural vulnerability and the risk of institutional violence. Disabled children have historically been the targets and objects of the "medical gaze" under the assumption that their bodies, by virtue of being classified as "aberrant," are open to interventions, critique, and investigation (Krogh and Johnson 2006). This "gaze" evidently transferred into institutional practices and, again, increased children's vulnerability to sexual abuse. Cindy's experience of feeling the "gaze" of multiple men on her as she lay naked on a bed, possibly during an enema procedure, is evidence of the embodied and emotional consequence of the medical gaze. And, for some children, the denial of bodily autonomy and being subjected to the gaze of institutional doctors resulted in sexual violence perpetrated by those doctors. The power imbalance that existed between these children/adults, inmates/ authority figures, doctors/laypeople exacerbated the children's structural vulnerability and heightened their risk of sexual abuse. The link between childhood and disability will be discussed further later in the chapter.

Popular opinion about children as needing strict discipline also likely influenced their experiences of violence within the HRC. Discipline was understood as an essential component of raising children to become "responsible" twentieth century citizens and to protect their "innocence" (Comacchio 1993). Although childhood was perceived as a "sacred" period, children were also understood to be "conniving creatures" (135) who required special discipline. Discipline was viewed as a necessary aspect of childrearing as it would "condition" children "to respond in the appropriate manner to parental requests" (131) or the requests of other authority figures. "All the advisers," Comacchio explains, "insisted on the centrality of discipline to any modern habit training program" (131). The view among some staff attendants of Ontario institutions in the 1960s that "there is a place for striking patients as part of acceptable application of restraint" (Dymond 1965, 1) certainly indicates that such "punishment" was perceived as a normative part of the "care" of all residents, not just children.

The testimony of one staff attendant, Richard Shunn, who worked at the HRC between 1947 and 1975, similarly indicates that the strict discipline of children was perceived as being a regular and "proper" part of their care. Shunn stated the following: "[My] experience in the military helped me to treat these [OHS] residents properly" (cited in Goodman 1994). It must be noted that Shunn was part of a high-profile OPP investigation into the abuse of children in the HRC in the 1950s and 1960s. Shunn was accused of extremely sadistic abuse of children between the ages of ten and sixteen years old. For example, four former HRC residents testified during the OPP investigation that Shunn "choked a resident, beat another with a broom handle, grabbed residents' private parts, beat up a resident accused of stealing $10, and kicked a resident in the groin" (Goodman 1994). Popular ideas about the need for disciplining "conniving children" evidently spilled over into institutional practice. However, it is also clear that the discipline children within the HRC experienced at the hands of Shunn and others went far beyond what would have been acceptable forms at the time. It can be presumed that beating children with the sole of a shoe, leaving them naked outside in freezing cold temperatures, and forcing children to watch animals being slaughtered were not "usual" disciplinary measures at the time. The evidence shows that the term "punishment" was more likely a narrative used to justify the abuse of children by staff within the facility. The exceptionality of the violence children in the HRC experienced was likely tied to the structural vulnerability they were subjected to resulting from the following circumstances: the discourse of innocence and vulnerability, the perception of children as "conniving creatures," and the extreme power imbalance institutionalized children experienced as both children and inmates. The violence they experienced resulted in a persistent dehumanization. The role of dehumanization in institutional violence in the HRC is discussed further below.

THE INTERSECTION OF CHILDHOOD AND DISABILITY

The idealized conception of childhood has played an important role in creating a rather widespread repugnance of any form of violence against children. This reality makes it difficult to understand how so many children admitted to Canada's custodial institutions, including the HRC, could be subjected to violence for over a century. A stunning contradiction, however, has been shown so far in this chapter. The status "child" and the language of childhood was actually at the root of institutional violence, in some respects. For example, the denial of certain entitlements to children in the HRC, such as the denial of privacy, autonomy, and consent, circumstances produced by the language of childhood, created violent consequences for children. But children admitted to the HRC also experienced increased structural vulnerability because they were simultaneously *excluded* from common conceptions of childhood, such as conceptions of the ideal child. The ideal child was the middle-class, white, Eurocentric, able-bodied child. "The distinction granted by age," Lafferty (2013) explains, "was carefully, and often consciously, demarcated by other social and cultural markers" (7). Lafferty summarizes the exclusivity of modern conceptions of child/childhood clearly: "The cosseted cherubs of Victorian nurseries, or early-twentieth-century kindergartens were certainly not blacks,

Native Americans, or other visible minorities, and these groups presented special challenges in a child welfare system that took this cosseted, white cherub as its standard of perfection" (7). Normative ideals of childhood contributed to the creation of the category "problematic child" and rather than being viewed through a discourse of innocence, children like those who did not live up to middle-class standards of childhood, were often perceived through a "discourse of evil" (Meyer 2007). Those children required special care to contain the "menace" they presented to the nation. The discourse of evil, like the discourse of innocence, legitimized the practice of admitting children to custodial institutions. "Problematic" children, such as those identified as physically, intellectually, and/or developmentally disabled, required a special kind of "care" that was designed to control and contain their nonconformity, care that could be found within the segregated institution. The structural vulnerability that children experienced *as children* was, therefore, convoluted by their subsequent construction as "problematic," "feeble-minded," "disabled," and or "mentally deficient." The intersection of dehumanizing rhetoric of disability and childhood pushed some children further into the margins of society, increasing their vulnerability and insecurity as citizens, humans, and children, and, therefore, intensifying their risk of experiencing institutional violence. Dehumanization, history tells us, is a prerequisite to violence.

Children with disability labels face an increased risk of violence "partly due to impaired defenses and partly due to social responses to disability that increase risk" (Sobsey 2014). These social responses to disability dehumanize and degrade children with disabilities, as will be discussed below. Children with disabilities are also more likely to be institutionalized, which creates additional risk of violence. The violence children experienced in the HRC stemmed from a long history or tradition of dehumanization; a "tradition" in which children with disability labels were precariously positioned in relation to humanhood and childhood, as mentioned above. Children with disability labels, for example, have historically been perceived as existing outside the boundaries of both humanhood and childhood. Discourses about "disabled" or "feeble-minded" children, especially during the early to mid-twentieth century, served as rationalizing language for the exclusion of those children from mainstream communities across Canada and their segregation within "specialized" facilities like the HRC. Those discourses sit at the root of the violence children experienced within those facilities. As well-known and celebrated Canadian doctor Helen MacMurchy stressed, "mentally defective children should be separated from the normal at an early age ... and what better place to send them than the asylum [HRC] in Orillia?" (cited in Wheatley 2013).

The bodies of children with disabilities have been discursively produced throughout history as odd, ugly, and generally monstrous (Goodley, Runswick-Cole, and Liddiard 2016, 771). Although children in general have often been viewed through a lens of monstrosity or animality by virtue of their inability to control their physical bodies (bowel movements, drooling, etc.), children with disabilities are further "monstered" because of their nonconformity to historical standards or norms of embodiment as they "grow" into adulthood. "The concept of the monstrous and the figure of the monster," Margrit Shildrick (2002) explains, "have haunted Western history from its earliest records" (9). Descriptions of children with disabilities, particularly those with visible physical "deformities," as monstrous can be traced to at least the early modern period, with the births of physically disabled children being described as "monstrous births" (Bates 2005). One of the earliest recorded instances of "monstrous birth" is found in the work of Michel de Montaigne (1580) who, in the late sixteenth century, witnessed the birth of a baby with a "parasitic twin," the baby was otherwise described as a monster. In the early modern period, "public exhibitions of monsters were commonplace ... and scholars such as Montaigne mingled with other curiosity-seekers in crowds that were sometimes so large that it was difficult to get close enough to see" (Bates 2005, 143). The equation of disability with monstrosity continued through to the freak shows of the nineteenth and twentieth century when persons with physical disabilities were displayed for a group of "normative" spectators looking on with equal measure of fascination, disgust, hatred, fear, and loathing (Clare 1999). The twentieth century saw the emergence of a new kind of freak show as medical authorities began to exploit the bodies of disabled children for medical research, and paraded those bodies in medical texts for curious viewers.

The dehumanization of marginalized children, especially those with developmental and/or physical disabilities is particularly evident in early twentieth-century medical and social literature. In medical journals, for example, disabled children were positioned precariously at the interstice between human and monster. Babies with Down syndrome were of particular interest to many twentieth century doctors in Canada and filled the position of the quintessential "monstrous" birth/child of previous centuries. Descriptions of children with Down syndrome in medical texts demonstrate the ideology of the disabled child as the "monstrous child." In 1914, for example, one doctor described a child with Down syndrome in the following way: "He is full of grimaces and facial contortions which are accompanied by wrinkling skin and are foreign to the normal child" (Tredgold 1914, 219). Such descriptions demonstrate a unique loathing of physical non-conformity. Children's so-called "peculiar" embodiments, as the texts written by Tredgold indicates, justified, in the minds of doctors at the time, the abuse of their bodies, for the purpose of medical research. Tredgold, for example, spoke enthusiastically about his experimentations with the bodies of babies with Down syndrome. Him and other doctors appeared to delight in exhibiting the bodies of disabled children in medical journals by sharing voyeuristic photographs. The bodies of disabled children have long been the physical sites of social loathing. It can be surmised that children's bodies continued to be the physical sites or objects of social loathing as they were rounded up by medical and social authorities, separated from their families and communities, and placed in facilities like the HRC. Considering the physical violence children like Brian and Henry were subjected to in the HRC, it can be speculated that children in the HRC were violently "punished" for their various non-conformities.

The dehumanization of children with disabilities in the twentieth century certainly had violent results. For instance, the lives of many children with disability labels were cut short because of a perception that disabled lives were simply not worth living. Between 1950 and 1971, twenty-seven babies born with Down syndrome and admitted to the Hospital for Sick Children in Toronto were denied "simple" medical procedures, such as surgery to fix a bowel obstruction, and were left to die (Ottawa [CP] 1979; Warren 1977). In 1977, a *Report on Human Life* was published, and it was argued within it that disabled babies should not be treated as human and should be denied life, at least in some cases. "An infant with severe neurological defects," the report emphasized, "may not be human ... and it is a fundamental error to treat it as human. It is natural to trust what we see, rather than what we know from the evidence of experience and medical science. We see that the creature looks like a human being, and it was born of woman, though we know that it cannot possibly develop humanhood (Report 1977, 11). Death for so-called non-human babies, according to the report, was necessary. Better to be dead than disabled, appears to have been a rather popular sentiment among some twentieth century Canadian doctors. "I'd sooner break the news to a mother that her child has fatal leukemia than that he will never be normal," one doctor from the Hospital for Sick Children stated in 1958 (Clare 1958). "I'd rather have to tell parents, 'Your child is dead,'" said another pediatrician from Kitchener, Ontario. And when death was not an option, institutionalization was believed to be a laudable substitute. For much of the twentieth century doctors asserted that disabled children should be institutionalized (Wright 2011). And, once admitted to an institution, the status of being an institutionalized child reified the dehumanizing perceptions of children and deepened the structural vulnerability they endured. Dr Alexander Beaton's statement that residents of the HRC were viewed by Orillia locals as "vile," "repulsive," and "dangerous creatures," certainly attests to the fact that the very act of being admitted to an institution reinforced and confirmed to onlookers their believed non-human social status.

The assertion that death was better than life for children with disabilities, who were excluded from notions of the ideal child and human, undoubtedly had a real impact on the violence children experienced in institutions like the HRC. The violent consequences of such rhetoric are particularly evident in HRC survivor recollections of play time. Despite the generally taken-for-granted assumption that play is synonymous with childhood, children with disability labels have historically been denied play due, in part, to the common understanding of those children as being unable to play "properly" (in a way that demonstrates "normative" child development) and by being perceived as unplayful as a result of disability (Goodley, Runswick-Cole, and Liddiard 2016). It is likely that these ideas shaped the play experiences of children in the HRC. Many survivors have shared that play was generally non-existent in the institution. For example, Cindy recalls the following: "I was in one little area. A small room where all the kids were playing. They had no toys no nothing. They would just play with their fingers and rock … I was pretty sad" (Remember Every Name 2016). Bev Link, another HRC survivor, explains that "if the children weren't toiling over hard labour or in the odd class, they'd spend their time in the 'playroom' – a square cell with only hard wooden benches lining the walls. There were no toys" (cited in Beattie 2016). According to Bev, "some kids would rock back and forth all day because there was nothing to do" (cited in Beattie 2016). The denial of play indicates that institutionalized children were excluded from understandings of childhood and were perceived as being underserving of the privileges granted to "normative" children, including playing.

Aside from the denial of play, the extent to which children in the HRC were dehumanized and excluded from normative understanding of childhood is strikingly evident in their experiences sexualized violence within the playroom. Brian and other survivors reveal that the playroom was the location of horrific sexual violence and humiliation, rather than a space symbolizing childhood. Bev Link notes that the playroom in her cottage was a space where more abuse than play occurred. "When staff members were bored," Beattie (2016) explains, "they'd line children up, and force them to take off their underwear and parade around the playroom." Link recalls staff "[making] kids go down the hallway stark naked." Marie Slark tells the same story: "If we got caught talking, we had to get up with our pants down and walk around the playroom with our pants down" (Loriggio 2013). Likewise, the playroom for Betty Bond was a location that caused incredible fear: "I was so scared to go in the playroom I would sit there frozen. I didn't want to be seen. We tried to hide, but we could never really hide" (Beattie 2016). Presumably, Betty is referring to the fact that the abuse children experienced in the playrooms was inescapable. Play time in the HRC provides a unique example of the violent consequences of the structural vulnerability that was borne by violent narratives of disability and childhood.

This uncertain position of children admitted to the HRC (in terms of their humanity and child status) influenced their experience of physical violence in the HRC, violence that was frequently disguised as punishment. While so-called "normal" children were believed to need strict discipline, as discussed earlier, corporeal punishment for non-normative children may have been seen as especially necessary. As discussed earlier, the language of childhood influenced the disciplinary practices used to control children during the twentieth century, such as the understanding of children as "conniving." This narrative of conniving children, and the widespread acceptance of corporeal punishment, likely influenced the practices adopted by the HRC in their "care" of children. But children deemed "problematic" in some way, those viewed as non-normative children, often faced more intense forms of discipline, and still do. Children with disability labels are often viewed as being inherently violent by virtue of being disabled

(Goodley and Runswick-Cole 2011). "A common functionalist trope" has historically influenced, and presently influences, how disabled children are viewed and treated by medical authorities: "the disabled subject that inevitably exhibits challenging behavior often manifesting itself through violence" (603). The perspective of children with disability labels as being inherently violent, they stress, is just one of the powerful discourses that produces violence against those children. The ableism that positions such children as a threat, a "menace" to themselves and others, has variously embodied consequences. The embodiment of such discourses is evident in the testimonies of the survivors who have shared their experiences of institutional disciplinary practices, namely the punishments described by former child residents as shared earlier. Other disciplinary practices adopted by the HRC included isolation and mechanical restraints such as straitjackets (Mechanical Restraints c. 1980). Brian, for example, was restrained using a straitjacket when he was just seven years old. The use of a straitjacket against a normative child would have likely been viewed as cruel, yet for Brian, who was understood as a "problematic" child, a straitjacket was perceived as acceptable and necessary. The dehumanization of children identified as disabled placed children like Brian, Cindy, Henry, David, and John at tremendous risk of institutional violence. If social, medical, and political authorities were saying that the lives of babies and children with disabilities were worth nothing – not even worth living – then what happened to them in life, and in the institutions to which many of them were sent, presumably, did not matter.

CONCLUSION

This chapter has identified key pathways to institutional violence against children who were admitted to the Huronia Regional Centre in the mid-1900s. It has recounted some violent experiences that former child residents had in the facility between 1960 and 1980. The experiences of these children exemplify the character of the facility, which was invariably violent. This chapter has highlighted the broader social and cultural context that laid the foundations for institutionalization, and therefore institutional violence, including the discursive construction of some children as needing segregated special care, and the generalized social loathing of children with disabilities and other non-normative labels. For example, it has highlighted how a discourse of innocence surrounding children in the twentieth century legitimized family separation and the admission of children to facilities like the HRC, under the pretence of protecting childhood innocence. It has demonstrated that the language of childhood – including discourse that positions children as innocent, weak, vulnerable, and nonautonomous – manufactured real structural vulnerability within the institutions to which children were sent, significantly increasing the risk of situational physical, psycho-emotional, and/or sexual abuse.

Furthermore, this chapter has established that the language of childhood as it intersected with dehumanizing rhetoric about disability increased some children's risk of institutionalization, their structural vulnerability, and therefore, their risk of interpersonal violence within the HRC. While the very fact of being children increased the risk of institutional violence for children admitted to the HRC, the simultaneous *exclusion* from ideal conceptions of child and childhood further heightened their structural vulnerability and risk of institutional violence. Overall, this chapter has demonstrated that the situational violence children were subjected to within the HRC was, in many ways, an embodiment of harmful discourses about children and disability. Dehumanizing discourses about children with disability labels in particular, and the social loathing that was directed at disabled children helped to construct those children as being unworthy of dignity, unworthy of respect, unworthy of love, and, ultimately, unworthy of life. These discourses translated into and were channelled through violent encounters between children and institutional staff. In other words, and as this chapter has argued, the bodies of children within the HRC became the sites upon which violent discourses and social loathing were physically enacted.

NOTES

1 The HRC was Canada's oldest and largest custodial institution for children and adults with disability labels. It was in operation between 1861, when it first opened as a branch of the Provincial Insane Asylum in Toronto, and 2009.

2 The experiences of former child residents of the HRC were a primary resource used to produce my doctoral dissertation, "The History and Legacy of the 'Orillia Asylum for Idiots': Children's Experiences of Institutional Violence."

3 The archival collection RG 4-154 contains documents used in the Huronia Regional Centre Class Action proceedings. Per the settlement agreement of 2013, the collection is digitally stored at the Archives of Ontario. The collection contains institutional policies, annual reports, resident case records, provincial inspection reports, contentious issue reports, news articles, and police investigation files, including case notes, resident and staff testimony, and final investigative reports, among other documents.

4 For an account of the broader systemic conditions of violence, conditions that allowed for the situational abuse of children to occur, please review my own dissertation (Viscardis 2020) and *Institutional Violence and Disability: Punishing Conditions* (Rossiter and Rinaldi, 2019).

5 Some survivors whose testimonies are shared in this chapter asked to remain confidential and so a pseudonym was allocated to them. Two survivors, Brian Logie and Cindy Scott, asked that their real names be used in my dissertation and future academic work.

REFERENCES

Australian Commission into Institutional Responses to Child Sexual Abuse. 2017. "Final Report: Preface and Executive Summary." Australia: Commonwealth of Australia. https://www.childabuseroyalcommission.gov.au/sites/default/files/final_report_-_preface_and_executive_summary.pdf.

Bates, Alan W. 2005. "Good, Common, Regular, and Orderly: Early Modern Classifications of Monstrous Births." *Social History of Medicine* 18, no. 2: 141–58.

Beattie, Samantha. "Locked Away and Forgotten: Muskoka Women Share How They Survived Institutionalized Childhood Abuse." *Bracebridge Examiner*, 18 May 2016. https://www.muskokaregion.com/news-story/6560028-locked-away-and-forgotten-muskoka-women-share-how-they-survived-institutionalized-childhood-abuse.

Chen, Xiaobei. 2005. *Tending the Gardens of Citizenship: Child Saving in Toronto, 1802–1920s*. Toronto: University of Toronto Press.

Chisolm, Christine Anna. 2019. "Life after the Scandal: Thalidomide, Family, and Rehabilitation in Modern Canada, 1958–1990." PhD diss., Carleton University.

Clare, E. 1999. *Exile and Pride: Disability, Queerness, and Liberation*. Boston: South End Press.

Clare, John. "A Better World for Retarded Children." *Maclean's Magazine*, 22 November 1958. https://archive.macleans.ca/article/1958/11/22/a-better-world-for-retarded-children.

Comacchio, Cynthia. 1993. *Nations Are Built of Babies: Saving Ontario's Mothers and Children, 1900–1940*. Montreal and Kingston: McGill-Queen's University Press.

Dymond, M.B. 1965. Memorandum. Striking of Patients. RG 4-154. File no. CR006547. 15 February 1965. Archives of Ontario. York University.

Ford, Carrieanne, and Kate Rossiter. 2017. "Trauma from the Past." *Canadian Journal of Disability Studies* 3, no. 3: 14–19.

Goodley, Daniel, and Katherine Runswick-Cole. 2011. "The Violence of Disablism." *Sociology of Health and Illness* 33, no. 4: 602–17.

– 2013. "The Body as Disability and Possibility: Theorizing the 'Leaking, Lacking and Excessive' Bodies of Disabled Children." *Scandinavian Journal of Disability Research* 15, no. 1: 1–19.

Goodley, Daniel, Katherine Runswick-Cole, and Kirsty Liddiard. 2016. "The DisHuman Child." *Discourse: Studies in the Cultural Politics of Education* 37, no. 5: 770–84.

Goodman, K. "Tales of Abuse 'Falsehoods,' Ex-attendant Tells Court." *Packet and Times*, 5 August 1994.

Gould, George M., and Walter L. Pyle. 1898. *Anomalies and Curiosities of Medicine*. London: The Rebman Publishing Co.

Gutnick, David. 2011. "Class Action: Ontario's Developmentally Challenged Go to Court." CBC News. https://www.cbc.ca/news/canada/class-action-ontario-s-developmentally-challenged-go-to-court-1.1022652.

Hall, M. 2002. "Law Commission of Canada, Restoring Dignity: Responding to Child Abuse in Canadian Institutions." *International Journal of Children's Rights* 10: 295–302.

Hutton, Sue, Peter Park, Martin Levine, Shay Johnson, and Kosha Bramesfeld. 2017. "Self Advocacy from the Ashes of the Institution." *Canadian Journal of Disability Studies* 6, no. 3: 31–59.

Krogh, K., and J. Johnson. 2006. "A Life without Living: Challenging Medical and Economic Reductionism in Home Support Policy for People with Disabilities." In *Critical Disability Theory: Essays in Philosophy, Politics, and Law*, edited by Dianne Pothier and Richard Devlin, 151–76. Vancouver: UBC Press.

Lafferty, R.N. 2013. *The Guardianship of Best Interests: Institutional Care for the Children of the Poor in Halifax, 1850–1960*. Montreal and Kingston: McGill-Queen's University Press.

Loriggio, Paola. 2013. "Class Action Lawsuit over Alleged Abuse at Ontario Institution Set to Begin." *Record*, 15 September 2013. https://www.therecord.com/news-story/4081519--1b-class-action-lawsuit-over-alleged-abuse-at-ontario-institution-set-to-begin.

Malacrida, Claudia. 2015. *A Special Hell: Institutional Life in Alberta's Eugenic Years*. Toronto: University of Toronto Press.

Mechanical Restraints. c. 1980. RG 4-154. File no. CR130676. Archives of Ontario. York University.

Meyer, Anneke. 2007. "The Moral Rhetoric of Childhood." *Childhood* 14, no. 1: 85–104.

Oliver. n.d. *My History in a Nutshell*. RG 4-154. File no. CR105811. Archives of Ontario. York University.

OPP (Ontario Provincial Police). n.d. *Ontario Provincial Police and Orillia Police Service Investigation into Allegations of Physical and Sexual Abuse at the Ontario Hospital School (Orillia) during the 1950s and 1960s*. CR213731.

Ottawa (CP). "Psychiatrists Condemn Practice of Letting Retarded Babies Die." *Globe and Mail*, 16 February 1979. ProQuest Historical Papers.

Police Statement. 1990. RG 4-154. File no. CR070216. January 26 1990. Archives of Ontario. York University.

Remember Every Name. 2016. "Cindy Scott: Huronia Regional Centre Survivor, Part 2." https://www.youtube.com/watch?v=jQZ10Kk5Y2k.

Report: Newborn Infant with Severe Neurological Defects. 1977. RG 4-154. File no. CR041169. 4 August 1977. Archives of Ontario. York University.

Rooke, Rodolph Leslie, and Patricia T. Schnell. 1983. *Discarding the Asylum: From Child Rescue to the Welfare State in English Canada (1800–1950)*. Lanham: University Press of America.

Rossiter, Kate, and Jen Rinaldi. 2019. *Institutional Violence and Disability: Punishing Conditions*. London: Routledge.

Scott, Cindy, with Jen Rinaldi. 2017. "That's My Story and I'm Sticking To It." *Canadian Journal of Disability Studies* 6, no. 3: 21–9.

Sobsey, Dan. 2014. "Violence and Disability." *Eugenics Archive*. Accessed 19 October 2021, https://eugenicsarchive.ca/discover/tree/535eee9d7095aa0000000262.

Shildrick, Margrit. 2002. *Embodying the Monster: Encounters with the Vulnerable Self*. London: Sage Publications.

Tredgold, Alfred Frank. 1914. *Mental Deficiency (Amentia)*. Toronto: The Macmillan Company of Canada.

Warren, J. "'Appalling Little Progress' in Treatment of Retarded." *Globe and Mail*, 5 March 1977. ProQuest Historical Papers.

Wheatley, T. 2013. "Huronia." http://www.thelmawheatley.com.

Wright, David. 2011. *Downs: The History of a Disability*. Oxford: Oxford University Press.

Zelizer, Viviana R. 1985. *Pricing the Priceless Child: The Changing Social Value of Children*. New York: Basic Books.

4

The Societal Underpinnings of Institutionalizing Othered Bodies

A Typology of Institutional Violence at the Huronia Regional Centre and the Mohawk Institute

ANNALISE CLARKSON

The bodies of Indigenous children that continue to be found on the grounds of former residential schools across Canada (Austen 2021; CBC News 2021; Reiss 2021) should not come as a surprise. Institutional survivors have made clear that mass graves are common to total institutions across the world. Take for instance the unmarked graves on the former site of the Huronia Regional Centre (HRC) in Orillia, Ontario. Or the whispers of bodies buried on the property of the Woodland Cultural Centre, site of the former Mohawk Institute (MI) in Brantford, Ontario (Leung 2015; Martin and Hill 2021). The presence of unmarked graves on sites of institutions symbolizes the violence that ultimately led to deaths of both Indigenous children and dis/abled children who were historically kept in government run institutions.

Indigenous and dis/abled people experienced comparable forms of collective loathing because Indigenous peoples threatened the homogeneity of the dominant culture while dis/abled children represented a societal burden. The MI's overarching goal was cultural genocide by killing the "Indian" in the child and training Indigenous children to be functional members of dominant society. Craft (2016) defines cultural genocide as the destruction of structures and practices that allow groups to thrive. In residential schools children were taught to despise Indigenous culture and traditions and to devalue all that is

Indigenous within themselves and their communities (Woodland Cultural Centre 2014). Residential schools worked to assimilate Indigenous children into an anti-Indigenous system, and in so doing the many forms of Indigenous knowledge were attacked. The understanding that there is an interconnectedness of living beings, that "there is a sacred nature to natural knowledge," a relational responsibility to knowledge (Gonzales 2020), the importance of stories and laughter (Woodland Cultural Centre 2010), and Indigenous forms of governance were buried so that if children left the school, they would no longer replicate Indigeneity.

Institutionalization of Indigenous children was explicitly a colonial and cultural attack while dis/abled children were removed and isolated from society using institutions that were given power over their care and containment. While it is important to note that Indigenous and dis/abled groups experience prejudice in multiple and distinct ways, there are certainly parallels in the institutional methods that were specifically used to isolate, control, and conform these othered bodies. A comparative analysis illuminates how institutional violence is rooted in othering, or social processes that remove, isolate, and train populations on the basis of a shared identity characteristic.

An important site for critical comparative analysis then, involves the experiences of institutional violence at two total institutions: the HRC in Orillia, a total institution that housed children with dis/abilities from 1876 to 2009 and was originally named the Orillia Asylum; and the MI in Brantford, the longest running residential school for Indigenous children in Canada between 1876 and 1969. I draw upon themes of institutional violence from literature related to the MI, which included historical and contemporary newspaper articles, Fletcher's (2004) thorough educational analysis of the MI's annual reports, and regular tours of the Woodland Cultural Centre that sits on the former site of the MI and works to preserve and promote Indigenous history; I then compare this body of work to primary documents from the HRC, including annual reports from 1919–52, doctors' meeting minutes from 1940 to 2007, newspaper articles about the HRC written between 1858 and 2013, and materials collected for the Recounting Huronia Community Archive.

In this paper I show that while there may be different grounds for othering (e.g., Indigeneity, intellectual disability), residential school and custodial facility spaces have similar mandates, funding, management, and administrative processes centred on conforming othered bodies. I then describe a typology of institutional violence that is entrenched in othering – whether that othering is the result of settler colonial or ableist histories. This typology includes "training" through mandatory heteronormative body presentations, low-quality education, and forced labour. Because of how processes of othering operate, these comparable conditions at MI and HRC are inherently violent, and they also give rise to more blatant experiences of violence, including the impacts of neglect and staff negligence, physical and sexual abuse, and the devaluation of the dead.

INSTITUTIONAL GOALS, FUNDING, AND MANAGEMENT

Despite their targeting of different identity markers (i.e., Indigeneity and disability respectively), the MI and HRC were both built on the broader assumption that isolating othered children was best for the wider society. In 1831, the contentious figure Joseph Brant requested that the New England Company (NEC) from London, England found the MI to "meet the specific needs of Six Nations Indians" (Brantford Expositor 1927, 42). Joseph Brant was a modernist who wanted the NEC to provide missionary and church education to Six Nations children (Fletcher 2004). The MI acted as a boarding school for the nearby reservation and trained Indigenous children in theoretical and practical work at the school, on the farm, and in domestic areas (Brantford Expositor 1927). The HRC, on the other hand, opened as an asylum before developing into a training school (Ironside and Grossmith 1984). In 1876 the Orillia Asylum opened as a training school for dis/abled folks and the community boasted about its comfort: "this place is a most complete, handsome, and well-conducted institution ... it is not a prison, but a home, a comfortable, carefully arranged home" (*Globe and Mail* 1891). Under the guise of comfort and care, both institutions were built to isolate and train othered children.

Methods used to target, control, and institutionalize were similar for Indigenous and dis/abled children though it is crucial to point out government and operational differences. These total institutions were funded by different government agencies, but the lack of bureaucratic accountability left funding a consistent issue throughout both histories. The MI was funded and managed by the NEC who set rules, appointed a Chief Missioner to Six Nations as an on-site representative, and hired employees and principals (Fletcher 2004). In 1891 the NEC asked the government of Canada to be part of their public-school system to receive an annual grant. The government forwarded quarterly cheques for the maintenance of pupils per capita, and the MI was granted $60 per child per year (Fletcher 2004). This agreement was renegotiated twice throughout the MI's history. The NEC exclusively managed the MI while the Department of Indian Affairs (DIA) developed policies for managing the school and conducted inspections and reports (Fletcher 2004). The two organizations had ongoing negotiations about which department held responsibilities for the care and management of MI throughout its history. Fletcher (2004) found no accountability for the funding that the NEC acquired from the government of Canada in the annual reports. When the DIA and NEC entered a new lease in 1929, the NEC stopped appointing principals and instead received reports from the DIA (Fletcher 2004).

Managing organizations and departments also dodged responsibilities throughout the HRC's history. The provincial government of Ontario, for example, was responsible for the care of children with disabilities when Orillia opened its asylum doors. Until 1931 the Department of Provincial Secretary held authority over asylums, charities, prisons, and public institutions; as the categorization of people with intellectual disabilities increased, the Department of Health took over the funding and management of the HRC (Rossiter and Clarkson 2013). After 1931, the Department of Public Works held responsibility for determining the size, location, design, construction, and renovations for the HRC but there was little coordination between the Departments of Health and Public Works (HRC Annual Reports 1919, 1928, 1937; Rossiter and Clarkson 2013).

MI principals and HRC superintendents monitored the quality of care and education, managed finances, and made administrative decisions (Fletcher 2004; HRC Annual Reports 1919–50) within the parameters set by funders. They often determined the type of training, quality of teachers and spent much of their time vying for additional funding to no avail. Dr Alexander Beaton, a leading authority on "mental retardation," served as the medical superintendent at HRC between 1876 to 1916 and advocated for better accommodations and training programs (Ironside and Grossmith 1984). Dr Beaton believed that intense education would benefit children at the HRC. Similarly, principals of the MI advocated for improved conditions that required additional funding but were repeatedly rejected by the DIA. Throughout the years, principals and superintendents who requested additional funding at the MI and HRC were often fired, and cooperative people were hired in their stead (Fletcher 2004; HRC Inspection Reports 1931, 1942).

The institutions' goals, management, and administrative processes may not be identical but are certainly comparable in how they function as tools of institutional violence. The MI and HRC were developed and managed with an emphasis on isolation, profits over care, assimilation, and conformity. The organizations and governing departments involved in the funding, control, and management of total institutions failed in their duty to care for institutionalized children. Managing departments of institutions evaded responsibilities and dismissed children's needs. Government records document the chronic underfunding and mismanagement of institutions that created climates of suffering for children at the MI and HRC (Fletcher 2004; HRC Annual Reports 1926, 1931; HRC Inspection Report 1942). The HRC and MI penetrated health and social spheres on the premise that removal of others bettered society.

FORCING CONFORMITY OF OTHERED BODIES THROUGH EDUCATION

In institutional settings, bodies are spatially and visually divided first by binary cis-gender norms and practices. Gender-specific dormitories housed gender-conforming bodies on either side of the main institutions' building. Gendered clothing and hairstyles were forced on HRC residents (Jackson and Rinaldi 2019a, 2019d) and MI students were forced to cut their hair and wear "modern" clothing (Woodland Cultural Centre 2004, 2010, 2014) specifically upon admission to the institution, for photographs, and on the rare occasion of visitors. Forced conformity is violent particularly in the context of cultural genocide. The institution mandated that Indigenous children's hair be cut, which is a particular kind of insidious cultural violence in the context of some Indigenous knowledge that understands Indigenous peoples' hair to be spiritually powerful ("Elders Talk" 2015; Woodland Cultural Centre 2004). Institutionalized bodies were forced to conform to settler society's patriarchal, and capitalist standards through education that prepared children for labour: "[Education] is always a hegemonic discourse. Through education, dominant culture in every society seeks not only to transmit a body of knowledge, but also values a "normative" hermeneutic. However, if all education is hegemonic discourse, Residential Schools have been uniquely so" (Fletcher 2004, 133). Educational institutions developed with the goal of assimilation, established through policies and practices that police the knowledge contradicting or impeding dominant society's progress. Thus, educating othered children through institutionalization is a form of indoctrination.

Throughout the 1940s, the principal at the MI insisted that the point of a residential school education was to prepare children to become part of dominant culture (Fletcher 2004). The HRC similarly became a training school for children with dis/abilities so they could become functional members of dominant society. Superintendent Beaton was fuelled by successful reports of educating children with dis/abilities (Park 1990; Williston 1971) while the MI was boasted as a training institute for Indigenous children in need (Brantford Expositor 1927). In 1928, the superintendent highlighted the effectiveness of the institution as a medical centre and school for dis/abled children. He congratulated seventeen nurses on completing the first half of their first year at the HRC on-site nursing school (HRC Annual Report 1928). In fact, the HRC changed its name from the Orillia Asylum to the Ontario Hospital School, Orillia in 1936 to emphasize training not only for residents of HRC but also as a teaching hospital (HRC Annual Reports 1936).

Despite the HRC's reputation as a training and hospital centre, and the MI's status as a boarding school, low-quality education, care, and training were reported throughout the years. According to Fletcher (2004), the MI hired teachers who would not be hired elsewhere because they were unqualified and would work for less. Students in Residential Schools across Canada were left barely literate (Barnes, Josefowitz, and Cole 2006; Fletcher 2004). Similarly, the HRC had trouble maintaining capable nursing staff through the 1920s (HRC Annual Report 1920, 1924, 1928). Workers from the HRC noted that administration remained the same for years while staff turnover was always high (HRC Annual Reports 1920–50; Recounting Huronia Community Archive 2022b).

Concerns about inadequate teaching and conditions at the MI were raised by the Brantford League of Christian Women (BLCW) in 1946 after a guided tour by the principal's wife when the principal was out of town (Fletcher 2004). The women compared the MI to the public schools that their children attended and were shocked because there were no music, art, or domestic science teachers, and no manual training instructors. The school lacked a proper library, there were no quiet spaces, no physical education facilities, and no proper classroom equipment. The Indian Agent at the time argued that the women were exaggerating but concerns were echoed by many voices throughout the years (Fletcher 2004, 143). Similar red flags were raised in relation to the HRC when Pierre Berton (1960) wrote the haunting article, "What's Wrong at Orillia": "In many respects it is an up-to-date institution with a dedicated staff fighting an uphill battle against despairing conditions. But should fire break out in one of those ancient buildings and dozens of small bodies be found next morning in the ashes, do not say that you did not know what it was like behind those plaster walls, or underneath those peeling wooden ceilings."

By the 1960s, the MI became a public school, and the teachers began receiving similar salaries and benefits as Ontario public school teachers. The student to teacher ratio became more appropriate but the demographics of the MI changed as most students were orphaned, delinquent, or disabled post 1961 and required other types of resources (Fletcher 2004). The BLCW, newspaper reporters, and inspectors have sounded alarms over the disgusting conditions of the MI and HRC. Survivor stories and public access to historical reports has provided a clearer picture of the experiences of institutionalization. Children housed at the MI and HRC were taught basic education in English reading, writing, and arithmetic, while the binary gender divide continued as boys were taught manual labour tasks, and girls were taught domestic skills. These educational practices were not only the bare minimum in providing for the needs of children who were deemed expendable in a developing capitalist, settler society, but also worked to prepare children for the institutions' work force.

CAPITALIZING ON THE WORK OF OTHERED BODIES

Both institutions utilized the human capacity of their residents through labour programs. In 1926 the superintendent of the HRC developed an Employment Services Program that ranked residents' abilities and taught job skills. The superintendent boasted about the savings to the institution when the residents were put to work (HRC Annual Report 1924). The boys worked on farms and did manual labour with maintenance staff (Jackson and Rinaldi 2019c), made shoes (ibid.), or formed gravestones (Jackson and Rinaldi 2019a) while the girls completed laundry and seamstressing (Jackson and Rinaldi 2019b). Similarly, the MI taught girls laundry and kitchen tasks, while the boys learned industrial labour (Fletcher 2004) and worked in the fields (Morritt-Jacobs 2021). Children residing at the HRC were ranked on skill and ability, then shipped off to the department that would benefit from that child's skill level. Children classified with higher skill levels were able to do intricate work within the institution but were determined unable to function within society's standards. It was important for the HRC to keep residents inside the institution, particularly when their skills were so valuable to its budget.

Other children, mostly girls that could work in the community, were exploited through off-property work programs (Fletcher 2004; Jackson and Rinaldi 2019b). In 1929, the HRC ran a probation scheme for fifty-three girls who went to work in the community. Some of the girls lived with their employers and others lived in the Colony House, where girls were sent to do housework. In 1932 the Colony House was burned down and never replaced (Morris and Hartley 1991). Similarly, the MI sent young Indigenous girls to work as servants for wealthy Brantford homes and the school received a stipend (Fletcher 2004). Both situations placed vulnerable children at the mercy of community members, which had disastrous consequences for young othered women. Institutionalized children were offered a double-edged sword when given the opportunity to work in the community because on the one hand children were able to leave the confinement of the institution and on the other, Indigenous children and dis/abled children were met with indifference in most communities, lacked protections, and often were violated with no consequence.

Institutional administration capitalized on the work provided by institutionalized children and used funding to maintain the institution but failed to improve conditions using funds from exploited labour. Colonial powers in Canada have historically policed labour practices to limit progress for non-normative folks. In the case of the MI, Indigenous children were offered sub-standard education and training such that their job options were limited once they left the institution. And residents of the HRC who could work outside the institution were held captive and received labour training. Education beyond entry-level workplace learning was denied to the children residing at the HRC and MI. Both institutions valued their residents for exploitable labour only and mirrored community neglect for the care and protection of othered children.

NEGLECTING OTHERED BODIES

The neglect, negligence, and disregard for the wellbeing of institutionalized children at the HRC and MI led to violence, abuse, suffering, and death. Both institutions are responsible for neglect because staff and administration failed to provide the necessities of life through poor environmental conditions, and denial of clothing and nutrition. The institutions' departments and organizations were negligent in their duties to care for the wellbeing of institutionalized children. Abhorrent and dangerous conditions at the MI and HRC were dismissed until social activists and journalists warned the public. Unsanitary conditions, inadequate education, and malnutrition was used by staff and administration to control and violate residents at both institutions. The following examples demonstrate devaluation of othered bodies through institutionalization. Neglecting othered children served colonialism by signalling clearly that unproductive bodies would be abandoned.

Superintendents of the HRC were diligent in buying and building infrastructure to house residents and staff, but the cost of maintaining such a grand-scale institution resulted in a chronic state of dilapidation (HRC inspection Reports 1924, 1928, 1935, 1940). Inspectors' reports for both institutions describe a dismal situation as damaged fire alarm systems and dangerous equipment posed serious safety concerns (Berton 1960; HRC Inspection Reports 1924, 1928, 1935; Fletcher 2004; Williston 1970). During their visit, the BLCW were appalled by the conditions of the MI building, and the inadequate sleeping and toileting facilities. They reported to the local newspaper that the MI was "abysmal and below any standard suitable to human living" (Brantford Expositor 1946, cited in Fletcher 2004, 139). A DIA inspection report, complete with graphic diagrams and photographs, described the unhealthy situation as toilets were in the open, too close to beds, had no toilet seats, and had inadequate plumbing and drainage. Residents had no privacy and there was no ventilation (Fletcher 2004). The inspector wrote: "Conditions are not good enough for a school whose objective is to raise the cultural and moral level of children who have already had a lower than average start. Conditions in the washrooms would by ordinary white standards be called degrading" (Fletcher 2004, 139). The government of Canada failed to act and in fact fired that Inspector shortly after writing the horrific report (Fletcher 2004). Conditions at the HRC were also sub-standard. Berton

(1960) and Williston (1970) publicly commented that the HRC was dirty and odorous while a 1942 inspection reported the institution had foul air (HRC Inspection Report 1942). Staff neglected sanitation in resident spaces. During a site visit to the HRC in October of 2014 a former employee commented that staff never used residents' bathrooms because they were putrid and dirty (Recounting Huronia Community Archive 2014c).

Public calls to improve conditions were limited at the MI and HRC because parents and visitors were discouraged to enter the closed institutions (Barnes, Josefowitz, and Cole 2006; Jackson and Rinaldi 2019a). It was not until social activists such as the BLCW visited the MI and the DIA in 1948 provided visual illustrations of the "sense of depression in the dormitories and playroom" of the MI (Fletcher 2004, 139). The HRC's conditions were hidden until Pierre Berton's (1960) scathing article described a "depressed state" at the HRC. Berton (1960) wrote about Orillia's appalling stench, that "no amount of cleansing would remove the odours of 70 years." The institution was "overcrowded and understaffed," and "Orillia's real problem," Berton (1960) condemned, "is one of public neglect." A visual depiction of othered children wandering aimlessly through the enormous institutions' halls has been described for both institutions (Fletcher 2004; Williston 1970) due to a lack of resources for children to occupy their time.

The institution also failed to provide other necessities of life. Children housed at the HRC and MI were refused proper clothing and nutrition. In 1939 an anonymous letter to the DIA reported that the children at MI were not adequately clothed: "the boys are still without underwear. They only received stockings one month ago. Light cotton clothes are worn summer and winter. Even the poor clothes they have are often dirty and ragged" (Fletcher 2004, 143). The BLCW complained about clothing as children were not provided with socks, winter coats or boots during Ontario winters. In 1955 there were 165 students at the MI. The principal, who argued that Indigenous children, "must be dressed as white children are" (Fletcher 2004, 142), was only able to clothe children using church donations. Children at the HRC were often nude or dressed in nightgowns (Lewis 1942). HRC survivor Brian Logie, for example, remembers wearing nightgowns while in the institution and only once being in clothes when a visitor came to the institution (Jackson and Rinaldi 2019a). Othered children who were institutionalized at the HRC and MI were denied their basic needs because they were not valued in settler society.

Malnutrition was a particular violence against Indigenous children. According to Fletcher (2004), inadequate nutrition was a concern raised by parents and outside inspectors of the MI. According to the MI's annual reports from 1948–50, thirteen children belonging to six different families requested their children be removed from MI and placed in Shingwauk School in Sault Ste Marie because of harmful conditions. The BLCW also complained about inadequate food and noted the lack of dental care (Fletcher 2004). Fletcher (2004) reports that in 1929 the principal of MI was diligent with dental care and asked for additional funding for a five-day dental clinic and better toothbrushes. The DIA would not authorize extra money for toothbrushes from the per-capita funding and objected to spending more on dental than other residential schools. In 1932 a dentist's report commented that the condition of the children's teeth improved after the principal bought the students new toothbrushes for Christmas with his own money (Fletcher 2004). The failure to provide hygiene resources followed through to the HRC. Survivors were forced to share toothbrushes and razors. Harold Dougall, an HRC survivor, remembers using his canteen money to buy the students in his ward toothbrushes (Jackson and Rinaldi 2019c). A chronic state of lacking resources meant children residing at both institutions were malnourished, lived in unsanitary conditions, and experienced emotional neglect.

Overworked staff, inadequate supervision, and an environment of neglect bred institutional violence and violation (Barnes, Josefowitz, and Cole 2006). The public is now learning about institutional violence through survivors' accounts of abuse but the suffering endured by institutionalized children is especially haunting. Rather than searching for the worst types of institutional violence, I consciously chose to remain within the parameters of my initial data collection. In this paper I refer to instances of violence that are exemplified in the HRC and MI annual reports, HRC patient files, public survivor accounts, and newspaper articles throughout the institutions' histories. What follows then, is not an exhaustive list of the types of violence that involved bodily contact in the institutions but rather a conscious selection that describes the horrors of the everyday lived experiences of institutionalized children at the MI and HRC. At times I chose to remove resident names out of respect for families while at the same time in describing other stories, I attempt to document the forgotten and provide space for the voices of public survivor advocates. Here I address the violence that is rooted in othering and perpetually replicated throughout institutional environments.

ABUSING OTHERED BODIES

Social hierarchies existed inside the institution at both the administrative and the peer-to-peer level. Residents of the MI and of the HRC developed social hierarchies that drove resident conflicts inside the institutions. New arrivals at the MI experienced violence at the hands of other students who maintained a social hierarchy that children learned from authorities (Moses 2016). According to HRC survivor accounts; social hierarchies existed amongst residents where those with higher status, usually the higher functioning residents, would coerce and intimidate others into following their established rules. One HRC survivor and advocate describes feeling like a hired goon for the staff and higher-status residents (Jackson and Rinaldi 2019c).

The following examples describe peer-to-peer violence and oppression at the MI that was detailed by Fletcher (2004; see also Charles and Lowry 2017 for a detailed analysis on the process of ethically and respectfully engaging with narratives of student-to-student abuse in Canada's residential school system). The example above illustrates the harm of inadequate supervision and the violence children experienced upon admission into these institutions. Othered children were taken from their homes and submerged into the colonial production line that involved institutional violence. Their introduction to the institution involved learning the social hierarchies that make up the basis of othering. Social hierarchies are established based on ideology that one person is better than another because they exist with qualities that align to settler norms. Children who existed further from the Western, able-bodied norm were oppressed where more normative children were exploited within the institution for labour. Peer-to-peer violence and oppression helped to maintain othering within the institution while a lack of supervision led to students' suffering and death.

An "accidental death" that involved damaged playground equipment demonstrates the harm that arises from neglect at the MI. Fletcher (2004) describes thirteen-year-old Effie Smith who resided at the MI in 1939. The MI had no playground equipment at that time except the May Pole which was used in the traditional European May Pole Dance. A steering wheel was affixed to the top of a pole which children used not only as a swing but also as peer punishment. Unpopular children would be strapped by the arms and swung until they vomited. An inquest found that Effie, a victim of neglect, died accidentally when the May Pole broke (Fletcher, 2004). Before being categorized as "accidental," Effie's death records would have been reviewed by several departments which are all culpable in the climate of neglect at the MI. Peer punishment mirrored the violence used as punishment by teachers and principals of residential schools.

Traditionally, Indigenous parental practices did not involve physical punishments like the methods used by staff and faculty at residential schools such as the MI (Stolen Lives 2015). A 1947 letter from the principal to the DIA recorded an incident of sexual assault where one "lad was holding down a younger lad and the third caught in the act while stripped" (Fletcher 2004, 145). Without proper supervision, the younger children at the MI were not protected from the older children who learned violent behaviour from staff and administration. For example, as punishment for the assault, which would regularly be a hand-strapping, the MI principal instead requested permission to use a behaviour modification technique based on pain and pleasure (Fletcher 2004) where desirable behaviours are rewarded, and undesirable behaviours are punished by inflicting pain. In this scenario, the authority inflicting pain would determine which acts or traits were undesirable. Essentially those that deviated from settler norms were deemed undesirable. Abuse was used not only as a form of punishment but also as a form of forced conformity. The HRC resident files also document staff's preoccupation with homosexuality and punishment methods to deter homosexual thoughts and actions (Jackson and Rinaldi 2019a, 2019c, 2019d).

Punishments went beyond hand strapping throughout the histories of both institutions. HRC survivors, for example, describe the following examples: "whacked with a wooden club for failing to pass [hygiene] inspections," "hit with a fly swatter and dunked upside down in ice water as punishment for not eating" and "residents [being] made to push a pink rubber eraser along the institution's floor with their noses (*Star* 2010). And over 500 feet of tramways meant staff and administration had access to every understaffed department from underground. HRC survivors describe the constant fear of being abused every night (Jackson and Rinaldi 2019a, 2019b). Othered bodies, particularly othered female bodies, are devalued through sexual exploitation. Evidence of sexual abuse is documented in the annual reports of the HRC and MI. Fletcher (2004) notes that the MI principal during the 1950s requested funding for improved laundry facilities, "to prevent the spread of venereal disease" (Fletcher 2004). HRC resident records document pregnancies of young women who were deemed disabled (HRC Resident Records: Cheryl 1969) and housed in a total institution where the only men who had access were administration and staff. Other young women institutionalized at the MI and HRC were farmed out to work on wealthy families' homes and returned pregnant (Fletcher 2004; HRC Resident Records: Cheryl 1969). Gross violations of othered bodies continued behind closed doors. The institutional model provides access to othered bodies and spaces for violation. Othering grants social permissions for violence against non-normative folks because the other is considered unnatural and inhuman, a burden on normative white society. Institutional othering signals that the bodies of the abused are impure and the institutional model is used to purify normative whiteness.

DEVALUING OTHERED BODIES IN DEATH

Purifying settler society demands the removal and devaluation of othered bodies through institutional violence. From assaulting othered children's bodies to the hidden and documented deaths of thousands of institutionalized children (Deer 2021; Remember Every Name 2022), institutional violence is predicated on devaluing othered bodies. Examples of sexual abuse, lack of funder accountability, and medical negligence illustrate institutional disregard for othered life.

In the case of the HRC, perpetual overcrowding and understaffing led to unnecessary deaths of children. The admission and painful death of four-year-old Lucas is documented in HRC resident records. Lucas, a toddler when admitted to the HRC in 1955 with a rash on his buttocks (Notice of Admission 1955) died two years after admission. After periods of isolation (Treatment Record 1956) and mismanaged diaper changes; Lucas died from "septic thrombus" (ibid.), a painful condition that spreads across the body. A Department of Health's Report on Death (Report on Death 1957) describes Lucas's right leg, penis, and scrotum as swollen with cyanosis (a condition where the skin turns blueish-purple due to lack of oxygen). Lucas' painful death was the result of outrageous failures on the part of care providers at the HRC.

Children's deaths were common until the HRC's closure. A 1971 HRC Medical Audit and Tissue Committee Meeting (HRC Reports 1971) describes the deaths of Annabelle, Charles, and Lucy (pseudonyms). Annabelle's autopsy found that her death resulted from "progressive deterioration" of an original condition, but Annabelle's file lacked a total care plan (HRC Reports 1971). The meeting minutes note a discrepancy between the diagnoses given by the HRC staff doctor and the coroner, a problem that appears twice, with no actionable items mentioned to rectify the discrepancies (HRC Reports 1971). This problem was important to note but not enough to make institutional changes.

Negligent medical care was covered up by institutional bureaucracy. Charles died, according to the 1971 meeting, because "he had kidney involvement since his admission" but received only one urinalysis that tested normal at that time (HRC Reports 1971). A doctor suggested that more urinalyses be done upon admission of residents, but this recommendation was implemented only four years before the HRC closed. Often children were forgotten and notes in the files were lacking. Lucy's cause of death, for example, was redacted with nothing "peculiar or noteworthy in this case" (HRC Reports 1971), though I fail to see how the death of any child would not be noteworthy. From the limited information available in this report, the death of disabled children seemed commonplace and medical negligence at the HRC was never reprimanded. The lack of accountability within the institutional model is apparent in the rising death tolls of institutionalized children (Morritt-Jacobs 2021; Recounting Huronia Community Archive 2022d).

Fletcher (2004) describes the death of Wilhemina Hill, a student of unknown age, represented by a number to the DIA, was orphaned and had tuberculosis. The MI principal unsuccessfully sought authorization to send Wilhemina to the sanitorium in Brantford for $1 per day, which was "considerably more than the per capita allowance for her to live at MI" (Fletcher 2004, 141). Wilhemina ended up dying while others contracted TB. Fletcher (2004) highlights a gap in medical care at the MI that is not the case for the HRC. The HRC and MI institutions' medical expenses were covered by different branches of the Canadian government. Children residing at the HRC were covered under the provincial government of Ontario while Indigenous peoples have always been funded through the federal government. On the ground, this meant that medical emergencies at the HRC were taken care of within the institution or at the nearest local hospital. On the other hand, medical emergencies from the MI were transported roughly twenty kilometres away to the Lady Willingdon Hospital in what is now called Ohsweken. For severe situations, the MI principal could request special permissions from the DIA to use additional funding from the per capita grant to pay for the fee charged by the

Brantford Hospital. Children often suffered at MI as conditions worsened while the principal waited for permissions that were not always granted (Fletcher 2004). The institutional model bureaucratizes healthcare and decides who gets to live and who dies based on financial considerations (Fletcher 2004).

Othered bodies of children at the HRC and MI were subjected to degradation before and after death. The institutional model treated the dead as they treated the living: with indifference and disrespect. HRC death certificates and medical logs document deaths and excuse staff of mistreatment. Institutionalized children died from disease, neglect, abuse, and other forms of violence; then a devaluation of the dead continued institutional violation. The final devaluation of othered bodies is represented through mass burial sites and unmarked graves. Only 32 per cent of the students who died in the residential school system in Canada are documented in any official capacity (Leung 2015) but for MI residents, their names are etched into the brick of the former residential school (Morritt-Jacobs 2021) to document their institutionalization. Numbered gravestones form a cemented rectangle that represents the bodies of children buried on the grounds of the HRC. The gravestones, though placed back in the cemetery, were previously repurposed as patio stones until a Chaplain ordered they be returned to the HRC cemetery (Recounting Huronia Community Archive 2022a). The audacious cruelty of the institutional system on an othered child's life is amplified by the devaluation of the othered child's death.

CONCLUSION

This chapter shows how institutional violence is rooted in othering. Others, those who deviate from social norms in terms of race, dis/ability, gender, age, and class, are deemed inferior and exploited because of their difference. The problem here is settler notions of hierarchy and difference where those deemed "normal" hold the characteristics of a perfect person – that only exists within capitalist, patriarchal, and settler structures. As a result, an enormous number of children were subjected to violence and degradation on the basis that their difference deserved violation and exploitation. Othered bodies, considered inferior, were neglected by the institution because their existence threatened settler and abled society while the process of othering resulted in violence and institutional death.

Themes of institutional violence rooted in othering are found within institutional administrative processes, methods for targeting, controlling, and educating othered bodies, and the abusive treatment, neglect of, and negligence toward othered bodies at the MI and HRC. Movement towards justice and healing for institutional survivors begins with mindful efforts from individuals, communities, policymakers, and stakeholders to push back against systemic racism, oppression, and inequity that is inherent in institutionalization. By acknowledging the lived experiences of institutionalization, people, communities, and organizations can be held accountable for their disregard for children who were not white, not able-bodied, and deemed abnormal. This typology demonstrates the ways that institutional violence is deeply socially patterned that highlights the need to apply a careful eye on future institutional practices.

REFERENCES

Abbas, Jihan, and Jijian Voronka 2014. "Remembering Institutional Erasures: The Meaning of Histories of Disability Incarcerated in Ontario." In *Disability Incarcerated: Imprisonment and Disability in the United States and Canada*, edited by Liat Ben-Moshe, Chris Chapman, and Allison C. Carey, 121–38. Palgrave Macmillan.

Austen, I. 2021 "How Thousands of Indigenous Children Vanished in Canada." *New York Times*, 7 July 2021. https://www.nytimes.com/2021/06/07/world/canada/mass-graves-residential-schools.html.

Barnes, Rosemary, Nina Josefowitz, and Ester Cole. 2006. "Residential Schools: Impact on Aboriginal Students' Academic and Cognitive Development." *Canadian Journal of School Psychology* 21, nos 1–2: 18–32.

Ben-Moshe, Liat, Chris Chapman, and Allison C. Carey, eds. 2014. *Disability Incarcerated: Imprisonment and Disability in the United States and Canada*. Palgrave Macmillan.

Berton. Pierre. 1960. "What's Wrong at Orillia." https://www.thestar.com/news/insight/2013/09/20/huronia_pierre_berton_warned_us_50_years_ago.html.

Brantford Expositor. 1927. "Semi-Centennial Edition, 1877–1927." Brantford, Ontario.

– 2011. "Six Nations Sets Record Straight on Woodland Cultural Centre." Accessed 10 November 2016. http://www.rcav.org/uploadedFiles/Six%20Nations%20 denies%20info%20sent%20to%20Annett.pdf.

Burghardt, Madeline C. 2018. *Broken: Institutions, Families, and the Construction of Intellectual Disability*. Montreal and Kingston: McGill-Queen's University Press.

CBC News. 2021. "Survivors, Community Honour 751 Unmarked Graves at Sask. Residential School Site with Vigil," 27 June 2021. https://www.cbc.ca/news/canada/saskatoon/survivors-community-honour-751-unmarked-graves-at-sask-residential-school-site-with-vigil-1.6082063.

Charles, Grant, and Glen Lowry. 2017. "Toward a Creative-Critical Approach to Narratives of Student-to-Student Abuse in Canada's Indian Residential School System." *Cogent Arts and Humanities* 4, no. 1: 1410081.

Craft, Aimee. 2016. *A Knock on the Door: The Essential History of Residential Schools from the Truth and Reconciliation Commission of Canada*. Winnipeg: University of Manitoba Press.

Daly, Kathleen. 2014. "Conceptualising Responses to Institutional Abuse of Children." *Current Issues in Criminal Justice* 26, no. 1: 5–29.

Deer, Ka'nhehsí:io. 2021. "Why It's Difficult to Put a Number on How Many Children Died at Residential Schools." CBC News. https://www.cbc.ca/news/indigenous/residential-school-children-deaths-numbers-1.6182456.

Duric, Donna, Lynda Powless, Jarrett Chase. 2012. "'Mush-Hole Kids' Finally Get to Tell their Story to History." *Turtle Island News*. Six Nations of the Grand River.

"Elders Talk About the Significance of Long Hair in Native American Culture." 2015. http://www.whitewolfpack.com/2013/08/elders-talk-about-significance-of-long.html.

Fletcher, Wendy. 2004. "The Canadian Experiment with Social Engineering, A Historical Case: The Mohawk Institute." *Historical Papers*.

The *Globe*. 1844–1936. 18 December 1877. ProQuest Historical Newspapers: *Globe and Mail*.

Gonzales, P. 2020. "Water-Womb-Land Cosmologic: Protocols for Traditional Ecological Knowledge." *Ecopsychology* 12: 84–90.

Graham, Elizabeth. 1997. *The Mush Hole: Life at Two Indian Residential Schools*. Heffle Pub.

HRC Annual Reports. 1919–52.

HRC Inspection Reports. 1924, 1928, 1931, 1935, 1940, 1942.

HRC Reports. 1971. HRC Medical Audit and Tissue Committee Meeting.

HRC Resident Records: Lucas. 1955. Notice of Admission. *Recounting Huronia Community Archive*.

– 1956. Treatment Record. *Recounting Huronia Community Archive.*
– 1957a. Notice of Admission. *Recounting Huronia Community Archive.*
– 1957b. Notice of Death. *Recounting Huronia Community Archive.*
– 1957c. Report on Death. *Recounting Huronia Community Archive.*
– 1969. Resident Records: Cheryl. *Recounting Huronia Community Archive.*
Hutchinson, Christina. 2017. "Languages Are Multiple: From Turtle Island to Africa – Combatting the Cultural Violence of Colonialism in Residential School and Christian Missionary School." In *New Framings on Anti-Racism and Resistance*, edited by Ayan Abdulle and Anne Nelun Obeyesekere, 35–55. Brill Sense.
Infrastructure Ontario. 2017. *Discussion on the Huronia Regional Campus' Unused Land Kitchen Table Conversation* – PARTICIPANT'S GUIDE. Toronto: Lura Consulting.
Ironside, Allan, and J.T. Grossmith. 1984. *Anecdotes of Olde Orillia: A Collection of the Works of Allan Ironside*. Orillia Historical Society.
Jackson, Kim, and Jen Rinaldi. 2019a. "Speaking Back to the Institutional Record: An Interview with Brian Logie." *Recounting Huronia Community Archive.* https://exhibits.wlu.ca/s/huronia/page/speaking-back-to-the-institutional-record.
– 2019b. Speaking Back to the Institutional Record: An Interview with Carrieanne Tompkins. *Recounting Huronia Community Archive.* https://exhibits.wlu.ca/s/huronia/page/speaking-back-to-the-institutional-record.
– 2019c. "Speaking Back to the Institutional Record: An Interview with Harold Dougall." *Recounting Huronia Community Archive.* https://exhibits.wlu.ca/s/huronia/page/speaking-back-to-the-institutional-record.
– 2019d. Speaking Back to the Institutional Record: An Interview with Pat Seth. *Recounting Huronia Community Archive.* https://exhibits.wlu.ca/s/huronia/page/speaking-back-to-the-institutional-record.
Koleszar-Green, Ruth. 2018. "What is a Guest? What is a Settler?" *Cultural and Pedagogical Inquiry* 10, no. 2: 166–77.
Leung, Marlene. 2015. "Aboriginal Children at Residential Schools Often Buried in Unmarked Graves, Report Reveals." CTV News, 15 December 2015. http://www.ctvnews.ca/canada/aboriginal-children-at-residential-schools-oftenburied-in-unmarked-graves-report-reveals-1.2701373.
Lewis, C.H. 1942. Inspection of the Ontario Hospital School. Orillia. HRC Inspection Reports.
Martin, M., and K. Hill. 2021. "'We Need to Find the Children:' Survivors of Former Residential School in Brantford, Ont. Call for Criminal Investigation into Unmarked Graves." CTV News Kitchener.

https://kitchener.ctvnews.ca/we-need-to-find-the-children-survivors-of-former-residential-school-in-brantford-ont-call-for-criminal-investigation-into-unmarked-graves-1.5517385.

Mohawk Institute (ON). The University of British Columbia. Indian Residential School History and Dialogue Centre. https://collections.irshdc.ubc.ca/index.php/Detail/entities/1146.

Morris, Joan, and Virginia Hartley. 1991. "The Dark Side of Mariposa: The Asylum at Orillia." *Beaver* 71, no. 5: 44–9.

Morritt-Jacobs, Charlotte. 2021. "Six Nations Prepares to Move Forward with Grounds Search of Former Mohawk Institute Residential School." APTN *News*. https://www.aptnnews.ca/national-news/six-nations-prepares-to-move-forward-with-grounds-search-of-former-mohawk-institute-residential-school.

Moses, J. 2016. "Russell Moses Memoir." *Canadian Journal of Children's Rights/Revue Canadienne* 3, no. 1: 9–15.

Moses, R. 2016. "Map – Mohawk Institute (1942–1947)." *Canadian Journal of Children's Rights* 3, no. 1: 8.

Recounting Huronia Community Archive. 2014a. *Final Site Visit Discussions*. 23 October 2014.

– 2014b. HRC *Cemetery Visit Discussions*. 23 October 2014. https://exhibits.wlu.ca/s/huronia/page/final-site-visit.

– 2014c.. *Putrid and Dirty*. 22 October 2014.

– n.d. HRC Cemetery Map. *Recounting Huronia Community Archive*.

Reiss, R. 2021. "182 Human Remains Discovered in Unmarked Graves Near Former Residential School." CNN, 2 July 2021. https://www.cnn.com/2021/07/01/americas/unmarked-graves-human-remains-british-columbia/index.html.

Remember Every Name. 2022. "The History." https://www.remembereveryname.ca/the-history#:~:text=Death,people%20died%20behind%20its%20walls.

Rogers, Glen, Shelagh DeGagné, Mike Dewar, and Jonathan Lowry, eds. 2013. *Speaking My Truth: Reflections on Reconciliation and Residential School*. Ottawa: Aboriginal Healing Foundation.

Rossiter, Kate, and Annalise Clarkson. 2013. "Opening Ontario's 'Saddest Chapter': A Social History of Huronia Regional Centre." *Canadian Journal of Disability Studies* 2, no. 3: 1–30.

Rossiter, Kate, and Jen Rinaldi. 2019. *Institutional Violence and Disability: Punishing Conditions*. London: Routledge.

Schmitt, Michael T., Scott D. Neufeld, Stephanie A. Fryberg, Glenn Adams, Jodi L. Viljoen, Lyana Patrick, Clifford Gordon Atleo, and

Sheri Fabian. 2021. "'Indigenous' Nature Connection? A Response to Kurth, Narvaez, Kohn, and Bae." *Ecopsychology* 13, no. 1: 64–7.

Stolen Lives: The Indigenous Peoples of Canada and the Indian Residential Schools. 2015. https://www.facinghistory.org/stolen-lives-indigenous-peoples-canada-and-indian-residential-schools/chapter-4/punishment-and-abuse.

Wildcat, D.R. 2009. "Red Alert! Saving the Planet with Indigenous Knowledge." Golden: Fulcrum Publishing.

Woodland Cultural Centre. 2004. Woodland Cultural Centre Guided Tour.

– 2010. Woodland Cultural Centre Guided Tour.

– 2014. Woodland Cultural Centre Guided Tour.

SECTION TWO

Loathing in the Transinstitutional Era

5

Invisible Institutions

Institutionalization of People Labelled with Intellectual/Developmental Disabilities

MEGAN Q. LINTON

Care services for people labelled as having intellectual and developmental disabilities in Canada were once centralized in custodial institutional spaces, often referred to as total institutions. Many of these spaces have been closed or minimized, leading to a mistaken belief that institutionalization is over. Rather, present-day institutions are reconstituted to be smaller, privately operated, and more widely dispersed across jurisdictions and ministerial mandates. Survivors of institutionalization often interconnect these continuities of incarceration, as Patrick Worth, survivor and deinstitutionalization movement organizer, summarized: "An institution is not just a place; it is the way people think" (Worth n.d.). Abolitionist and disability justice theorist Liat Ben-Moshe (2020) understands this way of thinking as *carceral ableist logic*, "the praxis and belief that people with disabilities need special or extra protections, in ways that often expand and legitimate their further marginalization and incarceration" (7). This logic is deeply tied to the logic of institutional violence, or the twinned forces of care and loathing described in the introduction of this collection.

While deinstitutionalization significantly impacted the size of institutions across Canada, carceral ableist logic maintains this praxis and belief, presently manifested in diverse locales of confinement. Today these locales may be diverse in name and function, however, institutional scholars Kate Rossiter and Jen Rinaldi unite these institutions in recognition of the shared violence inherent to their foundation. The goal of this paper is to provide a descriptive typology of transinstitutionalization across Canada such that we may better identify potential sites of institutional violence, and locales in which the logic of institutional violence bears out today. As such, this chapter takes an overview of a Pan-Canadian survey of institutionalization, which seeks to identify the expansive nature of the institutional system. The expansive nature of this system is one of many mechanisms employed by the state to obfuscate the dark realities of disability confinement (Linton 2021a).

The provision of care for people with disabilities is currently comprised of a complex web of services, service providers, jurisdictional boundaries, and responsibilities that together make up the decentralized transinstitutional landscape within Canada. Decades of governmental reports and audits have identified that one must be an expert in these policies to understand the system of services (Dubé 2016; Sylph et al. 1976; Welch 1973; Williston 1971), meaning that the current system, such as it is, is deeply inaccessible both from the position of a service user, and from the perspective of community engaged scholarship that seeks to illuminate violent practices and to make change.

For this reason, this research makes several key contributions to the field of institutional violence and disability justice efforts. First, disabled people should be able to know who is administering their care. Disabled people and their communities should be able to know who is responsible for receiving complaints and concerns. Disabled people and their families should be able to make informed decisions about where they live and what supports they receive. Informed decisions are only possible with a complete picture of the various systems and supports. Many disabled people are not given the opportunity to decide where they live, who provides their services, and what services they receive. It can help for individuals to is can at least help identify rights, accountability processes, and policies within this complex system. Beyond practical considerations, understanding how service provision does (or does not) operate in the Canadian context allows scholars, activists, and disability justice organizers to agitate against institutionalization and its many interconnected forms (Fritsch, Monaghan, and van der Meulen 2022). As this typology bridges gaps between sites of incarceration, it provides a pathway for prison abolitionists, psychiatric liberation movements, elder advocates, neurodivergent movements, and institutional survivors to build coalitions against institutionalization and engage in disability justice worldbuilding (Ben-Moshe 2020; Fritsch, Monaghan, and van der Meulen 2022).

The typology I present here is an important contribution to gaps in academic and political literature. This typology unfolds as follows: first, I begin with a description of my methodology, and a brief description of the populations who find themselves at risk of experiencing contemporary forms of institutional violence. Next, I lay out my typology in which I describe the state of institutional care for people labelled of having intellectual and developmental disability. Finally, I provide analysis linking this typology to the kinds of persistent violence that occurs within institutional settings.

METHODOLOGY

The vast nature of these institutions and the uniquity of their roles requires a set of factors to determine what is/is not an institution. Through this chapter, I use indicators set out by the United Nations Committee on the Rights of Persons with Disabilities (2017), which gave a more robust definition of an institution in order to better evaluate state parties' status of deinstitutionalization. These indicators are not all encompassing – there are many more possible shared qualities of institutions – but they do offer a beneficial framework to allow me to be able to identify institutions. The indicators include obligatory sharing of assistants and support workers; residents receive an institutional allowance in lieu of disability income from the province; rigid routine/schedule; set menu/meal schedule; limitation or regulation of visitors; set roommates; lack of choice in housing; residents do not get to choose their living arrangements (art, furniture, storage); identical activities in the same place. In addition to these indicators, I include shared regulatory capacities to identify institutions, which includes the use of a Behaviour Support Plan (Spivakovsky 2017); regulated use of chemical, mechanical, or physical restraints; and the presence of isolation rooms/solitary confinement.

These indicators are then used to evaluate contemporary systems of disability confinement. I approach these systems to allow for a complete overview of a complex ecosystem of services and supports (OECD 2017). Systems in this context refer to the ministerial and funding arrangements for the various programs of disability confinement. System mapping is a generative way to construct a typology as a tool of the systems approach, which "makes complex systems more approachable" (Canadian Centre on Substance Abuse 2014, 1), this is particularly important "given the scope of services and supports involved in a comprehensive continuum of treatment" (1). In order to construct the system map, I first surveyed literature and policy to identify the various systems that have been included in disability confinement: the carceral system (Isaacs et al. 2014; Ware et al. 2014), the forensic psychiatric system (Joseph 2015a), geriatric system (Lunsky et al. 2014; Ouellette-Kuntz et al. 2017), and the homelessness system (Joseph 2015b). Following the identification of institutions, a thorough review of relevant policy, literature, and open datasets provided foundational details for the systems mapping process. For institutions absent from literature, web-scraping – the extraction of data from websites – helped fill out further details.

I pay specific attention to the institutionalization of people labelled with intellectual or developmental disabilities. This is intentional, as the label of intellectual and developmental disability has an important history of institutionalization, which Rossiter and Rinaldi (2019) point to, the "growth of such institutions was concomitant with, and similar to, the design and development of institutions for people with other diagnoses" (4).

POPULATIONS AT RISK

As of 2022, the size of the population of people labelled with intellectual and/or developmental disabilities living in congregate group settings in Canada is relatively unknown. In 2009–10 Statistics Canada recorded 35,078 residents in residential care facilities for people with mental disorders (Crawford 2008; Statistics Canada 2011). In 2021, the population of residents in facilities for mental disorders is 57,230 residents. That signifies a growth of 22,152 people in ten years. However, these are aggregate numbers for all residential care facilities for all mental disorders, including mental health and substance use facilities, and developmental disability facilities. Currently, Statistics Canada does not publish the disaggregated data from the *Residential Care Facility Survey*.

Alongside this population of 57,230 people living in the residential mental disorders, it is important to include in assessments of the size of the institutionalized I/DD the breadth of institutionalization into various residential care facilities such as long-term care institutions, hospitals, and emergency shelters (Statistics Canada 2021). Presently, there are 542,500 people with disabilities living in residential care and nursing facilities in Canada. Including emergency shelters, residential services, and correctional facilities, there are 620,680 people living in congregate settings in Canada (Statistics Canada 2021).

TYPOLOGY: PRESENT DAY INSTITUTIONAL SPACES

This chapter focuses on two different types of institutional systems that are currently used to house and deliver supports and services for people labelled with intellectual/developmental disability. As such, services are divided into three broad categories: developmental services, aggregate services, and services related to the criminal justice system – more specifically, developmental services, those designed specifically for people labelled with I/DD, and aggregate disability services, not designed for people labelled with I/DD.

Developmental Services

Developmental services are services exclusively for people labelled with intellectual/developmental disabilities. These services are mostly regulated by the provincial ministry responsible for social services. Some jurisdictions, such as British Columbia, Ontario, and Saskatchewan, operate crown corporations responsible for regulation and oversight. Non-governmental and/or non-profit organizations are primarily responsible for service delivery (Agranoff 2013; Sonpal-Valias 2019).

CONGREGATE SETTINGS

Congregate settings are typically long-term residential services where multiple people labelled with intellectual/developmental disabilities live and share common spaces. The most common model for congregate settings is group homes, while some larger institutions continue to exist in Canada. Group homes are segregated, congregate settings that typically have capacity for between three and one hundred people labelled with intellectual and/or developmental disabilities.

Larger segregated institutions for people labelled with developmental disabilities continue to exist in Manitoba, Nova Scotia, Alberta, PEI, and Newfoundland and Labrador. Developmental service agencies delivering congregate services can utilize restrictive interventions against people labelled with intellectual/developmental disabilities (Gaskin et al. 2013). These interventions can include use of pharmaceuticals, restraints, and seclusion. Restraints are any manual method used to immobilize or reduce mobility of a person, whereas seclusion or secure isolation, sometimes called "time-outs," are the confinement of a person in a room that they cannot leave (Saini and Busch 2022). Congregate developmental settings have higher rates of inappropriate antipsychotic usage (Lunsky et al. 2018).

DUAL DIAGNOSTICS SERVICES

People labelled with I/DD and concurrent psychiatric disabilities are typically given the label of "Dual Diagnosis." As of 2012, there are an estimated 440,000 people labelled with Dual Diagnosis in Canada (Gough and Morris 2012). Dual Diagnostic labels have resulted in the creation of segregated psychiatric units for people labelled with I/DD. Dual diagnosis adds the challenging layer of requiring and navigating two systems (Gough and Morris 2012). The segregated units alongside the already institutional structure of psychiatric institutions make these sites of institutionalization for people labelled with I/DD. Some dual-diagnosis settings have the right to involuntarily detain people labelled with psychiatric, intellectual, and/or developmental disabilities under provincial Mental Health Acts (Browne 2010).

Along with segregated units, some provinces, such as British Columbia, have developed segregated dual diagnosis facilities. The Provincial Assessment Centre in BC is an inpatient unit for people over fifteen labelled with I/DD and an assumed psychiatric diagnosis (Community Living BC 2021). The PAC is one of several high intensity, complex care congregate settings developed by the province for acute hospitalization, as such the average length of stay is twenty-one days, in BC there is a maximum length of stay of three months (ibid.). In several jurisdictions, notably Ontario, Alberta, and Nova Scotia, people labelled with dual diagnosis have been unable to be discharged for months (Dubé 2016) or years (Tutton 2021) because of gaps in residential and support services. These service gaps result in inappropriate ongoing institutionalization and worsened psychological and psychosocial outcomes.

DUAL DIAGNOSTIC FORENSIC PSYCHIATRIC SETTINGS

The forensic psychiatric system is governed under the Mental Health Act (1990) and the Criminal Code (1985). Forensic psychiatric institutions are a unique form of institutions specifically for people labelled with mental disorders. Some intellectual/developmental disabilities are mental disorders as per the Diagnostic and Statistics Manual 5 definitions and contemporary case law (*R. v. Minassian* 2021). The different forms of institutionalization include psychiatric hospitals, forensic psychiatric institutions, group homes, hospital psychiatric wards, and community-based forensic psychiatric settings.

People labelled with intellectual/developmental disabilities are disproportionately represented in forensic psychiatric settings. For instance, in Ontario one in five forensic psychiatric beds are occupied by people labelled with I/DD (Woodbury-Smith, Furimsky, and Chaimowitz 2018). Forensic psychiatric settings constitute a form of institutionalization for people labelled with I/DD given the overrepresentation of labelled people, the segregation of people with disabilities apart from the population, the disproportionate length of sentences for labelled people, the removal of autonomy and choice. Increasingly, forensic psychiatric services are integrating dual diagnosis programs which segregate labelled people.

Compared with their incarcerated peers without I/DD, people labelled with I/DD on average have longer sentences within forensic psychiatric institutions (Lin et al. 2017). One of the challenges to being released from forensic psychiatric institutions is the lack of housing and supported living environments for people labelled with dual diagnosis who have interacted with the justice system. Life within forensic psychiatric units is characterized by the highest rates of both surveillance and limited access to liberties (Joseph 2015a). People labelled with I/DD within forensic psychiatric settings may be subject to clinical seclusion because of their assumed risk status and the negative impact of incarceration on responsive behaviours (Office of the Correctional Investigator 2013). Clinical seclusion is "is the involuntary confinement alone in a cell/room of a seriously disordered inmate/patient who presents an imminent risk of physical harm to self or others. The expert consensus is that seclusion should be used as a last resort and discontinued at the earliest time possible" (Office of the Correctional Investigator 2013, 15).

Aggregate Services

While not specifically intended to provide care for people labelled as intellectually or developmentally disabled, aggregate services are often used to compensate for the shortages in developmental services. Services and spaces related to the criminal justice system are not meant to provide care for people with intellectual or developmental disabilities, however, given the enormous gaps in service provision often inadvertently fulfil this role.

PSYCHIATRIC INSTITUTIONS

While some provinces operate services specifically for people with co-occurring dual diagnosis, other provinces rely upon generalized psychiatric services. People are admitted to psychiatric institutions (whether wards or hospitals) either voluntarily or involuntarily through provincial *Mental Health Acts*. Alongside involuntary psychiatric hospitalization, challenges with discharge and readmission are central trends in psychiatric institutionalization for people labelled with I/DD or dual diagnosis.

People labelled with intellectual/developmental disabilities alongside psychiatric disabilities are institutionalized in segregated, congregate settings in both psychiatric hospitals and psychiatric wards. Psychiatric wards, hospitals, and institutions are primarily short-term, acute, institutional settings for people with psychiatric or mental health disabilities. Institutionalization through psychiatric settings can result in increased reliance on chemical restraints (Lunsky et al. 2018), loss of community housing placement (*Disability Rights Coalition v. Nova Scotia* 2021), removal of rights through involuntary admission and isolation (Gough and Morris 2012).

As of 2006, psychiatric conditions were the primary cause of hospitalization for people labelled with I/DD, representing 42 per cent of all hospitalizations (Lunsky and Balogh 2010). Many provinces have guidelines for admitting people with developmental disabilities in psychiatric settings (see for instance, Byrne and Hurley 2007). Research finds that people labelled with dual diagnosis report experiences of judgment, disempowerment, and belittlement by service providers within psychiatric settings (Venville et al. 2015). While service-providers report experiences of jurisdictional inconsistency between Ministries of Health, who are responsible for providing psychiatric services, and Ministries of Social Services who are responsible for providing developmental services (Gough and Morris 2012). Many jurisdictions have as a primary challenge an insufficient number of community beds, which prolongs release, and makes individuals increasingly reliant on institutional settings (Dubé 2016).

LONG-TERM CARE INSTITUTIONS

There is minimal federal data on the use of long-term care institutions for people labelled with intellectual and developmental disabilities. According to Inclusion Canada's (2008) Crawford Report, "Customized data received from Statistics Canada indicate that about 1,200 people with intellectual disabilities were living in residential care facilities designated for seniors in 2001–2002" (8). Twenty years since that data point, in Ontario alone more than 3,200 people labelled with intellectual/developmental disabilities are institutionalized in LTC facilities (Lunsky et al. 2014). LTC facilities are highly institutional environments where people are unable to choose when or what they eat, how they spend their time, who provides their care, and who they live with. There is minimal Canadian research on the characteristics of younger people labelled with I/DD living in LTC facilities, however research from Australia characterizes the population as those with comorbidities and needs for specialized nursing care (Wilson et al. 2020). LTC facilities are residential institutions, designed to accommodate people with complex support needs who require twenty-four-hour support. Thus, the shared characteristic of all LTC facility residents is underlying disability, not age. Often, they are places of last resort for people labelled with I/DD, when there are no spaces in developmental services (Orosz et al. 2016).

One response to the support needs of younger adults with disabilities has been the creation of specialized wings of long-term care facilities for younger people. People living in LTC facilities have decreased health and social outcomes alongside higher-than-average mortality rates compared to their peers in community-based settings (Lane et al. 2019). Long-term care centres are associated with increasing rates of disablement, including increased rates of bone breakage, increased rates of depression or depressive symptoms (Dening and Milne 2011; Smith-MacDonald et al. 2019).

RETIREMENT HOMES

Retirement homes are privately owned residential buildings. The Canada Mortgage and Housing Corporation (2009) defines retirement homes by the following indicators: a) majority of residents (<50 per cent) are over the age of 65, b) have at least one unit that is not subsidized, c) offer a meal plan, d) provide some care services, and e) have at least ten units. There are more than 251,830 people living in retirement homes and communities (Statistics Canada 2020).

SHELTERS AND HOMELESSNESS SERVICES

Across Canada, services for unhoused people are a responsibility of municipal governments, overseen by provincial ministries of municipal affairs, and supported by federal anti-homelessness initiatives. High rates of poverty alongside extensive waitlists for housing and residential supports result can force labelled people into the homelessness system. Living in shelters, rooming houses, and hotels are associated with higher mortality rates (Hwang et al. 2009), higher rates of infection (Chambers et al. 2014), and injuries (Public Health Ontario 2019).

EMERGENCY SHELTERS

In the last fifteen years across Canada, the duration of stays within homeless shelters has increased, causing an increased demand for shelter beds (Employment and Social Development Canada 2021a). The pervasive issue of homelessness among people labelled with I/DD has resulted in widespread usage of emergency shelters as long-term institutional settings (Inclusion Canada 2019). There are 423 emergency shelters and 16,271 permanent beds in Canada (Employment and Social Development Canada 2021b). Aggregate research estimates between 12–39 per cent of the homeless population may live with an intellectual/developmental disability (Durbin et al. 2018).

Developmental service agencies when faced with no alternatives refer people labelled with I/DD to homeless shelters. Lougheed and Farrell's (2013) assessment of shelter usage among adults with dual diagnosis highlight the vulnerability of shelter settings for abuse and neglect. Homeless shelters are associated with minimal decision-making power – beds and meals are determined by staff and availability.

CUSTODIAL HOUSING

Over the last twenty years, custodial supports have been maintained through long-term supportive congregate housing for precariously housed people (Community Support and Research Unit 2012). These typically have shared rooms, bathrooms, and communal spaces, and twenty-four-hour staff. There is no choice in meals, rooms, staff, or service provision. As these are delivered municipally, there is significant variation in the type of support, size of residence, and name of the service. In Ontario, these institutions are known as Homes for Special Care and Domiciliary Hostels, which collectively house more than 10,000 people with disabilities (Linton 2021b). BC is shifting toward this model with their announcement of complex care facilities for between thirty to fifty people labelled with challenging behaviour, psychiatric disability, and/or addiction (Community Living BC 2021).

CARCERAL INSTITUTIONS

The carceral system in Canada is comprised of federal and provincial correctional institutions, overseen by provincial Office of the Solicitor General and federal Attorney General. There are 37,854 adults in provincial/territorial and federal custody per day (Public Safety Canada 2020). Limited research has been conducted on the size of the I/DD populations within the criminal justice system in Canada, and as a result there is significant variability of data. A 2007 prevalence study of intellectual disability in a Quebec pre-trial detention facility found between 19–28 per cent of incarcerated people met the criteria of intellectual disability (Crocker et al. 2007). While 2018 research of Ontario provincial correctional facilities found an over-representation of persons with developmental disabilities (Whittingham et al. 2020), but substantially less than the 2007 study, with a prevalence of 2.2 per cent.

Prisons are institutional settings that have disproportionate over-representation of people labelled with intellectual and/or developmental disabilities. The report by Ontario Ombudsman Paul Dubé (2016) found that prisons have functioned as a "failsafe when the developmental services sector could not provide adequate supports" (255). The incarceration of people labelled with I/DD into correctional facilities as a result of their support needs is in contradiction to article fourteen of the UNCRPD, which prohibits incarceration based on disability. Within the correctional system, people labelled with I/DD are more likely to experience solitary confinement (Office of the Correctional Investigator 2013), require medical attention (Whittingham et al. 2020), and engage in self harm (Endicott 1991). People labelled with I/DD are incarcerated in both prisons, and within psychiatric institutions for incarcerated people. One of such institutions is the Regional Psychiatric Centre (RPC), a Correctional Services Canada facility in Saskatoon, Saskatchewan. In 2013, the Office of the Correctional Investigator released a report on the treatment of self-injurious behaviours among federally sentenced women at the

RPC. The surveyed focused on eight women among whom: six of the eight lived with some form of developmental disability, and seven of the eight were subject to "clinical seclusion" otherwise known as solitary confinement (Office of the Correctional Investigator 2013). The investigation found that "control interventions are generally disproportionate to the risk presented and often inappropriate from a mental health needs perspective" (Office of the Correctional Investigator 2013, para. 37). Among the justifications for the use of seclusion are self-injurious behaviours, and lack of responsiveness to orders, which can be difficult for people labelled with I/DD, particularly if they are maladapted to the carceral environment (Office of the Correctional Investigator 2013).

ANALYSIS: THE PATTERNS AND VARIABLES OF VIOLENCE

This typology makes evident the expansive system of institutionalization used to confine disabled people across Canada – varying from single person developmental disability institutions, such as specialized complex care services, to several hundred-person large long-term care institutions and prisons. This complexity and uniquity reasserts the definition of institutional violence as violence "endemic to the logics of institutionalization" (Rinaldi and Rossiter, this volume, 4). I am specifically concerned through this chapter with what Rossiter and Rinaldi remark on as the *oscillation* of institutions and the subsequent varying "in intensity depending on the conditions on the ground, the population in question, and their needs in the moment; yet these forces are co-constitutive in an equation that generates institutional violence" (ibid., 15). Through this analysis, I use the typology as a mechanism to take this proposed equation seriously, providing insight into the possible variables of institution size, population intended and served, the conditions on the ground that produce systemic and shocking violence.

Behavioural Markers

All institutions are founded on violent origins – whether the "historic anti-Black logics of state captivity" (Rodriguez 2019, 1582), or the white supremacist eugenic ideology foundational to total institutions for labelled people (Rossiter and Rinaldi 2019). Today, certain institutions have the jurisdictional power to imbue violence in policies through behavioural surveillance (Daley, Costa, and Beresford 2019; Orosz et al. 2016; Spivakovsky 2017). The practice and ability to label institutionalized, and incarcerated people with "challenging behaviours" marks certain disabled people as worthy of loathing (Rossiter and Rinaldi 2022; Spivakovsky 2017). Challenging behaviours include a wide range of behaviours ranging from self-harm, to not showering, or ignoring the institutional schedule (Spivakovsky 2017). As these markers are subjective, the practitioner engaging in the labelling a is of course making decisions that are "racial, gendered and intertwined with sexuality" (Ben-Moshe 2020, 100). This marker of "challenging" rationalizes the violence of isolation and restraint applied similarly across long-term care institutions (Orosz et al. 2016), developmental and dual diagnosis services (Spivakovsky 2017), carceral institutions (Power and Usher 2010), psychiatric institutions (Daley, Costa and Beresford 2019), and forensic psychiatric setting (Fish 2018; Murray and Holmes 2015). Some settings, such as homeless shelters and retirement homes, have less jurisdictional capacity to imbue violence in policy forthright through restraint and isolation. Instead, a homeless shelter may call the police on a disabled service user they have labelled as *challenging*, transferring the responsibility for violence onto police (Jama 2020).

Capacity for Confinement

Paying specific attention to the violence of isolation reveals the prevalence of this violence across this typology. Just as institutionalization is at the crux of care and loathing, seclusion can be read as a "transinstitutional linchpin" (Reiter and Blair 2015, 179), uniting sites of care and loathing in what Murray and Holmes (2015) understand as "an integral dimension of institutional behavior modification programs and part of a patient-inmate's mental health treatment regimen" (116). Together, solitary confinement, isolation and/or seclusion are unique forms of "punishment in institutional contexts explicitly labeled as non-punitive" (Koenig and Reiter 2015, 2).

This typology highlights the need for these sites to be read together despite their discrete, wide-ranging names – solitary confinement cells in prisons; in psychiatric units, "therapeutic quiet rooms"; in forensic psychiatric institutions, seclusion rooms; in developmental disability and dual diagnosis institutions, isolation rooms; and in long-term care institutions, specialized units. In prisons across Canada, the use of solitary confinement continues the murderous desires of the settler-colonial state, debilitating and killing Indigenous people at disproportionate rates (Kilty and Lehalle 2019; Razack 2015). While these deaths have begotten inquests, royal commissions, legal battles, and abolitionist campaigns (Parkes 2015; Sheldon, Spector and Birdsell 2019), federal promises to end the practice of solitary confinement have thus far only resulted in a renaming, now calling these cells administrative segregation. The adaptability of the names and sites of confinements are exactly what this typology makes clear – if one form of institution ends solitary confinement, the threat of isolation, seclusion and confinement will continue to haunt the spectrum of institutionalization.

LIMITATIONS

As a result of persistent data gaps and high rates of privatization, I had to narrow my scope to omit addiction treatment facilities, the community carceral system, and congregate settings for youth. As governments frequently change the names of institutions, there may be changes in name by the time you are reading this.

CONCLUSION

This chapter makes evident the need for an interconnected abolitionist and deinstitutionalization movement. The carceral system is intricately intertwined with the disability system – forensic psychiatry, and the developmental service systems' specialized care networks are entire systems dependent on the carceral system. Simultaneously, the carceral system is used as an institution of last resort for disabled people when there are no available beds or services elsewhere. If carceral logic persists, any type of institution can and will be used to contain disabled people. The benefit of institutions taking so many forms is that it obfuscates the harm perpetuated by the state. But whether the institution is a one-person, privately operated, government-funded group home, or a 600-person prison operated and funded by the province, these institutions are sites of violence. Different names, funders, ownership structures, legal capacities, and sizes, institutions are united and characterized by their capacity to deliver loathing under the auspices of care.

The different developments and renaming of institutions over more than 150 years of reforms makes explicit the fact that reform of carceral institutions is not possible. As long as institutions continue to exist, they will deliver violences that is inherent to their existence. Thus, we do not need alternatives to institutionalization that maintain carceral logic or structures (Ben-Moshe 2020). Instead, as abolitionist Liat Ben-Moshe argues, we need a politics of abolition that will chart a radical new path forward (ibid.). Abolition is a "project of building," that demands coalitional organizing (ibid., 283). Because while deinstitutionalization and abolition are about eliminating cages, it is a radical project of fighting for a fundamentally different world beyond capitalism and confinement.

REFERENCES

Ben-Moshe, Liat. 2020. *Decarcerating Disability: Deinstitutionalization and Prison Abolition*. Minneapolis: University of Michigan Press.

Browne, Alister. 2010. "Mental Health Acts in Canada." *Cambridge Quarterly of Healthcare Ethics* 19, no. 3: 290–8. https://doi.org/10.1017/S096318011000006X.

Byrne, Caron, and Anne D. Hurley. 2007. *Planning Guidelines for – Mental Health & Addiction Services for Children, Youth & Adults with Developmental Disability*. Victoria: BC Ministry of Health.

Canada Mortgage and Housing Corporation. 2009. "Methodology for Seniors' Housing Survey." https://www.cmhc-schl.gc.ca/en/professionals/housing-markets-data-and-research/housing-research/surveys/methods/methodology-seniors-housing-survey.

Canadian Centre on Substance Abuse, Alberta. 2014. "Systems Approach Workbook: System Mapping Tools." https://www.ccsa.ca/sites/default/files/2019-04/CCSA-Systems-Approach-System-Mapping-Tools-2014-en.pdf.

Chambers, Lori A., Saara Greene, James Watson, Sean B. Rourke, Ruthann Tucker, Jay Koornstra, Michael Sobota, Stephen Hwang, Keith Hambly, Doe O'Brien-Teengs, Glen Walker, and the Positive Spaces Healthy Places Team. 2014. "Not Just 'A Roof Over your Head': The Meaning of Healthy Housing Living with HIV." *Housing, Theory and Society* 31, no. 3: 310–33. https://doi.org/10.1080/14036096.2014.897643.

Community Living BC. 2021. "What Support Is Available." https://www.communitylivingbc.ca/what-support-is-available.

Community Support and Research Unit. n.d. "From This Point Forward: Ending Custodial Housing for People with Mental Illness in Canada." Toronto: Centre for Addiction and Mental Health. https://www.eenet.ca/sites/default/files/wp-content/uploads/2014/12/Community-Support-and-Research-Unit-2012-From-This-Point-Forward.pdf.

Crawford, Cameron. 2008. "No Place Like Home: A Report on the Housing Needs of People with Intellectual Disabilities." Canadian Association for Community Living.

Crocker, Anne G., Gilles Côté, Jean Toupin, and Bernard St-Onge. 2007. "Rate and Characteristics of Men with an Intellectual Disability in Pre-trial Detention." *Journal of Intellectual & Developmental Disability* 32, no. 2: 143–52. https://doi.org/10.1080/13668250701314053.

Daley, Andrea, Lucy Costa, and Peter Beresford, eds. 2019. *Madness, Violence, and Power: A Critical Collection*. Toronto: University of Toronto Press.

Dening, Tom, and Alisoun Milne. 2011. *Mental Health and Care Homes*. Oxford: Oxford University Press.

Disability Rights Coalition v. Nova Scotia (Attorney General). 2021 NSCA 70.

Dubé, Paul. 2016. "Nowhere to Turn: Investigation into the Ministry of Community and Social Services' Response to Situations of Crisis Involving Adults with Developmental Disabilities." Toronto: Ombudsman of Ontario. https://www.ombudsman.on.ca/Media/ombudsman/ombudsman/resources/Reports-on-Investigations/NTT-Final-EN-w-cover.pdf.

Durbin, Anna, Barry Isaacs, Dane Mauer-Vakil, Jo Connelly, Lorie Steer, Sylvain Roy, and Vicky Stergiopoulos. 2018. "Intellectual Disability and Homelessness: A Synthesis of the Literature and Discussion of How Supportive Housing Can Support Wellness for People with Intellectual Disability." *Current Developmental Disorders Reports* 5, no. 3: 125–31. https://doi.org/10.1007/s40474-018-0141-6.

Employment and Social Development Canada. 2021a. "The National Shelter Study – Emergency Shelter Use in Canada 2005 to 2016." Reaching Home. https://www.canada.ca/en/employment-social-development/programs/homelessness/publications-bulletins/national-shelter-study.html.

– 2021b. "Reaching Home: Canada's Homelessness Strategy – 2019 Shelter Capacity Report." https://publications.gc.ca/collections/collection_2021/edsc-esdc/Em9-3-2019-eng.pdf.

Endicott, Orville. 1991. "Persons with Intellectual Disability Who Are Incarcerated for Criminal Offences: A Literature Review." Ottawa: Correctional Services of Canada. https://www.csc-scc.gc.ca/research/r14e-eng.shtml.

Fish, Rebecca. 2018. "'Behind This Wall' – Experiences of Seclusion on Locked Wards for Women." *Scandinavian Journal of Disability Research* 20, no. 1, article 1. https://doi.org/10.16993/sjdr.59.

Fritsch, Kelly, Jeffrey Monaghan, and Emily Van der Meulen. 2022. *Disability Injustice: Confronting Criminalization in Canada*. http://public.eblib.com/choice/PublicFullRecord.aspx?p=6871670.

Gaskin, Cadeyrn J., Keith R. McVilly, and Jane A. McGillivray. 2013. "Initiatives to Reduce the Use of Seclusion and Restraints on People with Developmental Disabilities: A Systematic Review and Quantitative Synthesis." *Research in Developmental Disabilities* 34, no. 11: 3946–61. https://doi.org/10.1016/j.ridd.2013.08.010.

Gough, Heather, and Susan Morris. 2012. "Dual Diagnosis Public Policy in a Federal System: The Canadian Experience: Dual Diagnosis Public Policy." *Journal of Policy and Practice in Intellectual Disabilities* 9, no. 3: 166–74. https://doi.org/10.1111/j.1741-1130.2012.00347.x.

Hwang, Stephen, Shirley Chiu, and Emma Wilkins. 2009. *A Survey of Domiciliary Hostel Program Tenants in Ontario: Final Report*. Toronto: St Michael's Hospital. https://www.homelesshub.ca/sites/default/files/attachments/domiciliary_hostel_report.pdf.

Inclusion Canada. 2019. "Housing and People with Intellectual Disabilities." https://inclusioncanada.ca/housing.

Isaacs, Caroline. 2014. "Treatment Industrial Complex: How For-Profit Prison Corporations Are Undermining Efforts to Treat and Rehabilitate Prisoners for Corporate Gain." American Friends Service Committee. https://www.afsc.org/sites/default/files/documents/TIC_report_online.pdf.

Jama, Sarah. 2020. "The Need to Root Disability Justice into Movements." In *Until We are Free: Reflections on Black Lives Matter in Canada*, edited by Rodney Diverlus, Sandy Hudson, and Syrus Marcus Ware. Regina: University of Regina Press.

Joseph, Ameil J. 2015a. "The Canadian Forensic Mental Health System: An Overview." In *Deportation and the Confluence of Violence within Forensic Mental Health and Immigration Systems*, edited by Ameil J. Joseph, 43–54. London: Palgrave Macmillan UK. https://doi.org/10.1057/9781137513410_3.

– 2015b. "Introduction: Outlining the Problem – The Confluence of Mental Health, Criminal Justice, and Immigration in the Authorization of Deportation." In *Deportation and the Confluence of Violence within Forensic Mental Health and Immigration Systems*, edited by Ameil J. Joseph, 1–17. London: Palgrave Macmillan UK. https://doi.org/10.1057/9781137513410_1.

Kilty, Jennifer M., and Sandra Lehalle. 2019. "Mad, Bad and Stuck in the 'Hole': Carceral Segregation as Slow Violence." *In Madness, Violence and Power: A Radical Anthology*, edited by Andrea Daley, Lucy Costa, and Peter Beresford, 310–29. Toronto: University of Toronto Press.

Koenig, Alexa, and Keramet Reiter. 2015. "Introduction." In *Extreme Punishment: Comparative Studies in Detention, Incarceration and Solitary Confinement*, edited by Keramet Reiter and Alexa Koenig, 1–13. Basingstoke, UK: Palgrave Macmillan. https://doi.org/10.1057/9781137441157_1.

Lane, Natasha E., Therese A. Stukel, Cynthia M. Boyd, and Walter P. Wodchis. 2019. "Long-Term Care Residents' Geriatric Syndromes at Admission and Disablement Over Time: An Observational Cohort Study." *The Journals of Gerontology* A74, no. 6: 917–23. https://doi.org/10.1093/gerona/gly151.

Lin, Elizabeth, Howard Barbaree, Avra Selick, Elke Ham, Andrew S. Wilton, and Yona Lunsky. 2017. "Intellectual and Developmental Disabilities and Ontario's Forensic Inpatient System: A Population-Based Cohort Study." *Psychology, Crime & Law* 23, no. 9: 914–26. https://doi.org/10.1080/1068316X.2017.1346100.

Linton, Megan. 2021a. "Mind the Gap: Adults Labelled with Intellectual and Developmental Disabilities and Data Collection in Ontario." *Carleton Perspectives on Public Policy*, no. 7.

– 2021b. "Ontario's Hidden Institutions." *Canadian Dimension*, 24 February 2021. https://canadiandimension.com/articles/view/custodial-institutions-ontarios-hidden-victims.

Lougheed, Donna C., and Susan Farrell. 2013. "The Challenge of a 'Triple Diagnosis': Identifying and Serving Homeless Canadian Adults with a Dual Diagnosis: The Challenge of a Triple Diagnosis." *Journal of Policy and Practice in Intellectual Disabilities* 10, no. 3: 230–5. https://doi.org/10.1111/jppi.12041.

Lunsky, Yona, and Rob Balogh. 2010. "Dual Diagnosis: A National Study of Psychiatric Hospitalization Patterns of People with Developmental Disability." *Canadian Journal of Psychiatry* 55, no. 11:

721–8. http://search.proquest.com/docview/817565445/abstract/906EF4756F894A25PQ/1.

Lunsky, Yona, Robert S. Balogh, Virginie Cobigo, Barry Isaacs, Elizabeth Lin, and Hélène M.J. Ouellette-Kuntz. 2014. "Primary Care of Adults with Developmental Disabilities in Ontario." *Healthcare Quarterly*, 30 October 2014. https://www.longwoods.com/content/24026//primary-care-of-adults-with-developmental-disabilities-in-ontario.

Lunsky, Yona, Robert Balogh, Anna Durbin, Avra Selick, Tiziana Volpe, and Elizabeth Lin. 2018. "The Mental Health of Adults with Developmental Disabilities in Ontario: Lessons from Administrative Health Data." *Healthcare Quarterly* 21, no. 1: 6–9. https://doi.org/10.12927/hcq.2018.25521.

Murray, Stuart J., and Dave Holmes. 2015. "Seclusive Space: Crisis Confinement and Behavior Modification in Canadian Forensic Psychiatric Settings." In *Extreme Punishment: Comparative Studies in Detention, Incarceration and Solitary Confinement*, edited by Keramet Reiter and Alexa Koenig, 115–34. Basingstoke, UK: Palgrave Macmillan.

OECD. 2017. *Systems Approaches to Public Sector Challenges: Working with Change*. https://doi.org/10.1787/9789264279865-en.

Office of the Correctional Investigator. 2013. *Risky Business: An Investigation of the Treatment and Management of Chronic Self-Injury among Federally Sentenced Women: Final Report*. https://www.deslibris.ca/ID/239975.

Orosz, Zsofia, Amy Porteous, Melissa Donskov, Tracy Luciani, and Peter Walker. 2016. "Designated Specialized Units: How Ontario's Long-Term Care Homes Fill a Gap in Care." *Healthcare Management Forum* 29, no. 6: 264–8. https://doi.org/10.1177/0840470416659880.

Ouellette-Kuntz, Hélène, Lynn Martin, and Katherine McKenzie. 2017. "The Risk of Re-Institutionalization: Examining Rates of Admission to Long-Term Care among Adults with Intellectual and Developmental Disabilities Over Time." *Journal of Policy and Practice in Intellectual Disabilities* 14, no. 4: 293–7. https://doi.org/10.1111/jppi.12215.

Parkes, Debra. 2015. "Ending the Isolation: An Introduction to the Special Volume on Human Rights and Solitary Confinement." *Canadian Journal of Human Rights* 4: i–iv. https://heinonline.org/HOL/P?h=hein.journals/canajo4&i=1.

Power, Jenelle, and Amelia Usher. 2010. *A Qualitative Study of Self-Injurious Behaviour in Women Offenders* (Publication R 225). Ottawa: Correctional Service Canada.

Public Health Ontario. 2019. *Evidence Brief – Homelessness and Health Outcomes: What are the Associations?* https://www.publichealthontario.ca/-/media/documents/E/2019/eb-homelessness-health.pdf.

Public Safety Canada. 2020. *2019 Corrections and Conditional Release Statistical Overview*. Data set. https://www.publicsafety.gc.ca/cnt/rsrcs/pblctns/ccrso-2019/index-en.aspx.

R. v. Minassian, 2021 ONSC 1258.

Razack, Sherene. 2015. *Dying from Improvement: Inquests and Inquiries into Indigenous Deaths in Custody*. Toronto: University of Toronto Press.

Reiter, Keramet, and Thomas Blair. 2015. "Punishing Mental Illness: Trans-institutionalization and Solitary Confinement in the United States." In *Extreme Punishment: Comparative Studies in Detention, Incarceration and Solitary Confinement*, edited by Keramet Reiter and Alexa Koenig, 177–96. Basingstoke, UK: Palgrave Macmillan. https://doi.org/10.1057/9781137441157_10.

Rodriguez, Dylan. 2019. "Abolition as Praxis of Human Being: A Foreword." *Harvard Law Review* 132, no. 6: 1575–612. https://heinonline.org/HOL/P?h=hein.journals/hlr132&i=1596.

Rossiter, Kate, and Jen Rinaldi. 2019. *Institutional Violence and Disability: Punishing Conditions*. New York: Routledge.

Saini, Valdeep, and Louis Busch. 2022. "Restrictive Behavior Management Practices." In *Handbook of Autism and Pervasive Developmental Disorder: Assessment, Diagnosis, and Treatment*, edited by Johnny L. Matson and Peter Sturmey, 1081–96. Autism and Child Psychopathology Series. Cham: Springer International Publishing. https://doi.org/10.1007/978-3-030-88538-0_47.

Sheldon, C. Tess, Karen R. Spector, and Mary Birdsell. 2019. "Uncovering Law's Multiple Violences at the Inquest into the Death of Ashley Smith." In *Madness, Violence, and Power: A Critical Collection*, edited by Andrea Daley, Lucy Costa, and Peter Beresford, 196–220. Toronto: University of Toronto Press.

Smith-MacDonald, Lorraine, Lorraine Venturato, Paulette Hunter, Sharon Kaasalainen, Tamara Sussman, Lynn McCleary, Genevieve Thompson, Abigail Wickson-Griffiths, and Shane Sinclair. 2019. "Perspectives and Experiences of Compassion in Long-Term Care Facilities within Canada: A Qualitative Study of Patients, Family Members and

Health Care Providers." BMC *Geriatrics* 19, no. 1: 128. https://doi.org/10.1186/s12877-019-1135-x.

Sonpal-Valias, Nilima. 2019. "History of Developmental Disability Policy in Alberta." *School of Public Policy Publications* 12, no. 20. https://ssrn.com/abstract=3422206.

Spivakovsky, Claire. 2017. "Governing Freedom through Risk: Locating the Group Home in the Archipelago of Confinement and Control." *Punishment and Society* 19, no. 3: 366–83. https://doi.org/10.1177/1462474517703968.

Statistics Canada. 2011. "Residential Care Facilities 2009/2010." https://www150.statcan.gc.ca/n1/pub/83-237-x/83-237-x2012001-eng.pdf.

– 2020. "Nursing and Residential Care Facilities – Public." 3 February 2020. https://www23.statcan.gc.ca/imdb/p2SV.pl?Function=getSurvey&Id=1275735#a1.

– 2021. "A Profile of Nursing and Residential Care Facilities, 2019." 16 September 2021. https://www150.statcan.gc.ca/n1/daily-quotidien/210916/dq210916c-eng.htm.

Sylph, J.A., M.R. Eastwood, and H.B. Kedward. 1976. "Long-Term Psychiatric Care in Ontario: The Homes for Special Care Program." *Canadian Medical Association Journal* 114, no. 3: 233–7.

Tutton, Michael. 2021. "Nova Scotia Woman Won Human-Rights Case for People with Disabilities: BETH MacLEAN PLAINTIFF, 50." *Globe and Mail*, 1 October 2021, sec. Sports. https://www.proquest.com/docview/2578006846/citation/1C9946B3C1FB42DCPQ/1.

United Nations Committee on the Rights of Persons with Disabilities. 2017. "General Comment No.5 on Article 19 – the Right to Live Independently and Be Included in the Community." General Comment 5. United Nations Human Rights Office of the High Commission. https://www.ohchr.org/en/documents/general-comments-and-recommendations/general-comment-no5-article-19-right-live.

Venville, Annie, Anne-Maree Sawyer, Maureen Long, Niki Edwards, and Sara Hair. 2015. "Supporting People with an Intellectual Disability and Mental Health Problems: A Scoping Review of What They Say about Service Provision." *Journal of Mental Health Research in Intellectual Disabilities* 8, nos 3–4: 186–212. https://doi.org/10.1080/19315864.2015.1069912.

Ware, Syrus, Joan Ruzsa, and Giselle Dias. 2014. "It Can't Be Fixed Because It's Not Broken: Racism and Disability in the Prison Industrial Complex." In *Disability Incarcerated Imprisonment and Disability in the United States and Canada*, edited by Liat Ben-Moshe, Chris Chapman, and C. Carey. Camden: Palgrave Macmillan.

Welch, Robert. 1973. "Community Living for the Mentally Retarded in Ontario: A New Policy Focus." Ontario: Provincial Secretariat for Social Development. https://www.mcss.gov.on.ca/documents/en/mcss/dshistory/legislation/Welch%20Report.pdf.

Whittingham, Lisa, Anna Durbin, Elizabeth Lin, Flora I. Matheson, Tiziana Volpe, Parisa Dastoori, Andrew Calzavara, Yona Lunsky, and Fiona Kouyoumdjian. 2020. "The Prevalence and Health Status of People with Developmental Disabilities in Provincial Prisons in Ontario, Canada: A Retrospective Cohort Study." *Journal of Applied Research in Intellectual Disabilities* 33, no. 6: 1368–79. https://doi.org/10.1111/jar.12757.

Williston, Walter. 1971. "Present Arrangements for the Care and Supervision of Mentally Retarded Persons in Ontario." Toronto: Ontario Department of Health. https://www.mcss.gov.on.ca/documents/en/mcss/dshistory/legislation/Williston%20Report.pdf.

Wilson, Nathan J., Vivienne C. Riches, Tanya Riches, Seeta Durvasula, Renell Rodrigues, and Sonali Pinto. 2020. "Complex Support Needs Profile of an Adult Cohort with Intellectual Disability Transitioning from State-Based Service Provision to NDIS-Funded Residential Support." *Journal of Intellectual and Developmental Disability* 45, no. 4: 355–64. https://doi.org/10.3109/13668250.2020.1717069.

Woodbury-Smith, Marc, Ivana Furimsky, and Gary A. Chaimowitz. 2018. "Point Prevalence of Adults with Intellectual Developmental Disorder in Forensic Psychiatric Inpatient Services in Ontario, Canada." *International Journal of Risk and Recovery* 1, no. 1: 4–11. https://doi.org/10.15173/ijrr.v1i1.3355.

Worth, Patrick. n.d. "Dare to Dream." Toronto: Inclusion Press website. https://inclusion.com/inclusion-stories-news/life-stories/patrick-worth-says.

6

The Violence of Work

Sheltered Workshops in Ontario, Canada

SIOBHÁN SARAVANAMUTTU

> Why should working be considered so essential that disabled people are allowed to be taken advantage of, and, moreover, expected to be grateful for such an "opportunity?"
>
> (Taylor 2004)

Since after the First World War, sheltered workshops have been used as closed work settings for disabled people in Anglo-American welfare state societies. In early 1900s North America, they emerged as spaces used to rehabilitate injured soldiers to re-enter the labour market with a newly acquired disability (Galer 2018, 109). Later in the 1960s and 70s, as deinstitutionalization of total institutions[1] began to gain momentum in Canada, these work settings have existed as one element in an array of state and privately funded services operating in the community for intellectually and developmentally disabled[2] people. Sheltered workshops operated as work simulation environments for people deemed incapable of working in the broader labour market because of disability. Often paying workers nominal wages much lower than the minimum wage (Linton 2021), these state-funded sites of disability segregation were justified through vocational training and rehabilitation rhetoric. While framed as temporary and transitional to the labour market, disabled workers rarely shifted to paid work alongside non-disabled co-workers. Despite more recent advances in employment equity, accessibility, and human rights legislation enabling disability accommodations for some disabled people in the workplace, the longevity of sheltered workshops and corresponding pay inequity remained for intellectually and developmentally disabled workers.

Using the case study of Ontario, Canada, this chapter examines the institutional violence of sheltered workshops. Kate Rossiter and Jen Rinaldi's continuum of institutional violence describes the range of violence normalized within institutional spaces: from the "cold" dehumanizing practices of institutional efficiency (2019, 42–3) to "warm" punishment practices (2019, 46), and the very worst "hot" acts of sadistic physical and sexual violence (2019, 51). Rather than thinking of the closure of total institutions as a temporal stopping point for these practices of institutional violence enacted on disabled people, literature on transinstitutionalization encourages us to look for the ways that institutional and carceral logics employed in those settings have become dispersed throughout our communities across a multitude of spaces where disabled people live, socialize, and work.

This chapter focuses on the role of work in practices of institutional violence. To this end, I am narrowly concerned with thinking through violence as the discursive practices of loathing and devaluation of disabled people that beget institutionalization. I ask: how has work provided justification for the institutional practices of sheltered workshops? Further, what are the discursive practices equating work as necessary and rehabilitative for disabled people both in and beyond the walls of total institutions? Through a case study of the sheltered workshop system in Ontario and the corresponding normative emphasis on productivity, capacity, and normalization this chapter seeks to develop a theory of work *as* violence. The chapter comprises three parts. First, I engage in a brief overview of how disability and work are conceptualized by the state, a major provisioner of social policy and redistributive measures for disabled people in Ontario. The chapter then traces discursive practices of work and disability that enforce the bounds of productivity and capacity in total institutions. This provides the basis for linking the violence of institutions to their transinstitutional cousin: the sheltered workshop. The centrality of rehabilitation and normalization through Ontario's institutional and sheltered work periods demonstrates how crucial work has been to practices of social control, economic marginalization, and alienation of intellectually disabled people. It is therefore impossible, I argue, to conceive of work *without* acknowledging its fundamental violence, presenting critical impracticalities for the future of disability advocacy and organizing focusing on waged labour as necessary for disability justice.

DISABILITY, LOATHING, AND THE STATE

A historical materialist lens of disability offers a view of the rise of the medical model of disability and the institutional era considering the welfare state's need to regulate the supply of labour (Rosenthal 2019, 88). Pre-capitalist social and family arrangements saw disabled people living amongst the community and involved in sustenance activities, as appropriate (Carey 2009, 37; Rose 2017, 5). This changed with the introduction of industrial capitalism. Scientific and medical developments in psychology and psychiatry meant innovating the ability to hierarchize and categorize. A precursor to today's medical label of intellectual disability, the term "feebleminded" was not a natural and immutable biological category, but one that was created for social, institutional, and legal control of alienated communities strengthened by gendered and racialized stereotypes of deviancy and physical and cognitive inadequacy (Carey 2009, 65). This social and scientific category was quite loosely and flexibly defined to include broad groups of people that were seen to need to be under the purview and control of both medicine and the state.

When liberal theorists take up conversations of political citizenship vis à vis disability, questions of intellectual disability are often elided. The reason for this is the locating of liberal conceptions of the citizen in humanist ideology, which Nirmala Erevelles (2013, 150) says "emphasizes individual potential and its associated traits of autonomy, competence, and rationality as the necessary preconditions for being recognized as a citizen." This idea of the rational "self" taken up in liberal theory is the basis on which capitalist society is built. John Rawls (1998, cited in Erevelles 2013, 150) defines the citizen as "a fully cooperating member of society ... [with] the capacity to understand, to apply, and to act from the public conception of justice ... and to rationally pursue a conception of one's rational advantage or good." Rawls accordingly presents the caution that intellectually disabled and mad folks are not included in this definition of citizenship based on the assumption that their perceived impairments would restrict them from participating in society in the manner he suggests is normative.

Rawls seems to locate the loathing of intellectually disabled folks in political citizenship discourse in terms of their perceived impairment. It appears implicitly self-evident that intellectually disabled folks are, by virtue of their perceived biological impairments, prevented from undertaking the responsibilities accordant with political citizenship. Unexplored, or perhaps ignored by Rawls, is that the humanist logic which undergirds our ideas of what it means to be a citizen contributes to and perhaps upholds the pathologizing of intellectual disability that enables disabled people's othering. Erevelles' (2013, 151) analysis helps us understand that the necessary foil to the citizen-self upon which both liberal individualism and capitalism are erected is a deviant, "defective agent." In the text, this undesirable defective agent is primarily located as the disabled subject, but the archetype of the deviant other is often also racialized (Erevelles 2014, 88). Erevelles' work (2013, 154) presents a blistering critique of liberal citizenship scholarship that seeks to broaden notions of citizenship and its attendant civil rights. For her, this discourse of equality stops short of intellectual disability due to the privileging of humanist logic, which is fundamentally unable to account for a subject that is not "autonomous, competent and rational." Indeed, the emphasis on Universal Reason must be seen as being located within an "ableist paradigm" (ibid., 158) that enables the othering of intellectually disabled and mad folks. Pathologized tropes of cognitive ability and rationality mark people separate from normal on this basis.

Erevelles' work is an essential contribution because she demonstrates how discourses of rationality and competence have created barriers for notions of citizenship related to intellectually disabled people and that these discourses are bound up in the foundations of capitalist society. "In the specific historical context of laissez-faire capitalism, 'rational' behavior represents those behavior traits that maximize benefits, minimize costs, and contribute to the efficient realization of profit. Those who exhibit behaviours that prove counterproductive to capitalism's efficiency logic are marked as abnormal and are either punished and/or segregated from the "normal" populations. In other words, I argue there that notions of autonomy and rationality are, in fact, closely tied to the historical and material conditions of capitalism" (Erevelles 2013, 158). Not only are tropes of "competence" and "autonomy" barriers to political citizenship for intellectually disabled folks, but they justify social control because they undergird discourses of productivity and efficiency under capitalism. To be clear, intellectually disabled people have been socially constructed as deviant and outside the bounds of citizenship, not just for social control to its end. This deviance constructs the foil to the capitalist nation-state's productive, rational, and competent ideal citizen-subject.

The state's role vis-à-vis disabled people is further complicated by settler colonialism. For Griffin Epstein (2014, 5), the construction of intellectually disabled or mad people as other is critical to the very maintenance of the settler-colonial state. Certain people and communities are constructed as deviant specifically because they threaten the hegemony of the colonial state and its nation-building fiction. In this way, deviance is not simply a matter of physical, psychological, or psychiatric impairment, but one that exists with disability, racialization, and Indigeneity intertwined, challenging hegemonic national myths. Thus, racialized and disabled people *must* be constructed as deviant to manage the threat they pose to the idea that "the ideal/normal citizen is white, straight, and fit for manual/intellectual labor" (Epstein 2014, 5). Epstein (2014, 5) argues that deviance is used to justify three possible state responses to the threat of disability and race: elimination, quarantine, and rehabilitation.

Of particular interest to our discussion of sheltered work is rehabilitation, which seeks to remove deviance from certain body-minds. Through projects focussing on the extraction of labour from people previously thought to be outside the realm of productivity under capitalism, rehabilitation seeks "to 'straighten up' the 'sick' to 'functional productivity'" (Epstein 2014, 6). Through Epstein's discussion, we can perhaps see rehabilitation as a tool to mould deviant others towards the ideal of political citizenship. Of course, this begets questions about the bounds of productivity under capitalism and whiteness, and which deviant body-minds occupy this liminal space seen capable of being guided towards citizenship. Indeed, the history of residential schools, institutions, and "curative" psychiatric technologies like electro-shock therapy and lobotomy should have taught us that this rehabilitation project is far from benevolent or voluntary. Chris Chapman and A.J. Withers (2019, 241) note the connections between eugenics and rehabilitation, which they say both "reinforce the taken-for-granted-ness of a morally superior normality ... [and] they both aim to eliminate certain ways of being human." Indeed, one might consider that instead of Epstein's (2014, 5) three categories of elimination, quarantine, and rehabilitation, there are only two: quarantine and elimination. Rehabilitation becomes temporarily subsumed within quarantine with the desired end-state of elimination. For rehabilitation to be successful under the logic of the colonial nation-state, it must necessarily seek to eliminate the deviance within the racialized, mad, and/or disabled body-mind.

Thinking of disability from the state's perspective further illuminates the connection between medical professionals' categorizations of disabled people and state management of their labour. The administrative category "disability" itself mobilizes the medical model to define the boundary between which people are available to engage in waged work and those viewed as incapable of work. According to Stone, each category of labour market exemption must rest on a "culturally legitimate rationale for nonparticipation in the labour system" (1984, 22). The state accepts that under capitalism, disabled people's impairments prevent them from producing a profit at the expected rate, necessitating their exclusion from the labour market. It is important to note that this is a necessarily narrow model of disability that cannot account for the myriad ways disabled people exist beyond its bounds and fails to reconcile an embodied, social, or economic state of being and becoming disabled.

Nevertheless, through Stone, we can see the gatekeeping function made clear: the welfare state is not simply a generous benefactor but a protective guard and spendthrift. Of course, the primary goal here is not maintaining people's ability to live independently with dignity and out of poverty, but rather to provide *just enough* of a safety net to *as few people as possible* to ensure the maintenance of the system as a whole. Since deinstitutionalization, state disability policy at the federal and provincial/territorial levels has centred on income support for those who meet the labour force exemption criteria through direct payments, pensions, and tax mechanisms. Beyond income support and health care, provinces and territories download most service provisioning for disabled people to non-profit service agencies, many of which initially existed as parent and family advocacy organizations (Race 2007, 145).

Thus, in the eyes of the state, to be unable to work renders one vulnerable to social control, surveillance, and meagre redistributive measures. The dehumanizing array of responses to the disability "problem" are delimited by the devaluation and loathing associated with its construction as deviant and unfit for work. For intellectually and developmentally disabled people in Canada, this has meant a long history of interference and abuse by the medical and scientific community and decades of state-funded institutional incarceration.

DISABILITY AND REHABILITATION IN THE TOTAL INSTITUTION

In the late nineteenth and twentieth century, Ontario asylums and related institutions represented a critical state response to the management of disabled and mad people. Licia Carlson (2015, 141) discusses how intellectual disability[3] is a historically contingent category. During the institutional era, intellectual disability was defined as both "static" and "dynamic," depending on which story of disability was being told at a particular time. "Static" institutional inmates were those who were deemed to be inherently disabled and therefore incurable and unable to be taught behaviours seen to be normal, appropriate, and desired. On the other hand, those considered dynamic were seen to lack these desirable or normal traits but were considered amenable to being taught. At once, disability is seen to be both innate and malleable, requiring different strategies on the part of the state. Due to this duality of intellectual disability, institutions professed mandates that involved both quarantine and rehabilitation. Quarantine in the institution, through segregated incarceration, was justified through the language of protection. Inmates[4] are provided protection and care that they do not otherwise have access to in the care of family. Deeply intertwined with the medical establishment, institutions were seen to provide health care to disabled children and adults not otherwise available in the community. At the same time, institutions were also justified as a protective mechanism for those outside the institution – non-disabled members of society.

Further, eugenic notions of criminality and deviance tied to "low intellect," which are also inherently racist, added to the ideological justification of institutions. Institutions existed to provide their custodial function and as a reactionary response to the threat of potential harm disabled people present to the common social good. Disabled people seen to be "static" or incurable were positioned to necessitate the institution's carceral apparatus.

And so, although institutions were often justified as a "charitable response," they facilitated the ongoing disposability of disabled and mad people by the state. The development of carceral systems as a response to the "problem" of disability represented a move towards a "rehabilitative" model that sought to instill inmates with normative behaviours or skills they were seen to lack. The "dynamic" nature of some people's disabled-ness required the institution to engage in disciplinary and curative practices. For those with hope of "improving" into ideal citizens, the institution further fulfilled its mandate of protecting this social good through rehabilitation. Chapman and Withers (2019, 241) note that possessing rehabilitative potential is aligned with characteristics of the ideal citizen that go beyond disability, such as race and class. Verbal and physical violence were often enacted both to punish unruly inmates but also for rehabilitative ends. Rossiter and Rinaldi discuss one Ontario institution where "attending medical staff presumed the programs – involving nudity, solitary confinement, restraints, verbal confrontation, heavy sedation, and other physically taxing and humiliating techniques – would induce self-discovery and responsibility for poor behaviour" (2019, 30). Crucially, they demonstrate that this mandated aim of institutional reform of disabled people towards a "normal" citizen allowed for the elision of moral responsibility of institutional staff and administrators (Rossiter and Rinaldi 2019, 30).

In addition to attitudinal behaviour modification, institutions ran training and education programs. These quickly became an integral component of the institution's function and reproduction. Such programs often consisted of work activities such as cooking, cleaning, agricultural labour, or producing handicrafts for sale. Institutions relied on the dynamic notions of a reformable or dynamic disabled person to justify the exploitation of inmates' unpaid labour. "Institutional administrators consciously and deliberately used unremunerated patient labour and easily justified it as a form of vocational training" (Rossiter and Rinaldi 2019, 32). This flies in the face of common knowledge of disabled people, which suggested that intellectually disabled people could not be considered workers capable of producing value. Ruthie-Marie Beckwith illustrates the contradictions involved in deinstitutionalization in an American setting, where inmates' work was highly productive and often essential to institutions' financial survival:

"Prior to their return to the community, resident and patient workers had been integrally responsible for the day-to-day operation … While institutionalized, their productivity as resident and patient workers was only called into question when it became clear that the institutions would have to either pay them minimum wage or forego their labor" (Beckwith 2016, 114). Wolf Wolfensberger (1975, 61) confirms this, explaining that while work in institutions was justified as occupying inmates and supporting their self-sufficiency, it quickly became an exercise in money-saving. Because "the institution could not have functioned without unpaid captive labor" (ibid.), work was violently extracted for free, under the guise of the inmates' "best interest." Inmates who learned skills most adeptly were used to replace paid staff, rather than being released having achieved the ostensible aim of the institution (ibid.). Institutions at once created and perpetuated knowledge about disabled people that confirmed their inability to be productive while simultaneously benefitting from their labour using the language of rehabilitation and training.

In the same period that institutions for mad and disabled people were being developed and refined, residential schools for Indigenous children proliferated across Canada. Burghardt makes clear that while the justifications for residential schools and institutions differed, they both shared similar disciplinary and rehabilitative tactics: stating that residential schools were seen "as a site of Christianization and white citizenry; institutions as sites to foster productivity and reasonableness" (2018, 18).

WORK/VIOLENCE AFTER DEINSTITUTIONALIZATION

Beginning in the 1960s, a deinstitutional movement took hold across North America, as mad and disability rights activists, family advocate groups, and others worked towards independent living integrated in the community (Galer 2018, 46). Despite disability rights advocacy and a provincial report conducted by Walter Williston in 1971 recommending swift deinstitutionalization, it would not be until 2009 Ontario's final institution, the Huronia Regional Centre in Orillia, was closed (Burghardt 2018, 62; Rossiter and Rinaldi 2018, 11–13). Sheltered workshops were quickly taken up as common practice following widespread closures of institutions. In 1972, 105 sheltered workshops were being operated in the province of Ontario for intellectually and developmentally disabled workers (Department of Manpower and Immigration 1972, 69–94). These segregated workplaces have long been a key site of contestation for intellectually and developmentally disabled workers and their allies. These institutions shaped the lives and livelihoods of disabled workers deemed "too disabled" to participate in the labour market. Operated outside employment standards regulation, sheltered workshops in Ontario were funded by the provincial government and managed by community disability service organizations such as Community Living Ontario and its local partners.

Justified through the rhetoric of vocational training, sheltered workshops paid sub-minimum wages while rarely facilitating a transition to the labour market or to "independent living" (Galer 2018, 107, 123). Sheltered workshops represented a major stopgap to the presumed problem of the widespread unemployability of disabled adults in Ontario. They offered stipends below the mandatory minimum wage for "transitional" job-skills training subsidized by income supports such as the Ontario Disability Support Program (ODSP). While the Employment Standards Act exemption that allowed disabled workers to be paid less than minimum wage was repealed in 1986 (Ontario Human Rights Commission 2015), sheltered workers continued to remain exempt. The Ontario Employment Standards Act 2000 3(5)6 stated that the act does not apply to those who are in a "simulated job or working environment," which had the primary focus of a worker's "rehabilitation" (Employment Standards Act 2000). The exclusion from adequately compensated labour and the associated social benefits and entitlements are argued by disability advocates to perpetuate systemic poverty by ignoring the capabilities and potential productivity of disabled workers (Beckwith 2016, 122; Galer 2018, 121–2) while also subsidizing capital by reducing or eliminating the cost of this labour. Work undertaken in sheltered workshops varied from repetitive tasks like sorting small items for the manufacturing sector to municipal contracts for snow removal and cleaning of public transit sites.

Transinstitutionalization literature helps us understand that although deinstitutionalization meant closing the door on the physical total institution, much of its disciplinary and surveillance tactics became dispersed or transferred to spaces occupied by disabled people in the community (Haley and Jones 2020, 1), including the sheltered workshop. Unlike in the total institution, disabled sheltered workers could leave and go home at the end of the day. The management of personal care needs was not overseen by the sheltered workshop, as it had been in the institution. In many ways, however, the differences between the institution and sheltered workshop end here. Sheltered work involved repetitive tasks such as packing, sorting, assembling, and envelope stuffing (Department of Manpower and Immigration 1972, 70–3). The repetitive nature of these tasks was amenable to the sheltered workshop's highly controlled space, which demanded a prescribed set of behaviours. Apart from quasi-professional management staff, sheltered workers were segregated from their community and non-disabled workers. Despite the moniker of "community living" sheltered workers continue to exist in a space of quarantine, at least during working hours.

In addition to the structure and organizational tactics shared by sheltered workshops and total institutions, we must understand their shared mandate involving work as a central activity through which to control disabled individuals and shape collective knowledge about disabled people. Gill (2005, 622) argues that while sheltered work is said to operate to transition individuals with intellectual disabilities into the labour market and community after having provided valuable skills training, it is little more than a state-implemented mechanism of exclusion and exploitation of disabled people. Indeed, the purported need for and purpose of sheltered work reminds us of the simultaneous stasis and dynamism of intellectual disability (Carlson 2015, 140–1). Just as in the total institution, sheltered workshops are said to offer protective "shelter." Very simply, workshops offered a space for disabled people to spend time during the day – either as a respite from a congregate living environment or for family caregivers who themselves often worked during the week. Workshops also shelter workers who are said to be unproductive from the harshness of the competitive labour market. In this way, they are positioned to fill an important custodial need of disabled people once again viewed as "static" and unable to access properly compensated employment. It is also worth interrogating whom segregation of disabled people serves to protect, following decades of activism surrounding the need to live, work, and socialize in the community.

At the same time, sheltered workshops are imbued with the all-important rehabilitative function of vocational training. This is also justified by the dynamic understanding of intellectual disability, as in the total institution. The idea that *some* disabled people can be reformed into an ideal citizen justifies the need for rehabilitation. The desired outcome of sheltered work is to mould disabled people into productive workers. Thus, this "dynamic" figure of the disabled person justifies the sheltered workshop as a temporary site of training where workers will eventually move out of the sheltered workshop and into the open labour market. The provisional nature of this training is directly referenced in the Employment Standards Act, which justifies the payment of subminimum wages in the "simulated" nature of the sheltered work environment. For if the work is not real, why should wages be? Indeed in 1972, sheltered workshops reportedly remunerated intellectually disabled workers between $0.05 to $0.99 per hour – ranging from 3 per cent to 60 per cent of provincial minimum wage at the time (Department of Manpower and Immigration 1972, 69). Rates of pay as recent as 2018 were not much better, ranging from $0.46 to $2.00 per hour (People First of Canada 2018, 30). Just as sheltered workshops imported many of the disciplinary tactics of total institutions, so too were the myths of training and rehabilitation. Indeed, the term vocational "training" is an obfuscation, as workshops often neglected to promote workers to waged labour when their skills were so crucial to the reproduction of the workshop itself (Galer 2014, 14). Agencies often were in the position of competing for piecemeal manufacturing or assembly contract work, requiring the "best" and most productive sheltered workers to remain in the workshop indefinitely. Implied in the very existence of the sheltered workshops is a contradiction. All at once, it claims both to rehabilitate and normalize disabled people in the image of a productive worker while also requiring that this end goal never entirely be actualized. For if the sheltered workshop was indeed successful, its longevity and the expertise of its professionals are jeopardized.

Erevelles (2013, 166) argues that under capitalism, not only is whiteness property but so too is ability. This has justified the quarantine of intellectually disabled (and poor, racialized) children as early as elementary school through to adulthood. Those that can be rehabilitated through special education, educational assistants, testing, or therapy, may enter the workforce as adults and "(earn) the right of recognition as citizens" (Erevelles 2013, 167). Those who are unable or choose not to do so continue to be labelled as deviant through their lack of productivity and endure further quarantine in the sheltered workshop. These folks are often also social benefit recipients, marked as dependents rather than citizens of the state. Griffin Epstein's characterization of rehabilitation supports this analysis, which they define as the range of "technologies to extract labor from previously non-viable bodies – that is, people whose embodiments, language, cultural practice or behavior meant that they could not participate in the normative, legal workforce" (2014, 5). From this standpoint, Erevelles offers us the tools to understand why movements that might seek inclusion in liberal rights regimes or recognition from the state may not have the scope to tackle the complicated structures of ableism, whiteness, and cis heteropatriarchy. Ultimately these strategies are bound up in the structures and foundation of the capitalist colonial settler state, which foregrounds loathing of the unproductive disabled person: "neither formal justice nor discursive interventions that deconstruct reason and privilege dependency over autonomy will prove to be emancipatory for people with severe/cognitive disabilities because both reason and dependency are historically constituted within the laissez-faire economic structures of capitalist societies" (Erevelles 2013, 160).

The deinstitutionalization movement is a major victory for disabled people that cannot be understated. Experiences of abject violence and neglect experienced in institutional "care" are well-documented by academics and institutional survivors alike. Indeed in 2013, the Ontario government settled with survivors of the Huronia Regional Centre in a landmark class-action lawsuit led by Patricia Seth and Marie Slark (Burghardt 2018, 3; Rossiter and Rinaldi 2019, 27). From this precedent-setting victory, there has been a cascade of other class-action lawsuits brought by survivors of other institutions against the government of Ontario (Rossiter and Rinaldi 2019, 27). Despite the wins associated with the end to the wholesale warehousing of disabled people, the experience of sheltered workshops offers a view to the limits of this victory. It is worth asking why deinstitutionalization efforts, which so poignantly understood the violence of total institutions, failed to take up the centrality of work and rehabilitation within their purview. Ultimately, working within a framework that prizes a productive citizen from whom the maximum profit can be extracted will be insufficient to provide interdependence and community sufficient to recognize and value the social contributions of intellectually disabled people that is not viewed as relative to, or less than an "ideal citizen." Sheltered workshops have perhaps existed as spaces of confinement for as long as they did precisely because of these bounds of who is considered human – the liberal, rational, autonomous, productive citizen.

DISABILITY ACTIVISM AND WORK

In March 2014, the Ontario Human Rights Tribunal found that paying disabled workers sub-minimum wages for their work, legislated through the Employment Standards Act, violated the Ontario Human Rights Code (*Garrie v. Janus Joan Inc.* 2014). The following year, the Ontario Human Rights Commission cited this decision in its recommendation that the government reviews all Employment Standards Act exemptions for their alignment with human rights law (Ontario Human Rights Commission 2015). This seems to have led to the announcement in 2015 by then-minister Helena Jaczek, that service delivery agencies were to stop taking on new workers to sheltered workshop programs in 2016, tapering off to province-wide closures in 2019[5] (Ministry of Community and Social Services 2015). The province planned to segue disabled workers into the labour market through individualized employment supports (Ministry of Community and Social Services 2015). Service agencies also transitioned their activities to include a recreational and social focus. This striking change seems to bring intellectually and developmentally disabled workers in line with changing attitudes in favour of accessibility, representing a coalescing of disability rights advocates and neoliberal diversity and inclusion mandates. In the 1980s and 1990s, disability rights organizers began to focus on principles of independent living, which asserted the right for disabled people to live autonomously with complete control over decisions regarding care services and personal finances (Galer 2018, 93). Moving out of decades of institutionalization where care workers, the state, or members of people's families had complete control over every aspect of daily life, the independent living movement was a radical step for the disabled community in North America. The independent living movement argued that employment was central to enabling disabled people to live fully independent lives (Galer 2018, 93), as access to stable income would provide a complete degree of autonomy that could not be achieved if one was tied, or indeed dependent, on state-provided disability assistance.

Considerations of work have been central to disability organizing in the late-twentieth century and a central factor in disabled identity formation in Canada in the same period. As Dustin Galer shows, "a dissociative relationship between paid work and identity existed for many people with disabilities, exempting them from mainstream expectations to work, making them unable to fully incorporate labour into the process of identity development" (Galer 2018, 20). It is then perhaps disabled people's lack of access to this crucial aspect of neoliberal citizenship, in addition to the material disadvantages associated with not working, that have sustained its longevity as a political goal for disabled people in Canada. Despite widespread experiences of chronic un- and under-employment and poverty experienced collectively as a community, twentieth-century disabled activism in Canada predominantly focussed on solutions that prioritized contributions to society and the economy as the source of independence. A key figure in the independent living movement based out of Toronto, Beryl Potter: "Argued that people with disabilities must be incorporated into the workforce in more significant numbers so that 'we can become useful citizens and pay taxes too,' since a larger tax base provided by working disabled people would help pay for demands for greater levels of accessibility" (Galer 2018, 94). Many Canadian disability activists sought to politicize citizenship for disabled people, building on the rhetoric of capacity, productivity, ability, and inherent worth. Seeking to centre discussion of access and inclusion to challenge societies and states that have historically viewed disabled people outside the bounds of social and political citizenship, activists seek institutional justice and equality offered formally through the state (Prince 2009, 180). However, it is important to note the dissonance this discourse encounters when considering the current and long-lasting "social realities of prejudice and segregation" experience by disabled people systemically (Prince 2009, 180).

Canadian disability advocacy focused on state-based claims at the turn of the century has been located within a social liberal tradition (Prince 2009, 225), reflecting the mainstream liberalism of broader society. The ideological influence of disability organizing is significant to understand, as it colours the disability movement's targets for redistributive justice and defines the bounds within which it seeks action. This movement and community is inherently reformist: it seeks change for its constituents within the bounds of the current state, institutional, and social structures. To be direct, disability activism in Canada works within the bounds of capitalist society and its associated market relations, which it accepts as necessary – this is not an anti-capitalist movement (Prince 2009, 182). Indeed, central to claims-making against the state for disabled people in Canada is the issue of access to meaningful paid employment due to a history of sheltered workshops and volunteer work "masquerading as competitive and fair wage-based work" (Prince 2009, 182). Much effort is put into calling on the government to support access to employment through workplace accommodations regulations, employment equity, and employment supports. In tandem with this is the continued work of making claims on the state for more robust and fulsome disability benefits that allow disabled people to meet their needs securely and out of poverty. Given the earlier discussion concerning Stone's assessment of the dichotomy between work and need, I wonder if these two goals of disability activism – access to work and access to better benefits – conflict with one another? Indeed, from the state's point of view, relying on notions of individual self-sufficiency and attachment to the labour market could be seen to provide an easy justification for decreased attachment to the state and its benefits, which are often perceived as perpetuating the dependency of recipients.

Disability organizing in this period challenged structural barriers to employment seeking reforms and access without questioning or undermining how work under capitalism allowed for (or indeed required) ableism. Liberal disability movements have sought to reaffirm disabled people's productivity and therefore value to the labour market and capitalist society as a whole. Indeed, Dustin Galer's interviews with disabled workers in the Toronto area reveal a consistent disavowal of dependence – on the state, family, or charity – and a desire among disabled workers to seek independence through identifying with a strong work ethic despite being disabled.

Advocacy groups like People First of Canada and Inclusion Canada (formerly Canadian Association for Community Living [CACL]) have been vocal for many decades about the exploitative nature of segregated, subminimum wage employment in sheltered workshops. Inclusion Canada's many local partner-service agencies have been deeply involved in providing sheltered workshops from the very beginning. Despite their role in facilitating segregated labour, Inclusion Canada has been a vocal agent of advocacy, pushing for federal and provincial governments to end enclaved and exploitative work in favour of "Employment First" (CACL 2011, 16). A policy of Employment First for state-funded service agencies shifts the operational objective to paid employment for disabled people in the first instance. This mirrors the evolving United Nations Convention on the Rights of People with Disabilities "Right to Work" program, which articulates that access to paid employment is a fundamental human right historically denied to disabled people (Lachwitz 2018, 313).

These demands seek to end the long history of quarantine, exploitation, and poverty endemic to the disabled community. However, by setting their sights on employment, the various players amongst the disability movement in Canada have failed to recognize the centrality of work itself to the long history and present-day exploitation of disabled people.

CONCLUSION

In stark contrast to this status quo of organizing, Sunny Taylor (2004) contests the idea that disabled emancipation can or should occur through the labour market under capitalism. Articulating a conception of being disabled as a social and political state of being, Taylor (2004) argues that systemic oppression enabled by ableism cannot be individualized and needs collective and structural solutions. Arguing in favour of "the right not to work," Taylor (2004) challenges the rhetoric that disabled people's only or primary source of value must be found through their attachment to a capitalist labour market. This suggests not only a challenge to ideas of productivity, value, and independence ingrained in liberal conceptions of citizenship under capitalism but squarely defies the long-held political goals of liberal disability rights movements. The limits of the disability movement in Canada, including its inability to dismantle systematic oppression of disabled people, are rooted in its refusal to imagine a future outside of liberal norms of subject and citizen, and the ideal of employment for all. The disability movement's demands have evolved alongside the fetishization of work and the idea that our intrinsic value is linked to our ability to participate, independently, in the rigours of a labour market made to extract the maximum profit.

The ideal liberal citizen is wholly incompatible with many disabled and mad people due to its emphasis on norms of autonomy, rationality, and independence. Taylor obliterates these norms: "no one partakes in American capitalism independently; there is no such thing as a 'self-made' individual" (Taylor 2004). Instead, we might begin to make visible how dependence is a relative state of being. Indeed, the rhetoric of self-sufficiency as an ideal to strive for rather than dependence (on state social assistance) obfuscates the myriad ways we all depend on each other, including the waged labour relationship between worker and employer (Young 2002, 43). An emphasis on how we are all interdependent might begin to undo the mythmaking of the liberal citizen and all the ways it discourages considerations of access and "deviant" ways of being.

It is further worth rethinking how rehabilitation masks the violence of sheltered workshops and the assimilationist project of work. The language of rehabilitation and vocational training suggests a temporal rest. The sheltered workshop is an in-between space that claims to bridge the gap between the sub-human unproductive disabled person that was and the capacious worker that is yet to be made. Rehabilitation justifies the quarantine or segregation of disabled people from everyone else: segregated special education classrooms, total institutions, or sheltered workshops. It is crucial to this re-making project that it happens away from acceptable citizens – productive workers must not become "infected" with the ills of dependence. Moreover, the quarantine of deviance also serves to discipline all workers through its example: live to produce ... or else! Again, in a Rawlsian sense, disabled people and all others not able to meet the standard of autonomy and rationality serve as a reminder of what not to do and who not to be(come). Nevertheless, the language of rehabilitation also masks at its core the elimination project central to settler-colonial capitalism. Through rehabilitation, all that is non-normative must be eliminated, including divergent ways of being that are incompatible with profit accumulation in the first instance.

And so, I submit that through this recent history of the various institutional practices of control and regulation of intellectually and developmentally disabled people, work has been a through-line. By focussing on work as a conduit for various confinement and institutional violence methods, the limits of the deinstitutional movement are exposed. The focus on the spatial elements of incarceration means deinstitutionalization was unable to meaningfully combat the discursive and knowledge-making practices of disability that emphasize work as a strategy of rehabilitation and normalization. Work not only enables and necessitates violence but, at its core, is violence itself.

We are at a crucial turning point in Ontario where decades of advocacy against the extraction of unremunerated labour from disabled people in segregated work environments is being taken up. But is it enough to have shuttered the institutional setting of the sheltered workshop without addressing the centrality of work to decades of violence, loathing, and neglect? To be sure, strengthened workplace accommodation frameworks and funding for supported employment programs mean that some intellectually and developmentally disabled people engage in competitive, unsegregated employment. But are projects seeking employment as emancipation and a form of disability justice not recuperating the language of rehabilitation? Broadening the bounds of liberal citizenship to include some disabled people only reinforces those limits for the rest. The increased enfranchisement of some disabled people without an uncoupling of the propertied nature of ableism must necessarily mean the continued disenfranchisement of those who are still seen as "too disabled."

Can we imagine life otherwise? Sunny Taylor boldly offers one model to consider: "I have a confession to make: I do not work. I am on SSI.[6] I have very little work value (if any), and I am a drain on our country's welfare system. I have another confession to make: I do not think this is wrong, and to be honest, I am very happy not working. Instead I spend the majority of my time doing the activity I find the most rewarding and valuable, painting" (Taylor 2004).

Perhaps what is instead needed is a reassertion of the value of life beyond and without work. The value of contributions to our collective and interdependent lives cannot merely be measured in wages, salaries, or profit margins.

NOTES

Siobhán Saravanamuttu is supported in part by funding from the Social Sciences and Humanities Research Council and the S. Leonard Syme Training Fellowship in Work and Health from the Institute of Work and Health.

1 To avoid confusion between institutionalization and institutional practices in community settings, I will often refer to places where disabled people were warehoused and often were not allowed to leave as total institutions.

2 Language and its political implications are ever in flux. When writing about disability, I use "identity-first" language such as *disabled people* rather than "person first," such as *people with disabilities*. This choice reflects a social and materialist model of disability. These models understand disability not as a bio-medical impairment that individuals may possess. Instead, one is disabled by social, political, and economic structural conditions.

3 Carlson here uses "mental retardation," where I have substituted intellectual disability. Both terms are labels imposed by the state and medical apparatuses upon people. Carlson's use of the outdated term

mental retardation acknowledges that while it is no longer appropriate to refer to disabled people as such, the term holds analytical value. Many critical disability studies scholars who engage with our collective histories retain similarly outdated terms to understand how they inform knowledge about disabled people historically and today. While I understand this choice, I have made a different one. As a disabled scholar, I foreground the experiences of intellectually disabled people. The term "mental retardation" has been used as a boundary-setting label, but the "r-word" is also a common and hurtful slur used to demean disabled people. For this reason, I choose not to repeat this language in this chapter except for in direct quotations.

4 When referring to people who live or have lived in institutions, I use the term "inmate" rather than "resident" or "patient." This choice reflects the assertion made by institutional survivors that total institutions for mad and disabled people are inherently carceral spaces of imprisonment, abuse, and control, not homes nor benevolent spaces of medical care (Chapman et al. 2014).

5 The implementation of this plan for closures has not quite been unilateral across Ontario, with the Ford government failing to officially enforce its predecessor's policy on transition (Institute for Research and Development on Inclusion and Society 2021, 15).

6 SSI or Supplemental Security Income is a means-tested income benefit payment for disabled people of all ages as well as adults over age sixty-five in the United States (Social Security Agency 2022).

REFERENCES

Beckwith, Ruthie-Marie. 2016. *Disability Servitude: From Peonage to Poverty*. United Kingdom: Palgrave MacMillan.

Burghardt, Madeline C. 2018. *Broken: Institutions, Families, and the Construction of Intellectual Disability*. Montreal and Kingston: McGill-Queens University Press.

CACL (Canadian Association for Community Living). 2011. *Achieving Social and Economic Inclusion: From Segregation to"'Employment First."* June 2011.

Carey, Allison C. 2009. *On the Margins of Citizenship: Intellectual Disability and Civil Rights in Twentieth-Century America*. Philadelphia, PA: Temple University Press.

Carlson, Licia. 2015. "Docile Bodies, Docile Minds: Foucauldian Reflections on Mental Retardation." In *Foucault and the Government of Disability*, edited by Shelley Tremain, 133–52. Ann Arbor: University of Michigan Press.

Department of Manpower and Immigration. 1972. *Directory of Workshops in Canada Serving the Handicapped (Including Activity Centres and Business Enterprises)*. Government of Canada.

Employment Standards Act. 2000. S.O.2000, c.41.

Epstein, Griffin. 2014. "Refrigerator Mothers and Sick Little Boys: Bruno Bettelheim, Eugenics and the De-Pathologization of Jewish Identity." *Disability Studies Quarterly* 34, no. 3: 1–25.

Erevelles, Nirmala. 2013. "(Im)material Citizens: Cognitive Disability, Race, and the Politics of Citizenship." In *Foundations of Disability Studies*, edited by Matthew Wappett and Katrina Arndt, 145–76. New York: Palgrave MacMillan.

– 2014. "Crippin' Jim Crow: Disability, Dis-Location, and the School-to-Prison Pipeline." In *Disability Incarcerated: Imprisonment and Disability in the United States and Canada,* edited by Liat Ben-Moshe, Chris Chapman, and Allison C. Carey, 79–99. Palgrave MacMillan: New York.

Galer, Dustin. 2014. "'A Place to Work Like Any Other?': Sheltered Workshops in Canada, 1970–1985." *Canadian Journal of Disability Studies* 3, no. 2: 1–30.

– 2018. *Working towards Equity: Disability Rights Activism and Employment in Late Twentieth-Century Canada*. Toronto: University of Toronto Press.

Garrie v. Janus Joan Inc. 2014. HRTO 272.

Gill, Michael. 2005. "The Myth of Transition: Contractualizing Disability in the Sheltered Workshop." *Disability and Society* 20, no. 6: 613–23.

Institute for Research and Development on Inclusion and Society. 2021. *Help Wanted: Ending Sheltered Work in Canada*. Oshawa.

Lachwitz, Klaus. 2018. "Barriers and Opportunities for Persons with Disabilities to Change from Sheltered Employment Settings into an Open and Inclusive Labour Market – Positions of UN Bodies and Some Global, Regional and National Disabled People Organizations (DPOs)." In *The Right to Work for Persons with Disabilities: International Perspectives*, edited by Gudrun Wansing, Felix Welti, and Markus Shäfers, 313–26. Baden-Baden, Germany: Nomos Verlagsgesellschaft.

LeBlanc Haley, Tobin, and Chelsea Temple Jones. 2020. "Introduction: Sites and Shapes of Transinstitutionalization." *Canadian Journal of Disability Studies* 9, no. 3: 1–16.

Linton, Megan. 2021. "A Penny a Poppy." *Briarpatch*, 4 November 2021. https://briarpatchmagazine.com/articles/view/sheltered-workshops-poppies-disabled-workers.

Ministry of Community and Social Services. 2015. "Developmental Services: Spotlight on Transformation." December 2015. 51, 1–2. http://www.mcss.gov.on.ca/documents/en/mcss/publications/spotlight/DS-Spotlight_issue51_en.pdf.

Ontario Human Rights Commission. 2015. *Ontario Human Rights Commission Submission to Ministry of Labour Changing Workplaces Review.* 18 September 2015. http://www.ohrc.on.ca/en/ohrc-submission-ministry-labour-changing-workplace-review.

People First of Canada. 2018. *Devaluing Ontarians with Intellectual Disabilities.* 25 October 2018. https://communitylivingontario.ca/wp-content/uploads/2018/10/NewsReleasePFCResponsetoSheltered WorkshopsOct252018.pdf.

Prince, Michael J. 2009. *Absent Citizens: Disability Politics and Policy in Canada*. Toronto: University of Toronto Press.

Rose, Sarah F. 2017. *No Right to Be Idle: The Invention of Disability, 1840s–1930s*. Chapel Hill: The University of North Carolina Press.

Rosenthal, Keith, ed. 2019. *Capitalism and Disability*. Chicago, Illinois: Haymarket Books.

Rossiter, Kate, and Jen Rinaldi. 2019. *Institutional Violence and Disability: Punishing Conditions*. New York: Routledge.

Social Security Agency. 2022. *Understanding Supplemental Security Income (SSI) Overview – 2022 Edition*. https://www.ssa.gov/ssi/text-over-ussi.htm.

Stone, Deborah A. 1984. *The Disabled State*. Temple University Press: Philadelphia.

Taylor, Sunny. 2004. "The Right Not to Work: Power and Disability." *Monthly Review*, 1 March 2004. https://monthlyreview.org/2004/03/01/the-right-not-to-work-power-and-disability.

Wolfensberger, W. 1975. *The Origin and Nature of Our Institutional Models*. Syracuse, NY: Human Policy Press.

Young, Iris Marion. 2002. "Autonomy, Welfare Reform, and Meaningful Work." In *The Subject of Care: Feminist Perspectives on Dependency*, edited by Eva Feder Kittay and Ellen K. Feder, 40–60. United States: Rowman & Littlefield Publishing Group.

7

Institutionalizing Unfree Labour in Ontario's Seasonal Agricultural Worker Program Farmsteads

SHANTI FERNANDO AND JEN RINALDI

In the first six months of the novel coronavirus pandemic, Juan López Chaparro, Bonifacio Eugenio Romero, and Rogelio Santos Muñoz died of the condition. All three men had travelled from Mexico to Ontario to participate in Canada's Seasonal Agricultural Worker Program (SAWP) – "low-skilled" temporary employment that brings people predominantly from Latin American or Caribbean countries to carry out agricultural labour. Their deaths coincided with alarming spikes in COVID-19 infection rates at SAWP farms. The disproportionate amount of confirmed cases among seasonal agricultural workers compared to the province's general population was absolutely attributable to the living and working conditions they navigated.

The pandemic shone a spotlight on the plight of racialized migrant agricultural workers who kept the food supply chain flowing even during lockdowns. They were not subject to lockdown because they were deemed essential, and their working conditions exposed them to COVID-19. When these conditions were examined by investigative journalists, workers were found to be kept in crowded bunkhouses, with little personal freedom and long hours, without health or labour standards. The living conditions described are not actually new, and were well documented as problems that predate the pandemic (Binford 2009; Choudry and Smith 2016; Cohen 2019; Fernando 2012; Horgan and Liinamaa 2017; Marsden 2018; Reid-Musson 2017). These are what Choudry and Smith (2016), Cohen (2019), and Shantz (2014) have referred to as conditions akin to unfree labour. Shantz argues this is part of a global return to and expansion of slavery as an institution with the decline in support for labour protections. We see this return play out in Canada where the acceptance of the need for insourcing racialized agricultural workers is coupled with the dehumanization and control of workers. Walia (2010) refers to this phenomenon as "the flip side of the transnational phenomenon of capitalist outsourcing [where] migrant workers thus represent the 'perfect workforce' in an era of evolving global capital-labour relations: commodified and exploitable; flexible and expendable" (72). In this chapter we place this established framing of migrant labour as an extension of historical servitude in conversation with total institutional histories, to show how they share in common defining features that are borne out in the custodial relation. It is important to identify those features because they generate violence.

The program we specifically study here positions the employer and property owner as a kind of caregiver, only their care is attenuated with racial affect. The affects that attach to migrant populations and their employers facilitate workforce insourcing and its attendant violences. To illustrate how "affective economies" operate, Ahmed (2004) describes the example of the white Christian farmer as "endangered by imagined others whose proximity threatens not only to take something away from the subject (jobs, security, wealth), but to take the place of the subject" (117). This narrative rewrites history, such that "the labor of others (migrants, slaves) is concealed in a fantasy that is the white subject who 'built this land'" (117–18). Sustaining the fantasy, then, entails containing the racialized migrant worker, controlling their access to land and resources. Along these lines Vukov (2003) argues, "immigration is central to the affective epidemics of security" (339). She posits Canada can justify unfree labour through retaining an historically entrenched, xenophobic narrative of the nation-state, and securing the state against perceived threat. Fear over the perceived threat the migrant poses drives immigration restrictions and deportations, but in the case of labour insourcing migrants cannot be immediately driven out. They are instead subjected to this ongoing public aversion even while positioned in relationships of structured dependency.

In this chapter, we posit that the exploitative worker permits used in Canada's Seasonal Agricultural Worker Program – which give employers great power while providing few worker rights or protections – creates a custodial relationship that mirrors the institutional model in miniature. The level of control that farmstead owners are able to exert over workers enables adapted forms of institutional violence. We were able to identify the kinds of violence common on SAWP farmsteads by surveying Canadian investigative journalism. We ran keyword searches on the most popular online Canadian news sites. Those sources appear on "top ten" legacy media lists in the following order (Anglophone sources only): CBC (or Canadian Broadcasting Corporation), *Globe and Mail*, *Toronto Star*, CTV News (or Canadian Television Network), *Huffington Post Canada*, Global News, and *National Post*. We limited our search to a timeframe that provided a year-long snapshot into pandemic reporting: 15 March 2020–15 March 2021. We accessed stories that were behind firewalls so subscriptions did not constrain our data gathering. But we did limit our search to news and print reporting – which meant that we excluded opinion pieces as well as radio and podcast pieces. While all articles we turned up referenced Ontario Seasonal Agricultural Work, we only added to our dataset the stories that explicitly referenced working and living conditions. These search parameters yielded eighty articles in total, broken down accordingly: thirteen from CBC, sixteen from *Globe and Mail*, thirteen from *Toronto Star*, seventeen from CTV News, two from *Huffington Post Canada*, sixteen from Global News, and three from *National Post*.

This dataset provided an on-the-ground accounting of violence against seasonal agricultural workers, specifically inadequate living conditions and exploitative working conditions. These forms of violence may have been horrifically amplified through the COVID-19 pandemic, but they bear a striking resemblance to the violences found in total institutional models (Goffman 1961) designed to manage unfree labour. This finding signposts the fact that there is a structural problem with the SAWP that will persist past the pandemic, for as long as institutional models reproduce labour practices that rely on an insourced racialized workforce with few rights or protections.

THE SMALL-SCALE INSTITUTIONAL MODEL

Canada's temporary foreign worker program (TFWP) is designed to enable Canadian employers to hire foreign workers to meet labour shortages (Caxaj and Cohen 2019; Marsden 2018). The majority of program participants are classified as non-professional or low-skilled, filling positions in service, farming, food processing, and caregiving (Inouye 2012; Stasiulis 2020). Within the TFWP, the Seasonal Agricultural Worker Program employs migrant farm workers predominantly from Mexico and the Caribbean for eight-month installments, during planting and harvesting seasons. Workers come for their installments and return to their home countries (and usually their families) during the off seasons, often on this rotation for years. As James (2021) reasons, the fact that the SAWP was established through a Memorandum of Understanding (MOU) between Canada, Mexico, and ten Caribbean states as an "intergovernmental administrative agreement" rather than a binding international treaty makes it less transparent and less enforceable.

The Canadian government has created immigration policy through the SAWP that includes racialized migrant workers in programs that institutionalize migrant exploitation. Shantz (2010) contends that "Canadian migration policy is the result of a perfected system of social control, containment and expulsion" (90). In order to distance the state from this exclusionary border policing the government does not directly administer the SAW program. Instead it is run by the Foreign Agricultural Resources Management Service (FARMS): a non-profit private organization headquartered in Mississauga, Ontario (https://farmsontario.ca). The use of FARMS delegates governmental responsibility for this exploited and vulnerable population to the labour market. This abdication of centralized responsibility has meant that *employers* affiliated with the SAWP (rather than governments) have been able to enact strategies of control that were so endemic to classic total institutions. The way in which this program has been implemented makes clear that racialized migrant workers are not desirable subjects. As non-citizens, potentially unruly or ungovernable outsiders, they are subjected to control under farm owners. The farmer who better fits the cultural imaginary of the ideal citizen is put "in charge" of racialized migrant workers, tasked with managing them in ways that look like care. This is a relationship of forced dependency, one that may engender resentment for having to provide support, and that turns on the calculation of how much value can be extracted from migrant labour. Even in this care relation, the migrant worker faces loathing because they cannot escape their framing as threat – either to national security or to budgetary bottom lines.

There has been no pathway to permanent status, much less full citizenship, through the SAWP. As Nolen (2021) chronicled, there are migrant workers who have returned to the same farm for thirty years yet were unable to apply for Canadian immigration status. SAWP rules – including recruitment resting on employers' decisions, costs expected of workers versus partially recoverable costs for employers, and closed contracts the employer can cancel – favour the employer and are clearly meant to deter anything other than temporary migration from the prescribed countries. Key features of the program include the lack of a path to permanent residence, the lack of continuous work authorization (not available to workers whose permits are designed to expire), the lack of a right to remain in the country (which is either legally impossible or materially difficult), the lack of independence from sponsorship (in this case employers), and few rights related to social citizenship (such as legal or substantive access to employment insurance or healthcare service) (Goldring, Berstein, and Bernhard 2009; Marsden 2018). These conditions differentiate temporary migrant populations from citizenries, and the differentiation "opens the door to differential treatment, marginalization, and even abuse" (Baglay 2016, 123).

For seasonal agricultural workers, unfree migrant labour is tied to closed work contracts: contracts that employers initiate, and that bind workers to a single employer (Marsden 2018; Walia 2021). Workers must make arrangements for work before arrival in Canada, and any transfer to another employer while in Canada requires an application for a new work permit (Bhuyan et al. 2018; Inouye 2012). Their time in Canada is entirely contingent on their contracts, to the extent that when contracts end or are broken the migrant has no right to remain in the country. Closed work contracts thus engender an indentured working relationship. This forced dependency not only limits labour mobility, but also renders workers vulnerable to violence (Binford 2009; Taylor, Foster and Cambre 2012). In response to calls by migrants and migrant advocates to create open contracts, the Canadian government created a limited pathway to open contracts that was only available to migrant workers who were already in the country but had complaints about their current contract and were considered vulnerable due to abuse (Mojtehedzadeh 2020). There is little chance that a migrant worker would know about the pathway and then subsequently also be able to access the complaint process (which is only available online and only available in French and English with documentation requirements); even if this occurred, they are unlikely to be approved as vulnerable. This is an inadequate and almost laughable policy response to the problems of dependency that the closed contract generates (Mojtehedzadeh 2020).

The closed contract echoes the patterns of institutionalization. Total carceral or medical institutionalization has historically been tied to a singular, centralized authority, found in government control of large populations in brick-and-mortar buildings. This mega-bureaucracy might impose daily scheduling and manage shared space to meet some key organizational aim (for more on this originating concept, see Goffman 1961). Typically, total institutions constituted a state-enacted strategy to deal with populations that needed around-the-clock care or surveillance (as examples, disabled persons and prisoners, respectively). Racialized populations in Canada and the US historically experienced unfree labour as a practice that shares important parallels with and distinctions from Goffman's model. The transatlantic slave trade built and grew American economies, while at the same time devastating the economies of much of the African continent. As Pizzolato (2018) argues, slavery cast a long shadow where post-slavery agricultural practices "hid ways in which employers have used the racialization of labour hierarchies, the denial of citizenship rights and debt, to foster unfree labour relations" (474). This was just as true for Canadian agricultural development: "transient servitude, especially in the form of (im)migrant labour, had many of the advantages of slave labour, as employers maintained control of both the labour as well as the labourer" (73). This exact form of the master/slave relation no longer exists in Canada but the affects carry through to exploitative racialized labour, wherein the landowner maintains control over their workers' living conditions and movements.

Racial hierarchy vests (especially white) citizen-owned households and farmsteads with their own personal totalizing power, to the extent that they provide housing, they serve as a migrant worker's connection (or barrier) to community supports, they set work schedules, and they determine whether a migrant stays or returns to the country for work on a yearly basis. Employers in sum establish labour and living conditions for migrants (Binford 2009). This power serves the TFWP's organizational aim to have essential work completed without the promise of status – and all the entitlements that come with status. This makes every SAWP farmstead similar to Goffman's (1961) total institution, in miniature – a space where a figurehead with authority controls a population in service of an organizational aim, just smaller in scale, more widely dispersed across the country, and entirely contingent on the employer/worker relation. Bringing racialized migrant labour into conversation with the total institutional model offers a productive contribution to theories of institutionalization: we show in this comparative analysis what happens when racial affects inflect the institutional arrangement. By which we mean, an ugly nuance to the farmstead/institution comparison is how racialized migrant populations are distinctly treated: housed and fed and paid only to the point that their labour can be extracted, otherwise treated to distrust and hostility.

Where comparable institutional conditions thrive, violence follows. Evident in our research for this chapter, the institutional violence of SAWP farmsteads includes austere, often substandard cramped, dirty, and isolated living conditions, and exploitative labour conditions that are tolerated by workers who fear reprisal and dismissal. In what follows we present the forms of violence that SAWP workers have experienced (both before and during COVID), and we link those forms of violence to the living and working conditions on farmsteads that represent something akin to total institutionalization in which care and constraint coexist precisely because the need to control unruly migrant populations was embedded in the SAWP.

LIVING WITH CONDITIONS OF VIOLENCE

The living conditions that SAWP workers endure are sites of extreme isolation, restricted decision-making, compromised privacy, and material deprivation – all of which are key features of classic institutional living in which they are forced to accept violent forms of care. Employers are required under the SAW program to provide lodging, which they tend to build on their property – and it can be a spartan at best and substandard, cramped, and dirty at worst. The farms where SAWP workers are deployed are typically located some distance from local towns, such that workers depend on employers for access to resources or transportation into town (Horgan and Liinamaa 2017; Stasiulis 2020). These overlapping living and working conditions mean that workers and employers "live and work in close proximity to one another" (Reid-Musson 2017, 722), some ways away from potential oversight, support, and general social participation. This is reminiscent of historically exploitative working relationships (especially unfree working relationships) in which an employer can claim benevolence for treating workers well or providing living conditions, yet this benevolence is not guaranteed and cannot be demanded.

The spatial arrangement described above has had profoundly isolating and psychologically damaging effects, exacerbated by employer rules. In our dataset, seasonal agricultural workers reported that some employers only allowed them to leave the farm for two to three hours every two weeks, strictly for the purpose of grocery shopping (Kelley, Wirsig, and Smart 2020). Those rare days off may also be packed with other kinds of social activities like religious services, medical appointments, and visiting family. Employers are able to restrict migrant movement materially, to the extent that the only way off rural properties and into town is often an employer's vehicle. The closed contract between workers and employers also functions as a control on movement. A SAWP worker losing their job would result in deportation, and the rotational nature of the work means an employer has the privilege to decide against rehiring that same worker the following season. This means that SAWP workers comply with employer demands often due to fear of job loss, which is an obvious avenue for potential abuse.

The pandemic only further aggravated this deep isolation. Media reported that SAWP employers received emails from people in town complaining about migrant workers wandering about (Kelley, Wirsig, and Smart 2020). These complaints were fuelled by fear of COVID spread, a fear which has been especially racially inflected – evident in complaints that included racist slurs and open threats (CBC 2020c; Blaze Baum and Grant 2020a). Some employers responded by having workers "voluntarily" sign forms pledging not to leave the premises even for grocery runs (Taekema 2020; *Toronto Star* Editorial Board 2020; Martin 2021). The racialization and criminalization of migrant farm workers demonstrate how these processes result in migrants' exclusion from the nation-state and local communities (Cohen 2019, 130). This racist backlash has further institutionalized workers, who evoke the carceral state in their description of the indignities that they are forced to endure due to fear of reprisals. They are forced to accept violent forms of care from their employers. One worker who signed such a form was quoted in a summer news article: "We can't speak out. It's like shackles around our feet. We cannot say nothing, because we want to come back" (Grant 2020). Similarly, another worker declared, "Honestly, it feels like I am in prison" (ibid.). COVID has only laid bare that workers feel trapped, bound to their employment space, cut off from social engagement, and institutionalized in their servitude.

These quoted references to shackles and prisons signal that the living conditions on SAWP farmsteads in effect strip workers of autonomous decision-making powers, which is a violence against agency. The experience of being trapped comes with cascading effects where workers lose control over the tasks of daily living like grocery shopping, and are denied dignity. Employers further pushed techniques of isolation and coercion past all reasonable and humane limits by controlling quarantine measures when a worker was diagnosed with COVID. One worker described situations where people in quarantine were not fed: "Our people are literally starving. People are dying ... trapped in homes by employers who won't let them out because migrants are seen as carriers of disease" (Wright 2020).

Living quarters themselves are strikingly similar to the wards, cottages, and cells of historical institutions. SAWP employers tend to provide their workers with shared bunkhouses, or "barrack-style housing" (Jeffords 2020) for sleeping, eating, and resting. SAWP workers frequently pointed to conditions of overcrowding in bunkhouses, with as many as twelve people per room (CBC 2020c), or four people sharing two beds and a single bathroom (Gatehouse 2020). A summer article describes as many as forty farm workers sharing a single shower (Grant and Blaze Baum 2020). This chronic overcrowding illustrates the extent to which employers signal their aversion to workers, given employers are responsible for the substandard, packed-in living.

There are net effects to the overcrowding of living quarters that materially and physically impact workers. One key effect is that violations of privacy are inevitable and frequent (Keung 2020a). Given that all the spaces involved are shared There is no escaping people when sleeping, eating, even bathing, mirroring many carceral institutions. Further, these cramped spaces become impossible to keep clean. Workers reported to news outlets the inescapable smell of urine (Grant and Blaze Baum 2020), cockroach and bedbug infestations (Blaze Baum and Grant 2020a), as well as leaks and mould in the ceiling, walls, and plumbing (Keung 2020a). Others reported showers that only ran excessively hot water so in effect there was no way to clean themselves after long days of dirty work unless they wanted to scald themselves (Blaze Baum and Grant 2020c). The emotional and physical toll of these living conditions is an example of how the specific iteration of programs like the SAWP obscure the violence that they engender. These horrific conditions could be improved through employer investment, but the underfunding of living space is such an integral feature of this institutional living to the extent that it signals the abandonment of the institutionalized. This abandonment is only magnified through logics of segmented labour and austerity. There is no perceived value in improving working conditions if workers are not able to complain and compliance is not enforced, so it is entirely a matter of employer choice whether workers are given liveable conditions.

UNFREE LABOUR ON FARMSTEADS: WAGE AND WORKER ABUSE

What are often appalling living conditions can also be coupled with physically difficult work and abuses and manipulation of farmstead workers that take advantage of SAWP rules. The institutionalized working conditions of SAWP farmsteads yield egregious examples of exploitation, exposure to illness and injury, and financial abuse. SAWP workers are overworked when assigned long hours (Hari 2014), and assigned tasks that extend beyond program expectations. Some of this extra work has gone unpaid or has not been identified as overtime (which would result in higher pay), because it is not recognized under employment contracts (Bhuyan et al. 2018; Polanco 2014). Further, wages earned may be cut into via "worker debt" that is itself rooted in corrupt program processing fees (Bhuyan et al. 2018). These conditions lead Reid-Musson (2014) to call migrant agricultural labour "indentured or unfree" (164). Employers who went grocery shopping on behalf of workers through the pandemic had the tendency to overspend, thus overdrawing from workers' salaries, because workers were ultimately still financially responsible for the groceries they were barred from choosing. Employers also reportedly used worker funds to purchase culturally inappropriate food (Thomas 2020). These financial conditions and wage theft constitute abuse to the extent that they erode labour freedoms and increase exploitation and financial dependence.

Our dataset yielded clear examples of economic abuse. Workers speaking to media referred to seventeen-hour workdays (Kelley, Wirsig, and Smart 2020) and seventy-hour work weeks (Gatehouse 2020). They were under threat of deportation if they were unable to meet productivity quotas (Blaze Baum and Grant 2020a). All for substandard pay, well below Ontario's minimum wage (Gatehouse 2020). Workers also see direct deductions from their paycheques for expenses they had not agreed to – a structure which enabled employers to go grocery shopping on their behalf as was described above (Blaze Baum and Grant 2020a). The work becomes indentured service when it is so significantly undervalued that it can be coercively conducted. The financial abuse has emotional impacts, undermines agency, and contributes to the solidification of the SAWP as a total institutional model for managing migrant workers.

These working conditions have somatic impacts, including and especially significant risk of injury. Labour conditions on SAWP farms include "pesticide use and repetitive motions [that] may expose workers to musculoskeletal injuries, eye and skin problems, respiratory conditions, sexual health concerns, and mental health challenges" (Caxaj and Cohen 2019, 4). Even with heightened risk of illness or injury, temporary foreign workers lack access to healthcare and employment protections, either in policy or in practice. Workers who fall ill or incur injury run the risk of their recruitment program refusing their work permit in the next year, or run the risk of their employer not inviting them back on contract, and this reduces their likelihood to report or to seek care (Marsden 2018; Rajkumar et al. 2012). Employer treatment shows the lack of concern for the health of workers and again their disposable nature. They do not want to spend time or money on keeping migrant workers safe or allowing them access to medical help if they are injured or become sick due to the lack of safety.

These conditions and lack of care for worker safety and health were a "recipe for COVID-19 to spread like wildfire" (Blaze Baum and Grant 2020a). Workers reported being forced to work without personal protective equipment like masks and gloves (Gatehouse 2020; Jones and Thomas 2020; Blaze Baum and Grant 2020a). Employers told workers to continue working in groups without adequate social distancing, even while waiting for results from COVID testing (Keung 2020b). On some farms only workers sick enough to impede their work were granted access to testing, signalling a devaluation of workers, and an explicit tying of value to their labour (Simpson 2020). Employers also had workers continue their jobs when they tested positive for COVID but were asymptomatic (CBC 2020b). There were workers who refused or avoided testing for fear that a positive result would lead to their deportation (Barker 2020), and many did not request support when developing COVID symptoms because they assumed they were ineligible for testing and treatment (CBC 2020a). An investigative article described workers as "concerned about being sent home, not being able to come back to work in Canada" (D'Amore 2020), indicating the stakes to their employment were too high to ensure they could remain healthy. This lack of care for the physical welfare of migrants and the disregard for their psychological welfare or right to a safe workplace just highlights their *disposability* to most employers. The thin veneer of liberal tolerance and humanitarian benevolence seems to have all but disappeared during the pandemic, which actually created *greater* levels of total institutionalization, abuse, and social control of migrant workers.

There were many incidents where employers took advantage of the pandemic to engage in expanded wage theft by further garnishing wages, withholding quarantine pay (Keung 2020b), or denying workers the top-ups available to Canada's essential workforce (Wright 2020). This is ethically egregious behaviour. As reported in June 2020: "many migrant workers report that employers are using COVID to further clamp down on basic worker freedoms, breaking down support systems and social networks, and targeting outspoken workers by ensuring they remain confined to workplaces and bunkhouses" (Keung 2020b). Forced isolation was especially dangerous given the social control employers could exercise over workers. There were accounts of workers in quarantine who received no or insufficient food (Gatehouse 2020; Jones and Thomas 2020; Blaze Baum and Grant 2020b; Hunter 2021). Workers who died while in quarantine raised "questions about whether health care providers were regularly checking in with the workers while they were in quarantine, and whether workers were able to access help" (Grant and Bailey 2021). The SAW program allows for financial abuse that keeps labourers as captives and the law and policy supporting this abuse obscures the violence of this institutional model. In this particular type of social control, the program allows for a type of incarceration in which workers are forced to accept violent forms of care knowing that the violence of semi-benevolence has removed agency, dignity and choice.

CONCLUSION

The liberation of workers from farmsteads will depend on the removal of the charity model that demands supplications from them and contains no duty of care to provide living and labour standards that non-migrant workers would be afforded. The lack of agency given to them in this caretaker model is a direct result of the master-slave narrative that underpins all that they do. Without drastic changes that both remove financial burdens to be a part of the program and stop employer exploitation that has been enabled through closed worker permits as hallmarks of this program, there will be no way out of the institutional violence embodied by the SAWP. This reimagining could then add potential status for all and enforceable labour standards to create a truly equitable migration policy framework.

Given that the SAW program is currently premised on keeping particular racialized migrants from accessing citizenship while insourcing them to address ongoing labour needs, there needs to be a complete overhaul of the program. This should include a true open-permit option that workers can apply for before they come to Canada and use to give themselves choice and to remove the fear of deportation, which gives employers the power to abuse. There should also be a path to permanent residency that starts with a continuous legal status as soon as a SAWP worker enters Canada and then gives them clear access to applying for a pathway to citizenship if they wish to pursue it. This would mean that SAWP workers are considered essential workers and employees who have the skills to contribute to the economy in a meaningful way similar to the way in which provincial nominee stream immigrants are classified as fulfilling a specific need and are therefore part of an immigration stream (Immigration, Refugees and Citizenship Canada 2021a). There also needs to be *actual* oversight of farms and punitive measures for those farms who have inadequate housing and dangerous working conditions. Corrupt employers should not be able to access employees to abuse without consequences. The use of an arm's length non-profit agency like FARMS does not mean that the federal government can relinquish their obligations to prevent and address abuse of those within their borders.

Cohen (2019) posits that "access to permanent status would have immediate and positive impacts on the everyday lives of migrants; it would allow them greater access to social, political, and legal rights, labour mobility, and the right to remain united with their families" (145). In 2021, Canada's federal government did extend an "innovative pathway to permanent residence" to temporary workers (along with international graduates), provided that they were "actively contributing to Canada's economy" (Immigration, Refugees and Citizenship Canada 2021b). But the application process for this fairly modest and temporary program is expensive and complex, including the need for extensive documentation and language requirement testing (Nolen 2021). This was a far cry from the status-for-all policy that many advocates and SAWP workers had called for.

Migrant advocates and migrant advocate organizations have worked tirelessly to get status for all migrant workers but they are aware that they face difficult challenges and have to counter prevailing xenophobic narratives. Systemic racism is inherent in these prevailing narratives that dehumanize migrant workers and see them as undesirable and unruly immigrants who should be grateful for any opportunities given to them since their home countries offer few opportunities. These narratives also characterize any labour protections for migrant workers as unnecessary and cast employers as hard-working virtuous farmers, as we saw in Ahmed's affective economy, who are doing their best under difficult circumstances. This is naive at best, disingenuous at worst, and also ignores all studies of migrant worker exploitation over the past decades. There is also the problem of changing a longstanding program that by design favours employers without contemplating the fate of the workers considered disposable. The logics of the SAW program are premised on the denial of status and potential immigration pathways as its value for social control and border imperialism and securitization.

What are the counternarratives, and how can they be circulated? Canadians – advocates, researchers, journalists, political commentators, labour unions – can hold the state accountable for a state sanctioned legal program of violence and exploitation – which our data has shown is not something that can be denied as a reality. Canadians can shine a light on the troubling paradox of Canada presenting itself as a welcoming immigrant country with a robust public discourse of human rights as fundamental to its "values" while at the same time taking advantage of migrants through institutionalized servitude. Migrant workers should have immigration status, the right to collectively organize and unionize, full rights to labour protections, and full health and safety protections. SAWP workers need immigration status and they need labour protections that provide living wages and safe working and living conditions for all workers. Ultimately, we need to make these border-created worker divisions obsolete.

REFERENCES

Cited Sources from Data Set

CBC

Barker, Jacob. 2020. "Leamington, Ont., Rallies behind Migrant Workers as 96 Farm Workers Test Positive for COVID-19." CBC News, 28 June 2020. https://www.cbc.ca/news/canada/windsor/migrant-worker-march-caravan-leamington-1.5630551.

CBC. 2020a. "COVID Outbreaks on Farms Reveal Crack in System That Migrant Workers Slip through, Say Health-Care Workers." CBC News, 20 November 2020. https://www.cbc.ca/radio/whitecoat/covid-outbreaks-on-farms-reveal-crack-in-system-that-migrant-workers-slip-through-say-health-care-workers-1.5808489.

– 2020b."Experts Concerned about Asymptomatic Migrant Workers Being Allowed on the Job." CBC News, 26 June 2020. https://www.cbc.ca/news/canada/windsor/experts-concerned-about-asymptomatic-worker-rules-in-province-covid19-agrifarm-plan-1.5628074.

– 2020c. "Information Revealed about Video Showing Alleged Local Migrant Worker Living Conditions." CBC News, 18 June 2020. https://www.cbc.ca/news/canada/windsor/information-revealed-about-video-showcasing-local-migrant-worker-living-conditions-1.5618395.

Gatehouse, Jonathan. 2020. "How Undocumented Migrant Workers are Slipping through Ontario's COVID-19 Net." CBC News, 2 July 2020. https://www.cbc.ca/news/canada/leamington-migrant-workers-1.5633032.

Kelley, Mark, Karen Wirsig, and Virginia Smart. 2020. "Bitter Harvest." CBC News, 29 November 2020. https://newsinteractives.cbc.ca/longform/bitter-harvest-migrant-workers-pandemic.

Taekema, Dan. 2020 "Canada Will Allow Stranded Farm Workers to Apply for Open Work Permits, Access Supports." CBC News, 16 December 2020. https://www.cbc.ca/news/canada/hamilton/farm-workers-stranded-supports-1.5843369.

CTV NEWS

Jeffords, Shawn. 2020. "Migrant Workers Need More Protection During the Pandemic, Say Advocates." CTV News, 7 May 2020. https://toronto.ctvnews.ca/migrant-workers-need-more-protection-during-the-pandemic-say-advocates-1.4930127.

Jones, Alexandra Mae, and Molly Thomas. 2020. "Migrant Worker Who Got COVID-19 Says He Was Fired from Ontario Farm for Speaking out." CTV News, 30 July 2020. https://www.ctvnews.ca/canada/migrant-worker-who-got-covid-19-says-he-was-fired-from-ontario-farm-for-speaking-out-1.5046484.

Simpson, Krista. 2020. "Migrant Worker Says COVID-19 Outbreak Mishandled at Norfolk Farm." CTV News, 8 June 2020. https://kitchener.ctvnews.ca/migrant-worker-says-covid-19-outbreak-mishandled-at-norfolk-farm-1.4975059.

Thomas, Molly. 2020. "Migrant Farm Workers Allege Pressure to Sign away Movement Rights amid COVID-19." CTV News, 4 August 2020. https://www.ctvnews.ca/canada/migrant-farm-workers-allege-pressure-to-sign-away-movement-rights-amid-covid-19-1.5051299.

GLOBAL NEWS

D'Amore, Rachael. 2020. "Windsor-Essex is One of Canada's Worst Coronavirus Hotspots. Here's Why." Global News, 14 July 2020. https://globalnews.ca/news/7173993/coronavirus-windsor-migrant-workers.

Wright, Teresa. 2020. "Migrant Workers in Canada Stage Multi-City Protest, Call for More COVID-19 Protections." Global News, 4 July 2020. https://globalnews.ca/news/7138902/coronavirus-canada-migrant-workers-risk.

GLOBE AND MAIL

Blaze Baum, Kathryn, and Tavia Grant. 2020a. "Essential but Expendable: How Canada Failed Migrant Farm Workers." *Globe and Mail*, 16 June 2020. https://www.theglobeandmail.com/canada/article-essential-but-expendable-how-canada-failed-migrant-farm-workers.

– 2020b. "Migrant Farm Workers Call for Safety from Reprisals for Speaking Out." The Globe and Mail, 16 August 2020. https://www.theglobeandmail.com/canada/article-migrant-farm-workers-call-for-safety-from-reprisals-for-speaking-out.

– 2020c. "Third Migrant Farm Worker Dies as Canada Reaches Deal with Mexico." *Globe and Mail*, 21 June 2020. https://www.theglobeandmail.com/canada/article-third-migrant-farm-worker-dies-as-canada-reaches-deal-with-mexico.

Grant, Tavia. 2020. "Migrant Workers on Farms across Canada Are Being Told They Can't Leave, Raising Rights Concerns." *Globe and Mail*, 3 August 2020. https://www.theglobeandmail.com/business/article-migrant-workers-on-farms-across-canada-are-being-told-they-cant-leave.

Grant, Tavia, and Ian Bailey. 2021. "Five Migrant Farm Workers Have Died Since Mid-March, Four while in COVID-19 Quarantine, Advocacy Group Says." *Globe and Mail*, 5 May 2021. https://www.theglobeandmail.com/canada/article-five-migrant-farm-workers-have-died-since-mid-march-four-while-in.

Grant, Tavia, and Kathryn Blaze Baum. 2020. "Migrant Farm Workers Detail Dangerous Pandemic Conditions." *Globe and Mail*, 8 June 2020. https://www.theglobeandmail.com/canada/article-farm-workers-detail-dangerous-pandemic-conditions.

Hunter, Justine. 2021. "Rules across the Country Inconsistent for Keeping Migrant Farm Workers Safe." *Globe and Mail*, 11 March 2021. https://www.theglobeandmail.com/canada/british-columbia/article-bc-finds-success-by-quarantining-farm-workers-in-hotels.

TORONTO STAR

Keung, Nicholas. 2020a. "COVID-19's Heavy Toll Pushed Ottawa to Propose These Changes to How Migrant Farm Workers Are Housed." *Toronto Star*, 5 November 2020. https://www.thestar.com/news/canada/2020/11/05/covid-19s-heavy-toll-pushed-ottawa-to-propose-these-changes-to-how-migrant-farm-workers-are-housed.html.

– 2020b. "Migrant Farm Workers 'In Crisis' amid Pandemic, Report Says." *Toronto Star*, 8 June 2020. https://www.thestar.com/news/gta/2020/06/08/pandemic-makes-problems-of-migrant-farm-workers-worse-report-says.html.

Mojtehedzadeh, Sara. 2020. "Open Work Permits for Exploited Migrant Workers a 'Band-Aid Solution,' Critics Say." *Toronto Star*, 17 July 2020. https://www.thestar.com/business/2020/07/17/open-work-permits-for-exploited-migrant-workers-a-band-aid-solution-critics-say.html.

Martin, Max. 2021. "Some COVID-Stranded Migrant Workers Finally Flying Home to Trinidad." *Toronto Star,* 19 January 2021. https://www.thestar.com/news/canada/2021/01/19/some-covid-stranded-migrant-workers-finally-flying-home-to-trinidad.html.

Nolen, Stephanie. 2021. "Roots of a Dream." *Toronto Star*, 29 July 2021. https://www.thestar.com/news/atkinsonseries/2021/covid-19-migrant-farm-workers.html.

Toronto Star Editorial Board. 2020. "The Migrant Farm Workers Did Their Job. It's Time Ottawa Gets Them Home." *Toronto Star*, 10 December 2020. https://www.thestar.com/opinion/editorials/2020/12/10/the-migrant-farm-workers-did-their-job-its-time-ottawa-gets-them-home.html.

OTHER SOURCES

Ahmed, Sara. 2004. "Affective Economies." *Social Text* 22, no. 2: 117–39.

Baglay, Sasha. 2016. "Who is My Neighbour? The Duty of Care in the Immigration Context: A Perspective from Canadian Case Law." *Windsor Yearbook on Access to Justice* 33, no. 2: 117–39.

Bhuyan, Rupaleem, Lorrraine Valmadrid, Esel Laxa Panlaqui, Novabella L. Pendon, and Pearlita Jean. 2018. "Responding to the Structural Violence of Migrant Domestic Work: Insights from Participatory Action Research with Migrant Caregivers in Canada." *Journal of Family Violence* 33: 613–27.

Binford, Leigh. 2009. "From Fields of Power to Fields of Sweat: The Dual Process of Constructing Temporary Migrant Labour in Mexico and Canada." *Third World Quarterly* 30, no. 3: 503–17.

Caxaj, C. Susana, and Amy Cohen. 2019. "'I Will Not Leave My Body Here': Migrant Farmworkers' Health and Safety amidst a Climate of Coercion." *International Journal of Environmental Research and Public Health* 16: 1–14.

Choudry, Aziz, and Adrian A. Smith, eds. 2016. *Unfree Labour? Struggles of Migrant and Immigrant Workers in Canada*. Oakland: PM Press.

Cohen, Amy. 2019. "'Slavery Hasn't Ended, It Has Just Become Modernized': Border Imperialism and the Lived Realities of Migrant Farmworkers in British Columbia, Canada." ACME*: An International Journal for Critical Geographies* 18, no. 1: 130–48.

Daley, Andrea, Lucia Costa, and Peter Beresford. 2019. "Introduction." In *Madness, Violence, and Power: A Critical Collection*, edited by Andrea Daley, Lucia Costa, and Peter Beresford, 3–18. Toronto: University of Toronto Press.

Fernando, Shanti. 2012. "Mexican Labour in Canada: A Critical Assessment of the Seasonal/Guest Worker Program." In *Dynamics and Trajectories: Canada and/in North America*, edited by A. Nurse and M. Fox. Halifax: Fernwood Books.

Goffman, Erving. 1961. *Asylums: Essays on the Social Situation of Mental Patients and Other Inmates*. New York: Anchor Books.

Goldring, Luin, Carolina Berinstein, and Judith K. Bernhard. 2009. "Institutionalizing Precarious Migratory Status in Canada." *Citizenship Studies* 13, no. 3: 239–65.

Hari, Amrita. 2014. "Temporariness, Rights, and Citizenship: The Latest Chapter in Canada's Exclusionary Migration and Refugee History." *Refuge* 30, no. 2: 35–45.

Horgan, Mervyn, and Saara Liinamaa. 2017. "The Social Quarantining of Migrant Labour: Everyday Effects of Temporary Foreign Worker Regulation in Canada." *Journal of Ethnic and Migration Studies* 43, no. 5: 713–30.

Immigration, Refugees and Citizenship Canada. 2021a. "How the Provincial Nominee Program Works." https://www.canada.ca/en/immigration-refugees-citizenship/services/immigrate-canada/provincial-nominees/works.html.

– 2021b. "New Pathway to Permanent Residency for over 90,000 Essential Temporary workers and International Graduates." News release, 14 April 2021. https://www.canada.ca/en/immigration-refugees-citizenship/news/2021/04/new-pathway-to-permanent-residency-for-over-90000-essential-temporary-workers-and-international-graduates.html.

Inouye, Kimiko. 2012. "Conditional Love: Representations of Migrant Work in Canadian Newsprint Media." *Social Identities* 18, no. 5: 573–92.

James, Theresa. 2021. "COVID-19 Pandemic and Structural Barriers for Migrant Agricultural Workers in Ontario." *University of Western Ontario Journal of Legal Studies* 12, no. 1: https://doi.org/10.5206/uwojls.v12i1.13636.

Marsden, Sarah Grayce. 2018. *Enforcing Exclusion: Precarious Migrants and the Law in Canada*. Vancouver: UBC Press.

Nixon, Rob. 2011. *Slow Violence and the Environmentalism of the Poor*. Cambridge: Harvard University Press.

Pizzolato, Nicola. 2018. "Harvests of Shame: Enduring Unfree Labour in the Twentieth-Century United States, 1933–1964." *Labor History* 59, no. 4: 472–90.

Polanco, Geraldina. 2014. "Social Citizenship in an Age of Temporary Flows: Migrant Workers in British Columbia's Immigrant Settlement Sector." *Transactional Social Review* 4, nos 2–3: 193–206.

Rajkumar, Deepa, Laurel Berkowitz, Leah F. Vosko, Valerie Preston, and Robert Latham. 2012. "At the Temporary-Permanent Divide: How Canada Produces Temporariness and Makes Citizens through its Security, Work, and Settlement Policies." *Citizenship Studies* 16, nos 3–4: 483–510.

Reid-Musson, Emily. 2017. "Grown Close to Home™: Migrant Farmworker (Im)Mobilities and Unfreedom on Canadian Family Farms." *Annals of American Association of Geographers* 197, no. 3: 716–30.

Shantz, Jeff. 2015. "'Slave-Like Conditions': Abuse of Foreign Workers in Canada." *Employee Responsibilities and Rights Journal* 27, no. 3: 233–9.

Smith, Adrian A. 2013. "Racialized in Justice: The Legal and Extra-Legal Struggles of Migrant Agricultural Workers in Canada." *Windsor Yearbook of Access to Justice* 31, no. 2: 15–38.

Stasiulis, Daiva. 2020. "Elimi(Nation): Canada's 'Post-Settler' Embrace of Disposable Migrant Labour." *Studies in Social Justice* 14, no. 1: 22–54.

Strauss, Kendra, and Siobhán McGrath. 2017. "Temporary Migration, Precarious Employment and Unfree Labour Relations: Exploring the 'Continuum of Exploitation' in Canada's Temporary Foreign Worker Program." *Geoforum* 78: 199–208.

Taylor, Alison, Jason Foster, and Carolina Cambre. 2012. "Training 'Expendable' Workers: Temporary Foreign Workers in Nursing." *Globalization, Societies and Education* 10, no. 1: 95–117.

Vukov, Tamara. 2003. "Imagining Communities through Immigration Policies: Governmental Regulation, Media Spectacles and the Affective Politics of National Borders." *International Journal of Cultural Studies* 6, no. 3: 335–53.

Walia, Harsha. 2010. "Transient Servitude: Migrant Labour in Canada and the Apartheid of Citizenship." *Race and Class* 52, no. 1: 71–84.

– 2021. *Border and Rule: Global Migration, Capitalism, and the Rise of Racist Nationalism*. Halifax: Fernwood.

8

Danger, Safety, and the Rhetoric of Urban Crisis

Institutional Logics and Windsor's Downtown Core

JIJIAN VORONKA, ADRIAN GUTA, TINA (JORDAN) NGUYEN, GRACE SHAW, AND AMAN AHLUWALIA CAMERON

This chapter explores what has been described as a growing "urban crisis" in Windsor, Ontario. While Windsor is attempting to revitalize its downtown core through business-friendly policies, new cultural attractions, and building infrastructure, the downtown core has increasingly become understood as a risky neighbourhood experiencing a "crisis" of homelessness and poverty, characterized as an outcome of drug use and mental illness, resulting in an exodus of people and business. Media accounts frame urban renewal efforts as being undermined by street-involved individuals and the community health and social service organizations that are expanding to serve them. Through a discourse analysis of local media coverage about this "urban crisis," we show how notions of violence get pinned to individual bodies who are understood to pose risks to both economic re/development and public safety. And how understanding marginalized individuals as harbingers of violence legitimizes calls for increased surveillance, policing, and psy interventions that would criminalize, contain, or remove marginalized people from public space. Building on spatial analyses of the governance of abject bodies post-deinstitutionalization, we explore how the age of "community care" still relies on institutional logics that risk managing unruly bodies out of public life.

This chapter contributes to understandings of what has been described as a growing "urban crisis" affecting communities across North America marked by increasing social divisions, poverty, inequality, racial, and spatial segregation which have resulted from attempts to promote urban renewal and revitalization (Florida 2017a). In the Canadian context, this process has not only affected major metropolitan cities like Vancouver, Toronto, and Montreal, but also in smaller cities and suburbs (Florida 2017b). Rates of homelessness have been rising across Canada since the 1980s with varying levels of intervention (Gaetz et al. 2016), a source of greater concern in the context of the COVID-19 global pandemic (Tsai and Wilson 2020). Beyond commonly held views of homelessness as rooted in personal failings, homelessness has been attributed to neoliberal reforms and corollary wage stagnation, job loss, and divestments in affordable housing and social assistance (Willse 2010, 2015). Myriad cuts to Canada's social safety net have increased the risk of homelessness for many, but especially those with disabilities (Dej 2020; Gaetz et al. 2016; Wang et al. 2016).

Amping up surveillance, policing, and psy discipline interventions (those drawing on psychological/psychiatric technologies) to manage social injustice is not new. Key scholarship has documented the violence incurred by inmates in carceral sites during the age of disability institutionalization in North America, as well as how deinstitutionalization dispersed such violence in new ways through transinstitutionalization and community care (Dyck and Deighton 2017; Reaume 1997; Rossiter and Rinaldi 2019). These works effectively show how disability institutionalization was central to the management of abject bodies in Western modernity. For instance, Malacrida's work explores how moral and racial panics in the province of Alberta facilitated the establishment and normalization of institutionalization, as well as the sexual sterilization of those incarcerated as part of the wider project of white settler nation building (Malacrida 2015). Dehumanization, seclusion, restraints, and physical and sexual violence were some of the practices that constituted the routine violence normalized and documented at one of the province's disability institutions (Malacrida 2015). Further, scholars and activists documenting the violence incurred at the Canton Asylum for Insane Indians in South Dakota show how normalizing the practices of institutional violence operated through the logics of racial-ableism and worked to justify colonialism and secure white supremacy (Burch 2014; Yellow Bird n.d.). Constructing a federal institution to specifically target indigenous people resulted in separating those institutionalized from kin, community, culture, language, land, and "epidemics, unsanitary conditions, the threat of violence, and physical barriers" at the institution meant that the primary reason for discharge from the asylum was death (Burch 2014, 148).

Yet in the age of community care, institutional logics prevail through practices of transinstitutionalization as well as efforts to spatially regulate and manage unruly bodies who escape the confines of institutional regulation. The dehumanization and devaluation of street-involved individuals involved in activities such as drug use, panhandling, sex work, petty theft, or who refuse psychiatric and other medical interventions runs rampant. Further, attempts to intervene on, contain, and cure street-involved individuals remains a goal that sustains institutional logics into community care and public space. As this chapter demonstrates, public discourse understands and reconstitutes those involved in street-life activities as mentally ill, and/or drug addicts, who require medical intervention. The proposed solution is increased mental health and addiction treatment services, but how those services are imagined risk looking less like community care supports and more like in-patient treatment settings, which recall the logics of institutionalization.

Post-institutionalization, we rely on other violent discursive logics that enact similar goals minus the build space, including respectability politics. We use the language of degeneracy and respectability in this chapter to connote how individual subjects, entire sub-populations, experiences, and particular traits have either been valued or troubled within the Canadian settler colonial project. Fellows and Razack trace conceptualizations of respectability and its converse degeneracy back to nineteenth century "ideological language expressing relations of domination and subordination. Respectability became an assertion of membership in the middle class and the basis on which one had the right to dominate others, those classified as degenerate" (Fellows and Razack 1998, 346). In contemporary Canadian contexts, respectability mirrors notions of white civility which is perceived as always under threat by degeneracy (Coleman 2006). Degeneracy came to be understood as a kind of self-producing pathological process lurking and reproduced in the blood, the body, and the race (Pick 1989, 22), which threatened respectability and thus needed to be identified, contained, and potentially cured (Karschay 2015). In the past, part of this work was managed through disability institutionalization, whose logics continue to permeate culture and practice in community care and public settings.

Ben-Moshe (2020) offers an analysis of neighbourhood resistance to disability integration in the age of community care. She uses Ahmed's work on affective economies (Ahmed 2004) to explain how NIMBYism binds communities together through a matrix of racist, ableist, classist and other logics of belonging/unbelonging that together work to resist integration, including "safety/danger, paternalism, change in the makeup of the neighbourhood, and fear of decreased property values, all couched around notions of hetero-normative racial ableism" (162). Responses not only involve defending the boundaries of a community but *in affect* creates these borders and helps explain how "the 'community' constructs itself as qualitatively different from so-called deviant elements, such as those formerly imprisoned or institutionalized, disabled, mad, queer, or substance users, even though such populations have always been part of every community, whether it is acknowledged or not" (174).

Kawash's (1998) seminal work shows how the "homeless body" as an event denaturalizes the duality of public/private space and renders visible how public and private spheres are constructed and maintained. Homelessness does this by creating disorder by using public spaces for activities officially relegated to the private realm of home. The constant work of maintaining public space for proper use, and not for private use (sleeping, living, bodily expulsions), invites the creation and maintenance of "disciplinary architecture" and regulations that blocks bodies from the illegitimate use of public space: which in turn reveals how within public space, there is a "symbolic and material distinctionbetween proprietary inhabitants and illegitimate usurpers: in this process, the body emerges as the stake and the site of the contest over public space" (Kawash 1998, 323). Our chapter explores how these conditions are manifesting in Windsor, Ontario, where revitalization is competing with a "crisis" of homelessness (Cross 2017; Viau 2017). We describe Windsor, then orient readers to our understanding of the relationship between violence, institutionalized spaces and care, the methodological approach we took, and then offer a close reading of publicly available textual productions in the form of newspaper articles. By exploring how stories are told about "the homeless body" in public discourse, we show how the logics and practices of institutionalization continue to govern unruly bodies in public space through carceral, spatial, and psy regulations.

THE PROBLEM OF WINDSOR'S DOWNTOWN CORE

Windsor is a city of 214,000 located in southwestern Ontario and sits on the traditional territory of the Three Fires Confederacy of First Nations, comprised of the Ojibwe, the Odawa, and the Potawatomi Peoples. A border city to Detroit with a long history of auto manufacturing, post-2008 global recession, the city is currently experiencing an economic recovery, real-estate boom, and population growth (Brownell 2015; Pearson 2017a) but is struggling to meet the needs of its precariously housed/homeless population. The city's long-term mayor cites high opioid and mental health issues as the cause of increased homelessness, not poverty and rapid gentrification, and thus places responsibility on provincial and federal mental health and drug strategies to increase investments (CBC News 2017). Much of the responsibility for meeting the needs of those experiencing poverty/homelessness falls to health and social service organizations that work within the downtown core. Notably, The Downtown Mission (the Mission), a non-profit charity, offers emergency shelter services and support to residents of Windsor's downtown core. Because several community health and social services are located adjacent to the shelter, there is considerable traffic of homeless people traversing and assembling within a few square blocks of the downtown core. This increased spatial concentration and heightened visibility of marginalized people in the city's core has produced public concern and action in local mainstream community and public discourse. For instance, the *Windsor Star* often publishes stories that frame The Mission as a contributing factor to public sleeping, drug use, intoxication, and safety issues in the city's core, which according to The Downtown Windsor Business Improvement Association is "not good for business. It's not good for tourism" (Cross 2017). This revitalization/backlash reflects a growing pattern in formerly industrial "rust belt" cities trying to reinvent themselves in the current era (Kapp and Armstrong 2012; Manning 2015; Neumann 2016; Pottie-Sherman 2017).

CONCEPTUALIZING VIOLENCE IN COMMUNITY CARE

Before we turn towards just how the homeless body is constructed as violent, we want to foreground how we understand the impact of systemic violence of those made marginal by it. Three interlocking structural approaches to violence thread through the lives of those most subject to institutional logics: epistemic violence, slow violence, and slow death. Epistemic violence conceptually emerged through postcolonial scholarship to describe the processes by which marginalized knowledges become subjugated, as do subjects that hold such ways of knowing (Spivak 1988, 281). Mad (Kilty and LeHalle 2019; Sheldon, Spector, and Birdsell 2019) decolonial (Mignolo 2011; Temper 2019) and transdisciplinary studies (Mills and Lefrançois 2018) show how epistemic violence works to normalize and justify both spectacular and routine slow violence. Slow violence "foregrounds practices of violence that are reproduced through a broad time frame within which marginalization, discrimination, and impoverishment are enacted through government policies, economic systems, and colonial exercises of power" (Van Veen, Teghtsoonian, and Morrow 2019, 64). These ways of thinking and doing result in the slow deaths of populations who are subject to long histories of environmental, spatial, racial, sexual, gendered, disabling, and debilitating violence. As a process, Berlant (2007, 754) posits that "*slow death* refers to the physical wearing out of a population and the deterioration of people in that population that is very nearly a defining condition of their experience and historical existence ... the phenomenon of mass physical attenuation under global/national regimes of capitalist structural subordination and governmentality" (Voronka 2019, 84). The everyday living of populations relegated to slow death are deemed crises when they pose problems to economic growth and profit or state management (e.g., disability-related state benefits). Yet the rhetoric of crisis obscures the enduring subordination of populations made abject, distorting "the duration and scale of the situation by calling a *crisis* that which is a fact of life and has been a defining fact of life for a given population that lives it as a fact in ordinary time" (Berlant 2007, 760). When the violence of slow death begins to pose problems to respectability, solutions to contain and cure slow death target individual bodies, re-entrenching disabling systems of violence. How do the lives of those made abject through epistemic violence, slow violence, and slow death play out in local communities post-institutionalization? Ben-Moshe's *Decarcerating Disability* (2020) includes an exploration of how neighbourhood responses to the spatial integration of disability and Other difference is resisted, and how this resistance is rationalized post-institutionalization.

This research is part of a wider study that explores the experiences of service users and community stakeholders in the downtown core. As part of this research, we conducted a discourse mapping of Windsor-based media outlets (*Windsor Star* and CBC Windsor) using search terms related to revitalization efforts and the crisis of homelessness in the downtown core (e.g., The Mission, homelessness, poverty, the downtown core, downtown business, etc.). This search was done between October 2018–March 2019, although we also included key sources that date outside of this period to provide wider context, key events, and updates. What follows is a theoretical engagement with a sub-sample of the media we located.

DANGER AND SAFETY IN THE DOWNTOWN CORE

In local media coverage of Windsor's downtown core, the problem of "danger" posed by the homeless body is mostly articulated by politicians, residents, and business owners, contributing to epistemic violence. Media stories that cover the downtown core characterize degenerate bodies and their associated behaviours as out of place and obstructing redevelopment efforts: crime, public sex, public urination, sex work, drug use, stray shopping carts, mental illness, and more are cited as plaguing the core, and are attributed to individual corporeal acts. The danger posed is reputational, economic, personal, and proprietary. Some coverage posits that the homeless body poses a danger to themselves and deserve better care than is available in the community. As we show, by detailing the problem of danger, calls to action working towards securing "safety" largely invoke institutional logics that bring surveillance, the carceral state, and psy interventions to bear on those who are deemed not to belong to "the community" of the core.

"CRAZY, SCARY DRUG GHETTO": CHARACTERIZING DANGER IN THE DOWNTOWN CORE

In metanarrative accrual, marginalized bodies become what is hindering capitalism rather than the debilitation that results from it. First, the "growing number of desperate mentally ill people, addicts and the homeless," are described as a "growingly brazen and desperate bunch of thieves hitting the neighbourhood" who break into cars and businesses to steal "GPS devices, cameras, musical instruments, luggage, even shoes" (Jarvis 2018b). Residents and business owners speak of being "confronted with persons using drugs, exposing themselves, setting up makeshift tents, loitering and lying unconscious in public areas, arguing and fighting with each other at all hours and exhibiting other negative behaviours" (Chen 2018b). The city's "offering incentives worth millions to lure investment downtown" is juxtaposed with a resident's concern that "When I go downtown, I don't feel comfortable" (Jarvis 2018c). This discomfort can be attributed to the "explosion of homelessness" in the downtown core, and that "people aren't going to move downtown if they view it as a crazy, scary drug ghetto" (Cross 2017). The crisis of homelessness is framed as a reputational issue requiring action because as "an area of Windsor that has been the focus of significant investment," the problem of homelessness is "causing concern for residents, business owners, and visitors" (Chen 2018a). Repeatedly, systemized violence and its consequences are understood and attributed to individual acts of public degeneracy, including a resident witnessing "men in her back alley shooting up girls, used needles, fights breaking out, and the area around the mission 'totally engulfed' with shopping carts" (Cross 2017). Or "people sleeping within the park and using the facilities around the church as injection sites, using the hose to take a shower, using the flowerbeds to go to the washroom (Wilhelm 2017). The danger posed by the homeless body impedes the pleasures of the rightful resident who "moved to downtown Windsor to enjoy a life that allows her to walk throughout the city and be close to coffee shops and restaurants ... [but] ... didn't expect she'd be kicking prostitutes off her street and strangers out of her backyard or dealing with squatters doing drugs in the burnt out abandoned building beside her home" (Ensing 2017). Not only women, but children's safety too is cited as in jeopardy: one resident noting that "when her great-granddaughter comes to visit the family doesn't feel it's safe to let her play alone outside because of strangers on the street and people passed out in alleys (Roberts 2018b). Discourses of who belongs in the neighbourhood, who is a stranger and who is not, and respectable normalcy imperilled by the homeless body proliferate in these stories.

At times measures to secure respectability are framed as being out of concern for the danger that the degenerate pose to themselves. In a highly circulated story, a local resident witnessed a man in crisis outside of a public school, and after calling emergency services, "took out his phone to record the scene of Facebook Live, to show the public what he says he sees on a regular basis in the community (Georgieva 2018). The good Samaritan argues that he live-streamed video of the man in clear distress without his consent on Facebook because "he has seen the core of Windsor and nothing being done" and that "I am worried about the person's dignity as much as the child" (Georgieva 2018). When politicians respond to these issues, they must balance the demands of constituents' personal and economic interests while simultaneously appearing compassionate, as a city counsellor does here: "it's really unacceptable that the people who live there and own businesses there are being negatively affected by this. But saying that, I don't want to come off sounding like we don't have empathy ... Mental illness and homelessness are huge problems in the city" (Chen 2018b).

Yet, many of the same stakeholders blamed the health and social service agencies tasked with responding to the needs of those in crisis. For instance, one story profiles a resident's complaints about what happens after the mission closes at night: "you see escalating drug use on the street, injecting in the neck. You see young women laying on the concrete in the alley being shot up. It starts with two people and turns into four, six, eight. It's a traumatic thing to watch your neighbourhood being invaded by people you don't know" (Battagello 2018b). As the same resident notes, "We just want the chaos disbanded. There is a responsibility of the mission – maybe start a program indoors and get them off the street" (Battagello 2018b). Similarly, a business owner argues "the municipality should become more involved and take immediate measures to change the situation: "Find a bigger place. Try to help them out. Not only feeding them, you have to help them with their drug addictions, their mental health issues" (Chen 2018b). In these narratives, The Mission becomes the reason why these "stranger dangers" are in the downtown core, and thus should be made responsible for managing, surveilling, disciplining, and confining this body that doesn't belong continually towards securing safety.

SECURING SAFETY: INSTITUTIONAL LOGICS IN PUBLIC SPACE

What does securing safety look like in these stories that narrate the downtown core? Calls for increased surveillance through spatial regulation and policing are common interventions and are easy to identify as expansions of carceral logics in community settings. But the most "compassionate" solution oft-recited to address issues of safety is increasing mental health and addictions interventions available to the homeless body, moving from criminalizing and towards pathologizing, and pathologizing is rarely read as violent. Concerned business owners, residents, and local government alike posit that safety will only be secured through the containment management and cure of mental illness and drug use. The desirable solution to safety concerns is ridding the individual of biological and behavioural degeneracy – only then will public and community culture be cured of the danger that lurks in bodies of difference.

Business owners and residents report calling the police "everyday" (Ensing 2017) or "six times a day" (Cross 2017). Local residents also report taking political action like filing a petition with city council to increase police presence in the community because "We can't live like this" (Roberts 2018a). Calling police isn't the solution to safety: people don't want to be put in the position where they feel like they have to call the police. What they want is the problem to be evicted from public space, which would secure safety for both us and them: "A whole neighbourhood should not have to be jeopardized in order to help these people" (Roberts 2018c).

Some responses are spatial: Initiatives like the Downtown Windsor Business Improvement Association spending $40,000 to install twenty-five stadium-type LED lights on buildings and storefronts in response to increased safety and vandalism issues skyrocketing in the city's core "due to those suffering from addictions" (Battagello 2018a). Other responses work to spatially limit where and how people can use public space, such as calls to implement limits of where panhandlers can operate – which is conceived as doing "nothing to hurt panhandlers while making people feel safer and welcome downtown" (Boscariol 2018). Some socio-legal responses involve criminalizing activities in select public space, including attempts to pass anti-panhandler by-laws in the downtown core (Pearson 2015). A clear example of how issues of systemic poverty get rerouted as deviance is demonstrated in the story "Many Windsor panhandlers aren't homeless, say police." Aligned with metanarratives that those debilitated by the slow violence of late capitalism are actually just "fakers," a superintendent at the Windsor police force puts forward the "issue" that panhandlers who are "perceived to be homeless are, in fact, not homeless – but suffering from mental health issues" (Chen 2018c). Another reflects that "Absolutely (it's a mental health problem). Who in their right mind would want to pretend that they're blind, sitting outdoors, begging for money?" (Chen 2018c). Here, "faking homelessness/blindness" is narrated as pathological, but not in ways meant to engender sympathy from the reader. This example of epistemic violence shows how behaviours are scripted as mental illness rather than interpreted otherwise: for instance, as tactical use of statuses that may help to frame the panhandler as part of the deserving poor.

Through a culmination of these narratives, the homeless body comes to be a result of drug use and madness, and their routine conflation. Almost everyone agrees, including the mission's executive director, who notes that there is "a perception the mission is part of the problem, but we want to be part of the solution. The problem is mental illness and drug addiction" (Battagello 2018b). How do you solve the problem of unbridled madness and/or drug use? Policing is repeatedly acknowledged as necessary but not enough, rather "Downtown needs more than extra police officers and citizen patrols," which leads to local government "proposing hiring seven more outreach workers to try to help the mentally ill, addicts and homeless on the streets" (Jarvis 2018c). And "We need to deal with why they're on the street and how to get them off the street," he said. "We need to attack the issue properly and not just throw them in jail" (Jarvis 2018a).

Drug use is discussed as endemic to the homeless body, and is used to explain why people are homeless. This ignores efforts by the Homeless Coalition of Windsor-Essex County who attempt to counter narratives that drug use causes homelessness (Vander Doelen 2018). There's no doubt that there is an opioid overdose crisis in Windsor, and that "The total rate of opioid users in Windsor and Essex County is 18.9 per cent higher than the provincial average" (Pearson 2017b). Of note is that 64.9 per cent of accidental opioid-related deaths in Windsor and Essex County occurred in private residence (not public space) (Windsor-Essex County Health Unit 2017). The introduction of a rapid access treatment model to address opioid and alcohol dependence by offering assessments and medical treatments and referrals to existing psychiatric and addictions services is framed as "getting at the root of the issue," but ignores the hour-long journey by foot from the core to the clinic and the requirements of biomedical increased surveillance (e.g., urine screening) (Maru 2019).

Perhaps unsurprisingly then, harm reduction services are rarely offered as a solution to the crisis of homelessness in the core. Despite being derided by health and policing experts from across the province, the Windsor Police Service refused to equip its officers with naloxone (a drug that can reverse opioid overdoses) until spring 2021 (Molnar 2018). Relatedly, the Windsor-Essex County Health Unit has yet to secure approval for a supervised injection site (SIS) and continues to hold broad consultations (the last in December of 2020) (Windsor-Essex County Health Unit 2019). An SIS would likely reduce the visibility of drug use and paraphernalia, and contain drug-using bodies which should appeal to residents, business, and political stakeholders. How then to explain the lack of momentum behind these initiatives? These decisions are framed in terms of the imagined needs of regular citizens and never as examples of extraordinary violence (i.e., police and public health letting citizens die preventable deaths). The lack of action is because drug users are positioned as the problem, not opioid-related deaths.

While treatment of mental health and addictions is heralded as the solution to the homeless body, those health and social service organizations already working in the downtown core to meet the needs of street-involved individuals have already and continuously been constructed as part of the problem. So what marks this incongruity between blaming existing community health and social service organizations for the problem, while simultaneously calling for more mental health and addictions services and supports? What does that look like in the public imaginary when the public calls for more mental health and addictions services, while simultaneously critiquing those supports in the community? Is it because these services are understood as existing outside of community?

It may very well be that when the public demands mental illness and drug treatment facilities they understand this to entail in-patient closed sites. It may be in-patient psychiatric treatment where drug compliance/enforcement is expected until the mentally ill can self-govern to a psy regimen. Or that drug treatment facilities are conceived as in-patient abstinence-based programs that physically contain users until they can re-enter society. Removal and containment of the homeless body rather than preserving life is the most common call, with the goal of getting the homeless body tapped back into in-patient closed psychiatric and addiction treatment programs that operate away from core communities. What is rarely covered or called for in these media accounts of homelessness in the downtown core is addressing access to affordable, subsidized, and supported housing. The homeless body are fathomed as not "housing-ready" because of mental illness/drug use, not as a result of systemic racial-ableist economic violence and their endurance of it. “Help” that is already embedded in community settings endangers the community. But the “help” that is called for and yet to come is imagined as something other than what exists in communities and left untroubled. That closed care is unproblematized contributes to epistemic violence as it erases not only the collective knowledges of critical approaches to mental health, but also the lived experience of those in distress. These interventions are constructed as safe at a time when even longstanding bastions like the American Psychological Association recognizes their implications in systemic violence (2021). At the same time, resistance to basic harm reduction approaches to mental health and drug use is detailed in these same stories.

CONCLUSION

This chapter has shown how media discourses of Windsor’s downtown core draw on and draw out the logics of institutional violence to solve the problem of “danger” in community settings. Once danger is established, safety is offered in ways that recall not only institutional logics of but also institutional practices of carceral governance through discipline, surveillance, spatial regulation, segregation, policing, and the psy disciplines. Media descriptions of the crisis of homelessness in the downtown core contributed to institutional logics of violence which risk re/entrenching responses to systemic violence through increased surveillance, policing, and psy solutions. This shows how the logics of institutionalization persist, and in this case how they target the homeless body of those living in the downtown core towards violent state-sanctioned logics of management containment and cure. Media representations of the degenerate body (be they described as homeless, vagrants, deviant, criminal, addicted, mentally ill, or more) are often criticizing for their negative portrayals, but this isn’t about countering with more positive representations that humanize this body through resilience, recovery, and redemption narratives. We found both positive and negative representations focus on redeeming the individual through self-governance management and cure – and in doing so re-entrench and proliferate the logics and practices of incarceration, institutionalization, and psy powers. As McWade (2019) notes, “the distinction between positive and negative representations or beliefs about madness is problematic because it obscures the ways in which both can secure or reflect psy-discourse and power” (153).

In this way, these stories end up leading us towards solutions that position the problem of marginalization as solved through curing difference, and draw on psy powers surveillance and enforcement to do so, with the goal of containment and ensuring "the community" do not have to bear witness.

REFERENCES

Ahmed, Sara. 2004. "Affective Economies." *Social Text* 22, no. 2: 117–39.

American Psychological Association. 2021. "APA's Apology to Black, Indigenous and People of Color for Its Support of Structural Racism in Psychiatry." 18 January 2021. https://www.psychiatry.org/newsroom/apa-apology-for-its-support-of-structural-racism-in-psychiatry.

Battagello, Dave. 2018a. "Downtown BIA Moves to Install More Alley Lights." *Windsor Star*, 4 October 2018. https://windsorstar.com/news/local-news/downtown-bia-moves-to-install-alley-lights.

– 2018b. "Residents Urge Mission to Take Steps to Curb Night-Time Loitering." *Windsor Star*, 25 July 2018. https://windsorstar.com/news/local-news/residents-urge-mission-to-take-steps-to-curb-night-time-loitering.

Ben-Moshe, Liat. 2020. *Decarcerating Disability: Deinstitutionalization and Prison Abolition*. Minneapolis: University of Minnesota Press.

Berlant, Lauren. 2007. "Slow Death (Sovereignty, Obesity, Lateral Agency)." *Critical Inquiry* 33, no. 4: 754–80. https://doi.org/10.1086/521568.

Boscariol, Mark. 2018. "Educate Public about Panhandling and Protect Local Businesses." *Windsor Star*, 1 October 2018. https://windsorstar.com/news/local-news/educate-public-about-panhandling-and-protect-local-businesses.

Brownell, Claire. 2015. "Sneer All You Want, Vancouver and Toronto: Windsor, Ontario's Recession Ravaged Rust-Belt City Is Turning into the Country's Hottest Real Estate Play." *Financial Post*, 31 July 2015. https://financialpost.com/personal-finance/mortgages-real-estate/sneer-all-you-want-vancouver-and-toronto-windsor-ontarios-recession-ravaged-rust-belt-city-is-turning-into-the-countrys-hottest-real-estate-play.

Burch, Susan. 2014. "'Dislocated Histories': The Canton Asylum for Insane Indians." *Women, Gender, and Families of Color* 2, no. 2: 141–62.

CBC News. 2017. "Windsor-Essex in Crisis with 24 Opioid-Related Deaths in 2015, Says Health Unit," 2 March 2017. https://www.cbc.ca/news/canada/windsor/opioid-windsor-essex-1.4007016.

Chen, Dalson. 2018a. "Councillor's Call for 'No Panhandling' Zones Worries Homeless Coalition." *Windsor Star*, 8 April 2018. https://windsorstar.com/news/local-news/dilkens-calls-for-solution-to-panhandler-problem.

– 2018b. "Death Investigated in Windsor Neighbourhood with Homeless Problem." *Windsor Star*, 25 August 2018. https://windsorstar.com/news/local-news/death-investigated-in-windsor-neighbourhood-with-homeless-problem.

– 2018c. "Many Windsor Panhandlers Aren't Homeless, Say Police." *Windsor Star*, 3 November 2018. https://windsorstar.com/news/local-news/many-windsor-panhandlers-arent-homeless-say-police.

Coleman, Daniel. 2006. *White Civility: The Literary Project of English Canada*. Toronto: University of Toronto Press.

Cross, Brian. 2017. "Homeless Epidemic in the Downtown Is Taxing Residents and Service Groups." *Windsor Star*, 13 October 2017. https://windsorstar.com/news/local-news/homeless-epidemic-in-the-downtown-is-taxing-residents-and-service-groups.

Dej, Erin. 2020. *A Complex Exile: Homelessness and Social Exclusion in Canada*. Vancouver: UBC Press.

Dyck, Erika, and Alex Deighton. 2017. *Managing Madness: Weyburn Mental Hospital and the Transformation of Psychiatric Care in Canada*. Winnipeg: University of Manitoba Press.

Ensing, Chris. 2017. "A Hard Place: Living beside an Alley and an Abandoned Building in Downtown Windsor." CBC News, 12 October 2017. https://www.cbc.ca/news/canada/windsor/a-hard-place-living-beside-an-alley-and-an-abandoned-building-in-downtown-windsor-1.4350335.

Fellows, Mary Louise, and Sherene Razack. 1998. "The Race to Innocence: Confronting Hierarchical Relations among Women." *Journal of Gender, Race and Justice* 1: 335.

Florida, Richard. 2017a. *Canada's New Urban Crisis*. Toronto: Martin Prosperity Institute. https://www.deslibris.ca/ID/10098355.

– 2017b. *The New Urban Crisis: How Our Cities Are Increasing Inequality, Deepening Segregation, and Failing the Middle Class – and What We Can Do about It*. New York: Basic Books.

Gaetz, Stephen, Erin Dej, Tim Richter, and Melanie Redman. 2016. *The State of Homelessness in Canada 2016*. Toronto: Canadian Observatory on Homelessness. https://www.deslibris.ca/ID/10065873.

Georgieva, Katerina. 2018. "He Was in Distress: Video Has Windsor Man Asking for Help for the City's Most Vulnerable." CBC News, 29 October 2018. https://www.cbc.ca/news/canada/windsor/video-vulnerable-people-windsor-1.4853296.

Jarvis, Anne. 2018a. "Downtown Bar Owners Fight Unchecked Crime with Late-Night Patrols." *Windsor Star*, 21 October 2018. https://windsorstar.com/news/local-news/jarvis-downtown-bar-owners-patrolling-streets-to-combat-unchecked-crime.

– 2018b. "Jarvis: Downtown Bar Owners Patrolling Streets to Combat 'Unchecked' Crime." *Windsor Star*, 5 September 2018. https://windsorstar.com/news/local-news/jarvis-downtown-bar-owners-patrolling-streets-to-combat-unchecked-crime.

– 2018c. "Jarvis: The Issue the Candidates Aren't Talking About." *Windsor Star*, 11 September 2018. https://windsorstar.com/news/local-news/jarvis-the-issue-the-candidates-arent-talking-about.

Kapp, Paul Hardin, and Paul J. Armstrong, eds. 2012. *SynergiCity: Reinventing the Postindustrial City*. Urbana: University of Illinois Press.

Karschay, Stephan. 2015. *Degeneration, Normativity and the Gothic at the Fin de Siècle*. New York: Palgrave Macmillan. http://site.ebrary.com/id/11032281.

Kawash, S. 1998. "The Homeless Body." *Public Culture* 10, no. 2: 319–39. https://doi.org/10.1215/08992363-10-2-319.

Kilty, Jennifer M, and Sandra LeHalle. 2019. "Mad, Bad, and Stuck in the Hole: Carceral Segregation as Slow Violence." In *Madness, Violence and Power: A Critical Collection*, edited by Andrea Daley, Lucy Costa, and Peter Beresford, 310–29. Toronto: University of Toronto Press.

Malacrida, Claudia. 2015. *A Special Hell: Institutional Life in Alberta's Eugenic Years*. Toronto: University of Toronto Press.

Manning, Patrick. 2015. "Archiving the Rust Belt: Investigating Rust Belt Narratives of American Exceptionalism through Buffalo's Downtown Department Store." *Canadian Review of American Studies* 45, no. 3: 300–22. https://doi.org/10.3138/cras.2015.s09.

Maru, Sanjay. 2019. "Rapid Access' Treatment Model for Addiction Comes to Windsor." CBC News, 14 January 2019. https://www.cbc.ca/news/canada/windsor/radid-access-treatment-coming-to-windsor-1.4975089.

McWade, Brigit. 2019. "Madness, Violence and Media." In *Madness, Violence, and Power: A Critical Collection*, edited by Andrea Daley, Lucy Costa, and Peter Beresford, 150–64. Toronto: University of Toronto Press.

Mignolo, Walter D. 2011. *The Darker Side of Western Modernity: Global Futures, Decolonial Options*. Durham: Duke University Press. https://doi.org/10.1215/9780822394501.

Mills, China, and Brenda A. Lefrançois. 2018. "Child as Metaphor: Colonialism, Psy-Governance, and Epistemicide." *World Futures* 74, nos 7–8: 503–24. https://doi.org/10.1080/02604027.2018.1485438.

Molnar, Dale. 2018. "Windsor Police Only Service in Ontario Not Carrying Naloxone, Says MPP." CBC News, 16 November 2018. https://www.cbc.ca/news/canada/windsor/mpp-windsor-no-naloxone-1.4909541.

Neumann, Tracy. 2016. *Remaking the Rust Belt: The Postindustrial Transformation of North America*. Philadelphia: University of Pennsylvania Press. https://doi.org/10.9783/9780812292893.

Pearson, Craig. 2015. "Banning Panhandlers Likely Unconstitutional City Report." *Windsor Star*, 6 January 2015. https://windsorstar.com/news/banning-panhandlers-likely-unconstitutional-city-report.

– 2017a. "'Crazy' Windsor Real Estate Market Hottest in Decades." *Windsor Star*, 6 April 2017. https://windsorstar.com/news/local-news/crazy-windsor-real-estate-market-hottest-in-decades.

– 2017b. "Windsor-Essex Task Force Releases Proposed Opioid Strategy." *Windsor Star*, 11 October 2017. https://windsorstar.com/news/local-news/live-windsor-essex-task-force-releases-opioid-strategy.

Pick, Daniel. 1989. *Faces of Degeneration: A European Disorder, c. 1848 – c. 1918*. Cambridge: Cambridge University Press.

Pottie-Sherman, Yolande. 2017. "Austerity Urbanism and the Promise of Immigrant- and Refugee-Centered Urban Revitalization in the US Rust Belt." *Urban Geography* 39, no. 3: 438–57. https://doi.org/10.1080/02723638.2017.1342398.

Reaume, Geoffrey. 1997. "Accounts of Abuse of Patients at the Toronto Hospital for the Insane, 1883–1937." *Canadian Bulletin of Medical History* 14, no. 1: 65–106. https://doi.org/10.3138/cbmh.14.1.65.

Roberts, Meg. 2018a. "Backyard Vagrant Sparks Jackson Park Neighbourhood Petition to City Council." CBC News, 6 July 2018. https://www.cbc.ca/news/canada/windsor/jackson-park-neighbourhood-petition-homelessness-1.4735834.

– 2018b. "Downtown Mission's Move to Library Building Could Spark 'Renaissance' on Victoria Ave." CBC News, 6 March 2018. https://www.cbc.ca/news/canada/windsor/downtown-mission-windsor-library-ouellette-victoria-1.4564861.

– 2018c. "Neighbours Outraged after Woman Offers Backyard to Homeless Following Incident at Street Help." CBC News,

19 August 2018. https://www.cbc.ca/news/canada/windsor/backyard-homeless-neighbours-outraged-1.4791233.

Rossiter, Kate, and Jen Rinaldi. 2019. *Institutional Violence and Disability: Punishing Conditions*. Routledge Advances in Disability Studies. London: Routledge.

Sheldon, Tess C., Karen R. Spector, and Mary Birdsell. 2019. "Uncovering Law's Multiple Violences at the Inquest into the Death of Ashley Simpson." In *Madness, Violence and Power: A Critical Collection*, edited by Andrea Daley, Lucy Costa, and Peter Beresford, 196–220. Toronto: University of Toronto Press.

Spivak, Gayatri Chakravorty. 1988. "Can the Subaltern Speak?" In *Marxism and the Interpretation of Culture*, edited by Cary Nelson and Lawrence Grossberg, 271–313. London: Macmillan.

Temper, Leah. 2019. "Blocking Pipelines, Unsettling Environmental Justice: From Rights of Nature to Responsibility to Territory." *International Journal of Justice and Sustainability* 24, no. 2: 94–112. https://doi.org/10.1080/13549839.2018.1536698.

Tsai, Jack, and Michal Wilson. 2020. "COVID-19: A Potential Public Health Problem for Homeless Populations." *Lancet Public Health* 5, no. 4: 186–87. https://doi.org/10.1016/S2468-2667(20)30053-0.

Van Veen, Christopher, Katherine Teghtsoonian, and Marina Morrow. 2019. "Enacting Violence and Care: Neo-Liberalism, Knowledge Claims, and Resistance." In *Madness, Violence and Power: A Critical Collection*, edited by Andrea Daley, Lucy Costa, and Peter Beresford, 63–79. Toronto: University of Toronto Press.

Vander Doelen, Chris. 2018. "Vander Doelen: Don't Encourage Street Pests." *Windsor Star*, 4 October 2018. https://windsorstar.com/uncategorized/dont-encourage-street-pests.

Viau, Jason. 2017. "Windsor's Homeless Population Reaches 'Crisis' Levels, Says Aid Agency." CBC News, 18 September 2017. https://www.cbc.ca/news/canada/windsor/windsor-s-homeless-population-reaches-crisis-levels-says-aid-agency-1.4295720.

Voronka, Jijian. 2019. "Slow Death through Evidence Based Research." In *Madness, Violence and Power: A Critical Collection*, edited by Andrea Daley, Lucy Costa, and Peter Beresford, 80–96. Toronto: University of Toronto Press.

Wang, Linwei, Dimitra Panagiotoglou, Jeong Eun Min, Kora DeBeck, M.J. Milloy, Thomas Kerr, Kanna Hayashi, and Bohdan Nosyk. 2016. "Inability to Access Health and Social Services Associated with Mental Health among People Who Inject Drugs in a Canadian Setting."

Drug and Alcohol Dependence 168 (November): 22–9. https://doi.org/10.1016/j.drugalcdep.2016.08.631.

Wilhelm, Trevor. 2017. "Residents Gather to Discuss Drugs and Crime Plaguing Downtown." *Windsor Star*, 11 July 2017. https://windsorstar.com/news/local-news/residents-gather-to-discuss-drugs-and-crime-plaguing-downtown.

Willse, Craig. 2010. *Surplus Life: The Neoliberal Making and Managing of Housing Insecurity*. City University of New York.

– 2015. *The Value of Homelessness: Managing Surplus Life in the United States*. Minneapolis: University of Minnesota Press.

Windsor-Essex County Health Unit. 2017. "Opioid Misuse in Windsor and Essex County Report." https://www.wechu.org/about-us/reports-and-statistics/opioid-misuse-windsor-essex-county.

– 2019. "Supervised Injection Services Community Consultations Report." https://www.wechu.org/reports/supervised-injection-services-community-consultations-report.

Yellow Bird, Pemina. n.d. "Wild Indians: Native Perspectives on the Hiawatha Asylum for Insane Indians." https://power2u.org/wild-indians-native-perspectives-on-the-hiawatha-asylum-for-insane-indians-by-pemima-yellow-bird.

SECTION THREE

Care Qua Violence

9

Gendered and Disability Violence, Uninterrupted

Law's Formulation of and Complicity in Violence against Women Labelled with Intellectual Disability in Community-Based Institutional Settings

TESS SHELDON

This chapter explores the legal representation of, treatment of, and challenges to gendered and disability violence against women labelled with intellectual disabilities who reside in group homes. It does so by locating the site of that violence, its mechanisms, and institutional logics. This chapter has three aims. First, it offers contemporary examples of gendered disability violence: (i) failure to respond to sexual violence, (ii) menstrual management/suppression, (iii) inaccessibility and unavailability of relationship and parenting supports. Next, this chapter considers opportunities for legal redress to gendered and disability violence in group homes. Finally, the chapter closes with a call to define group homes as modern-day "institutions" that enact – and are – gendered disability violence.

Approaches to understanding institutional violence have often lacked a more nuanced understanding of the gendered dynamics of this violence. Disability is largely excluded from conversations about gender-based violence, sexual autonomy, and reproductive justice (Flores 2018; Neal 2018; Strike 2018). However, disabled women are more likely to be survivors of violence than people without disabilities (DAWN 2020). Persons labelled with intellectual disabilities are sexually assaulted seven times more often than people without disabilities (NPR 2018). These statistics are undoubtedly low, since persons with disabilities face barriers to reporting abusive experiences, when ableist stereotypes undercut assessments of their credibility. For many institutionalized women labelled with intellectual disabilities, violence is "part of everyday life" (Malacrida 2015; Spagnoulo and Boulanger 2018, 79).

Women labelled with intellectual disabilities are vulnerable to violence because of where they live. After the closure of the large institutions that warehoused people with disabilities, community-based services continue to be underfunded and over-subscribed (Jacobs 2021, para. 2.23). People labelled with intellectual disabilities continue to face barriers to accessing community-based services (Spagnuolo 2016). Community placements remain unsafe (Community Living Ontario 2013) without adequate oversight and resemble "present-day versions of the moribund institutions from a century ago" (Linton 2020). The violent residue of those large institutions remains.

Group homes are an ideal crucible to explore the meaning and persistence of institutional violence. A group home is defined by the *Services and Supports to Promote the Social Inclusion of Persons with Developmental Disabilities Act*, 2008, as "a staff-supported residence operated by a service agency, in which three or more persons with developmental disabilities reside and receive services and supports from the agency." Group homes are one of the only forms of supported accommodation available. Domiciliary hostels (also known as Housing with Supports) are private residences for adults, including with disabilities, who require support to live independently. Ontario's Host Family Program places residents in private family homes.

The Joint Task Force on Deinstitutionalization defines an "institution" as "any place in which people do not have, or are not allowed to exercise, control over their lives and their day-to-day decisions" (Institution Watch n.d.). Institutions are a "state of mind" (Links 1992), and "deinstitutionalization" requires more than a "change of address" (Bazelon Center 2009). An institution is not defined by its size (Institution Watch n.d.). Institutions will continue "as long as we live in an ableist society whose primary response to disability is confinement" (Linton 2020a). Group homes are "largely designed and managed by the same logic as total institutions" (Spangoulo and Boulanger 2018, 81).

Violence continues to be built into present-day institutions. Residents are at risk of physical, chemical, and environmental restraint, neglect, humiliation, and degradation. They are experienced as a "living hell" (ARCH 2008). Residents' privacy and movement may be restricted, and their healthcare needs may be neglected. Private, for-profit group homes are particularly dangerous (i.e., Berens and Callaghan 2006). Domiciliary hotels are not subject to licensing framework or inspection requirements (CBC News 2010; *Toronto Star* 2017). In 2017, a private member's bill proposed to license unregulated group homes, though it died on the order table (Jacobs 2021, para. 2.23). There are troubling reports about the safety and security of persons labelled with intellectual disabilities living with Host Families ("Verdict of the Coroner's Jury" 2015).

Jurisdictional confusion obscures and sustains violence in group homes. In Ontario, funding for disability support is split between ministries. Residential supports for adults labelled with intellectual disabilities are funded by the Ministry of Children, Community and Social Services. Residential supports are delivered by social service agencies. Municipalities regulate supportive housing facilities such as group homes through the application of zoning bylaws. Applications for residential supports are often duplicated, and administrative/reporting requirements are always cumbersome. Ontario's Develop mental Services Housing Task Force highlighted the "complexity of multi-ministerial services" and jurisdictional silos (Developmental Services Housing Task Force 2018). The Ontario Ombudsman called for increased partnership and inter-ministerial collaboration (Dubé 2016, 69).

I CONTEMPORARY EXAMPLES OF GENDERED VIOLENCE IN GROUP HOMES

Gendered disability violence is enabled by its geography. This paper offers three examples of gendered disability violence against women labelled with intellectual disabilities who reside in group homes: (i) failure to respond to sexual violence, (ii) menstrual management/suppression, (iii) the inaccessibility and unavailability of relationship and parenting supports. These examples should be unsurprising. They are historical, predictable, and deep-rooted. Reproductive violence was common in institutional settings. In *Buck v. Bell* (1927), the US Supreme Court upheld a Virginia law that authorized Carrie Buck's eugenic sterilization, a finding which has never been expressly overturned. In *Re: Eve* (1986), Eve's mother sought a declaration that Eve was incapable of understanding marriage, sexual relations, or caring for a child. The Eugenics Board of Alberta approved Leilani Muir's non-consensual sterilization in 1957 (*Muir v. Alberta* 1996).

The sterilization of Carrie, Eve, and Leilani was produced by their institutional placements. The superintendent of the Virginia State Colony for Epileptics and Feebleminded selected Carrie as the perfect subject for a test case about eugenic sterilization (Jones 2017). Eve lived at a boarding school, where she met someone whom she wanted to marry. The school identified the relationship and "talked to the male student and brought the matter to an end" (*Re: Eve*, para. 2; Savell 2004, 1125). The Provincial Training School for Mental Defectives was a "major centre" in Alberta where the Eugenics Board authorized about 25 per cent of sterilizations (Leung n.d.; Malacrida 2015, 4). The sterilization of these three women predicts the current landscape of violence in Ontario's mini institutions.

These institutions' "eugenic impulse" has manifested in different ways over time: forced sterilizations, restrictions on marriage, and then "discriminatory child welfare practices that presume unfitness" (Bagenstos 2020). Reproduction continues to be "weaponized to subjugate people with disabilities" (Powell 2022, 250; see also Gordon 2015). Violence against women labelled with intellectual disabilities is committed under the pretext of "care" though it is "intimately linked to attempts to contain and even eliminate people who are assumed to be economically unproductive" (Spagnoulo and Boulanger 2018, 76).

Accounts of "bad mothers" shock and spark moral panic. Bad mothers continue to be "scapegoated for social ills" (Darricades 2018, 38) and "are blamed for the marginal sociocultural context in which they are mothering" (Hughes-Miller et al. 2017; see also Seidel 2013). This is particularly true for disabled women, whose reproduction "has been a central aspect of disability oppression in America" (Bagenstos 2020, 285). Child policing authorities rely on stereotypes about disability when making decisions about the capacity to parent. Determinations about the capacity to parent are racialized. However, Black and Indigenous women have been excluded from "prevailing narratives around the fight for reproductive justice" (Baker 2020). The targeting of Indigenous women in eugenic sterilization programs is an ongoing colonial project. In Saskatchewan, a class action has been launched about the coerced sterilization of Indigenous women (Lady Science 2019; Zingel 2019).

Feminist theories have inadequately explained the experience of disability violence. Spaces and systems of violence specific to persons with disabilities have remained separate from the discussion of spaces and systems of institutional violence applicable to other equity-deserving groups, including people who identify as women who are survivors of sexual violence. Women with disabilities have been excluded from reproductive rights spaces, and their voices are often not part of strategies to challenge gendered violence (DAWN 2014). Approaches to understanding institutional violence have often lacked a more nuanced understanding of the gendered dynamics of this violence, "neglecting the intimate and reproductive lives of disabled people, and disabled women in particular" (Wiseman and Ferrie 2020, 319).

For women and girls with disabilities, the intersection between ableism and gender oppression has not been explicitly identified, examined, or addressed. The UN *Convention on the Rights of Persons with Disabilities* recognizes "the difficult conditions faced by persons with disabilities who are subject to multiple or aggravated forms of discrimination" and that "women and girls with disabilities are often at greater risk, both within and outside the home, of violence, injury or abuse, neglect or negligent treatment, maltreatment or exploitation" (United Nations General Assembly 2006, preamble). Article 6 recognizes that women and girls with disabilities are subject to multiple discrimination. Article 16 requires state parties to take "appropriate legislative, administrative, social, educational and other measures to protect persons with disabilities, both within and outside the home, from all forms of exploitation, violence and abuse, *including their gender-based aspects*" (emphasis added).

1 *Sexual Violence in Group Homes*

Women and girls with disabilities are at particular risk of gendered violence (Cotter 2018; DAWN 2014; Dhand 2021 at 127; NPR 2018). The most intense forms of violence are directed against women labelled with intellectual disabilities (Spagnuolo and Boulanger 2018; Spagnuolo and Earle 2017), particularly those who live in institutional settings since "sexual violence flourishes in an atmosphere of oppression" (Disability Rights Washington 2015). Disabled women are increasingly likely to be incarcerated where they are also at risk for being assaulted (DAWN 2020, 41, xl:1; Paynter, 2019). Women labelled with intellectual disabilities experience complex forms of violence (Carmody 1991; Curry et al., 2001; Martin 2006; NPR 2018), obscured by its geography.

These data do not reflect the actual prevalence of gendered disability violence since violence against women with intellectual disabilities is under-reported and under-prosecuted (Beaudry 2018; Casteel 2008). Survivors are more likely not to be believed (Benedet and Grant 2013; Davis 2011, 2). Stereotypes about women labelled with intellectual disabilities as suggestible, unreliable, or unable to answer complex questions impact the fairness of sexual assault proceedings (Benedet and Grant 2007, 2012; see also *R. v. DAI* 2012). In *R. v. Slatter*, the Supreme Court considered the heightened credibility requirement imposed upon complainants with intellectual disabilities and found that the "over-reliance on generalities can perpetuate harmful myths and stereotypes about individuals with disabilities" (*R. v. Slatter* 2020, para. 2; LEAF 2020). Barriers to the receipt of testimony from witnesses with disabilities also discourage reporting future offences (Benedet and Grant 2020).

Group home residents who report violence may fear being characterized as difficult, complainers, or troublemakers. Women who reside in group homes face heightened barriers to reporting violence, including interference with their access to communication devices. They may fear reprisals, including the withdrawal of support and services. Family members or support persons who report on their behalf may be trespassed from the group homes thereby leaving the resident further isolated and vulnerable to additional violence (Payne 2019).

Allegations of violence in group homes are investigated internally. Regulation 299/10 ("Quality Assurance Measures") to Ontario's *Services and Supports to Promote the Social Inclusion of Persons with Developmental Disabilities Act* requires all service agencies to have policies and procedures for preventing and reporting abuse ("Ontario Regulation 299/10" 2011, s. 8). Agencies remain responsible for rights enforcement (Quinlan and Smele 2017). While section 8.2 of the *Regulation* requires service agencies to provide mandatory training to persons with disabilities, service agencies are "in full control of the material they use to deliver the abuse education" and may not be "truly accessible to the persons who are to receive the education" (Letheren 2013, 29).

2 *Menstrual Management/Suppression*

Menstruation has become a "key site of violence" against women labelled with intellectual disabilities (Steele 2014, 469; Steele and Goldblatt 2020, 77). Menstruation is constructed as distressing or frightening, resulting from sexist fears of women's blood or menstruation itself. They are instead offered options to suppress or eliminate menstruation.

Health support strategies should be least restrictive and tailored to decision-making skills (Tracy et al. 2016). However, disabled women rarely receive reproductive health education that is accessible to them (Insogna 2015; Verlenden et al. 2019). Without accessible health education, their periods are managed by others and contraception be imposed even where there is no identified need to control menstruation, including for menopausal residents.

Oral contraception may be used in group homes to suppress menstruation and "could be replacing surgical interventions" (Wiseman and Ferrie 2020, 324). Depo-Provera is more often provided to women labelled with intellectual disabilities than women without disabilities, especially where there are questions about compliance with prescriptions (Verlenden et al. 2019) or concerns about menstrual hygiene (Shea 2007, 11; Dizon, Allen, and Ornstein 2005). These strategies have been used to manage menstruation but are also used as a "pretext for contraceptive sterilization" (WHO 2014, 12).

Women labelled with intellectual disabilities are more likely to undergo permanent methods of contraception (e.g., hysterectomies or endometrial ablation) than women without disabilities (Agaronnik 2020; Marquez-Gonzalez, Valdez-Martinez, and Bedolla 2018). Contemporary requests for involuntary sterilization, including Ashley Treatment,[1] are ostensibly made as a "protective mechanism." However, those requests have more to do with social factors, including group home staff shortages, caregiving burden, and lack of adequate and appropriate services to support parents with disabilities (Steele 2014).

These permanent methods continue to be a "standard procedure for many people with disabilities" in the US (Powell 2021, 11), Australia (Steele and Goldblatt 2020, 78), and the United Kingdom (Savel 2004). However, the Supreme Court of Canada set firm limits on the non-therapeutic sterilization of people determined to be incapable (*Re: Eve* 1986). The Canadian Medical Protective Association recommends that requests for non-therapeutic sterilization be refused since they expose physicians to professional liability (CMPA 2021). Nevertheless, the forced/coerced sterilization of persons with intellectual disabilities continues (Inclusion Canada 2019a). For example, People First of Canada and the Canadian Association of Community Living (2019) point to the castration of AR by his mother in 2002 and the chemical sterilization of women through forced use of Depo-Provera. Additionally, Shaw (2015) highlights the expansion of *Eve*'s therapeutic purpose test.

Disability advocates have long called for the prohibition of coerced sterilization (Inclusion Canada 2019a). Steele (2016) also calls for the explicit inclusion of court-authorized sterilization in all discussions about disability violence (1005). The sterilization of persons with disabilities without their consent constitutes a form of gendered violence (WHO 2014 at 5; CEDAW 2017). Article 23 of the CRPD requires state parties to "ensure that persons with disabilities, including children, retain their fertility on an equal basis with others" (see also General Comment 3, para. 44, in United Nations Committee on the Rights of Persons with Disabilities 2017).

Generally, mainstream period activism has excluded people with disabilities (*Crippled Scholar* 2016; Louise 2020). The "menstrual invisibility" of women with intellectual disabilities should be unsurprising (Wiseman and Ferrie 2020, 323). They have been and continue to be excluded from information about reproduction (Tilley et al. 2011) because of deeply held prejudices about disabled women's bodies and refusal to accept people with intellectual disabilities as parents or sexual citizens (Inclusion Canada 2019a).

3 Barriers to Relationships/Parenting Supports

Restrictive practices in relation to menstruation depend on persistent failures to recognize them as sexual citizens or potential parents (Sharp 2021). The choices of women labelled with intellectual disabilities are routinely constrained by barriers to reproductive health care, contraception, and information about sexuality. In particular, LGBTQQIP2SAA[2] disabled women are presumed incapable of comprehending information about sex or sexual orientation, as well as managing sexual relationships, or making decisions about family planning (Brady 2001). Without access to such information, disabled women are more likely to experience sexual assault, sexually transmitted infections, and unwanted pregnancy. Their sexual health is often overlooked (Dusome and Melrose 2015).

Institutional living means that women do not have opportunities to build relationships, meet people and learn about love and sex. Group home residents lack privacy and have fewer social networks (Gilmore and Malcome 2014; Martino et al. 2019). There is a general reluctance and discomfort among workers in settings like group homes to talk about sexuality (Hamilton 2009; Pebdani 2016). Residents may be "barred from sexual activity and isolated from those with whom they may have developed an intimate relationship" (Letheren 2013, 32).

Women with disabilities are not given the support needed, including socialization opportunities, to "enter into and maintain private intimate relationships" (Bernert 2011, 139; Kischkel 2019; Malik 2021; Smith 2019). Women labelled with intellectual disabilities do not receive sex education or are provided with education that focuses on avoiding pregnancy (Lunsky 2018). The failure to educate people with disabilities about their sexuality leaves them without the tools to make meaningful choices or to identify and report abusive relationships (Powel and Stein 2016; Servais 2006).

There are also troubling reports of students with disabilities who have been removed (or "excused") from sex education (CBC 2019; Henley 2017). Without access to accurate and age-appropriate information, they are placed at greater risk of sexually transmitted infections, unplanned pregnancy, and unable to report sexual assault. The removal of students from sexual education perpetuates rape culture. It can lead to violence, reflecting and reinforcing structural biases that isolate and infantilize persons with disabilities (Collie 2019).

Mothering is a long-standing site of social control, particularly for those labelled with intellectual disabilities who face barriers meeting racist, classist, and ableist norms of good mothering. Mothers with disabilities face increased scrutiny of their capacity to parent and disproportionate state interference in their families (DAWN 2013; WestCoast LEAF 2014) despite research demonstrating that disability is a poor predictor of parenting skills (Frederick 2014; Khan et al. 2021; Wilson et al. 2014;). In Ontario, one in twenty babies of women labelled with intellectual disabilities is directly discharged to child protective services after birth (Brown et al. 2018). Parents with intellectual disabilities are more likely than other parents to have their children removed and placed in care (Mayes and Llewellyn 2009; Llewellyn, McConnell and Ferronato 2003; McConnell, Llewellyn and Ferronato 2000; McConnell et al. 2011; McConnell et al. 2009).

Child policing authorities rely on stereotypes when making decisions about the capacity to parent, stereotypes that "emulat[e] those raised during the eugenics movement" (Powell 2021, 13; Booth, 1994; Mayes and Llewelyn 2009). Newgenics operates in "covert ways" and frustrates opportunities for sexual expression, reproduction, and parenting by erecting "systematic barriers to education, services, policy and supports for disabled people" (*Eugenics to Newgenics* 2018).

Mothers labelled with intellectual disabilities often have inadequate and inappropriate long-term parenting supports (Brown et al. 2019). There are few parental support programs for mothers labelled with intellectual disabilities, and those available are limited to large urban centres. Such mothers are more likely to live in poverty and have insufficient social support. They may also have had poor models of parenting and be trauma survivors. These systemic factors – rather than their disability – may impact their ability to cope with the demands of raising children (Khan et al. 2021; Wilson et al. 2014).

In particular, women who are group home residents face barriers to accessing parenting support. Upon the removal of a child who is determined to require protection, the court can order supervised access. Group home residents may face barriers to arranging supervised visits with their children in the group home – such homes may have restrictive rules about visitors or accessibility to private spaces. They may instead be required to arrange for visits to supervised access centres. There is a cost for this service, which may not be borne by the child welfare agency.

The CRPD requires more than "the prohibition of forced sterilizations" (Inclusion Canada and People First 2019). Rather than resorting to apprehension, Article 6 sets out that "women with disabilities have the right to found a family and be provided with appropriate assistance to raise their children" (United Nations Committee on the Rights of Persons with Disabilities 2017, General Comment 3). Articles 23(2) and 23(4) require States Parties to guarantee the provision of appropriate assistance to persons with disabilities in the performance of their child-rearing responsibilities. *Nova Scotia v.* CKZ (2016) considered the rights of parents with intellectual disabilities and the contested authority of the state to separate children from their families based on the parent's disability. The trial judge relied on the CRPD's requirement for the provision of "appropriate assistance to persons with disabilities in the performance of their child-rearing responsibilities" as it relates to and refines (rather than trumps) the best interests of the child standard. However, the Nova Scotia Court of Appeal overturned the trial judge's decision and determined that the children remained in need of protection.

II LAW'S ROLE TO REDRESS AND PREVENT GENDERED AND DISABILITY VIOLENCE

The law's attention to institutional violence has garnered recent attention in Canada, including the Truth and Reconciliation Commission, class actions about solitary confinement, a class action about the treatment of Crown Wards, and the National Inquiry into Missing and Murdered Indigenous Women and Girls. This section offers some examples of gender-based and disability violence prevention inspired by various sources including the West Coast LEAF Mothering project (WestCoast LEAF 2014), Australian Royal Commission into Violence, Abuse, Neglect and Exploitation of People with Disability (Royal Commission into Violence, Abuse, Neglect and Exploitation of People with Disability 2019) and the Joint Task Force on Deinstitutionalization (Institution Watch n.d.).

This section remains skeptical about the role of legal reform to challenging forms of gendered and disability violence. Law is indeed complicit and grounded in "therapeutic" violence against women (Steele 2020). Laws were a primary tool of eugenic ideology and practice (Dyck 2013). No single approach will define, resolve, and recompense the institutional violence experienced by women labelled with intellectual disabilities who reside in group homes. At the same time, this section recognizes the urgent need for action.

Any approach requires a fundamental shift to characterize persons with disabilities as "subjects of rights and rights-holders" (United Nations Committee on the Rights of Persons with Disabilities 2017, General Comment 5, para. 3). Individualized supports, like education, healthcare, and housing, must be considered a right instead of a form of medical, social, or charity care (ibid., para. 28). These supports are typically under-funded. However, persons with disabilities are guaranteed – by law – the tools needed to be free from sexual violence, form meaningful relationships, flourish as parents, and make meaningful decisions about their sexuality. As such, accessible parenting programs is a right, not a benefit.

Typically, rights language has been marshalled to support "negative rights" claims, that is, the right to non-interference from the state. However, for persons with disabilities, the right to equality requires action (i.e., positive rights) by the state rather than being left alone. The explicit recognition of a "positive right" to non-coercive disability supports aligns with substantive conceptions of disability justice

(ARCH 2021). The failure to deliver such upstream resources will lead to the application of more coercive state interference. For example, a "positive right" to accessible, appropriate, and effective parenting supports protects against the removal of children from the care of mothers with disabilities (Michielsen and Brockschmidt 2021; Surrey Place n.d.).

Human rights legislation may protect those parenting programs in the same way they have protected mother-child programs in correctional settings. In *Inglis v. British Columbia* (2013), the BC Supreme Court considered the constitutionality of the closure of a mother-child program. The applicants argued that a mother's status as a prisoner should not deprive her (or her baby) of the significant benefits of the newborn period. The BC Supreme Court required reinstatement of the program (West Coast LEAF 2013).

Accountability requires data. There is, however, a persistent paucity of research about disability violence (DAWN 2014; Invisible Institutions 2021; Linton 2021c). Such data are ignored in official statistics about "general populations" (Brown 2004, 46). Remarkably little is known about violence in institutional settings because it occurs out of the public eye. Reporting requirements remain unclear, and there are no financial (and other) penalties for service providers who fail to report violence. Legislative frameworks do not provide for independent review or monitoring (Joffe 2010, 118). The *Social Inclusion Act* does not address how to make a complaint about service received (Jacobs 2021, para. 2.19; McCauley and Matheson 2016, 6). This data deficit is compounded for persons living in "collective dwellings," including group homes (Data Libre 2021).

Human rights principles support the mandatory collection of disability data (OHRC 2013). Disabled Persons Organizations could be supported by legal requirements to create an inventory of reports about the prevalence and quality of violence (see LCC 2000 as an example). Indeed, community living organizations have "developed significant research mandates on issues affecting the disability community" (Jacobs 2021, 2.7). Data, however, can result in harming the very people and populations it claims to help, including surveilling persons with disabilities. When carefully mobilized, data can be used to support test case litigation and expose institutions that systemically cause harm.

Legal strategies that rely on criminal law powers are ill-suited for "shedding light on the systemic problems that may have allowed the abuse to occur in the first place" (LCC 2000, 4). They are intended to identify the liability of individual perpetrators. The criminal system has failed to support survivors labelled with intellectual disabilities to disclose and report sexual violence since the criminal law system is "not designed to help victims" (Bakhtiary 2019). Perpetrators are seldom held accountable, and women labelled with intellectual disabilities rarely obtain any form of redress (Steele 2020a). This section does not propose legal strategies to extend domestic violence services to group home residents by reconceptualizing the violence perpetrated in these living arrangements as "domestic" or "family" violence (Didi, Dowse, and Frohmader 2015, 10).

Most provinces and territories have some compensation/financial assistance programs for survivors of violence. However, the Alberta Victims of Crime Assistance Program was recently terminated, and the dissolution of Ontario's Criminal Injuries Compensation Board (CICB) was announced in 2019 (CBC 2019). Until its cancellation, the CICB accepted applications from victims of violent crime and made decisions about financial compensation for their injuries, including pain and suffering, loss of income, funeral expenses, and ongoing counselling costs (Cross 2019). An applicant was not required to report the crime. Since its cancellation, the CICB has been replaced by the Victim Quick Response Program (VQRP+). Financial assistance appears sparse "especially for survivors of adult sexual assault" (Cross 2019), and there is a cap on short-term counselling (Bakhtiary 2019). Most troublingly, applicants to VQRP+ are required to file a police report. As a result, women, especially those labelled with intellectual disabilities, are less likely to apply to the VQRP+.

On their own, criminal injury compensation schemes are limited and must be considered in combination with other forms of redress (LCC 2000, 6). Despite the CICB's limitations, immediate monetary compensation assists survivors of gendered and disability violence in practical ways. The reinstatement of the CICB should be accompanied by key reforms, including alternative routes for compensation that do not rely on individuals commencing their litigation.

III GROUP HOMES ARE *PER SE* VIOLENCE

Gendered disability violence is enabled by its geography. The lack of adequate and accessible housing in the community creates further isolation. Persons labelled with intellectual disabilities are regularly denied choice and control over where they reside. There is a dire lack of alternative accommodation options (Bach 2012; Spagnuolo and Earle

2017) as wait times for supports and services promised are extraordinary (Provincial Network on Developmental Services 2016). Accessible housing is "critical to enable people to move from institutions into the community" (Bazelon 2013, 8). It is a "necessary condition" for personal development and well-being (Bach 2012, para. 47) including challenging violence against women labelled with intellectual disabilities. Genuine and small-scale community alternatives assure a maximum level of self-determination and interdependence.

Housing is a fundamental and universal human right (CRPD at art. 19; ICCPR at art. 12; ICESCR at art. 11e; CEDAW at art. 15(4); OHRC 2011). Persons with disabilities have a right to live independently in their self-chosen communities in the least restrictive environment that meets their needs (United Nations Committee on the Rights of Persons with Disabilities 2017, General Comment 5). Article 19 states that people with disabilities must "have the opportunity to choose their place of residence and where and with whom they live on an equal basis with others and are not obliged to live in a particular living arrangement." General Comment 5 stresses independent living as an "essential part of an individual's autonomy and freedom." They have a right to organize their daily activities with assistance at the time they see fit (Jacobs 2021, para. 2.4).

Nevertheless, Canadian courts have repeatedly refused to recognize housing as a human right thereby making the right to community living has been a "hard-fought battle" (Jacobs 2021, para. 2.8). Vagrancy laws "prohibit people from performing basic life functions outdoors – creating an impossible situation for those who are unhoused" (Kanji and Withers 2021), including people with disabilities. A class action about the "serious operational flaws in the delivery of essential services and supports to eligible adults with developmental disabilities" is currently proceeding through Ontario courts (*Leroux v. Ontario* 2021, para. 2). In *Tanudjaja v. Canad*a (2014), Ontario's Court of Appeal refused to recognize a constitutionally protected right to housing.

Remarkably, the Nova Scotia Court of Appeal recently recognized systemic barriers to community inclusion for persons with disabilities (*Disability Rights Coalition v. Nova Scotia* 2021). The appellants relied on Article 19 of the CRPD to allege that the current patchwork of options for community living was based primarily on the needs of institutions, not individuals. The Court of Appeal found that these failures amounted to systemic discrimination.

Canada's CPRD obligations should be "incorporated as an indivisible dimension of a rights-based approach to housing in Canada" (Inclusion Canada 2018). Comprehensive housing strategies by both the federal and provincial governments must include the availability of individualized living arrangements that respond to individual needs and with "real choices about where they live, who they live with, and how they live their lives" (People First Canada and CACL 2010; Respecting Rights 2021). Inclusion Canada has proposed requirements that limit federal spending to housing options that meet principles of community living and inclusion (2019b). They have also proposed the prohibition of residential admissions to institutional facilities of all types.

Violence is inherent in the new and old forms of institutionalization, bred by oppressive conditions, including low levels of personal choice. In particular, vulnerability to violence increases dramatically where residents "do not have control over where and how they will live, and where they are socially isolated" (Bach 2012, para. 50). In segregated environments, residents are separated from their support systems, with limited access to the outside. They are located on the "geographical and socio-political periphery" (Rossiter and Rinaldi 2020, 74–5; Dream Team n.d.; Homecoming Community Choice Coalition n.d.). Indeed, any kind of "enforced cohabitation" is an outdated model of custodial care that separates residents from the outside and represents the failure of the community living movement.

These concerns about group homes arise regardless of their size. Even small group homes may "needlessly segregate their residents from the larger community" (Bazelon 2013; National Council on Disability 2012). Even individual homes cannot be called "independent living arrangements if they have other defining elements of institutions or institutionalization" (General Comment 5 2017, para. 16). Smaller environments are not necessarily better than large institutions "if overall control remains with supervisors" (Report of the Office of the United Nations High Commissioner for Human Rights 2014). Even if living arrangements seem more "home-like," the risk is substituting isolation "outside the community for isolation within the community" (People First of Canada and CACL 2019).

Group homes employ a casual and unregulated workforce with high turnover rates and burnout (Soucie-Vukmanich 2021). According to Spivakovsky (2017), staff in group homes "have come to use the logics and mechanisms of workplace health and safety rights to manage the risks" and that the "right to refuse unsafe work [has] become the everyday local policing tools provided to workers' (377). Improved job security and wages will improve the well-being of group home residents. Staff will have the opportunity to establish relationships, build rapport with residents, observe behaviour, and understand their needs and preferences.

New and old forms of institutionalization constitute violence, not only because violence occurs within their four walls. They are inherently violent in form. Group homes operate as alternative sites of detention and "targeted site of confinement" (Spivakovsky 2017, 367). Restrictive practices in group homes constitute a form of "lawful" violence analogous to imprisonment. Violence is built into the way things are done and maintained by a culture of non-reporting. Group homes are an extension (or acknowledgement) of the institutional order (Rossiter and Rinaldi 2020, 92). The violence of group homes is maintained through "reforms" that are – on its face – intended to make them more "therapeutic."

The modern-day institution enacts, is responsible for, and is, per se, violence. Residents are contained, where they are subject to multiple layers of control. Women are maintained in "subordinate positions, including physical or ideological, with regard to other people within her family, household or community" (General Comment 3 2016, para. 26). Their subordination is a result of its location.

CONCLUSION: THE LONG SHADOW OF GENDERED DISABILITY VIOLENCE

This chapter explored the endurance and evolution of institutional violence against women labelled with intellectual disabilities who reside in group homes. It did so by locating the site of that violence, its mechanisms, and institutional logics. Gendered and disability violence is often mischaracterized as an isolated tragedy resulting from individual fragility/dependence or as beneficial treatment/discipline. Such an individual focus obscures the structural conditions that are built to exclude (Withers 2021). Spagnuolo and Boulanger (2018, 78) stress the value of situating it within the "pervasive and corrosive" context of structural violence.

Individualized approaches also distort violence as care. "Care" is used as a pretext for institutional control, and the institution masquerades as a provider of care. Violent expressions of care (visitor restrictions to interfere with relationships, menstrual management) are justified for residents' own good. Group home residents are subjected to force "under the guise of "therapeutic treatment" (Australia 2015, xxvi). Legal or "good violence" is removed from mainstream feminist scrutiny (Steele 2014).

Part I reviewed the breadth and complexity of violence experienced by women labelled with intellectual disabilities who reside in group homes. The law has not responded to gendered disability violence (Steele and Dowse 2016, 188; Series 2015). This is not a failure since the law was not designed to protect women with disabilities. These institutional forms of violence are, in some cases, permitted and produced by law (Steele 2020). Despite law's complicity, gendered disability violence must be urgently redressed. Part II was premised on the recognition that restrictive practices must be eliminated rather than reduced by piecemeal reform. Confronting this persistent violence requires "us to radically transform our laws and policies" (Powell 2021, 28). Advocacy towards greater inclusion in these carceral spaces – including group homes – detracts from ultimate abolition goals.

The persistent subordination of women labelled with intellectual disabilities requires cross-movement solidarity. The increased recognition of sexual violence against women has remained separate from a discussion of spaces and systems of sexual violence against women and girls with disabilities. Query, for example, how the #MeToo movement would have taken up Carrie's, Leilani's, and Eve's claims. First-wave feminists in Canada supported the eugenic sterilization of persons with disabilities (de la Cour 2017). Instead, connections between reproductive and disability justice movements acknowledge that the violence faced by women with disabilities is complex and overlapping and that "reproductive justice is disability justice" (Sins Invalid 2019).

That coordinated movement must be accountable to survivors in a way that confronts anti-Blackness, settler colonialism, and racism. Traditional reproductive rights spaces have failed to centre the experience of racialized communities, including the pregnancy complications facing Black women (Esegbona-Adeigbe 2020), surveillance (though birth alerts) of Indigenous mothers (Ontario Association of Children's Aid Societies 2020), and separation of children from migrant women (Echavarri and Lanard 2020). Survivors' experiences must be centred in redress strategies (Rossiter and Rinaldi 2020, 75) to negotiate "the elements of the program, such as the harms covered, the validation process and the compensation and benefits offered" (LCC 2000, 8).

Building on survivors' resilience and strength, a comprehensive program must prevent and respond to violence. Leaders with disabilities can craft more effective interventions to disrupt "the longstanding systems that oppress disabled people's reproductive freedom" (Powell 2021, 18). Self-advocacy supports the development of a culture of rights in the developmental services sector (Hutton et al. 2017; McKhail 2010; People First Canada n.d.). Accessible rights education supports women and girls to identify violence and empower women to become "active participants and consumers of services" (Joffe 2010, 55). Self-advocacy promotes the healing process by "giving survivors control over the narrative of their own experiences and empowerment in preventing future abuses" (Hutton et al. 2017, 54).

Alarmingly, the "intellectual inertia of eugenics" has continuing influence (UCSB Department of History 2021). Britney Spears was prevented from having children because her conservator would not allow her to stop using contraception (Powell 2021). The re-emergence of new institutional settings, including group homes, suggests that "institutions are like hydras, as one head is cut off, two more emerge" (Linton, 2021).

There is political urgency to address these issues. Given COVID-19, women labelled with intellectual disabilities are isolated more than ever, economically marginalized, and are facing increased violence (Martino, 2020; Special Envoy of the Secretary-General on Disability and Accessibility 2020). Group homes are infectious hotspots (Jacobs 2021, paras. 2.24–5; Lupton, 2021). Given the risk of transmission in congregate living environments like group homes, "institutionalization is itself a public health concern" and is "the problem – not people's frailty" (Seniors for Social Action 2021). COVID-19 has made apparent that institutionalization is an ongoing reality, one that has posed a particular threat to women labelled with intellectual disabilities.

NOTES

1 The "Ashley Treatment" refers to a set of various procedures to arrest the physical growth (including high-dose estrogen, hysterectomy, and breast bud removal) of girls labelled with intellectual disabilities. The parents of a six-year-old girl named Ashley requested these interventions since, they argued, it would give Ashley a better quality of life and allow her parents to continue to care for her at home. Disability rights advocates oppose the

treatment and raise questions about underlying ableist presumptions about her physical integrity and sexuality/reproductive capacity.

2 The acronym stands for lesbian, gay, bisexual, transgender, queer, questioning, intersex, pansexual, Two-Spirit, androgynous, and asexual.

REFERENCES

Legislation and Case Law

ARCH. 2008. "Official Report of Debates." Comments to Standing Committee on Social Policy. 8 August 2008. Legislative Assembly of Ontario. https://www.ola.org/sites/default/files/node-files/hansard/document/pdf/2008/2008-08/committee-transcript-1-EN-08-AUG-2008_SP011.pdf.

Bach, Michael. 2012. Affidavit. Ontario Superior Court of Justice. *Tanudjaja v. Canada.* http://www.acto.ca/assets/files/cases/Afd.%20of%20M%20BACH,%20Exe%20Vice%20President,%20Canadian%20Association%20Of%20Community%20Living%20-%20FINAL.pdf.

Buck v. Bell. 1927. 274 U.S. 200. https://supreme.justia.com/cases/federal/us/527/581/

Correctional Service Canada. 2020. "Commissioner's Directive 768 Institutional Mother-Child Program." https://www.csc-scc.gc.ca/politiques-et-lois/768-cd-en.shtml

Disability Rights Coalition v. Nova Scotia (Attorney General). 2021. NSCA 70 (CanLII). https://canlii.ca/t/jjg28.

Inglis v. British Columbia (Minister of Public Safety). 2013. BCSC 2309. https://www.bccourts.ca/jdb-txt/SC/13/23/2013BCSC2309.htm.

Leroux v. Ontario. 2021. ONSC 2269. https://canlii.ca/t/jdz83.

Nova Scotia (Community Services) v. C.K.Z. 2016. NSCA 61. https://ca.vlex.com/vid/n-s-v-c-679846353.

Muir v. Alberta. 1996. CanLII 7287 (AB QB). https://canlii.ca/t/1p6lq.

Olmstead v. L.C. 1999. 527 U.S. 581 Ct. 2176. https://supreme.justia.com/cases/federal/us/527/581.

"Ontario Regulation 299/10: Quality Assurance Measures." 2011. *Services and Supports to Promote the Social Inclusion of Persons with Developmental Disabilities Act.* https://www.ontario.ca/laws/regulation/100299.

R. v. DAI. 2012. SCC 5, [2012] 1 SCR 149. https://scc-csc.lexum.com/scc-csc/scc-csc/en/item/7990/index.do.

R. v. Slatter. 2020. SCC 36. https://www.canlii.org/en/ca/scc/doc/2020/2020scc36/2020scc36.html.

Re: Eve. 1986. 2 SCR 388. https://scc-csc.lexum.com/scc-csc/scc-csc/en/item/170/index.do.

Tanudjaja v. Canada (Attorney General). 2014. ONCA 852. https://www.ontariocourts.ca/decisions/2014/2014ONCA0852.htm.

United Nations Committee on the Rights of Persons with Disabilities. 2017. "General Comment 5: Living Independently and Being Included in the Community." https://www.ohchr.org/EN/HRBodies/CRPD/Pages/GC.aspx.

United Nations General Assembly. 1966. "International Covenant on Civil and Political Rights." Treaty Series 999 (December): 171.

– 1966. "International Covenant on Economic, Social and Cultural Rights." December 1966.

– 1979. "Convention on the Elimination of All Forms of Discrimination against Women." (December).

– 2006. "Convention on the Rights of Persons with Disabilities."

"Verdict of the Coroner's Jury at the Inquest into the Death of Guy Mitchell." 2015. Ministry of Community Safety and Correctional Services. https://www.mcscs.jus.gov.on.ca/english/Deathinvestigations/Inquests/Verdictsandrecommendations/OCCInquestMitchell2015.html.

OTHER SOURCES

Abbas, Jihan, and Jijian Voronka. 2014. "Remembering Institutional Erasures: The Meaning of Histories of Disability Incarceration in Ontario." In *Disability Incarcerated: Imprisonment and Disability in the United States and Canada*, edited by Liat Ben-Moshe, Chris Chapman, and Allison C. Carey, 121–38. New York: Palgrave Macmillan.

Agaronnik, Nicole, Elizabeth Pendo, Tara Lagu, Christene DeJong, Aixa Perez-Caraballo, and Lisa I. Iezzoni. 2020. "Ensuring the Reproductive Rights of Women with Intellectual Disability." *Journal of Intellectual and Developmental Disability* 45, no. 4: 365–76.

Allen, Karma. 2019. "Arizona's Hacienda Healthcare Closing Unit in Wake of Rape, Pregnancy Scandal Hacienda Did Not Say Where the Disabled Patients Would Be Moved to Next." ABC News. https://abcnews.go.com/US/arizonas-hacienda-healthcare-closing-unit-wake-rape-pregnancy/story?id=60928427.

Allen, Lisa M., Christine Dizon, and Melanie Omstein. 2005. "Menstrual and Contraceptive Issues among Young Women with Developmental Delay: A Retrospective Review of Cases at the Hospital for Sick Children, Toronto." *Journal of Pediatric and Adolescent Gynecology* 18: 157–62.

ARCH. 2021. "Statement to CRPD Committee Consultation on Deinstitutionalization." Last modified 9 June 2021. https://archdisabilitylaw.ca/respecting-rights-statement-to-crpd-committee-consultation-on-deinstitutionalization.

Aunos, Marjorie, Maurice Feldman, David McConnell, and Narasimha Presad. 2011. "Parental Cognitive Impairment and Child Maltreatment in Canada." *Child Abuse and Neglect* 620, no. 35: 621–32.

Australia. 2015. "Violence, Abuse and Neglect against People with Disability in Institutional and Residential Settings, including the Gender and Age-Related Dimensions, and the Particular Situation of Aboriginal and Torres Strait Islander People with Disability, and Culturally and Linguistically Diverse People with Disability." Last modified 25 November 2015. https://www.aph.gov.au/Parliamentary_Business/Committees/Senate/Community_Affairs/Violence_abuse_neglect/Report.

Australia Royal Commission into Violence, Abuse, Neglect and Exploitation of People with Disability. 2019. "Group Homes." https://disability.royalcommission.gov.au/publications/group-homes.

Australian Disability Violence Commission. 2020. "Issues Paper: Violence and Abuse of People with Disability at Home." Last modified December 2020. https://disability.royalcommission.gov.au/system/files/2020-12/Issues%20paper%20-%20Violence%20and%20abuse%20of%20people%20with%20disability%20at%20home.pdf.

Bagenstos, Samuel. 2020. "Disability and Reproductive Justice." *Harvard Law and Policy Review* 14: 273–92.

Baker, Brea. 2020. "Women of Color Speak out against the Whitewashing of Reproductive Justice." ELLE, last modified 9 July 2020. https://www.elle.com/culture/career-politics/a33251077/intersectional-reproductive-justice-movement.

Bakhtiary, Shiva. 2019. "Why Ontario's Victim Compensation Bill Will Hurt Those It's Designed to Help." *Lawyer's Daily*. https://www.thelawyersdaily.ca/articles/14621/why-ontario-s-victim-compensation-bill-will-hurt-those-it-s-designed-to-help.

Barken, Rachel. 2013. "A Place to Call Home: Intellectual Disabilities and Residential Services in Nova Scotia." *Canadian Journal of Disability Studies* 2, no. 1: 51–70.

Bazelon Center for Mental Health Law. 2009. "Still Waiting … The Unfulfilled Promise of Olmstead." https://www.americanbar.org/content/dam/aba/events/homelessness_poverty/2013_Annual_Meeting_Medicaid/bazelon_report.pdf.

Beaudry, Jonas-Sébastien. 2018. "The Intellectually Disabled Witness and the Requirement to Promise to Tell the Truth." *Dalhousie Law Journal* 40, no. 1.

Bedolla, Miguel, Horacio Marquez-Gonzalez, and Edith Valdez-Martinez. 2018. "Hysterectomy for the Management of Menstrual Hygiene in Women with Intellectual Disability: A Systematic Review Focusing on Standards and Ethical Considerations for Developing Countries." *Frontiers in Public Health* 6: 338.

Benedet, Janine, and Isabel Grant. 2007. "Hearing the Sexual Assault Complaints of Women with Mental Disabilities: Consent, Capacity and Mistaken Belief." *McGill Law Journal* 52, no. 2: 243–89.

– 2012. "Taking the Stand: Access to Justice for Witnesses with Mental Disabilities in Sexual Assault Cases." *Osgoode Hall Law Journal* 50, no. 1: 1–45.

– 2013. "More than an Empty Gesture: Enabling Women with Mental Disabilities to Testify on a Promise to Tell the Truth." CJWL 25, no. 1: 31–55.

– 2020. "Sex-Assault Prosecutions Often Fail Women with Mental Disabilities." *Policy Options*, last modified 7 February 2020. https://policyoptions.irpp.org/magazines/february-2020/sex-assault-prosecution-often-fails-women-with-mental-disabilities.

Berens, Michael, and Patricia Callahan. 2016. "Suffering in Secret: Illinois Hides Abuse and Neglect of Adults with Disabilities." *Chicago Tribune*, last modified 21 November 2016. https://www.chicagotribune.com/investigations/ct-group-home-investigations-cila-met-20161117-htmlstory.html.

Bernert, Donna. 2010. "Sexuality and Disability in the Lives of Women with Intellectual Disabilities." *Sexuality and Disability* 29 (9 December): 129–141. https://doi.org/10.1007/s11195-010-9190-4.

Booth, Tim. 1994. "Parents with Learning Difficulties, Child Protection and the Courts." *Representing Children* 13, no. 3: 175–88.

Boulange, Josée, and Natalie Spagnuolo. 2018. "Unconscious Terrain of Habits." In *Violence in the Lives of Disabled Women*, edited by Michelle Owen, Diane Hiebert-Murphy, and Janice Ristock. Halifax: Fernwood Books.

Brady, Susan. 2001. "Sterilization of Girls and Women with Intellectual Disabilities: Past and Present Justifications." *Violence against Women* 7, no. 3: 432–61.

Brockschmidt, Laura, and Kristien Michielsen. 2021. "Barriers to Sexuality Education for Children and Young people with Disabilities in the WHO

European Region: A Scoping Review." *Sex Education* 21, no. 6 (3 January): 674–92. http://doi.org/10.1080/14681811.2020.1851181.

Bromwich, Rebecca, Tamar Hager, and Michelle Miller. 2017. *Bad Mothers: Regulations, Representations, and Resistance*. Toronto: Demeter Press.

Brown, Hilary. 2004. "Violence against Vulnerable Groups." *Council of Europe Publishing*. https://www.corteidh.or.cr/tablas/r25587.pdf.

Brown, Hilary, Momina Khan, Yona Kunsky, Kate Welsh, Susan Havercamp, Laurie Proulx, and Lesley A. Tarasoff. 2021. "A Socio-Ecological Approach to Understanding the Perinatal Care Experiences of People with Intellectual and/or Developmental Disabilities in Ontario, Canada." *Women's Health Issues* 31, no. 6: 550–9.

Brown, Hilary, Yona Lunsky, Lynne Potvin, and Simone Vigod. 2018. "Maternal Intellectual or Developmental Disability and Newborn Discharge to Protective Services." *Pediatrics* 142, no. 6.

CACL (Canadian Association for Community Living). 2020. "Position on Housing." https://static1.squarespace.com/static/57f27c992994ca20330b28ff/t/5e84b9942e188c3fecebf696/1585756564812/CACL+-Position+Statement+on+Housing+-+2020.pdf.

Canadian Press. 2018. "Government Cost-Cutting Left People with Disabilities without Housing, N.S. Inquiry Told." *Toronto Star*, 4 June 2018. https://www.thestar.com/halifax/2018/06/04/government-cost-cutting-left-people-with-disabilities-without-housing-ns-inquiry-told.html.

Carmody, Moira. 1991. "Invisible Victims: Sexual Assault of People with an Intellectual Disability." *Australia and New Zealand Journal of Developmental Disabilities* 17, no. 2: 229–36.

Casteel, C., S.L. Martin, J.B. Smith, K.K. Gurka, and L.L. Kupper. 2008. "National Study of Physical and Sexual Assault among Women with Disabilities." BMJ *Journals* 14, no. 2: 87–90.

CBC News. 2010. "Group Homes Need Oversight: Ottawa Councillor." 12 July 2010. https://www.cbc.ca/news/canada/ottawa/group-homes-need-oversight-ottawa-councillor-1.884187.

– 2017. "Group Home Operator Wants Training Not Jail Time after Fatal Fire and Repeat Fire Code Violations." 20 March 2017. https://www.cbc.ca/news/canada/windsor/group-home-operator-wants-training-not-jail-time-after-fatal-fire-and-repeat-fire-code-violations-1.4033495.

– 2019a. "Doug Ford Government Scrapping Law That Compensates Crime Victims." 12 April 2019. https://www.cbc.ca/news/canada/toronto/doug-ford-ontario-crime-victim-compensation-1.5095827.

– 2019b. "Sex Ed Program for Young Adults with Developmental Disabilities Gets $33k." 19 March 2019. http://www.cbc.ca/news/canada/kitchener-waterloo/sex-ed-youth-developmental-disability-shore-centre-kitchener-1.4279246.

CMPA (Canadian Medical Protective Association). 2021. "Consent: A Guide for Canadian Physicians." Last modified April 2021. https://www.cmpa-acpm.ca/en/advice-publications/handbooks/consent-a-guide-for-canadian-physicians.

– 2022. "Informed Consent: Helping Patients Make Informed Decisions." Last revised November 2022. https://www.cmpa-acpm.ca/en/education-events/good-practices/physician-patient/informed-consent.

Collie, Meghan. 2019. "Young People with Disabilities Aren't Being Taught Sex-Ed – And It's Putting Them in Danger." Global News, 3 December 2019. https://globalnews.ca/news/6247887/disabled-youth-sex-education.

Committee on Adolescent Health Care. 2016. "Menstrual Manipulation for Adolescents with Physical and Developmental Disabilities." *National Library of Medicine*. Last modified August 2016.

Community Living Ontario. 2013. "Preventing the Neglect of Vulnerable Victims: Jamie Hawley's Death by Neglect." Last modified 30 August 2013. https://www.newswire.ca/news-releases/preventing-the-neglect-of-vulnerable-victims-jamie-hawleys-death-by-neglect-512863751.html.

Cotter, Adam. 2018. "Violent Victimization of Women with Disabilities, 2014." *Canadian Centre for Justice Statistics*. https://www.dawncanada.net/media/uploads/news_data/news-234/violent_victimization_eng.pdf.

Crippled Scholar. 2016. "Let's Talk about Disability, Periods, and Alternative Menstrual Products." Last modified 8 July 2016. https://crippledscholar.com/2016/07/08/lets-talk-about-disability-periods-and-alternative-menstrual-products.

Cross, Pamela. 2019. "Racing against the Clock." Last modified 24 September 2019. https://pamelacross.ca/racing-against-the-clock.

Curry, Mary Ann, Dena Hassouneh-Phillips, and Anne Johnston-Silverberg. 2001. "Abuse of Women with Disabilities." *Violence against Women* 7, no. 1: 60–79.

Darricades, Karen. 2018. "Bad Mothers: Regulations, Representations, and Resistance." *Herizons* 32, no. 1: 37–8.

Davis, Leigh Ann. 2011. "People with Intellectual Disabilities and Sexual Violence." *Arc*. https://thearc.org/wp-content/uploads/forchapters/Sexual%20Violence.pdf.

DAWN. 2013. "DisAbled Mothering – Building a Safe and Accessible Community." https://www.dawncanada.net/main/wp-content/uploads/2013/03/DisAbled-mothering-Jewelles-Smith.pdf.

– 2014. "Women with Disabilities and Violence." Last modified January 2014. https://www.dawncanada.net/main/wp-content/uploads/2014/03/English-Violence-January-2014.

– 2020. "Girls without Barriers: An Intersectional Feminist Analysis of Girls and Young Women with Disabilities in Canada." Last modified May 2020. https://dawncanada.net/media/uploads/page_data/page-64/girls_without_barriers.pdf.

– n.d. "The Only Parent in the Neighbourhood: Mothering and Women with Disabilities." *Disabled Women's Network of Canada*. https://www.dawncanada.net/ppbdp-en/the-only-parent-in-the-neighbourhood-mothering-and.

de La Cour, Lykke. 2017. "Eugenics, Race and Canada's First-Wave Feminists: Dis/Abling the Debates." *Atlantis* 38, no. 2.

Developmental Services Housing Task Force. 2018. "Generating Ideas and Enabling Action: Addressing the Housing Crisis Confronting Ontario Adults with Developmental Disabilities." http://webps.ca/wp-content/uploads/2019/09/HTF-Final-Report-2018_Generating-Ideas_Enabling-Action_FINAL.pdf.

Dhand, Ruby. 2021. "Women and Girls with Disabilities: Gendered Disability Discrimination." In *Law and Disability in Canada: Cases and Material*, edited by Laverne Jacobs, Ruby Dhand, Freya Kodar, Richard Jochelson, David Ireland, and Odelia Bay, 125–44. Toronto: Lexis Nexis.

Didi, Aminath, Leanne Dowse, and Carolyn Frohmader. 2015. "Preventing Violence against Women and Girls with Disabilities: Integrating a Human Rights Perspective." *Women with Disabilities Australia*. Last modified September 2015. https://wwda.org.au/wp-content/uploads/2013/12/Think_Piece_Revised_Edition.pdf.

Disability Rights Washington. 2015. "Understanding Disability Rights and Sexual Assault in Resident Advocacy." September 2015. https://www.disabilityrightswa.org/reports/understanding-sexual-rights-sexual-assault-resident-advocacy.

Dizon, Christine D., Lisa M. Allen, and Melanie P. Ornstein. 2005. "Menstrual and Contraceptive Issues among Young Women with Developmental Delay: A Retrospective Review of Cases at the Hospital for Sick Children, Toronto." *Journal of Pediatric and Adolescent Gynecology* 18, no. 3: 157–62.

Dowse, Leanne, and Linda Steele. 2016. "Gender, Disability Rights and Violence against Medical Bodies." *Australian Feminist Studies* 31, no. 88: 117–24.

Dream Team. n.d. "Advocacy." https://www.thedreamteam.ca/advocacy.

Dubé, Paul. 2016. "Nowhere to Turn: Investigation into the Ministry of Community and Social Services' Response to Situations of Crisis Involving Adults with Developmental Disabilities." Toronto: Ombudsman of Ontario. https://www.ombudsman.on.ca/Media/ombudsman/ombudsman/resources/Reports-on-Investigations/NTT-Final-EN-w-cover.pdf.

Dusome, Debra, and Sherri Melrose. n.d. "Sexuality." In *Supporting Individuals with Intellectual Disabilities and Mental Illness*. https://opentextbc.ca/caregivers/chapter/chapter-seven-sexuality.

Dyck, Erika. 2013. *Facing Eugenics: Reproduction, Sterilization, and the Politics of Choice*. Toronto: University of Toronto Press.

Earle, Kory, and Natalie Spagnuolo. 2017. "Freeing Our People: Updates from the Long Road to Deinstitutionalization." Last modified 4 July 2017. https://www.policyalternatives.ca/publications/monitor/freeing-our-people-updates-long-road-deinstitutionalization.

Echavarri, Fernanda, and Noah Lanard. 2020. "ICE Asked Parents to Choose between Family Separation and Prolonged Detention – During a Pandemic." *Mother Jones*, 21 May 2020. https://www.motherjones.com/politics/2020/05/ice-family-separation-detention-flores-settlement-coronavirus.

Esegbona-Adeigbe, Sarah. 2020. "COVID-19 and the Risk to Black, Asian and Minority Ethnic Women during Pregnancy." *British Journal of Midwifery* 28, no. 10: 718–23.

Eugenics to Newgenics. 2018. "What is Newgenics?" https://eugenicsnewgenics.com/2014/05/14/what-is-newgenics.

Ferrie, Jo, and Phillippa Wiseman. 2020. "Reproductive (In)Justice and Inequality in the Lives of Women with Intellectual Disabilities in Scotland." *Scandinavian Journal of Disability Research* 22, no. 1: 318–29.

Flores, Emily. 2018. "The #MeToo Movement Hasn't Been Inclusive of the Disability Community." *Teen Vogue*, 24 April 2018. https://www.teenvogue.com/story/the-metoo-movement-hasnt-been-inclusive-of-the-disability-community.

Fraser, Laura. 1998. "Sterilization: Choice, Right or Requirement? A Comment on the Best Interests Test in Re Eve." *Dalhousie Journal of Legal Studies* 7, no. 1: 163–88.

Frederick, Angela. 2014. "Mothering While Disabled." *Sage Journals* 13, no. 4: 30–5.

Gilmore, Linda, and Laura Malcolm. 2014. "Best for Everyone Concerned Or Only as a Last Resort? Views of Australian Doctors about Sterilization of Men and Women with Intellectual Disability." *Journal of Intellectual and Developmental Disability* 39, no. 2: 177–87.

Gordon, Tonie. 2015. "To 'Fill the Comfortable Cradles and Empty the Gutters': Maternalist Eugenics and Reproductive Inequalities in the United State." PhD diss., University of Virginia, May 2015. https://libraetd.lib.virginia.edu/downloads/bc386j61k?filename=Gordon_Tonie_2015.pdf.

Grover, Sonla, Sandra Macgibbon, and Jane Tracy. 2016. "Menstrual Issues for Women with Intellectual Disability." *Australian Prescriber* 38, no. 2: 54–7.

Hamilton, Carol. 2009. "Now I'd Like to Sleep with Rachael – Researching Sexuality Support in a Service Agency Group Home." *Disability and Society* 24, no. 3: 303–35.

Hasham, Alyshah. "Ontario Budget Cuts Millions in Compensation to Victims of Violent Crime, Advocates Say." *Toronto Star*, 18 April 2019. https://www.thestar.com/news/gta/2019/04/18/ontario-budget-cuts-millions-in-compensation-to-victims-of-violent-crime-advocates-say.html.

Henley, Ariel. "Why Sex Education for Disabled People Is So Important." *Teen Vogue*, 7 October 2017. https://www.teenvogue.com/story/disabled-sex-ed.

Homecoming Community Choice Coalition. n.d. "Yes in My Backyard." https://yesinmybackyard.ca.

Hutton, Sue, Peter Park, Martin Levine, Shay Johnson, and Kosha Bramesfeld. 2017. "Self-Advocacy from the Ashes of the Institution." *Canadian Journal of Disability Studies* 6, no. 3: 31–59. https://cjds.uwaterloo.ca/index.php/cjds/article/view/365/596.

Inclusion Canada. 2018. "A Right to Housing for All: Ensuring A Human Rights Approach Inclusive of All Persons with Developmental Disabilities." https://inclusioncanada.ca/wp-content/uploads/2019/09/2019_Federal_Election_Strategy.pdf.

– 2019a. "Forced and Coerced Sterilization of Individuals with an Intellectual Disability." https://inclusioncanada.ca/2019/06/19/forced-coerced-sterilization-of-individuals-with-an-intellectual-disability.

– 2019b. "A National Disability Action Plan." https://inclusioncanada.ca/wp-content/uploads/2019/09/2019_Federal_Election_Strategy.pdf.

Inclusion Canada and People First. 2019. "Letter to the Senate Standing Committee on Human Rights." 17 May 2019. https://sencanada.ca/content/sen/committee/421/RIDR/Briefs/RIDR_CACLPFC_e.pdf.

Insogna, Iris. 2015. "Sterilization as Last Resort in Women with Intellectual Disabilities: Protection or Disservice?" *American Journal of Obstetrics and Gynecology* 212, no. 1: P34–6.

Institution Watch. n.d. "Definition of an Institution." Joint Task Force on Deinstitutionalization. https://www.institutionwatch.ca/task-force/definition-of-an-institution.

Invisible Institutions. n.d. http://invisibleinstitutions.com.

Jackson, Kenneth. 2020. "There is No Timetable: Courts Refuse to Let These Three Moms See Children during Pandemic." APTN News, 13 April 2020. https://www.aptnnews.ca/national-news/there-is-no-timetable-courts-refuse-to-let-these-three-moms-see-children-during-pandemic.

Jacobs, Laverne. 2021. "Examining the Right Community Living for People with Disabilities in Canada." In *Law and Disability in Canada: Cases and Material*, edited by Laverne Jacobs, Ruby Dhand, Freya Kodar, Richard Jochelson, David Ireland, and Odelia Bay, 45–72. Toronto, Lexis Nexis.

Joffe, Kerri. 2010. "Enforcing the Rights of People with Disabilities in Ontario's Developmental Services System." *Law Commission of Ontario*. Last modified 30 June 2010. https://www.lco-cdo.org/wp-content/uploads/2010/11/disabilities_joffe.pdf.

Jones, Sarah. "Trump Has Turned the GOP into the Party of Eugenics." *New Republic*, 15 February 2017. https://newrepublic.com/article/140641/trump-turned-gop-party-eugenics.

Kanji, Azeezah, and A.J. Withers. 2021. "Encampment Evictions: Another Face of Colonial Violence in Canada." *Al Jazeera*, 20 July 2021. https://www.aljazeera.com/opinions/2021/7/20/encampment-evictions-another-face-of-colonial-violence-in-canada.

Kelly, Fiona. 2011. "Enforcing a Parent/Child Relationship at All Cost? Supervised Access Orders in the Canadian Courts." *Osgoode Hall Law Journal* 49, no. 2: 277–309.

Kendrick, Michael. 2018. "Why Group Homes Are No Longer Optimal: A Commentary." https://www.family-advocacy.com/assets/d673bafd49/Why-Group-Homes-Are-No-Longer-Optimal.pdf.

Kischkel, Sam. 2019. "Teaching 'Yes Means Yes' Can Make Sex Education More Inclusive for the Disability Community." *Rooted in Rights*, 17 April 2019. https://rootedinrights.org/teaching-yes-means-yes-can-make-sex-education-more-inclusive-for-the-disability-community.

Lady Science. 2019. "Decades after Forced Sterilization Native American Women in the US Still Face Rejection and Retraumatization in Healthcare." https://www.ladyscience.com/features/forced-sterilization-native-american-women-face-rejection-retraumatization-in-healthcare.

Lauriault, Tracey. 2021. "Open Data for Results: Disability." http://datalibre.ca.

Law Commission of Canada. 2000. "Restoring Dignity: Responding to Child Abuse in Canadian Institutions." https://www.attorneygeneral.jus.gov.on.ca/inquiries/cornwall/en/hearings/exhibits/Peter_Jaffe/pdf/Restoring_Dignity.pdf.

LEAF. 2020. "Announcement: Supreme Court of Canada Recognizes Harmful and Ableist Myths about Women with Disabilities Have No Place in Sexual Assault trials in *R. v. Slatter*." Last modified 16 November 2020. https://www.leaf.ca/news/r-v-slatter-decision.

– n.d. "*Tanudjaja v. Attorney General* (Canada)." https://www.leaf.ca/news/tanudjaja-v-attorney-general-canada-2.

Letheren, Laurie. 2013. "Obtaining Services for Persons Who Have Been Labelled with an Intellectual Disability: A Primer." ARCH *Disability Law Centre*. https://www.archdisabilitylaw.ca/sites/all/files/DISABILITY%20LAW%20PRIMER%20-%20English%20(PDF).pdf.

Leung, Colette. n.d. "Provincial Training School." *Eugenics Archive*. https://eugenicsarchive.ca/discover/institutions/map/517da50e9786fa0a73000001.

LINKS. 1992. "Living in New Kinds of Situations." April 1992. http://www.universallifestiles.com/An_Institution_April.pdf.

Linton, Megan. 2020. "Institutional Legacies of Violence: Neoliberalism and Custodial Care in Ontario." https://canadiandimension.com/articles/view/institutional-legacies-of-violence-of-custodial-care-in-ontario.

– 2021a. "Mind the Gap: Data Gaps and Adults with Developmental Disabilities in Ontario." *Carleton Perspective on Public Policy* 7. https://ojs.library.carleton.ca/index.php/cpopp/article/view/3182.

– 2021b. "Ontario's Hidden Institutions." *Canadian Dimension*. Last modified 24 February 2021. https://canadiandimension.com/articles/view/custodial-institutions-ontarios-hidden-victims.

– 2021c. "Vaccinate + Deinstitutionalize Now: Residential Service Homes and the Failure of Independent Living." *Disability Justice Network of Ontario*. Last modified 14 January 2021. https://www.djno.ca/post/

vaccinate-deinstitutionalize-now-residential-service-homes-and-the-failure-of-independent-living.

Llewellyn, Gwynnyth. 2012. "Mothers with Intellectual Disability and Their Babies: A Population Warranting Special Consideration." *Acta Obstetricia Et Gynecologica Scandinavica* 91, no. 12: 1353–6.

Loew, Morgan, Catherine Meija, and Briana Whitney. 2019. "Woman in Vegetative State Gives Birth at Hacienda Healthcare in Phoenix." AZ *Family*, 4 January 2019. https://www.azfamily.com/news/woman-in-vegetative-state-gives-birth-at-hacienda-healthcare-in/article_9342c7c4-0fb2-11e9-8138-4fcd53869faf.html.

Louise, Shona. 2020. "Is There Space for Disabled People in the Period Positive Movement?" *Rooted in Rights*, 27 October 2020. https://rootedinrights.org/is-there-space-for-disabled-people-in-the-period-positive-movement.

Lunsky, Yona. 2018. "Speaking of Sex-Ed – How About We Develop Some for Students with Developmental Disabilities?" CBC News, 24 September 2018. https://www.cbc.ca/news/opinion/sex-ed-students-1.4834984.

Lupton, Andrew. 2021. "Group Home Shutdown in St Thomas, Ont., Rekindles Debate about Provincial Licensing." CBC News, 9 July 2021. https://www.cbc.ca/news/canada/london/group-home-shutdown-in-st-thomas-ont-rekindles-debate-about-provincial-licensing-1.6094930.

Malacrida, Claudia. 2015. *A Special Hell: Institutional Life in Alberta's Eugenic Years*. Toronto: University of Toronto Press.

Malik, Aisha. 2021. "The Double Hurdle of Consent for Disabled Canadians. *Refinery29*. https://www.refinery29.com/en-ca/2021/10/10660318/consent-sex-disabled-women.

Martin, Sandra, Neepa Ray, Daniela Sotres-Alvarez, Lawrence L. Kupper, Kathryn E. Moracco, Pamela A. Dickens, Donna Scandlin, and Ziya Gizlize. 2006. "Physical and Sexual Assault of Women with Disabilities." *Violence against Women* 12, no. 9: 823–37.

Martino, Alan Santinele. 2020. "COVID-19 Has Isolated Disabled People from Family, Love, Sex." *Conversation*. Last modified 5 August 2020. https://theconversation.com/covid-19-has-isolated-disabled-people-from-family-love-sex-142262.

Matheson, Duncan, and Karen McCauley. 2016. "Perspective: From Institution to Community Living, to Social Inclusion – Unrealized Policy Promises." *Journal on Developmental Disabilities* 22, no. 1: 3–9.

Mayes, Rachel, and Gwynnyth Llewellyn. 2009. "What Happens to Parents with Intellectual Disability Following Removal of their Child in Child Protection Proceedings?" *Journal of Intellectual and Developmental Disabilities* 34, no. 1: 92–5.

Mays, Jennifer. 2007. "Feminist Disability Theory: Domestic Violence against Women with a Disability." *Disability and Society* 21, no. 2: 147–58.

McConnel, David, and Callie Westad. 2009. "Child Welfare Involvement of Mothers with Mental Health Issues." *Community Mental Health Journal* 48, no. 1: 29–37.

McKhail, S. 2010. "What Is Self Advocacy?" https://selfadvocatenet.com/what-is-self-advocacy.

Méndez, Juan. 2013. "Report of the Special Rapporteur on Torture and Other Cruel, Inhuman or Degrading Treatment or Punishment." United Nations General Assembly. https://www.ohchr.org/documents/hrbodies/hrcouncil/regularsession/session22/a.hrc.22.53_english.pdf.

National Council on Disability. n.d. "Institutions: Definitions, Populations and Trends." https://ncd.gov/publications/2012/Sept192012/Institutions.

National Housing Strategy. n.d. "Human Rights-Based Approach to Housinghttps://www.placetocallhome.ca/en/human-rights-based-approach-to-housing.

National People with Disabilities and Carer Council. 2012. "SHUT OUT: The Experience of People with Disabilities and their Families in Australia." *National Disability Strategy Consultation Report*. https://www.dss.gov.au/our-responsibilities/disability-and-carers/publications-articles/policy-research/shut-out-the-experience-of-people-with-disabilities-and-their-families-in-australia.

Neal, D'Arcee. 2018. "The #MeToo Movement Has Ignored Disabled People, But We Need It More Than Ever." *Them*, 16 April 2018. https://www.them.us/story/me-too-movement-must-include-disabled-people.

Nowak, Manfred. 2008. "Interim Report of the Special Rapporteur on Torture and Other Cruel, Inhuman or Degrading Treatment or Punishment." United Nations General Assembly. https://www2.ohchr.org/english/bodies/hrcouncil/docs/10session/A.HRC.10.44AEV.pdf.

NPR. 2018. "Abused and Betrayed." https://www.npr.org/series/575502633/abused-and-betrayed.

Olesen, Colleen. 1994. "Eve and the Forbidden Fruit: Reflections on a Feminist Methodology." *Dalhousie Journal of Legal Studies* 3, no. 1: 231–40.

Ontario Association of Children's Aid Societies. 2020. "The Practice of Birth Alerts in Ontario is Ceasing October 15th. What's Next for Child

Welfare Agencies and Their Approach to Working with Expectant Mothers?" www.oacas.org/2020/10/the-practice-of-birth-alerts-in-ontario-is-ceasing-october-15th-whats-next-for-child-welfare-agencies-and-their-approach-to-working-with-expectant-mothers.

Ontario Human Rights Commission. 2011. "In the Zone: Housing, Human Rights and Municipal Planning." http://www.ohrc.on.ca/en/zone-housing-human-rights-and-municipal-planning.

Ontario Ministry of Children, Community and Social Services. 2013. "Interrupted Childhoods: Over-representation of Indigenous and Black Children in Ontario Child Welfare." https://www.ohrc.on.ca/en/interrupted-childhoods.

– n.d. "Residential Supports." https://www.mcss.gov.on.ca/en/mcss/programs/developmental/servicesupport/residential_supports.aspx.

Paransky, Ora, and Robert Zurawin. 2003. "Management of Menstrual Problems and Contraception in Adolescents with Mental Retardation: A Medical, Legal, and Ethical Review with New Suggested Guidelines." *Journal of Pediatric and Adolescent Gynecology* 16, no. 4: 223–35.

Payne, Elizabeth. 2019. "Investigate Use of Trespass Law to Limit Visits in Retirement, Long-Term Care Homes: Ottawa MPP." *Ottawa Citizen*. https://ottawacitizen.com/news/local-news/ottawa-mpp-wants-investigation-into-use-of-trespass-law-to-limit-visits-in-retirement-long-term-care-homes.

Paynter, Martha. "Sexual Assault in Prison: Vulnerable Women Prisoners Have Few Protections and Face Reprisal for Reporting Attacks." *Halifax Examiner*, 24 May 2019. https://www.halifaxexaminer.ca/featured/sexual-assault-in-prison-vulnerable-women-prisoners-have-few-protections-and-face-reprisal-for-reporting-attacks.

Pebdani, Roxanna. 2016. "Attitudes of Group Home Employees Towards the Sexuality of Individuals with Intellectual Disabilities." *Sexuality and Disability* 34, no. 3: 329–39.

People First of Canada. n.d. https://www.peoplefirstofcanada.ca.

People First of Canada and CACL (Canadian Association for Community Living). 2010. "The Right Way: A Guide to Closing Institutions and Reclaiming and Life in the Community for People with Intellectual Disabilities." Last modified March 2010. https://inclusioncanada.ca/wp-content/uploads/2018/05/The-Right-Way.pdf.

– 2019. Submission to Senate Standing Committee on Human Rights. https://sencanada.ca/content/sen/committee/421/RIDR/Briefs/RIDR_CACLPFC_e.pdf.

Perreault-Laird, Jordyn, and Alan Santinele Martino. 2019. "I Don't Know If I Can Talk about That: An Exploratory Study on the

Experiences of Care Workers Regarding the Sexuality of People with Intellectual Disabilities." *Disability Studies Quarterly* 39, no. 3. https://dsq-sds.org/article/view/6383/5407.

Plan International. 2017. "Girls with Disabilities Kept in Dark about Sexual and Reproductive Rights." Last modified 1 December 2017. https://plan-international.org/news/2017-12-01-girls-disabilities-sexual-reproductive-rights.

Pomeranz, Thomas. 1992. "Living in New Kinds of Situations." http://www.universallifestiles.com/An_Institution_April.pdf.

Powell, Robyn. 2021. "From Carrie Buck to Britney Spears: Strategies for Disrupting the Ongoing Reproductive Oppression of Disabled People." *107 Virginia Law Review* 246. Last modified 18 October 2021. http://dx.doi.org/10.2139/ssrn.3902743.

Powell, Robyn M., and Michael Ashley Stein. 2016. "Persons with Disabilities and Their Sexual, Reproductive, and Parenting Rights: An International and Comparative Analysis." *Frontiers of Law in China* 11, no. 1: 57–8.

Provincial Network. 2016. "All Together. Now. Improving the Lives of Ontarians with a Developmental Disability." August 2016. https://provincialnetwork.ca.

Quinlan, Andrea, and Sandra Smele. 2017. "The 'Problem' of Abuse in Ontario's Social Inclusion Act: A Critical Exploration." *Critical Social Policy* 37, no. 1: 85–104.

Remember Every Name. n.d. https://www.remembereveryname.ca.

Report of the Office of the United Nations High Commissioner for Human Rights. 2014. "Thematic Study on the Right of Persons with Disabilities to Live Independently and be Included in the Community." United Nations. Last modified 12 December 2014. https://www.ohchr.org/EN/HRBodies/HRC/RegularSessions/Session28/Documents/A_HRC_28_37_ENG.doc.

ReportON. 2018. "What's ReportON?" Last modified 9 March 2018. https://www.mcss.gov.on.ca/en/mcss/programs/developmental/reportON.

Rossiter, Kate, and Jen Rinaldi. 2019. *Institutional Violence and Disability: Punishing Conditions*. London: Routledge.

Savell K. 2004. "Sex and the Sacred: Sterilization and Bodily Integrity in English and Canadian Law." *McGill Law Journal* 49, no. 4: 1093–141.

Seidel, Linda. 2013. *Mediated Maternity: Contemporary American Portrayals of Bad Mothers in Literature and Popular Culture*. Lexington Books.

Seniors for Social Action. 2021. "Get Them Out! And Keep Them Out!" Last modified 18 September 2021. https://d5bb3c6f-31a3-47ef-a85b-5c06ab03f844.filesusr.com/ugd/c73539_f15405246c7242768bb382843e16fe88.pdf.

Series, Lucy. 2015. "Mental Capacity and the Control of Sexuality of People with Intellectual Disabilities in England and Wales." *Disability Research Today* 1. https://www.taylorfrancis.com/chapters/edit/10.4324/9781315796574-20/mental-capacity-control-sexuality-people-intellectual-disabilities-england-wales-lucy-series.

Servais, Laurent. 2006. "Sexual Health Care in Persons with Intellectual Disabilities." *Mental Retardation and Developmental Disabilities Research Reviews* 12: 48–56.

Setzer, Rachel. 2020. "Decolonization as a Strategy for Accommodating Disabilities." https://disabilityvisibilityproject.com/2020/07/19/decolonization-as-a-strategy-for-accommodating-disabilities.

Sharp, Sonja. 2021. "Disabled Mothers-To-Be Face Indignity: Do You Have A Man? Can You Have Sex?" *Los Angeles Times*, 30 September 2021. https://www.latimes.com/california/story/2021-09-30/how-modern-medicine-neglects-disabled-mothers.

Shaw, Joshua. 2015. "De-recognition of Disability: Canadian *Parens Patriae* Jurisdiction and Sterilization. *Windsor Review of Legal and Social Issues* 36: 147–74.

Shea, Laura. 2007. "Reflections on Depo Provera: Contributions to Improving Drug Regulation in Canada." *Women and Health Protection*. https://whpapsf.ca/pdf/reflectionsOnDepoProvera.pdf.

Sheehy, Elizabeth. 1999. "Equality without Democratic Values: Why Feminists Oppose the Criminal Procedure Reforms." *Canadian Woman Studies*: 7–21. https://ssrn.com/abstract=2262364.

Sins Invalid, ed. 2019. *Skin, Tooth and Bone: The Basis of Movement is our People: A Disability Justice Primer*, 2nd ed. San Francisco: Sins Invalid.

Smith, Jennifer. 2019. "Inside the Fight for Developmentally Disabled People's Right to Sex." VICE, 19 March 2019. https://www.vice.com/en_us/article/7xnad9/developmental-intellectual-disability-sex-education-consent.

Social Rights in Canada. n.d. "Charter Challenge to Homelessness and Violations of the Right to Adequate Housing in Canada: SRAC and CERA intervene in *Tanudjaja*, CERA *et al. v Canada and Ontario*." http://socialrightscura.ca/eng/legal-strategies-charter-challenge-homlessness.html.

Soucie-Vukmanich, Katelyn. 2021. "Burnout of Direct Support Workers of Adults with Intellectual and Developmental Disabilities: A Systematic Review." MA thesis, Brock University, 2021. https://dr.library.brocku.ca/bitstream/handle/10464/15165/Brock_SoucieVukmanich_Katelyn_2021.pdf.

Spady, Amy. 2008. "The Sexual Freedom of Eve: A Recommendation for Contraceptive Sterilization Legislation in the Canadian Post Re Eve Context." *Windsor Review of Legal and Social Issues* 25: 33–67.

Special Envoy of the Secretary-General on Disability and Accessibility. 2020. "Women and Girls with Disabilities and Older Women in Relation to the COVID-19 Pandemic." United Nations. Last modified 28 April 2020. https://www.un.org/development/desa/disabilities/wp-content/uploads/sites/15/2020/04/covid19-joint-statement-women-girls-disabilities-olderwomen-covid19.pdf.

Spagnuolo, Natalie. 2016. "Building Backwards in a 'Post' Institutional Era: Hospital Confinement, Group Home Eviction, and Ontario's Treatment of People Labelled with Intellectual Disabilities." *Disability Studies Quarterly* 34, no. 4. https://dsq-sds.org/article/view/5279/4480.

Spagnuolo, Natalie, and Josée Boulange. 2018. "An "Unconscious Terrain of Habits": Structural Violence against Women Who Labelled with Intellectual Disabilities." In *Not a New Problem, Violence in the Lives of Disabled Women*, edited by Michelle Owen, Diane Hiebert-Murphy, and Janice Ristock, 76–96. Halifax: Fernwood Books.

Spivakovsky, Claire. 2017. "Governing Freedom through Risk: Locating the Group Home in the Archipelago of Confinement and Control." *Punishment and Society* 19: 366–83.

Standing Senate Committee on Human Rights. "Human Rights Committee to Study the Forced and Coerced Sterilization of Persons in Canada." Last modified 27 March 2019. https://sencanada.ca/en/newsroom/ridr-human-rights-committee-study-forced-coerced-sterilization-persons-in-canada/.

Steele, Linda. 2014. "Disability, Abnormality and Criminal Law: Sterilisation as Lawful and Good Violence." *Griffith Law Review* 23, no. 3: 467–97.

– 2016. "Court Authorized Sterilisation and Human Rights: Inequality, Discrimination and Violence against Women and Girls with Disability." UNSW *Law Journal* 39, no. 3: 1002–37.

– 2020. *Disability, Criminal Justice and Law: Reconsidering Court Diversion*. London: Routledge.

– 2021. "Sites of Conscience Redressing Disability Institutional Violence." *Incarceration: An International Journal of Imprisonment, Detention and Coercive Confinement*.

Steele, Linda, and Beth Goldblatt. 2020. "The Human Rights of Women and Girls with Disabilities: Sterilization and Other Coercive Responses to Menstruation." *Palgrave Handbook of Critical Menstruation Studies*: 77–91. https://link.springer.com/content/pdf/10.1007%2F978-981-15-0614-7_8.pdf.

Strike, Anne. 2018. "Disabled Women See #MeToo and Think: What about Us?" *Guardian*. https://www.theguardian.com/commentisfree/2018/mar/08/disabled-people-metoo-womens-movement-inclusion-diversity.

Surrey Place. n.d. "Parenting Enhancement Program." https://www.surreyplace.ca/directory/parenting-enhancement-program.

Tilley, Elizabeth. 2012. "The Silence is Roaring: Sterilization, Reproductive Rights and Women with Intellectual Disabilities." *Disability and Society* 27, no. 3: 413–26.

Toronto Star. 2017. "Despite 'Deplorable' Conditions, Police and Health Officials Allow Homes Offering Services to Vulnerable Residents to Stay Open." 16 July 2017. https://www.thestar.com/news/gta/2017/07/16/despite-deplorable-conditions-police-and-health-officials-are-ignoring-residences-that-offer-services-to-vulnerable-residents.html.

Track, Laura. 2014. "Able Mothers, The Intersection of Parenting, Disability and the Law." Last modified September 2014. http://www.westcoastleaf.org/wp-content/uploads/2014/12/2014-REPORT-Able-Mothers.pdf.

– 2018. "Mothering with Disabilities." In *Not a New Problem: Violence in the Lives of Disabled Women*, edited by Michelle Owen, Diane Hiebert-Murphy, and Janice Ristock, 16–34. Halifax: Fernwood Books.

UCSB Department of History. "California Eugenics Legacies Symposium." 4–5 June 2021 https://www.history.ucsb.edu/events/california-eugenics-legacies-symposium-june-4-5-2021.

UN Secretary-General. "Report of the Special Rapporteur on Adequate Housing as a Component of the Right to an Adequate Standard of Living, and on the Right to Non-Discrimination in this Context." Las modified 12 July 2017. http://www.socialrights.ca/SR/R2H%20of%20PWD%20A.72.128.pdf.

Verlenden, Jorge, Jeanne Bertolli, and Lee Warner. 2019. "Contraceptive Practices and Reproductive Health Considerations for Adolescents and Adult Women with Intellectual and Developmental Disabilities: A Review of the Literature." *Sexuality and Disability* 37: 541.

West Coast LEAF. 2021. "Inglis v Ministry of Public Safety and Solicitor General of BC [2013]." http://www.westcoastleaf.org/our-work/inglis-v-ministry-of-public-safety-and-solicitor-general-of-bc-2013.

WHO (World Health Organization). 2014. "Eliminating Forced, Coercive and Otherwise Involuntary Sterilization. An Interagency Statement." https://www.who.int/reproductivehealth/publications/gender_rights/eliminating-forced-sterilization/en.

– n.d. "Gender and Human Rights." https://www.who.int/reproductive-health/topics/gender_rights/sexual_health/en.

Wilson, S., K. McKenzie, E. Quayle, and G. Murray. "A Systematic Review of Interventions to Promote Social Support and Parenting Skills in Parents with an Intellectual Disability." *Child Care* 40, no. 1: 7–19.

Withers, A.J. 2012. "Violence and Abuse against Disabled People." https://stillmyrevolution.org/2012/01/01violence-and-abuse-against-disabled-people.

Zingel, Avery. 2019. "Indigenous Women Come Forward with Accounts of Forced Sterilization, Says Lawyer." CBC News, 18 April 2019. https://www.cbc.ca/news/canada/north/forced-sterilization-lawsuit-could-expand-1.5102981.

10

The List as Deterrent for "Others"

ALEX TIGCHELAAR

The list is a critical support technology of discipline in how it delimits spaces and assists in prescribing the articulation of elements within them. It is indeed a tool for caring for the mundane minutiae; it is the web that does not let details slip through the cracks, forcing classification on living beings, things, and events into discipline's enclosures. In this way, the list serves discipline in how it provides an underpinning structure for the materialization and visual inspection of whatever discipline might analyze, break down, and prescribe. Discipline lists, and once listed, components can be seen and prescriptions can be made for their order.

Kenneth Werbin, *The List Serves*

Deterrence is a feature of our criminal justice system, but we usually leave that to the sentencing process.

Abby Deshman, Canadian Civil Liberties Association (MacDonald 2016)

Historically and in the present day, throughout every legislative model that has criminalized their labour, Canadian sex workers report institutionally sanctioned violence in almost all aspects of their lives. This violence materializes in coercive workplace encounters with multiple divisions of law enforcement (by-law officers, Canadian Border Services, municipal, provincial, and federal police), harmful experiences with the medical industry (forced experiments and sterilization, anti-prostitution sentiments during healthcare), threatening experiences with Child Protection Services (wherein the status of sex-working mother is conflated with an abusive home setting), and capricious criminal legislation. Canada's laws have done everything from classifying and imprisoning sex workers as vectors of disease (Backhouse 1985), to issuing "nuisance injunctions" (Lohman 1989, 19) that prohibit them from accessing certain geographical locations, to, more currently, disciplining them by proxy as de facto victims of sex offenders.

This chapter looks at institutional violence that is adaptive and mobile – *sites*-specific rather than *site*-specific – but still shares many characteristics of institutional violence experienced and reported in bricks and mortar locations. Like the Huronia Regional Centre, "built to impress the public from afar" (Rossiter and Rinaldi 2018, 9), Canada's sex work laws are written and widely circulated with an eye for public approval and dissuasion from critical analysis. Common also is that the laws are "ostensibly designed to provide care for people deemed vulnerable" (1–2), yet they have proven to support further violence from those who administer them.

Institutional violence against sex workers is interdisciplinary, not only because it contributes to associative discourses formed on the sex-working body (long a location where fields of study meet to debate and establish sociological, legal, and cultural traditions), but also because sex workers are regulated through an interconnected and interdependent process. They are, effectively, "interdisciplined" via a constellation of law-enforcement officers contracted by various levels of government. Additionally, this enforcement interpellates ordinary citizens, soliciting them to report goings-on related to sex work (situated in this discourse as human trafficking) in their neighbourhoods, hotels, and in other urban locations they visit. When media accompanies enforcement officers on raids, these campaigns are often publicly broadcast as acts of care. These raids are rarely if ever experienced by sex workers as care.

In investigating this type of sites-specific, interdisciplinary institutional violence, this chapter demonstrates how sex workers are, against their will, constituted, regulated, and circulated through Canada's criminal codes as victims of sexual exploitation. It does so by way of a case study that reveals how the clients of sex workers are now constituted, regulated, and circulated through Canada's criminal codes as de facto sex offenders.

In 2014, the Conservative government introduced *The Protection of Communities and Exploited Persons Act* (PCEPA) as the legal basis to criminalize sex work in Canada. They did this even though the Supreme Court acknowledged that the criminal offences connected to prostitution in the *Bedford* decision contravened sex workers' charter rights. PCEPA has resulted in sex workers, clients, and third parties being criminalized. This enactment, amended the Canadian *Criminal Code* to, among other things:

a) create an offence that prohibits purchasing sexual services or communicating in any place for that purpose;[1]
b) create an offence that prohibits receiving a material benefit that derived from the commission of an offence referred to in paragraph (*a*);
c) create an offence that prohibits the advertisement of sexual services offered for sale and to authorize the courts to order the seizure of materials containing such advertisements and their removal from the Internet;
d) modernize the offence that prohibits the procurement of persons for the purpose of prostitution; and
e) create an offence that prohibits communicating – for the purpose of selling sexual services – in a public place, or in any place open to public view, that is or is next to a school ground, playground or daycare centre. (*Protection of Communities and Exploited Persons Act* 2014)

The chapter uses the list – long a crucial "support technology" (Werbin 2008) employed by institutions to negatively capture, depict, surveil, and punish – as one highly efficient site of institutional violence. The list that is the focus of this chapter is one compiled and given at a press conference by the Cape Breton Regional Police Department police department on 8 September 2015, nine months after the ascendance of PCEPA. This list contains the names, ages, and residential locations of twenty-seven men. These men had been caught in an undercover sting operation called "Operation John Be Gone," wherein Constable Ashley MacDonald posed as a sex worker in public and engaged them in conversation about paying her for sex. It was under the purview of the new PCEPA legislation, again, one that situates all sex workers as victims of exploitation and "purchasers of sexual services" as criminals "for their role in the prostitution transaction" (justice.gc.ca) that this operation took place.

THEORY, METHODOLOGY, AND LEGISLATIVE HISTORY

Lynch argues that in the United States, "the sociocultural frenzy over sex-related criminality is not isolated to our contemporary period; it has been an episodic feature of our social, moral, and legal landscapes for more than a century" (2002, 533). Indeed, sex-related criminality in Canada shares this same episodic and recurring quality. The "pervert" of late nineteenth-century "medical-professional and legal realms" (534), who showed "a proclivity toward sex acts that did not lead to procreation" (534), is the very same one referred to by Justice Minister Peter MacKay in Canada (Davies 2015, 82) when he introduced PCEPA, and named the clients of sex workers as such.

Prior to PCEPA, sex work itself was not a criminal act. Nevertheless, the laws surrounding it made working safely difficult. One could not conduct business in the presence of other sex workers, one could not hire people to assist in one's business, and one could not work indoors at a location designated for sex work. It was these laws, along with communicating in public for the purpose of selling sex, that three sex workers in Canada brought to a charter challenge in 2007. The argument was simple: if one was legally permitted to be a sex worker, one should have access to safe working conditions.

Reaching back further in Canadian history, nineteenth-century prostitution laws "took three distinct approaches" (Backhouse 1985, 387). Legislators and social reformers

> Attempted to regulate the trade in sexuality through a Canadian Contagious Diseases Act, which sought to control venereal disease in prostitutes. They attempted to prohibit the commercial sale of sex through systemic criminal enactments meant to abolish all features of prostitution, from the selling and buying of sexual services to the procuring, pimping and profiteering from the business. They attempted to rehabilitate prostitutes and would-be prostitutes by establishing asylums, women's prisons and juvenile detention institutions. None of these approaches was ultimately successful and each worked substantial injustice upon individual prostitutes (387).[2]

A body circumscribed by criminal laws that are ceaseless and mutable exists in a state of perpetual submission to this institutionalized criminality, and by virtue, in a state of ritualistic and unrealistic wishful thinking. For example, sex workers might believe, "if I ask the client if he's a cop he has to say he is" or "police officers are not allowed to have sex with us as a means of entrapment." Clients also perform their own rituals as they face uncertain exchanges: checking websites that include reviews of workers, following them on social media to ensure they are who they say they are. This type of identity checking has recently become increasingly more difficult as a result of The Stop Enabling Sex Traffickers Act and Allow States and Victims to Fight Online Sex Trafficking Act (SESTA-FOSTA), which "established a criminal liability for websites that operate a 'facility or means of interstate or foreign commerce … with the intent to promote or facilitate the prostitution of another person,' leading many websites like Instagram and Tumblr to remove all adult content to avoid prosecution" (Tichenor 2020, 102). In 2018, sex workers universally lost access to Backpage.com by powerful American anti-sex work lobbyists, including now-vice-president Kamala Harris. This was their most affordable and widely read online advertising platform. These initiatives were widely framed as an attempt to prevent trafficking for the purpose of sexual exploitation and like all initiatives that are framed as an attempt to prevent trafficking for the purpose of sexual exploitation, they had a deeply negatively impact on sex workers everywhere, including in Canada.[3] Though roundly criticized even by anti-trafficking organizations, they came into effect in July of 2018 and had an immediately devastating impact: "Within one month of SESTA-FOSTA's passage, thirteen sex workers were reported missing, and two had committed suicide. The law also placed many independent online workers at risk of exposure to law enforcement due to technology companies' use of facial recognition and other tools for taking punitive anti-trafficking measures aiming to abolish prostitution" (102).

Given ongoing state control over the presence and movement of sex workers and their clients and how dualistically, their lives are determined by the "administrative apparatus" (Namaste et al. 2012, 37), institutional ethnography provides a serviceable framework to analyze and interpret data in this study. As Walby argues, institutional ethnography "is neither a theory nor a methodological technique per se; it is more like an agenda for inquiry that is guided by particular theoretical and methodological commitments" (2013, 141). It "treats people not as the object of analysis but as an entry point into understanding organisational processes" (132).

Institutional ethnography also seeks to reveal, "how people's experience of the everyday social world is structured by larger institutional relations" that "affect our everyday experience of the world" (Namaste et al. 2012, 35). It "is a project wherein matters of knowledge are central and where one examines the intimate connections between specific forms of knowledge and ruling" (39). Specific methods differ, but may "include interviews, analysis of policy documents, and participant observation of relevant sites" (39). Critical discourse analysis is also a guiding approach in this chapter, as "discourse figures alongside bodily behaviour in constituting particular ways of being, particular social, or personal identities" (Fairclough 2003, 27).

SOURCES USED AS QUALITATIVE RESEARCH AND LITERATURE REVIEW

The material used in this chapter to investigate the "John Be Gone" list from an institutional ethnographic and critical discourse analysis perspective includes local and national media reports on the arrests in Sydney, governmental reports on substance use and sub-populations, judicial transcripts, and personal communication with attorney T.J. McKeough, who represented several of the men charged. Parker Donham, a reporter in Cape Breton who attended one trial and who lives close to Sydney, also provided valuable information.

The study is informed by scholarship on lists that includes Werbin's *The List Serves* (2008), research on shame as a deterrent for crime (Harvard Law Review Association 2003), Erving Goffman's pivotal studies on stigma (1963), and Judith Butler's theories on grievable lives (2009). It includes the historical and current framing of Indigenous women[4] within the context of the Canadian Criminal Code and sex work (Hunt 2013, 2015–16), as well as evidence gathered by sex worker rights organizations, specifically but not limited to, post-PCEPA law enforcement interventions (Canadian Alliance for Sex Work Law Reform 2014, 2017a, 2017b). It is also supported by the community-based research of Elene Lam. Lam is the executive director of Butterfly: The Asian and Migrant Sex Worker Support Network, a community-based group that organizes with and provides support to over 5,000 Asian workers who work in massage parlours and the sex industry across Canada. Butterfly includes permanent residents, refugees, and non-status women.[5]

Over the past four years I have also been employing Google Maps Street View searches in both my creative and scholarly research on the built environment and sex worker presence. Many urban, suburban, and rural spaces have been documented by this technology since 2007. A virtual slider in the top left-hand corner of the Google Map Street View allows one to view changes in a neighbourhood, now over a period of fourteen years. As neighbourhoods become more gentrified (inevitably leading to the removal of street-involved populations and economies), one may see adult-related commerce literally slide into more "family- and student-friendly" businesses, and condominiums. A Google Map Street View search of the neighbourhood related to the "John Be Gone" investigation (specifically in September of 2015)[6] was employed as a means of getting a sense of the locations cited in news articles. A thorough examination showed no obvious sex trade. It is difficult to ascertain whether this documentation was made before or after the arrests – Google Map Street View only offers the month of documentation, not specific dates. Various signs advertising bands and food specials suggested documentation took place around 5 September 2015.

Still, from an experiential sex worker perspective, it is clear why this area would appeal to street-engaged women. Multiple parking lots behind buildings and overgrown former lots provide suitable space to provide vehicle or alfresco service while still be close enough to human activity to feel safe. One thing that stood out was the presence of a YMCA (399 Charlotte Street), which offers childcare, within criminalizing proximity of the offending activity. The current laws would permit police to arrest women for working in this vicinity. Indeed, Regional Chief of Police Peter McIsaac stated that surveillance and attempts at moving the trade out began three years ago, but that the current group of women was particularly difficult to remove (CTV Atlantic 2015). Given their refusal to leave, using the new legal rhetoric of exploitation was, it may be argued, significantly advantageous to their expulsion. McIsaac himself stated that surveillance and attempts at moving the trade out began three years ago, but that the current group of women was particularly difficult to remove (ibid.). Given their refusal to leave, using the new legal rhetoric of exploitation was, it may be argued, significantly advantageous to their expulsion.

"There are enduring lessons to be drawn about moral accountability in the face of modern bureaucracy," Bowker and Star argue, regarding devastating race classification and reclassification under South African apartheid (2000, 196). As an early career scholar who will be regularly conducting research with human subjects – specifically sex workers and their clients – I am also attempting to model in this chapter a more ethical way to study and distribute data that was obtained and circulated deceitfully. In this case, and again from an experiential perspective,[7] this means not publishing the names, ages, and neighbourhoods of people whose social circumstances have been made more challenging by the dissemination of this list. *The Tri-Council Policy Statement on Ethical Conduct for Research Involving Humans* makes this claim:

> The welfare of a person is the quality of that person's experience of life in all its aspects. Welfare consists of the impact on individuals of factors such as their physical, mental and spiritual health, as well as their physical, economic and social circumstances. Thus, determinants of welfare can include housing, employment, security, family life, community membership, and social participation, among other aspects of life. Other contributing factors to welfare are privacy and the control of information about the person, and the treatment of human biological materials according to the free, informed and ongoing consent of the person who was the source of the information or materials. A person's or group's welfare is also affected by the welfare of those who are important to them (Secretariat on Responsible Conduct of Research 2018, 7–8).

Though *The Tri-Council Policy Statement on Ethical Conduct for Research Involving Humans* (specifically the test required to receive one's certification) could use a more nuanced analysis of sex working populations and vulnerability, it provides the standard by which we, as academics working with human subjects, measure our interactions as ethical. While I have not interviewed these men personally, using their stories indirectly may cause them additional harm.[8] Moreover, several have themselves identified the publication of their arrests as personally damaging (*R. v.* ████ 2016; McKeough 2018). Though it may be argued that "most people who observe a shaming penalty fail to link its imposition to the offender's identity because they have no preconceived idea of who the offender is," and that that this chapter itself "may be responsible for stimulating interest" (Harvard Law Review Association 2003, 2196), this is a standard I would like to set in my research going forward.

That the sources and literature review contain little direct experiential research conducted with clients themselves post PCEPA, speaks to a dearth of scholarship on the topic. Though there is ample research that centres clients' experiences directly (Atchison 2010; Bernstein 2007; Blevins and Holt 2009; Brown 2011; Milrod and Weitzer 2012), as Khan notes, much of it "is based on interviews and empirically driven to get at *the truth* [her emphasis] of the male client demographic, or it looks only peripherally at the construction of the male client in legal and popular discourses" (2015, 14). Bernstein argues that "drawing on field data and interviews, qualitative researchers have generated typologies of clients and consumer motivations" (2007, 131). My research looks at the typologies generated by the institutions of criminal law, law enforcement, and media, pre- and post-PCEPA.

Like Khan's, my project focuses "on the male client as a construct whose significance has legal and political effects" (2015, 14). Where Khan interrogates "*the regulation and representation* [her emphasis] of male clients in both law and culture" and "explores how these two fields interact" (14), I question how their regulation and representation are contingent on the new legal paradigm of sex worker as victim. I argue that this provides a means of maintaining the criminalization of sex work through a care model that masks harm. I believe it is imperative that the current criminalization of clients through the current reframing of sex workers as "exploited" be more thoroughly analyzed, and weighed against the principles of those who implemented it. For example, at a senate hearing for Bill C-36 (now known as PCEPA), Senator Donald Neil Plett made this comment: "And so, Miss Pacey,[9] well I think maybe both of you have talked a number of times about how this is making it more dangerous for prostitutes. Well of course we don't want to make life safe for prostitutes, we want to do away with prostitution. That's the intent of the bill" ("Plett" 2014). One would be hard-pressed to find a more transparent admission as to the purpose of the new laws, and the violent impact they are intended to have on sex workers.

THE "JOHN BE GONE" LIST

Regional Chief of Police Peter McIsaac stated in media reports that his department was encouraged to deal with sex workers in Sydney after businesspeople in the downtown core complained about prostitution activity taking place in front of their stores (Shannon 2015).

Initial reports have McIsaac stating that charges had been "laid against female prostitutes in 'three or four' instances over the past several months" and that "If we have enough evidence, we're certainly going to lay charges in every instance that we can because we can't have this kind of activity happening on the main street of our municipality" (ibid.).

Within a few days of the first articles, McIsaac stated that clients would be the ones targeted and that the police force would "be trying everything in our power to identify those individuals" (CTV *Atlantic* 2015). And they did: since 8 September 2015, the list of men apprehended during "John Be Gone" has been accessible online, on various news outlets, and on the Sydney police website itself. Ensuing details about the cases must be obtained through more thorough research (*Cape Breton Post* 2015, 2017a, 2017b, 2017c; McKeough 2018). To wit: six men paid fines of $693.95 immediately and were required to submit a DNA sample to yet another list, the national DNA registry.[10] Five men had their charges dismissed, two men were found not guilty, and one left the country and will be arrested if he re-enters Canada. The remaining thirteen were found guilty after hearings and forced to pay fines ranging from $500.00 to $693.95, along with providing a DNA sample to the national DNA registry. One of these men took his case further, claiming that the use of a "police officer to pose as a prostitute to enforce section 286.1(1) of the Criminal Code and in holding a press conference announcing the names, ages and places of residence of those charged, constitutes an abuse of the criminal justice process," and that this infringed his rights under s. 7 of the Charter of Rights and Freedoms (*R. v.* ██████ 2016). The accused man described the press conference as a "public shaming" by the police and contends that this was an abuse of process. "The accused, age ██, in his testimony on the *Voir Dire*, stated he had never used a prostitute before. He testified that as far as he was concerned it was entrapment. He told the court that his wife and friends found out by "word of mouth" of his being charged by the police when it appeared in the local newspaper" (*R. v.* ██████ 2016).

This man lost his case, but the sustained deployment of the new legal category of the sex worker as victim in his case file and in press interviews with McIsaac toward the fall of 2015 is instructive in building an understanding of this particular list as a deterrent for those seeking sexual services (and by extension those providing them) in downtown Sydney and beyond. As with home-addressed letters sent to men caught driving through neighbourhoods where sex work is known to take place (Khan 2015), the apparent goal of this list was "to produce a docile body, inculcating the panoptic fear that the next time the suspect" or any other potential client, "cruises for sex work, he will likely find himself again under the police gaze" (21). In essence this list attempts to produce a docile body by displaying ones that have been deemed abusive. A press interview (Gyapong 2017) with PCEPA supporter and former Conservative MP Joy Smith quotes her as saying, "The fact that they were shamed, well that's too bad," and "What are they are doing behind the backs of their wives? So they are caught and they feel ashamed." Smith praises, "the police for doing their job" and that this will "save countless lives of young girls."

Lists must be understood in the context "of the specific temporal, cultural, political, and moral setting in which they occur" (Lynch 2002, 531) and indeed, it is the recent reclassification of the sex worker in the Criminal Code as exploited that has made the "John Be Gone" list what it is: a registry of abusers. How else to describe someone who attempts to engage the services of someone who is now legislatively defined as exploited? This exploited person, up until nine months prior to these stings, was legally construed as a nuisance, but as Butler argues, "content is framed by shifting time and place" (2009, 10–11). New conditions are established to achieve new goals by provoking "astonishment, outrage, revulsion" (11) and subsequently, demarcating public disgrace. "Some power manipulates the terms of appearance and one cannot break out of the frame; one is framed, which means one is accused, but also judged in advance, without valid evidence and without any obvious means of redress" (11). Setting aside issues with the measures employed to create and disseminate the list, there are, in fact, seven men who were found not guilty or had their charges dismissed who remain on this list, without amendment. Regardless of ensuing convictions, they all continue to be framed with the same disgracing intentionality by association. Though McIsaac argued that they, "didn't publish the names to shame anyone," and that, "once the formal information is sworn before the court, that name becomes public knowledge," he also stated that, "by the very nature of the offence, there is a certain amount of public shame that comes with it. If that acts as a deterrent moving forward, so be it" (CBC News 2015). In fact, however, it is by the very nature of this action being *named* an offense that there is a certain amount of public shame expected to occur with it. These men have been strategically communicated as offenders. The state-produced identity of abuser and subsequent discourse of antipathy used by lawmakers, politicians, media, and anti-trafficking advocates circulates the image of the client as shameful, not worthy of respect.

SHAMEABLE LIVES

Butler asks "when is life grievable?" (2009), and argues that "specific lives cannot be apprehended as injured or lost if they are not first apprehended as living. If certain lives do not qualify as lives or are, from the start, not conceivable as lives within certain epistemological frames, then these lives are never lived nor lost in the full sense" (1). Prior to this recent framing, sex workers were not institutionally situated as grievable beings. This is illustrated by decades of persuasive documentation recounting apathetic to violent to deadly exchanges between law enforcement and sex workers (Ferris 2015; Gwendolyn 1990; Network of Sex Work Projects 2015). This documentation is now being collected in the post-PCEPA context both in Canada and in other countries where similar laws exist, such as Sweden, Norway, France, and Northern Ireland. One may ask how is this new label of "victim" any different than the former one of "nuisance"? It is still a form of discrimination, which positions law enforcement as the administrators of sex workers as people without agency: "The initial response by the Cape Breton Regional Police to complaints about prostitution in the downtown Sydney area was to generally treat it as a nuisance problem and try to move it away from the complaint area. As the police talked to the sex trade workers they became increasingly aware of the hardships, stigma and violence to which they were exposed. The Police Community Safety Unit, headed by Sgt Jodie Wilson, came to see first-hand how these workers, who were largely aboriginal, were often disadvantaged and vulnerable along race, economic and gender lines" (*R. v.* █████ 2016, 17).

It is difficult to believe that the Cape Breton Regional Police Department was unaware – prior to talking to local, largely Indigenous sex trade workers – that they suffered immense violence and stigma. It is equally difficult to conceive that they would be unaware that this violence and stigma was often overlooked and facilitated by their own confreres. One of the most famous and widely publicized cases about police indifference to sex workers in recent history is that of a serial killer who preyed on street-based sex workers on Vancouver's downtown east side for decades (Hunt 2015–16). McIsaac himself was listed as a contributor to a handbook published in 2012 by the Canadian government that glibly connects sex work, Indigeneity, and drug use. The handbook highlights "promising practices in integrated approaches to policing substance users" (Public Safety Canada 2012, 2), including an initiative that McIsaac headed up.

The sudden mobilization of the grievable lives of sex workers by juridico-disciplinary institutions is disingenuous. It is worth considering that the police in Cape Breton were precipitously using words like "vulnerable" and "marginalized" to describe sex workers, and the work they were performing alongside this was being foregrounded both in media and in judicial documents:

> The police sought and received specialized training on the new prostitution offences, on human trafficking and on undercover operations. The police then employed improved policing techniques by offering the women strategies and information regarding community treatment programs for addictions, mental health and abuse suffered by them. The police also offered supportive relationships with them to promote future contacts and safety planning including information about potentially violent johns. The new legislation, for the most part, decriminalizes prostitutes in recognition of their marginalized and vulnerable positions and criminalizes the johns who buy, or attempt to buy, and the pimps and human traffickers who exploit, and profit from, coercing women into the sex trade. As the police learned more about the dangers to which these women were exposed, they came to the conclusion that they could no longer use a "band-aid" approach to the problem. The new law had shifted the focus away from the women who were seen as victims to the johns and pimps on the demand and exploitative side. (*R. v.* ■■■■ 2016)

Expanding on Butler's concept of an ungrievable life, I ask "when is a life shameable?" When is a life so deprived of merit that it is fit for public defamation? What institutional mechanisms are put in place for this to occur? How are lists then used both to construct and circulate a shameable life? "How does the list serve to fracture threatening populations, and at the same time act as the primary instrument for their management and policing?" (Werbin 2008, 32). By extension, whose lives are denoted as exploited and used as acceptable collateral in the shaming of those with whom they associate? Is a life shameable in the service of the subterfugic criminalization of another life? And finally, from a social and legal standpoint, is there value in using shame as a deterrent for purchasing sexual services?

Central to the above questions is the qualification of and right to both public and private space. Lynch contends that policymaking around sexual predation "is not simply motivated by a rational drive to manage the risk posed by this class of offenders, but rather it is seeped in a constellation of emotional expressions of disgust, fear of contagion, and pollution avoidance, manifested in a legislative concern about boundary vulnerabilities between social spheres of the pure and the dangerous" (2004, 532). This disgust, ciphered through the new institutionalized construct of exploiter foisted on clients, is one step in ensuring that their presence in public space will be carefully monitored: "Because of the emotional power of disgust – it is strongly felt both physically and psychologically – its influence on the social order can be dramatic" (Lynch 2004, 539). Offsetting this with the many media reports focusing on police officers building trust with exploited women provides an excellent emotional counterbalance. Subsequently, community members are interpellated as valuable, caring citizens through initiatives such as "Say Something If You See Something," instituted by the Cape Breton Regional Police in January of 2017:

> Police officers in Nova Scotia are equipping their communities with tools to help identify potential victims of human trafficking and sexual exploitation. It's part of the "Say Something If You See Something" education and awareness campaign, aimed at employees in the hospitality and transportation industries. Human trafficking and sexual exploitation takes place in all kinds of properties, from budget motels to luxury hotels and resorts, and air and ground transportation is often used to carry out these criminal acts. For those reasons, employees in these industries can play a positive role in preventing these offences, by reporting their concerns to police. (Kent 2017)

These tools include pamphlets with lists of "signs to watch out for" that are often overbroad and easily misread. This type of community surveillance that interpellates people through concern is identified as highly problematic by organizations that support Asian and migrant sex workers, who, again, are often viewed by the public as trafficked and/or exploited from the outset (butterflysw.org). In Montreal, police operations like RADAR (implemented in 2019) tells hotel staff to keep an eye on "out-of-ordinary behaviours" such as "a large amount of condoms left in a room after somebody checked out or people that stay in their rooms for several days without leaving" (CBC News 2019). These initiatives, which included raids on strip-clubs where twenty to thirty police officers arrived, lined women up asked for their identification, and documented their tattoos and piercings, are widely condemned by organizations like Stella, l'amie de Maimie. Sandra Wesley, the organization's executive director, stated police "stamped their wrists when they were done," and "said they were creating a database" (Maratta 2019).

Werbin describes "milieus of circulation" where "good circulation was intended to be maximized and bad circulation was intended to be diminished and nullified through mathematical and statistical techniques involving calculations, probabilities, risk assessments, and the delimitation of populations" (2008, 21): "On the one hand, it delimits a class called 'threat,' carving out the fundamental caesuras of 'us' and 'them,' on the other hand, the list serves as the primary instrument for the identification and policing of the movement of the very threats it contains; all the while self-elaborating itself in the 'truthful' fabrication of threatening 'facts'" (2008, 27). To reiterate, within the institutional scope of local and mass media, these police investigations were enacted using the very recent constitutional interpretation of street involved sex workers as "vulnerable" and "exploited." Sarah Hunt's research with Indigenous street-involved women and colonial law provides an important entry point of reflection into this current interpretation. As Hunt argues, regarding research she had completed prior to the implementation of PCEPA, "because women in Vancouver's Downtown Eastside and other urban centres are socio-legally constructed as non-citizens or "less-than" as a result of their supposedly degenerate status – seen as impoverished sex workers, drug addicts, and racialized – they are rendered outside of society" (2015–16, 33). The technical paper preceding PCEPA, written by then-Justice Minister Peter MacKay, the architect of the current laws, proposed, "law reform that would signal a significant shift in prostitution-related criminal law policy from treatment of prostitution as a nuisance toward treatment of prostitution for what it is: a form of exploitation" (*Technical Paper* 2014). The technical paper also claimed that "the impact of the new prohibitions would be borne predominantly by those who purchase sex and persons who exploit others through prostitution" and were intended to "reduce the demands for prostitution, which disproportionately impact on society's most marginalized and vulnerable." Currently, all women who engage in sex work for trade or money are now named by the Canadian legal system as exploited, with Indigenous women marked as especially "marginalized and vulnerable." This is arguably little more than a paternalistic version of "less-than."

As Bowker and Star argue, "political and socially charged agendas are often first presented as purely technical and they are difficult even to see. As layers of classification system become enfolded into a working infrastructure, the original political intervention becomes more and more firmly entrenched. In many cases, this leads to a naturalization of the political category, through a process of convergence" (2000, 96). Nine months after their implementation, the wording crafted by MacKay was being mobilized at every turn in the investigation that produced the "John Be Gone" list. Judge Brian Williston, who presided over the charges laid on the twenty-seven men, stated: "The police actions were a legitimate response to a need to protect society's most *marginalized and vulnerable* [my emphasis] members in focusing their attention on the men driving demand. As well, the effort by the police in disseminating information to the sex trade workers on safety issues, social services, drug and alcohol rehabilitation and treatment programs related to abuse, is encouraging" (*R. v.* 2016, 17).

As Pratt argues, "The relation between the production of citizenship and the state's sovereignty over life is therefore not incidental but productive and fundamental" (2005, 1053). The state's production of all sex worker citizens as vulnerable is indeed a productive status: it hinders them from working, as it is work that PCEPA argues renders them vulnerable. "Inclusion within the law as sex workers is simultaneously an act of exclusion" (2005, 1059). Though Pratt made this claim nine years prior to the enactment of PCEPA, it supports the argument that these laws are circular and episodic. Though sex workers are not legally construed as a nuisance, they remain under the constraint of criminal laws: a nuisance by proxy, a nuisance that must be eliminated.

As presented above, the police in Cape Breton, along with Judge Brian Williston who presided over cases, bring forward evidence that sex workers are now experiencing a more trusting relationship with them. Conversely, evidence gathered universally by sex worker rights organizations shows that law enforcement support of and exchanges with sex workers has always been measured by sex workers with great caution, as these efforts often prove to be little more than methods of violent deception (Network of Sex Work Projects 2015). Pertaining to law enforcement interactions post-PCEPA, The Canadian Alliance for Sex Work Law Reform states that between 11–15 October 2017, "police forces across Canada conducted their yearly raids" (2017b, 1) on sex worker establishments such as hotels and homes. These raids were "intrusive and intimidating" and were conducted "under the auspices of an anti-trafficking initiative" (1). The communications,

> Begin with a male or female police officer posing as a client and booking an appointment with a sex worker. Several police officers then appear at the sex worker's place of work, ostensibly to ensure that no coercion is taking place, but with the impact of intimidating sex workers, violating their right to privacy and putting their confidentiality and safety at risk. Sex workers across Canada who are victims to this Operation also report feeling confused, frightened, stressed and traumatized after these interactions with police, followed by intense feelings of mistrust in the overall police system. (1)

Further, the alliance argues that "Operation Northern Spotlight has also undermined sex workers' health and safety. To avoid the greater scrutiny and law enforcement surveillance, interrogation, harassment, detention, deportation and arrest associated with such campaigns, sex workers are forced to work in greater isolation and secrecy, reducing their capacity to earn money and their ability to negotiate safer working conditions with clients and with third parties" (1). Sex workers maintain that the "provision that makes no distinction between clients and perpetrators of violence" is not only incorrect, "but also extremely harmful, as it trivializes actual violence when it does occur" (Alliance 2017a, 37).

According to Pratt, "The state administers the health of the national body through and in the name of the health of individual bodies" (2005, 1056). When sex workers are named as harmed rather than harmful, they have essentially been legally divested of their physical autonomy, placing them in the context of "the victim trope, so familiar in justifications for colonialism and echoed in 'interventions' by dominant groups 'for their own good.'" This trope can be, "used as yet another silencing strategy" (Hunt 2015–16, 34). Again, in all documents related to the "John Be Gone" list, no sex workers were interviewed directly. Police and the presiding judge state that they were too frightened to make direct statements, because of "retaliation from johns and pimps." Yet when reported from the perspective of sex workers in a climate where their clients are criminalized, it is law enforcement that is often perceived as retaliatory: "In a survey of Asian sex workers in Toronto and Vancouver, 95 per cent of respondents indicated that they never seek help from law enforcement – even if they experience violence, abuse, harassment or exploitation. In Toronto, not a single respondent indicated that they trusted the police" (Canadian Alliance for Sex Work Law Reform 2017b, 1).

As Hunt argues, "If sex workers or Indigenous women always need others to speak for them in order to legitimize their appeals to law, their marginal status will remain intact" (2015–16, 34). The new reassessment of sex workers as "exploited" rather than "nuisance" continues to enforce this marginalization while doing little to prevent in any meaningful way what is disparagingly referred to as "demand" by sex work prohibitionists. For example, twelve years after the Sex Purchasers Act was enacted in Sweden (this is the model that PCEPA is based upon), studies show that client criminalization has done little to protect sex workers, particularly those who are street-involved: "When the law was introduced, there were voices in the debate in Sweden that expressed concern that sex work may move underground, and that sex work could become more dangerous. Those in favour of the law said that there would not be negative impacts, and since the law criminalised only clients, sex workers would be shielded from harm. This has not been the case. The reality is that sex workers face increasing difficulties"(NSWP 2015). As the Canadian Alliance for Sex Work Law Reform argues, "Despite its stated intentions, the Swedish model does not reduce, much less eliminate, prostitution. This is supported by the three Swedish government reports affirming that the sex industry has not diminished but been displaced to more isolated spaces" (2014, 1).

SHAME AND CRIMINALITY AS DETERRENTS FOR THE PURCHASE OF SEXUAL SERVICES

"The Greeks, who were apparently strong on visual aids, originated the term *stigma* to refer to bodily signs designed to expose something unusual or bad about the moral status of the signifier. The signs were cut or burned into the body and advertised that the bearer was a slave, a criminal, or a traitor – a blemished person, ritually polluted, to be avoided especially in public" (Goffman 1963, 1). When the issue of public shaming in the case of the "John Be Gone" list was raised both by Canadian Civil Liberties representatives and one of the men charged, Janine Benedet, a University of British Columbia law professor lawyer, an anti-sex work advocate and a vocal supporter of PCEPA argued, "We now have a very clear law in Canada that obtaining or offering to obtain sexual services for consideration is a criminal offence. And so, if that's what it is that these men are looking for, then they are breaking the law" (Weeks 2016).

As Khan states, "Those who criminalize and discipline clients do not just gather information, but also package and perform this constructed knowledge to accomplish ideological, political, and latently perverse goals (2015, 12). Formerly, this entailed John School, which is comprised exclusively of "men were busted in sting operations on the street" (11). Attendees would be streamed into John School through the courts if they chose to plead guilty, the cost of which was five hundred dollars. Khan attended one for research and provides this description: "A police officer equates all prostitution with sex trafficking; a sexual health nurse shows menacing slides with close ups of herpes and genital warts; a recovering sex addict invites the men to view their behaviour as a mental health problem; a community representative admonishes the men for bringing prostitution into 'decent' neighbourhoods; a client's wife bemoans the destruction of her marriage because of her husband's infidelity; and a former prostitute narrates how drugs, abuse, and poverty – not choice – drove her into the trade" (11).

Though this was costly, meant taking time off work, and took the same shame-based approach as the current model, their names were not revealed in easily circulated media documents. Men could attend John School and additionally have their charges expunged.

Benedet argues that the sting operation, "doesn't meet the legal definition of entrapment" because "entrapment really involves a situation in which the police orchestrate and convince otherwise law-abiding citizens to commit a crime" (Weeks 2016). Additionally, "entrapment can only be argued after an accused has been found guilty of an offence charged and not before" (*R. v.* ████ 2016, 19). McIsaac also argued that the entrapment interpretation was unfair, and that revealing names was something his police force did in all large investigations (Weeks 2016). This is quantifiably untrue. The Cape Breton Regional Police Force website has media releases for all its investigations and at least one large investigation does not name all those arrested and charged (Cape Breton Regional Police 2017).

In one article, McIsaac was paraphrased as saying the list was meant to act "as a deterrent for others" (King 2015). This is a phrase to which I want to draw attention: "A deterrent for others." Post-colonial theorists such as Edward Said (1977) have long articulated the powerful concept of the Other. The men on this list, now constituted as "other," provide strong symbolic representation to those who now know the penalty by association. The list provides "the junction between that which is perceived as real, and the consequences of that perception." (Bowker and Star 2000, 224). Effective shaming strategies must involve "communicating the status of an offender to a large audience" (Harvard Law Review Association 2003, 2194) and though it may seem that "modern communities are simply too diffuse and complex for shaming penalties to create an effective link between the imposition of shame and the identity of the offender" (2194), the list these men appear on, again, is available online forever. The numbers of institutions that have now reached into their lives as a result of their actions is astonishing: law enforcement, the legal system, the national DNA database and the media, and now academia. How will this impact them? "Although most of the people whom the shamed offender encounters in daily life will be ignorant of his stigmatized identity, the offender nonetheless constantly faces the possibility that some know his 'true' status. Every time he applies for a new job, meets a new love interest, or even engages in a conversation at a party, he will have to decide whether to hide his true identity. It is this discreditable identity with which the shamed offender must struggle, and it is here that the implications of shaming penalties are most likely to manifest themselves" (Harvard Law Review Association 2003, 2194–5). This alienation "may further criminal behavior by alienating offenders from their communities and steering them toward criminal subcultures" (2195). Again, studies done in Sweden, where the model that criminalizes clients has been in place since 1999, show that trade has simply moved to less detectable spaces in order to avoid the disciplinary gaze of law enforcement. In Northern Ireland, where sex work is guided by the Human Trafficking and Exploitation (Criminal Justice and Support for Victims) Act, research "has concluded it is unclear that criminalisation will change the behaviour of male purchasers, many of whom thought that their actions were already illegal" (Network of Sex Work Projects 2015). A recent study states that most sex workers "interviewed reveal that the criminalisation of clients has in practice been more detrimental to themselves than the previous laws against soliciting" (4). This includes "increased impoverishment, especially among people already living precariously" (4).

Meanwhile, in Sydney, journalist Parker Donham says, "the very low-end trade that flourished on Charlotte Street has pretty much dried up. At least, it's no longer obvious to me" (Donham 2018). But where has it gone?

Khan, borrowing from Foucault, states that "laws against sex work do not repress pleasure or instinct; instead, the prohibitions incite new articulations of sexuality" (2015, 12). An example of this in the current prohibitive climate would be sex worker led mobilization around SESTA-FOSTA, signed into law on 11 April 2018 and making "any website that hosts third party content liable for 'knowing conduct' that could 'assist, support or facilitate' sex trafficking" (Wolbers 2017). "Sex workers from Australia quickly built a social media platform hosted out of Australia called Switter. As of 8 April 2018, Switter had close to twenty thousand members, many expressing relieved gratitude at this new option by and for sex workers and their allies. Vital advocacy groups like SWOP behind Bars, which services imprisoned sex workers with book programs, pen pals, and post-incarceration clothing, gift cards and cell phones, moved their website hosting out of the United States" (Tigchelaar 2018, 5). What we may garner from this is that prohibitions incite new articulations of both separation and connectivity. Regardless of prohibitions, sex workers will continue to work.

CONCLUSION

When considering the deployment of the new sex work laws in Canada and how local law enforcement are using them, one may return to Backhouse's words regarding nineteenth century Canadian sex work laws: "None of these approaches was ultimately successful and each worked substantial injustice upon individual prostitutes." There is established evidence that the decriminalization of the sex trade makes work safer for sex workers. More importantly, it is what sex workers want. With women who trade sex for commodities or money viewed solely as desperate or exploited, it is important to look to the institutional frameworks that draw them into the criminal law system to begin with, that brand their bodies and those with whom they do business criminal entities. We must be circumspect about what it means to put bodies on lists, and consider the multiple cautionary histories of this inclination, and the impact this has on those listed. "Like with statistics, the list serves to materialize populations, and at the same time, in materializing populations it provides a way of delimiting and policing the movement of risks and threats to populations, through disciplinary normalization" (Werbin 2008, 27).

The power to deprive someone of civil rights arises from the institutionalized power to name someone civil or uncivil: "The dominant discursive framework in Canada is shaped by an adversarial parliamentary and legal system and a debate approach to moral and political issues, as well as sensationalist and conflict driven mass media. These approaches encourage the belief that there are always two and only two sides to every issue. We are encouraged to vilify villains and rescue victims. Complex issues are oversimplified and forced into a pro and con structure framed by familiar and equally over-simplified moral and political questions" (Davies 2015, 79). The "vilify villains and rescue victims" narrative "is always given over to others, to norms, to social and political organizations that have developed historically in order to maximize precariousness for some and minimize precariousness for others" (Butler 2009, 2–3). McKeough himself describes the whole case (including the fines, whose monetary value suggested that the offences did not occur in a public place) as "ridiculous" (McKeough 2018).

In June 2022, two years after the deadline they were given to produce it, the House of Commons Standing Committee on Justice and Human Rights released the report "Preventing Harm in the Sex Industry: A Review of the Protection of Communities and Exploited Persons Act." The committee held a series of hearings, which included the testimony of sex workers, their allies, and those ideologically devoted to the complete prohibition of sex work. As reported by the Canadian Alliance for Sex Work Law Reform "While certain recommendations in the report address issues of concern to sex workers, the report has serious and dangerous shortcomings: namely its failure to break from Canada's ongoing use of criminalization as the primary tool for addressing sex work at the expense of sex workers' safety, autonomy and equality" (Canadian Alliance for Sex Work Law Reform 2022). Additionally, the report does not acknowledge the hostile and negative presence of police in the lives of sex workers who suffer the worst repercussions of anti-sex work immigration laws and criminalization.

As of October 2022, Canadian sex workers are once again returning to court to sue their government for failure to protect their constitutional rights. On the list of plaintiffs are the twenty-five sex-worker led and allied organizations across Canada that make up the alliance, as well as half a dozen other individuals.

NOTES

1 The communicating offense prior to PCEPA modifications put the criminal onus both on sex worker and client, but more often sex workers were charged (Rotenberg 2016, 4). They were also not legally situated as "exploited." This reframing changes the tone and criminality of the charge significantly.

2 Velma Demerson writes in depth about how this injustice continued in early to mid-twentieth century Canada in her book *Incorrigible* (2004). Demerson was imprisoned in an institution in 1939 for living with her Asian boyfriend. While institutionalized, Demerson, along with women accused of prostitution crimes, were subject to non-consensual experiments that Demerson believes were related to the contagion and treatment of venereal diseases.

3 Even sex workers in New Zealand where sex work has been "relatively incorporated" into the country's conventional labour force, felt the repressive measures, reporting a rollback of workers' rights they had not experienced since sex work was decriminalized there in 2003 (Tichenor 2020, 108).

4 Statistics offered by the police state that 80 per cent of the women were Indigenous and drug using.

5 Elene Lam has observed through over five years of research that 30 per cent of women who use the services of Butterfly report violence from the various levels of law enforcement that interfere in their lives

(Butterfly 2022). Lam's research also demonstrates that migrant women who use the services of Butterfly are not the unwitting targets of trafficking for the purpose of sexual exploitation often circulated in multimodal media discourse. Rather, women report the majority of violence they encounter is a result of criminal legislation against migration and sex work, which prevents them from seeking appropriate support, and through the various levels of law enforcement they encounter in their day-to-day. Since 2012, women migrating to Canada as students, visitors, and temporary workers must sign documentation agreeing they will not do sex work in Canada.

6 Google street maps began its documentation of Sydney in 2012, with a three-year gap between the most recent documentation in September of 2015.

7 By this I mean the importance consigned in sex working communities to discretion. If we conduct ethical scholarly work around sex work, I would argue we must respect established sex worker community standards. "Operation John Be Gone was initiated using undercover police officers posing as sex trade workers. The police were not able to use the actual sex trade workers themselves since they were reluctant to participate in prosecutions for fear of reprisals from the johns or pimps. The police utilized trained police officers to minimize any risk of harm to the street workers" (*R. v.* 2016, 18). Given centuries of asymmetrical power relations between police and sex workers, I would prefer to hear from sex workers directly on the matter of publishing client names. Without their direct input, I would argue, as a sex worker, that they would not want names of clients, none of who were charged with violence or robbery, to be revealed.

8 Sex workers are not allowed into the United States. As for convicted clients, T.J. McKeough "looked at the issue of travel to the United States at length, the Judge even did his own research, however no one could give us a straight answer." Prostitution falls under Crimes against Moral Turpitude in that country, "but it is unclear if people convicted under this new law fall under that" (McKeough 2018).

9 Plett is addressing Katrina Pacey, the former executive director of Pivot Legal, which "works in partnership with communities affected by poverty and social exclusion to identify priorities and develop solutions to complex human rights issues." Pivot's "work is focused in four policy areas: police accountability, health and drug policy, homelessness, and sex workers' rights" (Pivot Legal Society 2016).

10 Our attention may be drawn here to Dorothy E. Smith's use of "the metaphor of DNA as a means of illustrating how socially organized knowledge invented by the ruling apparatus in one location becomes packaged in texts and then is replicated either electronically or in hard-copy format in multiple locations as a means of regulating local activities and organizing the working relationships among people" (Deveau 2016, 312–13). McKeough says, "The DNA registry is basically a modernization of fingerprinting. Everyone charged with an offence can be required to give fingerprints but only people convicted of certain offences can be required to give a sample of their DNA. There are two parts to it, offender database and crime scene database. They are constantly matched against each other so when someone new is added they are instantly compared to unmatched samples from crime scenes. Being on the registry has no practical implication unless you committed an unsolved crime in the past or plan to commit more crimes in the future. We have a separate Sex Offender Registry for sex crimes. This offence does not require you to be registered on it" (McKeough 2018).

REFERENCES

Atchison, C. 2010. "Report of the Preliminary Findings for Johns' Voice: A Study of Adult Canadian Sex Buyers." January 2010. https://tinyurl.com/y9rbphax.

Backhouse, C. 1985. "Nineteenth Century Canadian Prostitution Law: Reflection of a Discriminatory Society." *Social History* 18, no. 36: 387–423.

Bernstein, E. 2007. *Temporarily Yours: Intimacy, Authenticity, and the Commerce of Sex*. Chicago: University of Chicago Press.

Blevins, K.R., and T.J. Holt. 2009. "Examining the Virtual Subculture of Johns." *Journal of Contemporary Ethnography* 38, no. 5: 619–48.

Bowker, G., and Leigh Star 2000. *Sorting Things Out: Classification and Its Consequences*. Cambridge, MA: MIT Press.

Brown, C. 2011. *Paying for It: A Comic-strip Memoir about Being a John*. Montreal: Drawn & Quarterly.

Butler, J. 2009. *Frames of War: When is Life Grievable?* London: Verso.

Butterfly. 2022. Asian and Migrant Sex Worker Support Network. https://www.butterflysw.org/legal-information-for-services-prov.

Canadian Alliance for Sex Work Law Reform. 2014. "What Canada Can Learn from Sweden's Laws That Criminalize the Purchase of Sexual Services." https://www.safersexwork.ca/wp-content/uploads/2014/06/WhatCanadacanlearnfrom.pdf.

– 2017a. "Safety, Dignity, Equality: Recommendations for Sex Work Law Reform in Canada." March 2017. http://sexworklawreform.com/wp-content/uploads/2017/05/CASWLR-Final-Report-1.6MB.pdf.

– 2017b. "Turn off the Spotlight: Sex Workers and Allies Urge an End to Operation Northern Spotlight." 19 October 2017. https://www.hivlegalnetwork.ca/site/turn-off-the-spotlight-sex-workers-and-allies-urge-an-end-to-operation-northern-spotlight.

– 2022. "Media Release: Failure to Act: National Sex Workers' Rights Groups Respond to Parliamentary Report on Sex Work Laws." 27 June 2022. https://sexworklawreform.com/media-release-failure-to-act-national-sex-worker-rights-groups-respond-to-parliamentary-report-on-sex-work-laws.

Cape Breton Post. 2015. "Cape Breton Men Fined for Prostitution." 5 October 2017. https://www.saltwire.com/cape-breton/news/local/cape-breton-men-fined-for-prostitution-153323.

– 2017a."Fine Issued to Sydney Man in Prostitution Case." Last updated 2 October 2017. https://www.saltwire.com/cape-breton/news/local/fine-issued-to-sydney-man-in-prostitution-case-14913/

– 2017b. "Sydney Judge Delivers Guilty Verdict in Prostitution Case." Last updated 2 October 2017. https://www.saltwire.com/cape-breton/news/local/sydney-judge-delivers-guilty-verdict-in-prostitution-case-14408.

– 2017c. "Sydney Prostitution Sting Survives Constitutional Challenge." Last updated 2 October 2017. https://www.saltwire.com/cape-breton/news/local/sydney-prostitution-sting-survives-challenge-1366.

Cape Breton Regional Police. 2017. "Media Releases: Police Seize over $200,000 Worth of Drugs, Charge Three." 3 December 2017. https://www.cbrps.ca/police-seize-over-200-000-worth-of-drugs-charge-three.html.

CBC News. 2015. "Sydney Prostitution Crackdown Will Continue, Says Cape Breton Police Chief." 9 September 2015. https://www.cbc.ca/news/canada/nova-scotia/sydney-prostitution-crackdown-will-continue-says-cape-breton-police-chief-1.3220927

– 2019. "Montreal Police Enlist Taxi Drivers, Hotel Staff in Campaign against Sexual Exploitation." 28 May 2019. https://www.cbc.ca/news/canada/montreal/spvm-radar-sexual-exploitation-1.5152323.

CTV *Atlantic*. 2015. "Sydney Business Owners Concerned about Brazen Prostitution." 5 March 2015. https://atlantic.ctvnews.ca/sydney-business-owners-concerned-about-brazen-prostitution-1.2265052.

Davies, J. 2015. "The Criminalization of Sexual Commerce in Canada: Context and Concepts for Critical Analysis." *Canadian Journal of Human Sexuality* 24, no. 2: 78–91.

Demerson, V. 2004. *Incorrigible*. Ontario: WLU Press.

Deveau, J. L. 2016. "Using Institutional Ethnography's Ideological Circle to Portray How Textually Mediated Disability Discourse Paralysed a Supreme Court of CanadaRuling." *Culture and Organization* 22, no. 4: 311–29.

Donham, Parker. 2018. Personal communication via email. 22–3 April 2018.

Fairclough, N. 2003. *Analysing Discourse: Textual Analysis for Social Research*. London: Routledge.

Ferris, Shawna. 2015. *Street Sex Work and Canadian Cities: Resisting a Dangerous Order*. Edmonton: University of Alberta Press.

Goffman, Erving. 1963. *Stigma: Notes on the Management of Spoiled Identity*. New York: Touchstone Edition.

Gwendolyn, dir. 1990. *Prowling by Night*. ONF/NFB. Film.

Gyapong, D. 2017. "Anti-Trafficking Experts Applaud Prostitution Sting." *Catholic Register*, 14 September 2016. https://www.catholicregister.org/item/23082-anti-trafficking-experts-applaud-sydney-prostitution-sting.

Harvard Law Review Association. 2003. "Shame, Stigma, and Crime: Evaluating the Efficacy of Shaming Sanctions in Criminal Law." *Harvard Law Review* 116, no. 7: 2186–207.

Hunt, S. 2013. "Decolonizing Sex Work: Developing an Intersectional Indigenous Approach." In *Selling Sex: Experience, Advocacy, and Research on Sex Work in Canada*, edited by Victoria Love, Elya Durisin, and Emily Van der Meulen, 82–100. Vancouver: UBC Press.

– 2015–16. "Representing Colonial Violence: Trafficking, Sex Work, and the Violence of Law." *Atlantis* 37, no. 2: 25–39.

Kent, B. 2017. "'Say Something If You See Something': Police Press Release." Transition House Association of Nova Scotia. 10 January 2017. https://thans.ca/say-something-see-something-police-press-release.

Khan, U. 2015. "'Johns' in the Spotlight: Anti-Prostitution Efforts and the Surveillance of Clients." *Canadian Journal of Law and Society* 30, no. 1: 9–29.

King, N. 2015. "Prostitution String Nets 27 Charges." *Cape Breton Post*, 9 September 2015. https://www.pressreader.com/canada/cape-breton-post/20150909/281492160092834.

Lowman, J. 1989. *Street Prostitution: Assessing the Impact of the Law, Vancouver*. Ottawa: Department of Justice.

Lynch, M. 2002. "Pedophiles and Cyber-Predators as Contaminating Forces: The Language of Disgust, Pollution, and Boundary Invasions in Federal Debates on Sex Offender Legislation." *Law and Social Inquiry* 27, no. 27: 529–66.

MacDonald, M. 2016. "Cape Breton Prostitution Sting Raises Public Shaming Concerns." CBC News, 1 September 2016. https://www.cbc.ca/news/canada/nova-scotia/cape-breton-prostitution-sting-public-shaming-1.3743981.

Maratta, Alessia Simona. 2019. "'A Violation of Their Basic Rights': Sex Worker Advocacy Group Says Police Violated Their Privacy." Global News, 9 June 2019. https://globalnews.ca/news/5371358/sex-worker-advocacy-group-says-police-violated-privacy.

McKeough, T.J. 2018. Personal communication via email, 17–18 April 2018.

Milrod, C., and R. Weitzer. 2012. "The Intimacy Prism: Emotion Management among the Clients of Escorts." *Men and Masculinities* 15, no. 5: 1–21.

Namaste, Viviane, Tamara Vukov, Nada Saghie, Robin Williamson, Jacky Vallee, Mareva Lafreniere, Marie-Josee Leroux, Andre Monette, and Joseph Jean Gilles. 2012. HIV *Preventions and Bisexual Realities*. Toronto: Toronto University Press.

Network of Sex Work Projects. 2015. "Community Guide: The Real Impact of the Swedish Model on Sex Workers." https://nswp.org/resource/nswp-publications/community-guide-the-real-impact-the-swedish-model-sex-workers.

Pivot Legal Society. 2016. "Our Story." http://www.pivotlegal.org/our_story.

"Plett – We Don't Want to Make Life Safe for Prostitutes." 2014. Posted by sexworker 416 to YouTube. 12 November 2014. https://www.youtube.com/watch?v=q18rMJo1YKw.

Pratt, G. 2005. "Abandoned Women and Spaces of the Exception." *The 2005 AAG Antipode Lecture*. Oxford: Blackwell Publishing.

Protection of Communities and Exploited Persons Act. 2014. Statues of Canada 2014, Chapter 25. https://laws-lois.justice.gc.ca/PDF/2014_25.pdf.

Public Safety Canada. 2012. "Promising Practices in Policing Substance Users: A Handbook of Integrated Models and Practices." https://www.publicsafety.gc.ca/cnt/rsrcs/pblctns/prmsng-prctcs-plcng/prmsng-prctcs-plcng-eng.pdf.

R. v. ████. 2016. NSPC 48. Provincial Court of Nova Scotia.

Rossiter, Kate, and Jen Rinaldi. 2018. *Institutional Violence and Disability: Punishing Conditions*. London: Routledge.

Rotenberg, C. 2016. "Prostitution Offenses in Canada: Statistical Trends." Canadian Centre for Justice Statistics. Last modified 10 November 2016. https://www150.statcan.gc.ca/n1/pub/85-002-x/2016001/article/14670-eng.htm.

Said, Edward. 1977. *Orientalism*. New York: Vintage.

Secretariat on Responsible Conduct of Research. 2018. *Tri-Council Policy Statement on Ethical Conduct for Research Involving Humans*. https://ethics.gc.ca/eng/policy-politique_tcps2-eptc2_2018.html.

Shannon, Chris. 2015. "Sydney Business Owners Say Prostitution Driving Customers Away." *Cape Breton Post*, 3 March 2015. https://www.saltwire.com/cape-breton/news/sydney-business-owners-say-prostitution-driving-customers-away-8449.

Technical Paper: Bill C-36, Protection of Communities and Exploited Persons Act. 2014. https://www.justice.gc.ca/eng/rp-pr/other-autre/protect/p1.html

Tichenor, E. 2020. "'I've Never Been So Exploited': The Consequences of FOSTA-SESTA in Aotearoa New Zealand." *Anti-Trafficking Review* 14: 99–115.

Tigchelaar, Alex. 2018. "Wish You Would Hear: Sex Worker Visibility and Perceptibility from Postcards to the Virtual Space." Unpublished paper for HUMA 889, Concordia University.

Walby, K. 2013. "Institutional Ethnography and Data Analysis: Making Sense of Data Dialogues." *International Journal of Social Research Methodology* 16, no. 2: 141–54.

Weeks, J. 2016. "Sydney Prostitution Sting Subject of Charter Challenge." CBC *News*. 11 February 2016. https://www.cbc.ca/news/canada/nova-scotia/sydney-prostitution-arrest-charter-challenge-1.3442649.

Werbin, K. 2008. *The List Serves: The Apparatuses of Security and Governmentality*. PhD thesis, Concordia University.

Wolbers, Rachel. 2017. "Techfreedom + Engin: How SESTA Fails to Counter Sex Trafficking." Engin. 7 November 2017. https://www.engine.is/news/category/techfreedom-engine-how-sesta-fails-to-counter-sex-trafficking.

11

We Want You to Listen

The Shelter Video Project Collective on Colonial/Capitalist Violence

THE SHELTER VIDEO PROJECT COLLECTIVE: KIM JACKSON, SHIRLEY BERRY, SANDIE GUIGNARD, ASIL LAVOIE, LISA LABLANC, MINUTET NIMA, OPAL SPARKS, MARLENE BLUEBIRD STICKINGS (AND MANY PARTICIPANTS WHO REMAIN ANONYMOUS)

SB: All homeless means is being without a home, not having enough money for a home. But people seem to equate homelessness with all kinds of negative traits. Somehow there's something seriously or fundamentally wrong with you because you are homeless.

TL: You people look at us like clowns, people to laugh at. You don't take us seriously. Just because we're homeless does not mean we're not smart, we're not capable, we're not caring. We're human beings who come from all different walks of life. The stereotypes of homeless people are completely wrong and biased. If you come to a shelter here and you apply for housing, you're waiting five to ten years to get a place. Five to ten years to get a place!!! So, you're going to be stuck either homeless or on the streets.

XA: Food and shelter are basic human rights. When you strip away those things to the bare bones, you strip away the person as well.

Shelters for the "homeless" or what we now, more respectfully, call the unhoused,[1] are perceived largely to be places of care, however, testimonies from residents tell of the institutional violence that they endure in the shelter system. In 2016, a series of interviews were conducted with folx[2] living at a shelter designated for "women" in a gentrifying Toronto[3] neighbourhood, the Junction, for a video project by a group of advocates for the unhoused.[4] While the original intention of the video project was to critique the city government about the lack of shelter space, interviewees spoke instead to the dehumanizing shelter conditions that they endure. Thus, it was decided to use the footage to make a separate video about the shelter as a site of institutional violence. The Shelter Video Project (SVP) collective was formed made up of the authors of this chapter – a smaller group out of the fifteen plus folx who were originally interviewed. Collective members are activists, artists, researchers, community builders, allies, and former/current shelter residents. Together we have resilience and see joy and creativity as integral for survival and resistance. The video, *We Want You to Listen: Shelter Video Project* (SVP) centres the critical lived expertise (a term introduced to our discussion by Opal Sparks) of the shelter residents who inhabit different economic, social, and cultural intersections of race, class, Indigeneity, gender, sexuality, and disability. In SVP, community members speak at great risk to themselves and with conviction and vulnerability in order to give empirical evidence and details of the everyday workings of the shelter system and critical assessments of the systemic and relational loathing and violence that they are subject to. The following chapter is comprised of excerpts from a transcript of the video framed with further analysis of the issues of institutional violence and the carceral continuum that are raised in the video. With this chapter, we seek to validate and value the unfiltered knowledge of those with lived expertise by centring the text around the transcript.

As folx in the project articulate, society considers those marginalized by the system as "failures," as "Other," as not "normal" and thus to blame as individuals (Anonymous in Daley et al. 2019; hooks 2000; Lyon-Callo 2002) for the conditions of existence that capitalism/colonialism has put on them: "it's that it's very hard to feel good about yourself. It's very hard to hold your head up and present yourself in a positive way when you're constantly being reminded that you're nothing and no one and continually treated with contempt" (SB, Shelter Video Project Collective 2021). Theorists refer to the phenomenon of blaming the victim as "symbolic violence" (Bourdieu 1993). Symbolic violence then makes it possible to dismiss and discredit the critical knowledge of marginalized peoples (hooks 1990; O'Leary & Ben-Moshe in Daly et al. 2019), what Amanda Fricker (2007, 1) identifies as "epistemic injustice": "a wrong done to someone in their capacity as a knower." According to Fricker (2007) epistemic injustice is an attack on a persons' fundamental being and often leads to physical harm and or assault by others, for instance when a low-income person is disbelieved in an emergency room or by the police and they end up dead. In worst-case scenarios, when marginalized peoples' knowledge is irrefutable, the public just doesn't care, they revert to the social loathing Rinaldi and Rossiter identified in the introduction to this volume. And thus, as described by many in the video, despite a plethora of "research" the conditions of violence in the shelter that exist now are the same as thirty years ago: "No One Listens!" (Shelter Video Project Collective 2021).

In the absence of believability of low-income folx, relatively privileged people are the ones constructing knowledge about the marginalized, either through their own limited experience of the marginalized, or through surveys and secondary sources. Thus, the picture of social reality that is being produced is distorted, especially because those with relative privileges have biases, prejudice and/or ignorance about poor people and investments in the dominance of their privileged worldview (hooks 1990, 2000; Swanson 2001). Indeed, Amanda Fricker (2007, 20) points out that those who are privileged experience an "excess of credibility" due to the presumption of superiority and respectability that follows from relative "success" in a system of capitalist/colonial values. Symbolic violence and epistemic injustice are key instruments in normativizing the unequal power that characterize institutions (and the strata of society they serve) making the abuse of unhoused people totally acceptable and thus laying the ground for institutional violence. The SVP, and this chapter, on the other hand, hopes to restore epistemic privilege and agency to those with experiential knowledge of the shelter system and to centre their critiques as the beginning of an abolitionist praxis that addresses the many causes of institutional violence in the shelter system.

INSTITUTIONAL VIOLENCE

Institutional violence can be understood as ongoing, everyday physical, mental, and emotional harms to persons in the context of the normal and sanctioned functioning of an institution understood both as a physical site of containment (shelter, prison, residential school, foster care, hospital, social housing) and of resource access (food bank, church, social services, social work, welfare, disability, law). Institutions are marked by a one direction flow of power between those employed to run them, their rule book, and the society they represent, *and* those who have been re-cast as "clients" under neoliberalism, those whose economic and political agency have been diminished to the point that they are un- or under waged, unhoused, and forced into a position of perceived "dependence" on institutions for survival (Russell and Malhotra 2002). Institutional violence takes the form of both rules and regulations that are sanctioned by the organization *and* of individually corrupt behaviours on the part of those in positions of power. The experience of institutional violence can be understood as the deprivation of control over one's life choices, community, identity, sense-of-self, one's knowledge, the ability to protect oneself, and one's bodily integrity and to heal and survive. Being positioned as subject to socio-economic disenfranchisement means that one is treated as a statistic and vulnerable to violence (Horii 1996; Swanson 2001) and, historically speaking, various forms of extermination, genocide, and eugenics.

The SVP collective members speak to forms of institutional violence experienced by folx in the shelter system as multiple, across scales and from every direction. From the state and its legal arms, social work/health care organizations, the public at large as well as lateral violence within the unhoused social strata. In the institution itself, on the embodied level, there is: nutritional starvation; lack of sleep or disturbed sleep; overcrowding; sustained levels of high stress; surveillance; regulation of daily life; lack of harm reduction; threat of eviction onto the streets where one is vulnerable to further physical harms (weather, police harassment and violence, physical assault). On the psycho-emotional level there is: little to no *effective* support resources including for finding housing in an inflated market; favouritism; arbitrary rules; inconsistent and punitive enforcement of rules; punitive measures against people who stick up for themselves; lack of conflict resolution; lack of privacy;

divide and conquer tactics; false accusations with punitive consequences; infantilization; stigmatization; stereotyping; and medicalization (hooks 2000; Lyon-Callo 2000, 2008; Swanson 2001). On the political level: unhoused people's agency is stripped from them; there is no effective complaints process and no political or legal representation for the interests of low-income/unhoused peoples and the abuses they endure. Outside of the institution, unhoused people are subject to social exclusion; judgment; fear; gentrification (which constantly threatens their spatial support networks); segregation; over policing and lack of appropriate crisis intervention; lack of access to everyday needs and desires such as mental health supports, housing, community, family, recreation, and culture.

Society has normalized the violence and trauma that they witness every day on the streets towards unhoused/unwaged peoples (Kawash 1998; Lyon-Callo 2000). Despite having experienced the tragedy and trauma that brought one to the shelter, residents are subject to shame and blame from workers, their friends and family as well as the general public.

> MN: I came to Canada eight years ago. When I came here to the shelter I thought I was expected to pay for the service, but they told me that I don't have to pay so I was grateful for that. I stayed only four weeks and I rented my own place. After that year, I started hearing many complaints from other people about shelter problems. So, I start questioning why is this happening? Is it a shortage of resources why people are not getting basic services as I assume housing is a basic need. Then I saw a guy sleeping by a roadside walkway beside a big building. It was in the middle of winter, there was a mountain of snow beside him. And because that was my first time in Canada during winter time, I was just really shocked that people were walking by without giving any attention to the person laying down there. At the same time, across the street, inside that big nice building, very energetic slim healthy looking people were doing exercise. So, I start thinking that in my culture, people give priority to human beings over animals. They also like animals, but there is priority given to people. So I said, why in this country do people give priority to animals, because, if that person was a pet animal, I assume that those people walking by would give some attention. But they didn't for the human being. I was so sorry.

SB: You cannot tell how you will behave when you're sleep deprived and hungry. When your belly is full, and you're living in a comfortable home it's easy to say, well, I certainly wouldn't have found myself in that situation. Rather than people wanting to help me pick up the pieces and build another life, it was as though people wanted to punish me for not behaving as they believe they would have in a similar situation.

OS: People assume I must be either selling my body, selling drugs, doing drugs, or mismanaging, or mentally ill, or whatever. All of the labels that we give people when they're going through situations.

AL: I always try to find myself a place as fast as I can. And sometimes it's more of a dump than the shelter but at least I'm not with a bunch of women being mentally abused.

OS: Homeless people should be allowed to make their own decisions, rise or fall, just like everybody else in humanity, and not to be surveilled, stigmatized, and vilified in the way that we are.

SHELTER CULTURE

Collective members speak to a variety of reasons on how they came to live at the shelter. Many folx end up at the shelter because of loss of housing due to physical, mental, and domestic violence. Personal health issues also can cause a loss of and/or a denial employment, housing and/or economic stability. Others have had to cope with failing health and/or the death of a family member for whom they were the primary care giver. Some are refugees and others carry the trauma of colonization. Others just don't fit the normative demands of wage labour society.

While on the surface, shelters claim to be helping unhoused people, once in the shelter, residence must endure a culture of negativity and abuse of power that constructs a certain kind of shelter subject: helpless, childlike, incapable, needy, undeserving, and depraved.

SG: So the day that I had, you know, problems. I was, I guess, kind of sleeping on everybody else's couch … and, you know, people have their own lives, so I made that phone call. I was relieved. I was like, wow, I have a place. I don't have to be a burden to anybody. No! Clearly, I'm a burden to the shelter system, the one that I was in anyway.

LL: I've grown through the shelter experience, but I've also suffered because I'm a product of childhood trauma so it's very traumatizing to be in the shelter system. There's a lot of oppression, there's a lot of blame, and belittlement. If you don't do some work on yourself while you're in the shelter system, it can really take a toll on your person, who you are, your identity, and your self-esteem.

OS: I really learned how people are treated in the shelter system. People are confrontational, judgmental, they sneer at you, they bark at you. There's little cliques, with staff and specific residents, or not.

LL: When you ask for things the answer is usually no. And it's almost like you're asking them to give it to you from their pocket. I have a lot of food allergies, so that's a huge struggle because they don't really want to make accommodations when you have such extreme allergies. I walked into the shelter system using a cane because I had vertigo, and I'm leaving the shelter using a walker. And my allergies are all heightened. Everything is heightened and extremely sensitive now. And I know that all of these sensitivities and allergies that I'm having are a trauma response.

SHELTER CONDITIONS

While the shelter in question underwent a renovation, this benefitted the staff and public areas of the building and not the areas inhabited by residents. The physical structure does the bare minimum to create an illusion of care for a public who don't want to have to deal with the "homeless problem" (Kawash 1998; Swanson 2001) while the persistent degraded physical conditions of the shelter and lack of maintenance reflect the degrading treatment of residence.

XA: We have three bathrooms during the hours of 9 am till 12:30 for almost 100 women and it's ridiculous. And most of the time they're not even open.

SA: When it comes to your washrooms, there's mold in the bathrooms, there's feces left in the toilets in the basement over the weekend.

KE: I find that although they have cleaning staff, they don't actually clean properly. Like once in a while I'll smell some bleach, but most of the time it just seems like water in a bottle. And it doesn't even seem to be hot. They may say it's disinfectant, but it's hard to believe them when you go and you touch it and it still seems to be dirty or greasy or dusty.

SG: My concerns are for people with disabilities. We've had the elevator not working for probably about five out of seven days. There's no air conditioning on the floors where the women live. There's air conditioning where the staff are and that's it. We're forced to sleep in our rooms with no outlets near our bed. We're not allowed to have any fans.

XC: The air conditioning vent that is beside my room that air conditions the hall, but not the rooms, is just black with mould. It's just absolutely terrible.

XD: One woman refused to wear a tampon, and she bled all over a couple of different seats. It took them, I guess, two or three days to clean it.

SG: The physical conditions are bad, but let's talk about the mental and emotional environment. It breaks your spirit. It breaks you down.

KE: They treat the mentally ill[5] extremely badly and they treat everybody else like they're mentally ill. They say they have mental health training, but I haven't seen them do anything. I remember one worker dealing with a woman who was bugging them at the desk, but that's their job. And the worker gave her a book to read saying "why don't you go read a book." The book was on Mexico and the mentally ill woman got so upset, she said "I don't want to go to Mexico." She was crying and the worker started antagonizing her, like, "oh, what's wrong? Don't you want to go to Mexico?"

MH: You know, they create problems for me, and I don't even do anything. In the morning I stay out of the shelter till nighttime. When I come back there's still a problem. I don't know what I should do? Like, if they can help me to look for housing so I can get out of there, maybe I'm okay. If I stay over there now it will make me more crazy. I have bipolar because those people in the shelter make me sick like that. You know, they just hurt me badly and badly. I'm just waiting for them to look for housing for me and I get out of there. Or if they don't, I should go outside and sleep on the street. That may be better than living in there.

LL: When we go through difficult times and we have different emotions to deal with, we have nowhere to go where we can deal with them on our own, in private, to maybe cry, maybe scream. We have nowhere, leaving us to feel maybe we need to bury these emotions, put a tough outer shell on so that nobody sees us and we're not feeling vulnerable, leaving us prey to be picked on, or humiliated, or put down, or whatever.

XB: Enter that place and see what you come out like because you will not be yourself. You will not be the same person who went in. You will not have the heart and soul that you went in with. You cannot bond in there. You cannot be emotional in there. It's taken as weakness. And you get warnings for that. You're written up for not being strong or nasty. If you're nice, you're weak. You're just fed to the sharks, written up.

LL: Every day I've been thinking I'm in the twilight zone, I'm in a nightmare that's never ending. Sometimes I just want to kill myself just to end this madness.

SG: What do you do as a woman when you're struggling with mental health issues and you're homeless? Mental health and addiction are usually concurrent disorders.

SB: So people often equate homelessness with drugs and alcohol. It's commonly believed that people are homeless because they are on drugs or alcoholic. But, what I've learned about being homeless is that sometimes it's being in the homeless situation that causes people to begin taking drugs and alcohol. It's a way of coping with the fear and the pain.

SG: And I found that I almost relapsed in there, just because there was no support. I would say a good amount of the women in the shelters have turned to substances or have already been using substances. I mean, how worse can it get when you're on the street and you go into a shelter and the shelters treat you worse than the people on the street do, you know? If you look around, people are dying everywhere from an overdose. People did use while I was there, and people were just basically, you know, left to fend on their own. And then, if you got caught, instead of having support, you got evicted and hence you're back to the same routine again, on the streets, or back in the abusive relationship. I kept six[6] for women that were using, because I didn't want them to use in a laneway or out on the street. People that use substances are people first and substance users after. They wouldn't treat somebody that had cancer that way with their medication. People are struggling in the world, let alone when you've been put on the street, when you've been in an abusive relationship, and you can't just stop addiction. So harm reduction is a way of stopping harm to anybody who uses drugs, whether it be through education, or whether it be through bringing awareness, or whether it be through having clean supplies, or safe injection clean supplies. Simple things like Naloxone kits were not available. Naloxone kits save lives.

LL: People have asked me to stop telling my story because it's too painful to hear. But I live this every day. It's more painful for me.

SB: It's very sad to see. They need help. They need someone to come in and provide counselling and care. But instead they're just being warehoused.

Bodies carry the trauma of surviving the maldistribution of resources for survival, and are re-traumatized by institutionalization. Shelter residents report that the institutional violence of the shelter causes their mental and physical health to decline, causing suicidal ideation, self-harm. recourse to substance use as a survival strategy, and actual suicide.[7] Social determinants of health tell us that poverty and its stresses are the biggest factor influencing a person's life span (Mikkonen and Raphael 2020). Institutional violence can be understood as a necro-political economics of accelerated death (Mbembe 2003; Montag 2005; Razack 2015), what Puar (2017) refers to as debilitation, the maiming of expendable bodies/populations through structural violence.

SHELTER DISCIPLINE AND THE CARCERAL CONTINUUM

Once in the shelter, life is regulated by schedules and rules, which are different for every shelter. Meal times, counsellor appointments, when you have to be in and out of your room, medication time, curfew, and bed checks. The schedule is announced through a loudspeaker that continually interrupts the day. Individual residents are called to the front desk for meetings, mail, if there is a visitor or to be disciplined. Residents are also expected to take turns helping to clean the kitchen after mealtimes. Rules include: adhering to the schedule, no food or beverages in your room, limited number of belongings, sign up for laundry, sign in and sign out when coming and going from the shelter, speaking respectfully to staff (even though staff may not be respectful), no helping fellow shelter residents, etc. Notice is given for rules infraction, three notices and you are evicted onto the street. The shelter does not adequately accommodate for the disability that most residents experience, whether that be aging, mobility, food allergies, mental/emotional crisis, and/or addiction. Individuals can find themselves on the street because they are viewed as "unmanageable," non-compliant, conflict prone, and/or are considered to complain too much. Power dynamic between staff and residents allow for abuse, arbitrary enforcement, and playing favourites among residents. Staff power and control is enforced through surveillance cameras in all common spaces.

> SG: Women were obeying partners out of fear prior to leaving an abusive relationship, and it got even worse when they went into the shelter. You know, because it wasn't any better. Obey, obey, obey.

> SB: We're not supposed to have food in our room. Well, if my blood sugar drops, I need to be able to have access to something to eat immediately, which I can't do without breaking the rules.

So what do I choose to do? Of course there's always the threat that if you're breaking the rules, however necessary it is to break the rules, then you run the risk of not even being able to stay in the shelter.

MBS: Well, I was staying in a shelter with my daughter and I had a friend in there, she also had a son. And she wanted to go out, so I babysat her son. And so, when I had to go out to look for an apartment, she was looking after my daughter and this was inside the shelter. Next thing I know, I come back and one of the staff had called Children's Aid on me because I left my daughter unattended. I said "no," and she was just very, very rude. And, I heard today about how staff is pretty rude and neglectful to the residents so that's pretty much the same as the story thirty-five years ago.

SG: A lot of women had to give away their children to go in there! CAS (Children's Aid Societies) was involved because they had an abusive relationship. Can you imagine? They're traumatized before they get there! Definitely! And then you're ordered to meet with a counsellor once a week. You had to be there when they required you. So you're going to this counsellor who doesn't know shit about lived experience or addiction. You're sitting there because I guess they need to get paid, and they're just naming off all the stuff that you've done wrong. I shit you not! Well, there was a thing you were written up for, you didn't get out of bed at this time, we found this in your room, or you came in drinking. There was always a reprimand for everything.

SB: They can call us in and put us on reprimand or give us notice for the slightest infractions, like leaving a bag where it shouldn't be left. But somebody's screaming in the hallway, somebody's fighting, shouting "I'm gonna kill you, I don't care if I go to jail, I'm gonna throw you out the window" and where are the staff when that's going on?

SB: As soon as I start walking towards the shelter, I feel such anxiety inside, such tension. And then, by the time I reach the shelter and go to sign in, I can barely breathe. The people behind the desk won't even look at you. When the staff talk to us, it is usually with contempt. I've actually said to a staff member, is there some reason you're talking to me that way? Have I done something or said something? And she said "I talk to everybody that way!" as if that was an explanation. I said: "well, out in the hallway you have a list of values posted on your wall. One of the top values listed is respect and I certainly am not feeling it here!"

XB: It makes you nasty. And the staff encourages this. They don't want you to be helpful to anyone. They don't want you to be nice to people. I'm becoming a very nasty person inside the shelter in order to follow the rules. I challenge anybody to go in there and not be totally changed, by just seeing, living, and experiencing the nastiness that you have to put up with just to survive, and just to survive the staff. Like the girls in there are so nice, but they're not allowed to be nice. You'll get written up for boundary violations. You can't even help somebody who's got physical problems carry their bags up the stairs. They make you stop and put that bag down and have the individual with the health problems make five trips when you being a healthy person can do it yourself. It's just something that I never thought I would experience, and now that I have, I am an absolutely different person. And I don't want to change. I don't want to be a hard person.

XC: And you are treated as if you are in kindergarten, like okay, pat on the head run along now. Or, if you mention something of concern, you get written up and given a warning.

SB: I have trouble going down for meals because of the contempt of the serving staff. I just feel somehow, like I'm lower than low just by being there. I was late for dinner once because of an appointment downtown. I went into the dining room and tried to explain. But because they had started to put things away, there is a long argument about whether to give me food. One woman finally says to the other: "yeah, give her the food." So she takes the dish, comes over, slams it on the counter.

SG: And there were all women working on the staff except for one man. I don't understand it. As women, we're supposed to have each other's back!

LL: We're very fortunate to be in a shelter where we only have to be out of our bed for three and a half hours then we can go back to our room in the afternoon. But in some shelters, the women have to be out of the shelter from nine a.m. until five p.m. And I've been in one shelter where you had to be out of your room between nine and five, but you could stay in the building. So each shelter that you go to has different rules, different hours, different regulations. When you move around from shelter to shelter, you're going to get confused with hours and rules and staff and everything. It's very hard to keep your mind thinking straight.

XE: I find there seems to be a lot of workers at the shelter, but they're all in the office. Nobody does anything, like nobody! They're not much help.

SG: I just wanted to say that the staff themselves won't go up onto the floors. I've personally heard them saying "I'm not going up there." They spend their time sitting behind a desk using the intercom to call clients down. Like, when it was too hot they don't monitor the floors. They don't come up and ask or see how everybody's doing.

SB: Throughout the night, staff shine a flashlight in the room to make bed checks. Some of the bed checks are quiet and the flashlight is directed at the floor. But often staff shine the flashlights in our faces and most of the time I'm woken up. Then it's hard to get back to sleep. A thin sheet barely covers the cold plastic covering of the mattress. The thin top sheet barely covers your body. And then, once again you are aware you're sleeping within arm's reach of a stranger. Someone that you don't know and you may or may not get along with.

XC: I have found my stuff that has been rummaged through. I'm not sure if it's staff or if it's the cleaning ladies.

SG: If they're coming up, it's strictly to write you up. Or to complain about something like "get your feet off the chair," "don't do this, don't do that." There's no positive energy coming from them. We come in there in a crisis. And as another woman was saying, we leave feeling a lot worse.

MH: They racist or something? They deal under the table, whatever ... it's like you're not the same style as what they are, and you get hurt.

LL: So how do you stay healthy? How do you move on with your life? When you're climbing a hill like this? And you're carrying this huge bag of rules and regulation, and you have fallen into a depression? And you can't do this and you can't do that and we never do anything right!

SG: So basically, it's like you're being punished, you're being punished for who you are. Who are they to judge who you are? Being punished for what? If you have a disability you're being punished. If you're an alcoholic or you're a substance user, you're being punished. If you use in there or if you are caught with anything, you get thrown out and you're back in the cycle, back into the violent relationship that you left, whether it be domestic or ... there was no chance. You had to conform to their rules. So if you were a woman who needed to escape either by drinking or using drugs, you were condemned for that, there was no sense even going to the shelter.

SB: I feel in this particular situation, there isn't an attempt to help people. No one says: this is a stepping-stone, we're going to take you from here and help you move to there. Instead, what we feel is this is our final destination.

LL: When I first got into the shelter system, I figured, after a couple of weeks I'll find myself a place to live and then I'll be fine. Here I am, almost six years later, and I'm still in the shelter system.

In our discussions of the violence of the shelter system, members of the group compared the shelter to being in prison (De Ward and Moe 2010). As prisons are places of punishment, a juxtaposition of prisons and shelters shows us how poverty and homelessness are treated as a crime (Swanson 2001). As such, we began to think about the "carceral continuum" of institutions, which manage and contain unhoused/unwaged populations deemed dependent, undeserving, unworthy, and unwanted by "respectable" society (Foucault 1979). The carceral continuum looks at the punitive logic, which originates with the prison and is disseminated throughout the institutional network. Importantly, the continuum also includes privileged sites (such as universities and workplaces) that use a similar punitive logic (w different means and objectives) to train a class of citizen "guards" who enact superiority to hold captive those who are excluded from, or non-conforming to, the wage labour system: no prisoner exists without a guard.

Poor people's whole lives are spent interfacing with a multitude of institutional sites as they move from patriarchal family structures to foster care, from group homes and youth detention to welfare and disability support payment programs or precarious employment and the army, then potentially the shelter, the prison, detox, and rehab where they are subject to rehabilitative programs such as life skills, anger management classes, and other mental health and social work strategies, to social housing, psych wards, hospitals, long-term care homes, and finally palliative care. This serial institutionalization is referred to as "trans-incarceration" (Ben-Moshe 2011, 11). Each of these spaces in the carceral continuum contain people in an environment that is degrading and punitive while at the same time claiming to rehabilitate them into conforming citizens (Chapman and Withers 2019; Stark 1994). SVP collective members evoked the Stanford Prison Experiment to understand the relational violence they were experiencing in the shelter. In 1971, in the basement of the psychology department of Stanford University, a mock prison was created and students were randomly divided into the roles of "guards" and "prisoners." The experiment had to be stopped part way through because the "prison guards" became so abusive and the "prisoners" were being traumatized. The Stanford Prison Experiment showed how unequal social power leads to abuse, how "care" can become social loathing.

> XC: It's like we are herded like cattle when it comes to calling us for our meals and what have you, we are herded like cattle, and we are treated with no dignity.

> XB: Human rights. There are none. We're not even treated like human beings.

> KE: They don't really treat you like you're a person. If you complain about anything, they'll call you a complainer. They'll give you warnings. They'll threaten to kick you out, tell you that

you are lucky you're getting fed after all, even if it's just garbage you're being fed.

MH: Okay, you don't do anything, but they just say you did that, you do that, and you did that, and after, you lose. That's why they kick you out. You have to move to another shelter. And at the other shelter, they just do exactly the same thing like that. They say "ok, I talked to you. You have to listen. You don't listen. You're no good," something like that.

KE: If they want you out and you haven't got any warnings, they'll just say, oh, well, you got in an argument with so and so and you got a warning, they just didn't tell you. And they'll make up two or three different warnings that they've given you which you didn't actually get so that they have a reason to kick you out.

MH: One time, two years ago, they discharged me with only ten minutes' notice to go out on the streets on New Year's Eve. The snow comes up to your knees and they don't even let me go back to my room to take my things or my walker. I tried to talk to them. What happened? They discharged me because one of my roommates had a bad migraine headache and they can't see the bright light coming in the windows. I open my blind a little bit. She went to complain to the counsellor and they discharged me in ten minutes.

XD: Sometimes they kick people out of the shelter and refuse to let them collect their things out of their room or their locker. And so the staff goes in and puts all their stuff in a plastic bag and throws it into a locker. It's a human rights violation. They should give a person twenty-four hours to find someplace else to stay or find something else to do, you know, with where they're going to live right?!

SG: I've seen people leave and say, you know what, eff this! I'd rather sleep on a bench, I'd rather go in the park. I'd rather, you know … I can't do this. I can't do this because you're getting beat and beat down. You know, insulted, judged. You know, you're terrified all the time, you say the wrong thing, do the wrong thing, don't get up in time.

LL: It takes your hope away, your self-worth, your dignity. It's like you've been raped. This is no exaggeration. That feeling of being stripped of your dignity, your autonomy, self-respect, independence and that part seems almost deliberate.

MBS: You feel so helpless and there's no place to go. You're stuck in a kind of prison system. And you get abused. When you want to escape you can't because of those brick walls. In shelters where there are no walls, the walls are invisible. You have the freedom to leave but where are you going to go? There is no place to go. You will be on the streets. You have that fear of being out there. It's not safe. There's that invisible wall.

POLITICAL ECONOMY OF SHELTERS

Colonial/capitalism represents a system of relational violence where private property and wage labour relations create a social strata who live with debilitating conditions of poverty (Marx 1976). Those who are not able to sell their labour and acquire property are consigned to a network of institutions, which are seen as a drain on the economy (Russell and Malhotra 2002) and are thus, in the last few decades, are subject to neoliberal rollbacks that lead to conditions of warehousing (Lyon-Callo 2000; Wacquant 2009). The poor must be punished for not contributing to profit production. Punishment must be painful (Chapman and Withers 2019) in order to coerce peoples who are able bodied into what are often dreadful, immiserating, and unfulfilling forms of labour (Fracchia 2008; Russell and Malhotra 2002). Ultimately, the poor and non-conforming are treated as disposable, meaning there is an overarching social desire for their death (Blaney and Inayatullah 2012; Jones and Jarelle 2021; Russell and Malhotra 2002).

While poor people experience the symbolic violence of being considered to be a drain on the system,[8] in reality, they spend every cent that they earn in the market economy and thus contribute to it. Furthermore, they prop up the massive social services and institutional employment sector (who guard them) (Linton 2021; Russell and Malhotra 2002) through which, again, money is cycled back into the economy via middle-class consumption. Collective members are very keen to the reality that those employed in the shelter industry are making money off their oppression.

SG: It's all about money, I'm sorry to say that but it is. Where I was, they didn't care. They talk a good talk, right? Oh, we're going to support women, I think they do it for the funding. I'm going to say it straight out. It's for the funding.

SB: And your complaints are seldom taken seriously, if they're heard at all then they turn it back on you. You're a complainer. You're getting the food and the shelter for free. You know, we're not paying anything so beggars can't be choosers, right?

MBS: Get into a shelter and it's filthy so you want to get out of there as fast as you can. But then, to rent you usually need first and last month's rent and where are you going to get enough money to survive? It was difficult at that time.

SG: Some women have to sell, you know, sell sex to pay somebody to stay at their house. Right? So women aren't just paying through money, it's usually through sex. It's out of the frying pan and into the fire. It's worse.

SB: If you sincerely want women to be in these shelter situations temporarily, then you need to provide the resources to get them out. You need to provide the resources to improve their situation. And it's already been said many times, but we need affordable housing. And so what do you expect people to do if they don't have anywhere to live, and they don't have adequate food to eat? What are they supposed to do? They may think they are saving money by throwing starch and sugar at people, but ultimately the health costs are going to be astronomically higher than what they would pay in the first place if they just gave nutritious food. How can we function, how can we get up and do the things we need to do if we don't have the energy or the resources to do it.

Despite being subject to a neoliberal discipline of false individualism and independence, it is common knowledge that residents *are* the ones that support each other:

OS: One of the things I learned being homeless, it was mostly homeless people who helped me!

SB: I continued to volunteer at the homeless shelter where I was originally housed for an additional two years after I got out.

Shelter residents engage in mutual aid helping each other in navigating the shelter system, finding supports outside of the shelter, sharing necessities, being each other's first responders in a crisis (hooks 2000; Swanson 2001) and doing free labour to survive the system and sustain their communities where social work fails them (Chapman and Withers 2019). Mutual aid is a model for survival and resistance that has grown popular since COVID that operates outside of government and economic systems, which is by no means new to people who are poor and unhoused (Davis and Fayter 2020; Disability Justice Network of Ontario 2021; Hilliard 2008; Douglas et al. 2021). Collective members also put in a lot of free labour to get the SVP project off the ground, which we see as congruent with the mutual aid paradigm. Since receiving an Ontario Arts Council grant, we make sure that members are paid, have technological access and respond to each other's material, intellectual, psychological, and emotional needs as they arise in day-to-day life as a community. To ask marginalized people to share their knowledge without attending to the totality of social cohesion is to extract knowledge rather than nurture it. As such, SVP collective establishes an ethos of care and redistribution across difference. Supporting and building on the social reproduction labour of poor/unhoused peoples is an abolitionist gesture and one antidote to the institutional violence that is experienced.

WHAT'S IT GOING TO TAKE?

In the video, participants make repeated calls for people who are involved in the shelter industry to "come and live at the shelter and see what it's like." Such embodied lived experience is a unique form of knowing understood to be indispensable, profound, and urgent.

SG: People with addictions want to speak to somebody who knows what the hell they're going through. You can have a degree, you can have a diploma in whatever you want. If you have not lived it, then you'll have no friggin idea. People that have mental health issues, or women that have addictions, they need a peer support group, not the shelter counsellors there. If they don't have lived experience, then get the hell out.

SB: You know, there are people making rules and setting standards who have no idea what is going on. They have no idea what people are experiencing. They have no idea what the situation is. But they think because they've studied it from the outside or read somebody's written report, that they understand what's needed and what's wanted. And that's the crux of the problem. These people are making decisions that affect people's lives.

SG: Any committee, any board that makes decisions that affect people with lived experience of homelessness, women and substance users, people who use drugs, need people with lived experience to be sitting on that board. The board needs to consist of people who have lived this. People can't make decisions based on what they don't know. That's how it works. So I'd like to push for having women that have lived experience with mental health issues or with being homeless with substance abuse problems. Listen, people who are still using substances can function. I don't understand where they get the idea that people who use substances are bad people. Oh my gosh! It's just, it's the stigma. You know, we can fight as hard as we want, but we need, things to take place. And as women, we need to stick together. We need to really stick together.

The knowledge that is imparted by SVP collective members points to the ethical failure of this "liberal-democratic" society, what we don't want to face about ourselves and the complacency of those of us with the relative privileges of housing and economic resources. They see our ignorance, uncaring ways, and the violence of our charitable attitudes (Chapman and Withers 2019; hooks 2000) and claims to their knowledge. They propose that a restorative justice, abolitionist praxis to address the harms of institutional violence would include centring and materially supporting those with lived expertise in projects at every scale that are concerned with the lives of poor/unhoused peoples from local arts, academic, activist, and community-building projects to governmental reforms.

CONCLUSION

In the SVP transcript, folx who have survived poverty and insecure housing have relayed their lived expertise of institutional violence in a shelter in Toronto. Often work with marginalized communities is framed by a charity or a "doing-for" ethos (Boilevin et al. 2019; Chapman and Withers 2019; hooks 2000): short term, extractive, symbolic focused academic, activist, or arts projects are standard. The SVP project, on the other hand, is an effort to create a space of mending of the social fabric torn through the relational violence of colonial/capitalism, a space of collective healing, agency, and resistance. The SVP is rooted in long-term, committed relationships of community building rooted in a praxis of material redistribution that makes participation possible. In this way, the SVP radically departs from a dynamic of organizing poor people from above, a practice that reproduces the power imbalances that create the possibility of institutional violence to begin with. Thus, it is important to centre our work – our struggles for liberation – around those most marginalized, as we seek our own liberation from the constant threat of our own, further marginalization. The SVP collective works to imagine and practice a better way in the most exclusionary conditions of the present. Imagine the kind of society in which affordable housing and an adequate shelter system are a priority; where we practice a political economics of mutual care according to an ethics that recognizes the inherent value of all beings and institutions are finally abolished. This is a proposal for a world of respect, reciprocity, humility, and the valorizing of all beings. This is not a utopian world, but one that finds reference in pre-colonial and existing Indigenous societies of these Lands (Battiste and Henderson 2009; Hall 2015; Simpson 2011; Tuck and McKenzie 2015).

NOTES

Some voices from the Shelter Video Project remain anonymous. Also, video artist Rebecca Garrett was a part of the SVP collective and contributed to the conversation, which this chapter represents. Kim Jackson's participation in the Shelter Video Project was funded via a SSHRC-CMHC post-doc at Wilfrid Laurier University.

1 We have taken up the term unhoused to affirm that it is society that takes the action to deny housing to people. Also, that unhoused people still have a sense of "home" in multiple other senses. In a decolonizing understanding an Indigenous person can be without a house but still be at home on the land and/or their traditional territory (Thistle 2017). Where the video transcript represents the direct speech of SVP members who use the term "homeless" we have left it in.
2 We use the word "folx" to include those bodies who do not necessarily fit into the norms of gender proscribed by the institution of the "women's" shelter which also houses queer, non-binary, and trans people who may identify differently.
3 We recognize the SVP takes place on the unceded and stolen Lands of the Wendat, Haudenosaunee, and the Anishinaabe, and the Treaty 13 Lands of the Mississauga's of the Credit River. These lands are also covered by the Dish with One Spoon, Two Row Wampum, and the Nan Fan Treaty.
4 Bursting at the Seams.
5 The term "mentally ill" is used widely in community as well as among those who experience mental health issues themselves. The SVP collective understand "mental illness" as a fluid state of being that is, in low-income community, most often the result of experience of the intersectional oppressions, trauma, and re-traumatizing that folx are enduring/surviving/resisting within colonial/capitalism. Across society, mental health distress is something that can impact anyone at any time.
6 To "keep six" is to keep a look-out for staff.
7 The Toronto Homeless Memorial counted sixteen deaths of houseless people in August of 2021, and over half of those were in shelters.
8 In fact, the only class who are a drain on the system are those who are wealthy enough to hoard money in offshore accounts, investments, and in decadent consumption.

REFERENCES

Battiste, Marie, and J. Youngblood Henderson. 2009. "Naturalizing Indigenous Knowledge in Eurocentric Education." *Canadian Journal of Native Education* 32, no. 1: 5–18.

Ben-Moshe, Liat. 2011. "Disabling Incarceration: Connecting Disability to DivergeConfinements in the USA." *Critical Sociology*: 1–19.

Blaney, David, and Neeam Inayatullah. 2012. *Savage Economics: Wealth, Poverty, and the Temporal Walls of Capitalism*. London: Routledge.

Boilevin, Louise, Jules Chapman, Lindsay Deane, Caroline Doerksen, Greg Fresz, D.J. Joe, Nicolas Leech-Crier, Samona Marsh, Jim McLeod,

Scott Neufeld, Steven Phan, Laura Shaver, Patrick Smith, Martin Steward, Dean Wilson, and Phoenix Winter. 2019. *Research 101: A Manifesto for Ethical Research in the Downtown Eastside*. https://open.library.ubc.ca/cIRcle/collections/ubccommunityandpartners-publicati/52387/items/1.0377565.

Bourdieu, Pierre. 1993. *The Field of Cultural Production*. United Kingdom: Polity Press.

Chapman, Chris, and A.J. Withers. 2019. *A Violent History of Benevolence: Interlocking Oppression in the Moral Economies of Social Working*. Toronto: University of Toronto Press.

Daley, Andrea, Lucy Costa, and Peter Beresford, eds. 2019. *Madness, Violence, and Power: A Critical Collection*. Toronto: University of Toronto Press.

Davis, Simone Weil, and Rachel Fayter. 2020. "Mutual Aid as Abolitionist Praxis." *Citizenship Studies*.

De Ward, Sarah, and Angela M. Moe. 2010. "Like a Prison!": Homeless Women's Narratives of Surviving Shelter." *Journal of Sociology Social Welfare* 37, no. 1: 115–35.

Disability Justice Network of Ontario. 2021. *Cops Out of Care: A Summer Series. Interview with El Jones, Souheil Benslimane, Cyree Jarelle, Megan Linton*. https://www.youtube.com/watch?v=efoAHUKL-9s.

Douglas, Tanisha, Mimi Kim, Kirk James, and Cameron Rasmussen. 2021. *Abolitionist Social Work Possibilities Paradox and Praxis*. AK Books Video Series. https://www.youtube.com/watch?v=JZxUeSAmIXo.

Foucault, Michel. 1979. *Discipline and Punish: The Birth of the Prison*. New York: Vintage-Random House.

Fracchia, Joseph. 2008. "The Capitalist Labour-Process and the Body in Pain: TheCorporeal Depths of Marx's Concept of Immiseration." *Historical Materialism* 16, no. 4: 35–66.

Fricker, Amanda. 2007. *Epistemic Injustice; Power and Ethics of Knowing*. Oxford: Oxford University Press.

Hall, Laura. 2015. "My Mother's Garden: Aesthetics, Indigenous Renewal, and Creativity." In *Art in the Anthropocene: Encounters among Aesthetics, Politics, Environments and Epistemologies*, edited by Heather Davis and Etienne Turpin, 283–92. London: Open Humanities Press.

Hilliard, D.E. 2008. *The Black Panther Party: Service to the People Programs*. Albuquerque: University of New Mexico Press.

hooks, bell. 1990. "Marginality as a Site of Resistance." In *Out There: Marginalization and Contemporary Cultures*, edited by R. Ferguson, M. Gever, T.T. Minh-Ha, C. West, and G. Gonzales-Torres, 241–3. Cambridge, MA: MIT Press.

– 2000. *Where We Stand: Class Matters*. New York: Routledge.

Kawash, Samira. 1998. “The Homeless Body.” *Public Culture* 10, no. 2: 319–39.

Lyon-Callo, Vincent. 2000. “Medicalizing Homelessness.” *Medical Anthropology Quarterly* 14, no. 3: 328–45.

– 2008. *Inequality, Poverty, and Neoliberal Governance: Activist Ethnography of the Sheltering Industry*. Toronto: University of Toronto Press.

Marx, Karl. 1976. *Capital*. Vol. 1. New York: Penguin.

Mbembe, Achille. 2003. “Necropolitics.” *Public Culture* 15, no. 1: 11–40.

Mikkonen, Juha, and Dennis Raphael. 2010. *Social Determinants of Health: The Canadian Facts*. Toronto: York University School of Health Policy and Management.

Montag, Warren. 2005. “Necro-Economics: Adam Smith and Death in the Life of the Universal.” *Radical Philosophy* 134: 7–17.

Puar, Jasbir K. 2017. *The Right to Maim: Debility, Capacity, Disability*. Durham: Duke University Press.

Razack, Sherene. 2015. *Dying of Improvement: Inquiries and Inquests into Indigenous Deaths*. Toronto: University of Toronto Press.

Red Wagon Collective. 2012–13. *We Have a Story: Women, Disability and Homelessness*. Toronto: anagraphia press.

Russell, Marta, and Ravi Malhotra. 2002. “Capitalism and Disability.” *Socialist Register* 38: 211–28.

Shelter Video Project Collective, prod. and dir. 2021. *We Want You To Listen: Shelter Video Project*. Video. 70 minutes.

Simpson, Leanne. 2011. *Dancing on Our Turtle’s Back: Stories of Nishnaabeg Re-Creation, Resurgence and New Emergence*. Winnipeg: ARP Books.

Stark, Louise R. 1994. “The Shelter as ‘Total Institution’: As Organizational Barrier to Remedying Homelessness.” *American Behavioral Scientist* 37, no. 4: 553–62.

Swanson, Jean. 2001. *Poor-Bashing: The Politics of Exclusion*. Toronto: Between the Lines Press.

Thistle, Jessie. 2017. *The Definition of Indigenous Homelessness in Canada*. Toronto: Canadian Observatory on Homelessness Press.

Tuck, Eve, and Marcia McKenzie. 2015. *Place in Research: Theory, Methodology, and Methods*. London: Routledge.

Wacquant, Loïc. 2009. *Punishing the Poor: The Neoliberal Government of Social Insecurity*. Durham: Duke University Press.

12

Kaleidoscope

Hope-in-Action beyond Institution

MO KORCHINSKI, LYNN FELS,
AND RUTH ELWOOD MARTIN

When you listen carefully, you can hear a resonant song of hope …
To live with hope requires immense courage, forgiveness, and patience.
(Leggo 2019, viii)

Narratives of lives lived within and outside prison gates hold stories within stories within stories. To story a narrative of institutional incarceration and release is to attend to the multiplicities, complexities, and complicities of lived experience.

Jail[1]

most people think jail is hard
a sad place to be
but jail saved my life
jail gave me hope
a sense of belonging
a purpose to life
a new way to live
jail gave me a job
three meals a day
a warm bed to sleep in
clean clothes to wear

friends by my side
growing and healing
from the beat of the drum
on this new journey
called life.

In a discussion about imprisonment, rehabilitation, and freedom of mobility, Mo, a formerly incarcerated prison activist and social worker offered, "I know 400 women who will tell you that prison saved their lives."[2] What conditions of compassionate empathy and communal engagement did these 400 women encounter that saved their lives? Explained Mo, "It's a relief going in, you don't have to hustle, you have a place to sleep – you have a job, you have family, my best fondest memories come from prison, it's a community." Prison temporarily got women off the streets, away from drugs, offered a bed, food, and safety, and a possibility to begin anew. When asked how Mo knew that she was finished with incarceration, and drugs, and living on the street, she shrugged, "You know when you are done. It's as if there is a done button."[3]

Incarceration is a revolving door; women are repeatedly arrested for crimes that support substance use or daily survival, or parole infractions, many of them minor (Janssen, 2017). Challenges faced by the women whether incarcerated or seeking re-entry into their communities are numerous and alienating. Incarcerated, women must navigate the challenges of communal living, forced confinement, oppressive relationships, policies, and regulations that bind. Many are released but few women can survive; they continue self-medicating through substance use, with fentanyl poisoning the supply. They also return to unwelcoming communities: formerly incarcerated women encounter homelessness, unemployment or minimum wage jobs, stigma, broken families. Many have had their children removed from their care.

Community support, such as it may be, outside the gates is limited, indifferent, exclusive, inaccessible. Imagine trying to find a job, or secure an apartment, or make new friends, or rebuild a family, with a criminal record, carrying the weight of shame, and anger, that marks their return. Accompanying each precarious arrest and release is unaddressed trauma. As one woman recalls, "I remember how scary it was the first time I was dropped off at the bus loop. I had no idea how to get home or even where to begin. I didn't make it very far before

I ran into someone I knew, and the next thing I knew I was getting high. The minute I was released, I was set up to fail" (Korchinski, cited in Martin et al. 2019, 118).

Violence precedes arrest: systemic violence exists within familial and communal values, prejudices, actions within which hierarchical, gender-based, ableist, racist, capitalist power is reinforced; institutional violence is enacted by procedures, policies, requirements, rules, expectations, regulatory practices designed to enforce compliance; physical environments designed to restrain and contain. None of this surprises.

1 THE LITTLE PRISON THAT COULD

> You have a job, you have family, my best fond memories, from prison, it's a community ... released back to street and you have nothing."
>
> (Korchinski)

The Alouette Correction Centre for Women (ACCW) houses women sentenced to two years minus a day. Opened in 2004, under the leadership of its first warden, Brenda Tole, ACCW was designated as a new model of incarceration in British Columbia, where locked cells and institutional grays were replaced with bungalows and unlocked bedrooms; a recreation and learning centre; and a communal kitchen and dining hall. The women had their own keys to their room, which provided privacy. The Eagle Hut, a site for Indigenous ceremony and teachings, introduced and sustained Indigenous ways of knowing and being. A vegetable garden maintained by the women, for healthy eating and for the satisfaction of growing one's own food, and a meditation maze, for walking through difficulties, were tucked behind administration buildings located at the front gates.

Warden Tole was given the responsibility to redesign the old prison, and support relevant health, education, and workplace programming. Most critically, Warden Tole looked to hire employees who were able to bring a compassionate empathy and care to their workplace, in order to address employee absenteeism, mental wellness, and improve relationships between prison guards and the incarcerated women. "They were our champions ... they would say, you deserve better than this – they believed in me. I didn't want to let them down" (Korchinski, in conversation 2021). The women Warden Brenda Tole hired – Mary Fayant, a First Nations Elder fondly known as

"Holy Cow," and Alison Granger-Brown, a recreational therapist – and the community relations she nourished (such as that with a local Aboriginal post-secondary institution) were all committed to meet the women's needs and interests. Explained Lara-Lisa Condella, one of the teachers in the *Building Bridges for Woman: Community Reintegration through Education* program, "When asked to articulate their learning expectations, half of the group wanted to learn about their culture, 30 per cent simply wanted to be in a learning environment and 7 per cent recorded personal growth ... Every woman wanted to give back to her family and community ... There was hope and resiliency in their stories of despair and marginalization ... perhaps it was not what we were learning, but how we learned together that made a difference" (Martin et al. 2014, 184). Learning was experiential, arts-based, collaborative, and dialogic, based on Indigenous principles of learning.

The intention of the new warden of ACCW was to create an institution that did not punish or rehabilitate, but rather offer opportunities for education, health, recreational and work experiences to "treat the women as human beings, with compassion and empathy, not as pieces of garbage" (Korchinski, in conversation, 2021). As Warden Tole explained: "We had the opportunity to slowly move away from a security and control-focus model and towards a more social pro-social offender responsibility model ... we found the normalized environment made the centre safer for staff and inmates, and institutional violence and use of force incidents generally reduced when compared to correctional centres for women" (Tole, cited in Martin et al. 2014, 47). In the structural design and programming offerings, Warden Tole consulted closely with those delivering the services. On meeting the new warden, the prison doctor, Dr Ruth Elwood Martin writes: "Today I met the new warden, Brenda Tole ... she talked about wanting to create a therapeutic environment, about correctional staff working collaboratively with the health-care teams, so that together we can address the medical needs of the women in prison. It is so refreshing to meet a personable warden who seems to 'get it'! I am anticipating great things!" (Martin, cited in Martin et al. 2014, 47).[4] The warden and those working with her sought to create a physical, communal, and culturally sensitive environment. Based on a model of communal health and well-being, recreational, educational, and work opportunities were introduced. One of the favourite activities led by Alison Granger-Brown, the recreation therapist, was swimming in the nearby river, where women could be free from the constraints of uniforms and gates. The women were received as individuals who came from communities, families, and the street with stories of trauma, loss, drug abuse, and violence needing a place to heal; they were treated with respect and offered opportunities to live in community in meaningful ways. Each woman was recognized not as a number with a crime attached but by their name and what they could offer to the community.

On first viewing, ACCW looks like a summer camp, with women in blue checkered hoodies and sweatpants engaged in a variety of chosen jobs, such as cooking in the kitchen, tending the garden, training dogs, sorting clothes in an off-site second-hand store. The focus of work duties is meaningful work that serves members of the community and teaches relevant skills for employment beyond the gates. Women are relatively free to move throughout and between the buildings and outside areas, with the exception of count and after hours. Notwithstanding the twenty-foot fence topped with barbed wire encircling the compound, inside the fence, ACCW tried to establish a caring environment through its structural design and program offerings. Recognizing that the majority of the women were of First Nations heritage, an Eagle Hut was built on the property, and Holy Cow, the First Nations Elder, introduced the women to Indigenous ways of knowing, story, drumming, and ceremony. As noted, the incidence of self-harm and institutional violence was significantly reduced. As Warden Tole remarked: "If you expect the staff and inmates to treat everybody with respect and to exercise their responsibilities, people will rise to those expectations and do the right thing, at least most of the time … The more we gave people opportunities, the more they valued the opportunities and responded. The more we gave responsibility for doing things to the women themselves, and the more we talked to staff about our plans, the better the situation got" (Tole, cited in Martin et al. 2014, 47). As the years unfolded, many women experienced ACCW as a place where they were temporarily safe from the streets, from the life and abuse that haunted them. They made friends, worked at a variety of jobs, socialized, and created meaningful lives within the prison fence, while enduring mandatory counts and once-an-hour night checks by the guards. They could participate in a variety of activities, as they chose, as long as they chose something. Some worked in the garden, others in the kitchen. A number joined Alison, the recreation therapist, in afternoon jogs outside the gate. First Nations Elder Holy Cow gathered groups of women in the Eagle Hut for ceremonies, drumming, and singing. Those who wished could upgrade their high school credits and/or attend courses to learn about their Indigenous heritage. Many experienced a childhood they never had.

Hope Abecedarian[5]

Alison's office, Aboriginal Day, angel cards, acceptance
Barbeques, Baby Sierra, becoming healthy, belonging
Carnival, cotton candy, chalk drawings, connection, comfort, creativity
Drumming, dressing up, hip-hop dancing, dialogue in the research room
Eagle hut, Easter egg hunts, excited about making a difference, encouraging, energy
Forums for research, driving a forklift, finding a voice …
Games, Alison's graduation, gym
Holy Cow, Halloween party, Happy Tuesday, hanging out with dogs, hope, heart
Ice cream, Ignition[6]
Joining in
Karaoke, working in the kitchen, kindness
Living with three babies, living on Alder, loving
Mattresses in the gym, mill outside the gates
Nail-painting …
One-on-one talks
Puppet show, presents on the door, photos, parenting tips
Quiet
Running club, river, rocking chair, research team
Sweats, sports day, smoking, slip and slide, survey designing, safety, sharing, smiles
Tug (the dog)
Us
Volleyball, voice
Water fights, W2, wiener roasts, wanting to make a difference, warmth
Xmas parties
Yoga, dog yard
Zucchini in the vegetable garden

Warden Tole created an inmate advisory committee to meet with her every week, to contribute to the facility's operations. Mo, who had been incarcerated multiple times, was an active member of the committee. Committee members made suggestions, organized parties, influenced what happened in their environment. The advisory committee offered the women a platform where they were empowered to speak on behalf of the community, and agency to improve their situation. As Warden Tole notes, "The more responsibility they had, the better job they did. It wasn't without problems. People make mistakes – that's part of the reason that they're here – and it's a learning process. So when things went sideways, we just had a discussion with everybody, put things back on track, and away we went" (Martin et al. 2014, 47–8).

Being part of an advisory committee recognizes that expertise and learning arises from lived experience. In any group, learning arrives through holding spaces open to listen to the stories of lived experience and insights of those present in the room (Friere 1972). Listening to each other with mutual respect and compassion, and engaging in meaningful relevant ways, became practices that served everyone well.

When asked if she had advice for other correctional institutions based on her experience, Warden Tole identified good health care; opportunities for physical exercise and working outside in the fresh air; involvement in planning and organizing events in their lives; meaningful work and responsibilities to each other; and opportunities to connect with the community. She also emphasized how critical it is to have mutual respect between inmates and staff (Martin et al. 2014, 49). She noted that incarcerating women in a single provincial institution was not conducive to reintegration in their home community. The women "come from all over the province, they're so separated, they're so isolated from their families. The ideal situation would be to house them in a place like ACCW for a short time and then move them into facilities in the community" (49). And she recognized the power differential that runs a correctional centre: "The person who runs the show is the person who sets the tone. If the warden is running the show, then their basic principles and their philosophy are going to be reflected. And I don't know how you get around that, other than you pick the people. You can't mandate compassion" (49).

Giving Back through Research: Meaningful Engagement

In 2005, our participatory action research project on women's health in prison of which Ruth Elwood Martin was the principal investigator (and the prison doctor) entered through the prison gates, welcomed by Warden Tole.[7] The first hopeful action was to gather everyone in the centre's gymnasium. The microphone was passed in the manner of a talking stick from woman to woman around the circle as administration, university professors, and correctional guards listened, surprised and impressed by the stories, passion, and insights of the women speaking. Within the week, a participatory action research group was created, which women could join as part of their job duties. Over the next two years, over 150 women participated in the research inside the gates. A curious few joined the research team for a week, others for the length of their sentence.

The research was shaped by those who sat around the table. Thus, like ACCW's recreational and educational programming, which evolved over time to meet the needs of the women, our research was emergent, informed by the women, determined by their key interests and concerns. The initial intention of the research had been to investigate and improve women's health in prison. At the inaugural meeting, women were invited to speak to their issues; coding of the transcript resulted in the identification of nine key health goals. However, co-researchers dwelling inside the gates quickly redefined the focus of the research to *what do we do when we get out? And who will be there for us?* Between the years of 2005–07 we engaged in a unique participatory action research project that focused on releasing voice, through writing and hopeful action. The research was guided by the women inside the gates with an intent of reimagining what might be possible.

Our co-researchers each wrote a paragraph of passion stating what they wanted to research and why. Housing. Education. Family. Drug Rehabilitation. They organized information forums to present their research findings to the entire prison population, including guards, administration personnel, and outside community agencies. They wrote their life stories, and some named their drug of choice. As difficult as writing about their lives was, what emerged was recognition of the similarities in their life experiences: child abuse, sexual abuse, drug addiction, dropping out of school, crimes committed to support drug addiction. *Unresolved trauma was the undercurrent running across their stories*. They learned that they had all been incarcerated for what they had seen as personal failings, which had occurred within structures of family, school, institutions, and community.

The participatory action research we engaged in, inside and outside the gates, illustrates that actively engaging women through meaningful responsibility and opportunity, where their voices matter, creates a communal environment of unfolding possibilities. A community in the making – imperfect, yes, but one where hope was enacted daily one step at a time, laying down a path in walking (Varela, 1987).

2 WHEN ONE DOOR SLAMS SHUT, A CRACK IN THE WALL APPEARS

Disappointingly, the hope that was embraced by those revisioning what a correctional institution might become fell victim to neoconservative politics. Induction of a new warden, tightened rules and restrictions, and brutal construction of a narrow-windowed concrete building all cast shadows across the Eagle Hut. Permission for our on-site health research project was terminated. However, a number of formerly incarcerated women wanted to continue the research with Ruth and others outside the prison gates. Through this research, two key initiatives or actions-in-hope were initiated: *Women in2 Healing*, a women's support group for formerly incarcerated women[8]; and *Unlocking the Gates*, a peer mentorship program to ease transition and integration of women upon their release (McLeod 2020).

Through the years of research, as evident in the narratives and experiences of formerly incarcerated women, employment, health, family, and housing remain central issues. *Women in2 Healing* set up a website, Facebook page, and wrote newsletters for incarcerated and formerly incarcerated women. Communications between those on the outside and those in the inside were maintained through newsletters, and through women coming in and women going out. Formerly incarcerated women, who had engaged in participatory health research while inside the prison gates, now on the outside, designed and led research projects, co-authored academic articles and presented at academic conferences, wrote non-academic articles, held media interviews, and created movie documentaries.[9] Women learned that their voices and lived experience mattered. And this participatory and educational process was profoundly transformative for all involved – academics, service providers, and other stakeholders – as well as women with incarceration experience.

Hope-in-action embedded in research included a series of health awareness workshops for formerly incarcerated men and women; presentations at and the organization of conferences, notably an international conference, Bonding through Bars, for formerly incarcerated women and children in 2013. Two women, whose infants were taken away after birth, came forward to the British Columbia Supreme Court as complainants in *Inglis v British Columbia (Minister of Public Safety)*, a successful court case, for the reinstatement of a policy that permitted incarcerated women to keep their babies in prison with them (Martin, 2013). Women learned that their voices and lived experience mattered. *Unlocking the Gates*, initially a research project, developed into a peer mentorship program where formerly incarcerated mentors meet the newly released at the prison gates to ferry them safely to their home community.

Hopes for Release[10]

stay clean
stay clean
stay clean
stay clean

stay out of jail
stay strong
stay out of trouble
stay focused
stay out of jail
stay healthy
stay out of trouble
stay connected

stay alive

In 2020, *Unlocking the Gates* became a non-profit society, with Mo Korchinski, who has been closely involved throughout the years inside and outside the gates, as executive director. Initially Mo was a member of the prison advisory committee, and through the years she reconnected with her children, mentored formerly incarcerated women, made films, and completed a BA in social work. The experience of women newly released being greeted at the gates by mentors working with the

Unlocking the Gates project is evident in their responses to this question, "What was it like having a mentor the day you were released?"

Mentors: A Love Note[11]

awesome
my peer mentor gave me confidence
comforting
inspiring to have someone who has shared my struggles
great
she can relate to who I am and what I have gone through
happy
great to have someone help me adjust to being free
helpful
helpful to know someone who understands the difficulties
of getting out
understood
happy to have someone help me along the way
hopeful
she knows what I am going through
gratifying
awesome to be with somebody who doesn't judge you
pleasant
there is support for us to stay focused and to reach our goals
exciting
great having someone there to help me get home to the island
inspiring
she makes me feel like I matter
relieved
she gave me strength to stay sober
perfect
I'm relieved that someone can help me
blessing
she gave me a feeling of confidence that I can be a productive
member
of society
positive
she gives me better chances for staying clean and not relapsing
caring
comforting to have someone who knows what you're capable of

supportive
she really inspired me to do my best
friendly
perfect to get out and have someone there and not just be alone
excellent
I feel like a normal person, not a caged wild animal, not a government number.

Unlocking the Gates continues the hard work of identifying and addressing the needs of incarcerated and formerly incarcerated individuals, successfully partnering with the First Nations Health Authority and most recently with a new men's prison, where the warden is hiring only individuals who have not had previous prison-guard experience. The warden aims to create an institution that prioritizes mental health, communal well-being, mutual respect, and compassionate care.

Warden Tole's vision and the original research team's hope to engage in meaningful participatory action is now playing out in new arenas, inviting into being new possible worlds of communal renewal and hope-in-action. What initially began as a women's communal health and wellness initiative in the hope of recovery and healing has turned into social intervention, advocacy, and action.[12] As Mo writes, through hope arrives healing.

Hope[13]

hopeless
my life
hope
to die
hopeless
getting busted
hope
charges will be dropped
hopeless
going to court
hope
for short sentence
hopeless
off to jail

hope for ACCW
hopeless
turns to hope
hope
turns to healing

3 TEACHING STORY THROUGH FRAGMENTS OF LIVES LIVED

In between arrest and release there is a space ... and in that space there is the opportunity to choose. The support needed is simply to help the choosing process because in that choice lies freedom.

(Granger-Brown, cited in Martin et al. 2019, xiii)

Our participatory action research dwells in liminal spaces between what is imagined, and what is impossible – inside and beyond the gates. We chose, as researchers, to attend to possibility, renewal, and new beginnings in the midst of difficult narratives in difficult places. With all that arrived, two books, *Arresting Hope* (2014) and *Releasing Hope* (2019) were published, containing the stories and writings of women: the first book tells of the narratives within the prison gates; the second contains the difficult narratives of women seeking to re-enter their communities. In the compilation of both books, we offered a bricolage (Berry 2015) of arrested hope released, enacted in action and story with all its vulnerabilities and imperfections. We chose to empower this telling of women's lived experience within and beyond the prison gates through the women's writings. Mo's writings, poetry, artwork, and narratives are interwoven throughout both books, in recognition of the lived experience of those whose voices she has listened to over thirty years of incarceration and inquiry. As Mo says, "I am a woman of lived experience."

You might imagine our research and the two books that document our learning as a kaleidoscope of multi-voiced narrative inquiry, an interweaving of illustrations, stories, inquiry, and actions-in-hope that were undertaken by women formerly incarcerated, researchers within and outside the gates.[14] Mo's narratives, poetry, and illustrations signal the difficult journey outside the gate with those who have been released and yet who are imprisoned still by a society unwilling and/or unable to accept responsibility for the health and well-being of those it has imprisoned upon their release. Found poems, such as *Hopes for Release*, in which participants responded to the question, "What do you hope for after your release? were composed by scholar poet Carl Leggo from a series of research interviews conducted by our co-researchers, formerly incarcerated women. Themes of empowerment, voice, listening, being present, mutual respect, being received with compassionate care, relationship, and hope-in-action are threaded throughout the women' narratives, words, as they tread the thin edge of re-entry, recovery, wondering how they will be received, what their live might be outside the gates.

Hopes for Release[15]

    stay clean
stay clean
    stay clean
stay clean

stay out of jail
    stay strong
stay out of trouble
    stay focused
stay out of jail
    stay healthy
stay out of trouble
    stay connected

stay alive

Paulo Freire (1972) recognizes that within any community, knowledge is held and revealed within the stories of experience particular to each individual present. One cannot tell the complete story of a single institution or a life; each individual arrives in the midst of familial, communal, social, economic, cultural, institutional, and political narratives already in interplay. Within community dwell stories, perspectives, experiences, and insights that in the sharing and listening can reshape, contradict, and enlarge communal understanding and response. As poet scholar Carl Leggo writes in the introduction of *Releasing Hope*, "many of these texts are like fragments of coloured glass that reflect and refract the light in different ways as the glass is turned and seen from different perspectives" (cited in Martin et al. 2019, 3).

We sought through our research texts, in the spirit of poetic inquiry,[16] a performance of written fragments, moments, hesitations, poetic interjections of women's voices as they speak to hope, to violence, to action, to renewal, sounding melodies that interrupt the sound and weight of a gate locking behind.

MANIFESTO: LISTENING TO WHO YOU BECOME IN THE PRESENCE OF WHO ARRIVES

Perfect to get out and have someone there and not just be alone.

Formerly incarcerated woman

Listen to how you listen. Our chapter concludes with what we call our manifesto, *Listening to who you become in the presence of who arrives*, which invites you, as our reader, to reimagine what is possible. As we four editors neared the completion of our second book, our editing meetings located around the dining room table at Ruth's house, we paused, unsettled. "What questions have we asked as researchers during our meetings?" we wondered, during all our years together as we stitched our quilts of texts that simultaneously arrest and release hope-in-action. Ruth collated all our questions voiced through the two years, and Carl returned to us with this found poem, questions not to be answered, but to be a pause, a catalyst for reflecting on *the heart of what matters*.

Beset by Questions[17]

Who is served by incarceration?

Who are you?
Who are you becoming?
Who do you want to be?

Who has agency over writing your story?

Who is being released without any consideration for who will receive them?
What networks of support exist for those being released?

Where are the gaps?

Who is waiting for you?

Those in conversation with women incarcerated within, and those released, continue to seek meaningful ways to work with each other, in all our different roles, within an imperfect system of justice, within communities that support and hinder, resist and welcome. Warden Brenda Tole, Alison, Elder Holy Cow, Mo, and Ruth, along with countless others, have through the unfolding years worked tirelessly within and beyond the gates of ACCW to invite communities to engage with formerly incarcerated women as human beings with difficult stories, people not to be feared but rather welcomed. What arises are notions of empowerment, agency, voice, meaningful engagement, listening to what matters. Hope enacted through action[18] "enlarges the space of the possible" (Sumara and Davis 1997, 299).

We willingly recognize that our ongoing and past research has been fraught with relational dynamics born of familial and institutional violence and compliance, politics and policies, and at times, sheer human stubbornness, fear, broken hearts, substance use born of trauma, and all the messiness in between that is the human condition bounded by inequities. Our participatory health research with incarcerated and formerly incarcerated women through the past sixteen years has been bounded within a justice system and penal institution within and outside its gates, within the regulatory, financial, and social strictures of the university and community. The power differential between prisoner and prison guard, researcher and researched, even as co-researchers, is impossible to ignore. The university researcher restrained freely walks through the prison gates at the end of the day. Positionality matters. As Warden Tole noted in her interview, the philosophy and attitudes of those in position of power impact the policies and practices and relationships born inside and outside the gate. Mo offers her experience, her wisdom.

Keys to the Gates[19]

I've been watching women struggle with bridging the gap
between a life focused on crime, drugs, and prison
and a life

where they fit into mainstream society.
People need to know

it's not as simple as putting down the drugs
and getting on with your life.

The key to the gates of prison represents far more than just turning
the lock to open it on the days you are incarcerated or released.

For me, the day I was released
was the beginning of many unknown challenges
that I would have to face as I tried to find my place
in mainstream society.

So many barriers to moving forward in one's life
after many years of addiction that led to crime

Always on the outskirts of society and not sure where I fit
into this big wide world we live in

Actions-in-hope inside and beyond the gates are so often caged by prison policies and practices, communal resistance, homelessness and unemployment, substance use, unresolved trauma, and one's own self-sabotage borne of despair, disappointment, and loss. In our participatory action research with women incarcerated and formerly incarcerated, as Carl Leggo writes, "we have been surprised by hope … We seek to arrest hope in order to linger with hopefulness, we seek to acknowledge how hope arrests us so that we are always committed to radical transformation of individuals, institutions, communities, and social networks (Martin et al. 2019, 377).

What is possible when violence and locked cells, indifferent communities and inadequate support are disrupted by invitation, listening, and yes, love (hooks 2001)? We are all caged by visible and invisible bars, performing and performed by scripts and roles and language determined by those in power, by expectations, by habit – and yet, through hope-in-action, wide-awakeness (Greene 1978) seeks cracks in prison walls. As Carl writes, "prisons are not only places of punishment, marginalization and trauma, but they can also be places of hope, blessings even, where people with difficult lived experiences can begin to compose stories full of healing, anticipation, communication, education, connection and community" (Leggo, cited in Martin 2014, 4). To say, "yes and" ... and thus improvise another possible world into being.[20]

In the juxtaposition of voices, an orchestrated bricolage performs our experience in inquiry; recognitions of our learning spelled within and between the lines of knowing and not-knowing, doing and undoing.[21] Hope is fluid, navigated over time, constantly in peril. Our communal performative texts offer metaphorical, poetic, fragmented, lived and textual resistance to the dominant narratives of institutional violence[22] so that we might attend to another way of listening. How we receive each other in relationship and storying of stories matters. In the spirit of First Nation storytelling, in which the teachings are embodied in the story, the learning is the responsibility and work of the listener. In our offering, we chose to invite the reader's presence into the act of meaning making. To stand in front of the wire fence and wonder which side they, you, and we are positioned.

Hope is enacted – a precarious relationship where integrity, honesty, teamwork, comraderie, acceptance, and forgiveness of our imperfect presence guides our work. We sit in the difficulty, not knowing, undoing, recognizing the impossible within the possible (Salverson 2020; Frantzich 2013).

YES, AND

Releasing women from forced incarceration to live in co-created environments of compassionate care, communal responsibility, mutual respect, security from harm, with opportunities for learning, healing, agency, education, and meaningful work, where mistakes are a place for beginning anew, is now the hope of the work and communal responsibility that calls on each of us. ACCW in its time under the guidance of Warden Tole in relationship with the women who sought to reimagine their lives revealed what is possible. Mo's learning to survive from childhood abuse and journey into community leadership offers lessons yet to be unravelled. This chapter is our witnessing of emergent hope-in-action through communal care and mutual respect, enlarging the space of the possible as we attend to the voices and actions of women who choose to see each other, within an institution and in the community beyond, emboldened by practices of living inquiry (Meyer 2006) that create liberatory spaces of possibility.

Sustaining hope-as-action within community *is* a precarious in-between, an ever-shifting liminal space of possibility and yes, impossibility. Our research and this chapter speak of women's resilience in the midst of violence – relational and institutional. The resonant sound of the gate closing behind us whenever one of us entered or exited spoke simultaneously to both new possibilities and barriers of resistance. In between the stories told, the actions taken, we seek to listen to silences as yet to be recognized, impossible to behold the unspoken, the unsaid, the unspeakable (Salverson 2008,) and wonder what has yet to be said, who has yet to speak. Perhaps, the children of those with whom, and in whose absence, we have journeyed will prove our moral guide.

As we reflect on our research, we recognize that "a resonant song of hope" and "listening carefully" seems to be the lesson of this journey (Leggo, cited in Martin et al. 2019, 6). Poet Leonard Cohen writes, "Forget your perfect offering/there is a crack in everything/that's how the light gets in" (1993, 373). This chapter seeks the light revealed through women's narratives of what is possible when compassionate care, mutual respect, and a shared responsibility for a culturally sensitive commitment to practices of communal and individual health and wellness slip through the bars. In between spaces of policy and practice, reimagining incarceration as a healing place of community, welcome, and embrace will author new narratives, notwithstanding the challenges and heartbreak of lived experience. Hope turns to action, illuminating what is possible.

Throughout our engagement with our work inside and outside prison gates, we have wrestled with the Gordian knot of institutional containment and responsibilities of care. As evident throughout this collection of writings, an unconscionable number of individuals, groups, and communities have been and are being punished for reasons arising from political expediency, social devaluation, and economic ambition. An impoverished practice of containment and care has arisen in response to those with lived experiences of abuse, disavowal, greed, shame, and abandonment by families, schools, and incarceration facilities, which are all socially designed institutions whose primary responsibility is to care, to sustain, to nurture. Are we not all complicit? Communal loathing, shame, fear, and violence is all-encompassing: those who guard, restrain, limit, monitor, restrict another's freedom of agency are themselves incarcerated within systems and actions where power imbalances exist, and violence, in all its diversity of forms, recognized or not, is enacted.

Stories silenced, and institutional narratives written, of those who are unwanted, those who resist, those who are abused, and those who are restrained, beg to be interrogated. Our responsibility and call to action is to interrogate and reconsider the institutional, social, economic, political, and communal scripts that infiltrate our lives. To successfully interrupt what is perceived and experienced as institutional violence, we need to listen to *how* we listen (Armos 2020), and to be wide awake to how we are individually and collectively treated in turn.

How are we, you and I, being performed and by who? Whose script? For what purpose(s)? Who and what do we value, and why or why not? "What we do is what we know," writes Varela (1987), "and ours is but one of many possible worlds." Is improvisation possible? Are we open and willing to risk what is involved in co-creating new possible worlds? And to do so in recognition and reimagining of the impoverished institutions and policies that imprison? *This too is possible.*

What is hope?
What sustains our hope in this work?
What does it mean to be part of a community?
What does it mean to write a story?
What does it mean to offer a story?
What sustains health outside of prison?
What am I supposed to be learning?
What are the women given when they are released?
What can people do to better their lives coming out of prison?

How does telling one's story support healing?
How are you received?
How do you create a life?
    How will *you* respond?[23]

Imagine this. A warden who is not a warden is tasked to reimagine a prison that is not a prison in partnership with a caring and curious doctor, a First Nations Elder, a recreation therapist, guards who are not guards, and the women who arrive, all bearing stories. *Giving back and meaningful work matters. Being seen matters. Holding the space open matters.* Inside and beyond the gates women come together in a collective spirit of sharing healing stories, listening, collaboration, determination, resilience, resourcefulness, and promise, embodying hope-in-action, recognizing that their hearts may be broken, again and again.

And yet … between the cracks, hope prevails.

NOTES

We acknowledge that our work and learning have taken place on the traditional and unceded land of the Coast Salish peoples, including the shared traditional territories of the Sḵwx̱wú7mesh Úxwumixw (Squamish), Tsleil-Waututh, and xʷməθkʷəy̓əm (Musqueam) First Nations and south of the Fraser River numerous Stó:lō Nations, including the Kwantlen, Semiahmoo, Tsawwassen, Katzie, Kwantlen, Kwikwetlem, and Qayqayt First Nations.

We recognize the challenges experienced by women who have been incarcerated, their stories, and the hope that is released into our stewardship, whose voices contribute to *Arresting Hope* and *Releasing Hope*. We honour Luciana Ricciutelli, editor-in-chief of Inanna Publications and Education Inc, for her thoughtful oversight and expertise in making possible the publication of *Arresting Hope* and *Releasing Hope*. Inanna Publications has provided copyright consent for the re-printing of all images, quotations, poems, and extracts from *Arresting Hope* and *Releasing Hope* that are contained in this article. We hope her good work will continue with those who now tender her place. We thank Nelson Luk for his careful attention to detail and for his assistance in formatting this manuscript. And we honour Carl Leggo, whose voice and spirit, enthusiasm and heart, is so present in this writing.

1 Poem by Mo Korchinski, cited in Martin et al. 2019, 19.

2 This was a remark Korchinski made in conversation with co-author Lynn and co-editor Katherine Rossiter, 26 July 2021.

3 In conversation with Korchinski, leading to her poem, "Done Button." Cited in Martin et al. 2019, 355.

4 Ruth's journal is a constructed reflection of her experiences and feelings through the participatory action research that she led inside ACCW.

5 Poem by Carl Leggo, cited in Martin et al. 2014, 96. This Abecedarian was created from a mapping exercise undertaken by women participating in a writing workshop about their experiences and qualities that for them made ACCW a place of hope, hope-in-action, and possible renewal. Professor Leggo created the found poems chosen for this article, by

selecting lines, words, and phrases of formerly incarcerated women in response to interview questions from research projects over the years. A selective listening that the poet scholar engages in, attuning to the words of others, listening for the melodies of their temperatures. See Prendergast, Leggo, and Sameshima 2009; Barba 1995.

6 Ignition is a music group that performed at the correctional centre.

7 Our participatory action research continued outside the gates with women, formerly incarcerated, who encouraged the university research team to continue the research outside the prison gates. A number of research projects were initiated, notably Women in2 Healing and Unlocking the Gates, including the writing of *Arresting Hope* and *Releasing Hope*.

8 Women in2 Healing was a self-directed outreach group of formerly incarcerated women established to provide emotional support, friendship, and guidance to each other. With research funding, a Women in2 Healing newsletter was distributed to women within ACCW; a Facebook support group was initiated; and monthly meetings were held. Many of those who participated in Women in2 Healing became involved in the design and implementation of a variety of research projects.

9 See the extensive list of publications, conference presentations, media interviews, documentary films, etc. in *Releasing Hope*, 2019, 399–406.

10 Poem by Leggo, cited in Martin et al. 2019, 98.

11 Ibid., 161.

12 *Arresting Hope* (2014) and *Releasing Hope* (2019), document the collective experiences of women within and outside Alouette Correctional Centre for Women and the research projects that emerged. Each book is a bricolage (Kincheloe 2001) of the women's stories, poetry, interviews, poetry, extracts from Women in2 healing newsletters, reports, illustrations by Mo, paragraphs of passion and found poetry created by poet scholar Carl Leggo from interviews conducted by the women. All royalties and net proceeds are donated to the Vancouver Foundation Arresting Hope Education Fund, which provides educational awards for women with incarceration experience and their children. The Education Fund is run by the Vancouver Foundation (www.vancouverfoundation.ca/arrestinghope) and awarded recipients are selected by a committee hosted by Nicola Valley Institute of Technology.

13 Poem by Korchinski, cited in Martin et al. 2014, 155.

14 All quotes, poems, and text were originally published in *Arresting Hope* (2014) and *Releasing Hope* (2019). These are not primary data but rather offerings of participating women who chose to share their insights,

stories, and experiences so that their voices might be attended to as experts in their lived experience.

15 Poem by Leggo, cited in Martin et al. 2019, 98.

16 Poetic inquiry is a form of arts-based research that recognizes the writing of poetry as inquiry, and knowledge representation. See Prendergast, Leggo, and Sameshima 2009; Poetic Inquiry 2021.

17 Poem by Leggo, cited in Martin et al. 2019, 11. These questions emerged throughout our conversations together with Carl around Ruth's dining room table. They are not presented here to be answered but to serve as catalysts to action. We have chosen to divide the poem in two sections, so as not to overwhelm the reader with questions.

18 Hannah Arendt (1958) writes of different ways one can engage: task, labour, and action. In institutions, one can be engaged in time consuming, repetitive tasks, or in labour that maintains what already is. Action arrives when we look again at that which occupies us. To engage unthinkingly in tasks or labour to bureaucracies, governments, or industries without considering the consequences is to abandon our responsibility to ourselves and to others, to the health and well-being of our environment and our communities. Action as envisioned by Arendt asks of us critical, meaningful, and insightful presence in our relationships and what we choose to do. As poet Mary Oliver asks, "What do you plan to do with your one wild and precious life?" Hope-in-action enacts imagination that attends to the possibilities of hope that may be realized through our actions in relationship with and in the presence of others. To engage in hope-in-action is to be responsible to that which we may or may not yet imagined, and are willing to embody.

19 Poem by Korchinski, cited in Martin et al. 2019, 15.

20 Yes and ... is the invitation of improvisation. Improvisors must be willing to receive what is offered, and have the courage, imagination, willingness to improvise from *here and now*, not knowing what will arrive, but open and welcoming to all possibilities. The challenge of improvisation is not to relapse into stereotypes or scripts that lock the players and audience into the expected and the known. See Nachmanovitch (2002), who writes about improvisation as a musician, and in life.

21 See Frantzich (2013, 323) for discussion on undoing as a critical component to knowledge creation.

22 We use the term institutional violence deliberately as a two-pronged allusion to the hegemony of conventional academic text and the oppressions experienced within the towers of the academy.

23 Poem by Leggo, cited in Martin et al. 2019, 11. These questions emerged throughout our conversations together with Carl around Ruth's dining room table. They are not presented here to be answered but to serve as catalysts to action.

REFERENCES

Arendt, Hannah. 1977. *Between Past and Future*. New York: Penguin.

Barba, E. 1995. *The Paper Canoe: A Guide to Theatre Anthropology*. Translated by R. Fowler London: Routledge.

hooks, bell. 2001. *All about Love: New Visions*. New York: First Perennial.

Berry, K. 2015. "Research as Bricolage: Embracing Relationality, Multiplicity and Complexity." In *Doing Educational Research: A Handbook*, edited by Kenneth Tobin and Joe Kincheloe, 77–110. Leiden: Brill.

Frantzich, K. 2013. "Theater of the Psyche: The Emergence of Embodied Theater Ecology and the Stage as Home(be)coming." PhD diss., Pacifica Graduate Institute, Carpinteria.

Freire, Paulo. 1972. *Pedagogy of the Oppressed*. New York: Penguin.

Janssen P., M. Korchinski, S. Desmarais, A. Albert, L. Condello, M. Buchanan A. Granger-Brown, V. Ramsden, L. Fels, J. Buxton, C. Leggo, and Ruth Elwood Martin. 2017. "Factors That Support Successful Transition to Community among Women Leaving Prison in British Columbia: A Prospective Cohort Study." *CMAJ Open* 5, no. 3: E717–23.

Kinceloe, J.L. 2011. "Describing the Bricolage: Conceptualizing a New Rigor." *Qualitative Research* 7, no. 6: 679–92.

Martin, Ruth Elwood, Lynn Fels, and Carl Leggo. 2014. *Arresting Hope: Women Taking Action in Prison Health Inside Out*. Toronto: Inanna.

Martin, Ruth Elwood, Mo Korchinski, Lynn Fels, and Carl Leggo. 2019. *Releasing Hope: Women's Stories of Transition from Prison to Community*. Toronto: Inanna.

Martin, Ruth Elwood, and Brenda Tole. 2016. "Mother-Child Unit Supports Infants Born to Incarcerated Mothers." *Transition*. The Vanier Institute of the Family. Accessed 26 September 2020. https://vanier institute.ca/supporting-the-health-of-mothers-and-their-babies-in-the-context-of-incarceration.

McLeod K. E., M. Korchinski, P. Young, T. Milkovich, C. Hemingway, M. DeGroot, L. Condello, L. Fels, J.A. Buxton, P.A. Janssen, A. Granger-Brown, V.R. Ramsden, M. Buchanan, and R.E. Martin. 2020.

"Supporting Women Leaving Prison through Peer Health Mentoring: A Participatory Health Research Study." *CMAJ Open* 7, no. 4: E1–14.

Meyer, K. 2006. "Living Inquiry – A Gateless Gate and a Beach." In *Spirituality, Ethnography, and Teaching: Stories from Within*, edited by W. Ashton and D. Denton, 156–66. New York: Peter Lang.

Nachmanovitch, S. 2002. *Free Play: Improvisation in Life and Art*. New York. Penguin Putnam.

Poetic Inquiry. 2009. *Educational Insights* 13, no. 32. https://einsights.ogpr.educ.ubc.ca/v13n03/toc.html.

Prendergast, M., C. Leggo, and P. Sameshima, eds. 2009. *Poetic Inquiry: Vibrant Voices in the Social Sciences*. Rotterdam: Sense.

Salverson, J. 2008. "Taking Liberties: A Theatre Class of Foolish Witnesses." *Research in Drama Education* 13, no. 2: 245–55.

– 2020. "Loopings of Love and Rage: Sitting in the Trouble." *Canadian Theatre Review* 181 (Winter).

Sumara, D.J., and B. Davis. 1997. "Enlarging the Space of the Possible: Complexity, Complicity, and Action Research Practices." In *Action Research as a Living Practice*, edited by T. Carson and D.J. Sumara, 299–312. New York: Peter Lang.

Thomasson, A. 2017. "The Gardener, the Actor, and the Educator: Six Lessons towards Creating and Cultivating Spaces of Vulnerability between Theatre for Young Audiences and Education." MA thesis, Simon Fraser University.

Varela, F.J. 1987. "Laying Down a Path in Walking." In *GAIA, A Way of Knowing: Political Implications of the New Biology*, edited by W.I. Thompson, 48–64. Hudson, NY: Lindisfarne Press.

Index

The following abbreviations are used: ACCW *(Alouette Correction Centre for Women);* HRC *(Huronia Regional Centre);* I/DD *(intellectually/developmentally disabled);* PCEPA *(Protection of Communities and Exploited Persons Act); and* SAWP *(Seasonal Agricultural Worker Program).*

abolitionist movement. *See* prison and police abolitionist movement

abortion: institutional denial of access to, 28, 30, 32–3, 37–8, 40, 43n4

affect: and affective economy, 13, 160, 172, 182; and care/loathing as affective forces, 13–15; as force of circulation/transmission, 13; and white landowners/employers vs racialized agricultural workers, 160, 164–5, 172

aggregate services settings, for I/DD people, 122–6; carceral institutions, 125–6; custodial housing, 124–5; emergency shelters, 124; long-term care institutions, 123; psychiatric institutions, 122–3; retirement homes, 123–4; shelters/homelessness services, 124. *See also* intellectually/developmentally disabled (I/DD) people, institutionalization of, *and entries following*

Ahmed, Sara: on affective economies, 13, 160, 182

Alouette Correction Centre for Women (ACCW) (British Columbia): as compassionate institutional model, 20, 293–316; first warden's role in establishing/encouraging, 295–9; Indigenous spaces/activities at, 295–8; inmate advisory committee at, 299, 302; recreation at, 296–7; research project on women's health at, 300–1; research project's cancellation by new warden, 301; research project's continuation by formerly incarcerated women, 301–5. *See also entry below*

Alouette Correction Centre for Women, participatory action research project led by former residents of, 301–5; and Bonding through Bars conference, 302; and court case of incarcerated mothers, 302; as hope-in-action initiative, 301–2, 304, 306, 307–13, 315n18; manifesto of, 307–10; and publication of prison/community narratives, 305–6, 307, 314n7, 314n14; and *Unlocking the Gates* peer mentorship program/non-profit society, 301, 302–3, 304, 314n7; and *Women in2 Healing* support group, 301, 314nn7–8. See also *Arresting Hope*; *Releasing Hope*

American Psychological Association, 191

Arendt, Hannah, 10, 315n18

Arresting Hope (ACCW women's book), 313, 314n7, 314n14; as containing women's prison narratives, 305; Korchinski's contributions to, 304–6, 314n12; Leggo's poetry in, 298, 314n12

"Ashley Treatment," to arrest physical growth of I/DD girls, 207, 218n1

Australia: commission on institutional child sexual abuse in, 76; disability royal commission of, 211; Good Shepherd laundries/reformatories in, 47, 51, 54; permanent contraception for I/DD women in, 207; sex workers' social media platform and advocacy group in, 258; younger I/DD people at long-term facilities in, 122–3. *See also* Konstandinitis, Janice

Autumn (former Good Shepherd inmate): on extraction rather than filling of teeth, 50; on inmates as irredeemable/"worthless," 54–5; on resistance/self-preservation strategies, 59; on surveillance/scrutiny, 57; on use of holy cards to exchange information, 60; on weekly "instruction" sessions, 52

Backhouse, Constance, 239, 241, 258–9

Backpage.com (classified advertising website), 242

Baert, Kirk, 76–7

Beaton, Alexander, 84, 95, 97

Bedford case, on unconstitutionality of Canadian prostitution laws, 240

Benjamin, Walter, 10

Ben-Moshe, Liat: on carceral ableist logic, 115; on "carceral matrix," 9; on deinstitutionalization, 15; on neighbourhood resistance to disability integration, 182, 184; and prison abolitionist movement, 15, 115, 129

Ben-Moshe, Liat, Chris Chapman, and Allison C. Carey, eds, *Disability Incarcerated: Imprisonment and Disability in the United States and Canada*, 11

Berton, Pierre: article on HRC by, 98, 100–1

Bond, Betty (HRC survivor), 74, 85
Bonding through Bars (conference), 302
Bourdieu, Pierre, on symbolic/soft or "gentle" violence, 49–50, 51, 63; and "destiny effect" as legacy of, 54, 56; and gender domination, as paradigm of, 64n4; and "hidden persuasion," as exerted by everyday "order of things," 58, 65n15; and victim-blaming/loss of self-worth, 54–5, 56, 270. *See also* Good Shepherd laundries and reformatories for girls/women, *and entry following*
Bowman, Chaparral (former Good Shepherd inmate): on damaged/"broken" sense of self-worth, 55, 56; on legacy of self-estrangement, 61
Brantford League of Christian Women (BLCW): tour of Mohawk Institute by, 97–8, 100, 101–2
Buck, Carrie, and court case of, 203–4, 217
Butler, Judith, 243, 248; on grievable/ungrievable lives, 243, 249, 250–1
Butterfly: The Asian and Migrant Sex Worker Support Network, 243–4, 260n5

Canada Mortgage and Housing Corporation: on retirement homes, 123–4
Canadian Alliance for Sex Work Law Reform, 254, 255, 259–60
Canadian Association for Community Living (CACL), 207–8. *See also* Inclusion Canada
Canadian Charter of Rights and Freedoms, 247
Canadian Girls in Training (CGIT), 36, 44n7
Canadian Medical Protective Association, 207
Canton Asylum for Insane Indians (South Dakota), 180–1
Cape Breton Regional Police Department: prostitution sting operation of, 240, 246–9; "Say Something If You See Something" initiative of, 251–2. *See also* "John Be Gone," *and entry following*
capitalism: and colonialism, as forces of violence against unhoused people, 269–70, 285–7, 289, 290n5; and concept of autonomous liberal citizen, 153–4; as reinforced by justice system, 295; slow violence of, as used against unhoused people, 184, 186–7, 188; and state control/loathing of I/DD people, 139–43. *See also* sheltered workshops for I/DD people, *and entry following*; Shelter Video Project Collective on Colonial/Capitalist Violence (Toronto): *We Want You To Listen*
carceral institutions, I/DD people in, 125–6; in Ontario, 125; in Quebec, 125; in Saskatchewan, 125–6; self-injurious behaviours of, 125, 126; solitary confinement of, 125

care: and access to institutionalized bodies, 14; as affective force, 14–15; and degradation of institutionalized people, 14–15; and gendered disability violence, under pretext of, 204, 216–17; neighbourhood resistance to, for unhoused people, 182, 184; in settings of ostensible care, 5, 19–20; in total institutional orders, 5; in trans-institutional era, 5, 18–19. *See also entry below*; institutional violence
care and loathing, as drivers of institutional violence, 4–5, 13–15, 17–20; as affective forces, 13–15; and degradation of institutionalized bodies, 14–15; Gordian knot of, 5, 16, 311; and roots of total institutional violence, 5, 17–18, 27–112; in settings of ostensible care, 5, 19–20, 201–317; in Stanford Prison Experiment, 283; in trans-institutional era, 5, 13–14, 18–19, 115–17
Chaparro, Juan López, 159
Children's Aid Society (CAS), 71
Cohen, Leonard, 311
Community Living Ontario, 146
concentration camps, 7, 10
Condella, Lara-Lisa (teacher at ACCW), 296
congregate settings, for I/DD people, 119–20; group homes as, 119; inappropriate use of antipsychotic drugs at, 120; restrictive interventions used at, 119–20
contraception, forced: for I/DD women/girls, 207, 208, 218n1
COVID-19: and homelessness, 180; and I/DD women, 218; and mutual aid, 287; at SAWP farms, 159, 161, 165, 166–7, 169–70
Criminal Code: forensic psychiatric system and, 121; sex workers and, 239, 240, 243, 248
Criminal Injuries Compensation Board (CICB; Ontario), 213
criminal justice system, I/DD people in. *See* carceral institutions, I/DD people in; dual diagnostic forensic settings, for I/DD people
Crown wards, class action lawsuit on treatment of, 211
custodial housing, for I/DD people, 124–5; in BC, 125; in Ontario, 125

deinstitutionalization, 5, 137; and carceral archipelago/matrix, 9, 15; and dispersal of institutional methods/violence into community, 9, 115, 138, 146–7, 164, 180, 202; Joint Task Force on, 202, 211; and prison/police abolitionist movement, 15–16; and rehabilitative work, 137, 138, 142, 144–9, 154. *See also* intellectually/developmentally disabled (I/DD) people, institutionalization of, *and entries following*; transinstitutional era
Department of Indian Affairs (DIA): inspections/reports on Mohawk Institute by, 95, 100, 101, 104; and Mohawk Institute funding, 102, 106–7

Depo-Provera (contraceptive drug), 207, 208
Developmental Services Housing Task Force (Ontario), 203
developmental services settings, for I/DD people, 119–21; congregate settings, 119–20; dual diagnostic forensic psychiatric settings, 121; dual diagnostic services, 120. *See also* intellectually/developmentally disabled (I/DD) people, institutionalization of, *and entries following*
Diagnostic and Statistical Manual of Mental Disorders, 5th ed. (DSM-5), 121
Disability Rights Coalition v. Nova Scotia (Attorney General), 122, 214
DNA registry, for sex offenders, 247, 257, 261n10
domiciliary hostels, 125, 202, 203
Donham, Parker, 243, 258
Dougall, Harold (HRC survivor), 102
Down syndrome, children with, 82–4; surgical procedures denied to, 83–4
Downtown Mission (Windsor, Ontario), 183, 185, 186, 187, 189
Downtown Windsor Business Improvement Association, 183, 188
drugs, as used in institutional violence: antipsychotic, 120; as chemical restraints, 117, 122; contraceptive, 207, 208, 218n1; sedative, 71–2
drugs, illegal: former ACCW resident on, 294, 308–9; and sex work, 250, 256. *See also entry below*
drugs, illegal, as issue for unhoused people: in downtown Windsor, 179, 181, 183, 185–91; in shelters, 273, 276–7, 282, 288; and unavailability of harm reduction, 189–90, 191, 271, 277
dual diagnosis, of I/DD people, 120. *See also entries below*
dual diagnostic forensic settings, for I/DD people, 121; in Ontario, 121
dual diagnostic services, for I/DD people, 120
Dubé, Paul (Ontario Ombudsman), 125

emergency shelters, I/DD people in, 124
Employment Standards Act (Ontario), 146, 148, 150
Epstein, Griffin, 141–2, 148–9
Erevelles, Nirmala, 139, 140–1, 148–9
eugenics, 11, 271; and gendered disability violence, 14, 203–4, 209–10; and forced sterilization, 203–4, 207, 208; as "newgenics," 209–10; recent reappearance of, 218; and rehabilitation, 141–3; and white supremacism/settler colonialism, 15, 142. *See also* group homes, gendered disability violence in, *and entries following*; reproductive violence, against I/DD people; sterilization, forced, of I/DD people

Eugenics Board of Alberta, 203, 204
Eve (*Re: Eve*, 1986). See *Re: Eve*

Fayant, Mary ("Holy Cow"; ACCW First Nations Elder), 295–6, 297, 298, 308
Fletcher, Wendy, analysis of Mohawk Institute reports by, 93, 95, 104; on children's deaths, 103, 106; on poor nutrition/dental care, 102; on unqualified teachers, 97
Foreign Agricultural Resources Management Services (FARMS), 162, 171
Foucault, Michel, 258; and concept of carceral archipelago, 9, 13; on "heterotopias of deviation," 53, 64n10; Malacrida on, 41, 42; on power in total institutions, 35–6
Freire, Paulo, 306
Fricker, Amanda: on epistemic injustice, 270

Galtung, Johan, 10–11
Garrie v. Janus Joan Inc. (Ontario Human Rights Tribunal), 150
gendered disability violence, in institutions, 201–3; and background/history of eugenic sterilizations, 203–4; law's complicity in, 211, 212–13, 217; legal redress for/prevention of, 211–13; LGBTQ community and, 208; need for coordinated activism against, 216–18; and pretext of "care," 204, 216–17. *See also* group homes, gendered disability violence in, *and entries following*; reproductive violence, against I/DD people
Goffman, Erving, 16; on stigma, 243, 256; on total institutions, 7–9, 33, 41, 42, 161, 164. *See also* total institutional model; total institutions, as studied by Goffman
Good Shepherd, Sisters of, 47–8, 63n2. *See also entries below*
Good Shepherd laundries and reformatories for girls/women, 17, 47–65; industrial labour at, 49, 52, 53, 58; institutional violence at, as symbolic, 49–50, 51, 54–5, 56, 63; legitimizing "rescue"/"reform" mission of, 49–50; post-institutional legacy/exile borne by survivors of, 48–9, 50–1, 52, 53, 60–3; regulation booklets used at, 51–2; resistance/self-preservation strategies by inmates of, 58–61; victim-blaming by inmates of, as turning stigma into stigmata, 48, 54–7, 61–2. *See also* Magdalene laundries; *entries for former inmates, esp.* Autumn; Konstandinitis, Janice
Good Shepherd laundries and reformatories for girls/women, examples of institutional violence at: denial of education, 50; denigration/labelling, 55, 61; enforced silence, 48, 50, 51–2, 53, 56, 57, 58, 59, 60–1; extraction rather than filling of teeth, 50; humiliation/shaming, 48–9, 50, 51, 52, 54–7, 58, 61–2; infantilization, 50, 57; physical punishment, 51, 52, 62;

renaming/erasure of identity, 50, 56, 57, 60; segregation from families/communities, 53; surveillance/judgmental gaze, 56–7, 60; weekly "instruction" sessions, 52
Good Shepherd laundries and reformatories for girls/women, resistance/self-preservation strategies by inmates and survivors of, 58–61; breaking of silence through narratives of institutionalization, 48, 58, 60–1; exchange of information on holy cards, 59–60; self-injury in laundries, 58; skin-cutting, 58, 59; skin-inking/tattooing, 58, 59
Granger-Brown, Alison (ACCW recreational therapist), 296–7, 298, 305
group homes: definition of, 202; compared to domiciliary hostels/host family program, 202, 203; as institutions, 202; jurisdictional confusion over, 203; staff of, as unregulated/prone to high turnover and burnout, 215–16; violence as built into, 202–3, 213–16. *See also entries below*
group homes, gendered disability violence in, 14, 20, 201–19; as built into group home setting, 202–3, 213–16; contemporary examples of, 203–10; as enabled by geography, 203, 205, 213–14; legal redress for/prevention of, 211–13; and need for accessible community housing, 213–14; need for coordinated activism against, 216–18; as "part of everyday life," 201–2; and pretext of "care," 204, 216–17
group homes, gendered disability violence in, contemporary examples of, 203–10; and aim of preventing reproduction, 204–5; and background/history of eugenic sterilizations, 203–4; barriers to relationships/parenting supports, 14, 20, 201, 203, 208–10; menstrual management/suppression, 14, 20, 201, 203, 206–8; sexual violence, 20, 205–6. *See also* eugenics; menstruation, methods of managing/suppressing, in I/DD people; reproductive violence, against I/DD people; sterilization, forced, of I/DD people
group homes, gendered disability violence in, law's role in, 203–19; as complicit, 211, 212–13, 217; and eugenic sterilization cases, 203–4, 207, 208; and jurisdictional confusion over group homes, 203; and legal redress/prevention, 211–13; for survivors of violence, 213

harm reduction, lack of, 271, 277; for Windsor's unhoused population, 189–90, 191
Harris, Kamala, 242
Hill, Wilhemina (TB victim at Mohawk Institute), 106
Homeless Coalition of Windsor-Essex County, 189
Hospital for Sick Children (Toronto), 83–4

Host Family Program (Ontario), for I/DD people, 202, 203
House of Commons Standing Committee on Justice and Human Rights: "Preventing Harm in the Sex Industry: A Review of the Protection of Communities and Exploited Persons Act" (report), 259–60
Hughes, Everett C., 7
human trafficking: and Canadian sex work legislation, 239, 250, 251–2, 254, 261n5; and US sex work legislation, 242, 258
Huronia Regional Centre (HRC) (Orillia, Ontario): about, 87n1, 94; Berton's article on, 98, 100–1; as "built to impress the public from afar," 239; closure of, 68, 145; and false narratives told by official files at, 12; as former asylum, 82, 87n1, 93, 94, 95, 97; government involvement at, 95; lawsuit against, by former residents, 68, 149; as model for other Canadian institutions, 6; off-property work programs run by, 99, 105; poor hygiene/sanitary conditions at, 100–2; preventable deaths at, 105–6; as teaching hospital, 97. *See also entries below; entries for* HRC *survivors, esp.* Logie, Brian; Scott, Cindy
Huronia Regional Centre, institutional violence against children with disabilities at, survivors' stories of, 3, 17, 68–88; and discourse of childhood innocence/vulnerability, 75–80, 86–7; and discourse of evil/dehumanization of "problematic" children, 80–6, 87; and extreme power imbalance, 76–7, 79, 80; and isolation from family/friends, 76–7; permanent legacy of, 74–5; and pretense of discipline, 70–2, 79–80, 85–6
Huronia Regional Centre, institutional violence against othered bodies at, as compared to Mohawk Institute, 17–18, 92–108; as capitalizing on forced labour, 98–9; and devaluation/degradation in death, 105–7; and forced conformity through education, 96–8; and institutional goals/funding/management, 94–6; and neglect/negligence, 100–2; and presence of unmarked graves, 92; and sexual abuse, 104–5; and social hierarchies of abuse, 103–4
Huronia Regional Centre, specific types of institutional violence at: as accompanied by drugs/sedatives, 71–2; in communal showers, 72, 77–8; forced nakedness/denial of privacy, 71, 73, 77–9, 80, 85, 101; forced participation in "games"/activities for staff entertainment, 71–2, 85, 104; forced viewing of farm animals' slaughter, 70–1, 74, 80; physical violence, under guise of punishment, 70–2, 79–80, 85–6; at play time/in playroom, 84–5; psycho-emotional violence, 74–5; sexual violence, 69, 72–3, 77–9, 85; use of straitjacket, 86

Huronia Regional Centre cemetery: gravestones for, as made by boys, 98; repurposing of numbered gravestones at, as patio stones, 107; unmarked graves at, 92; as used to threaten children, 74

Inclusion Canada (formerly Canadian Association for Community Living), 123, 124, 152

Indigenous people: loathing of, as leading to cultural genocide, 92–3; and missing/murdered women and girls, 211; and sex work, 249–50, 252–3, 255. *See also* Alouette Correction Centre for Women (ACCW), *and entry following*; Mohawk Institute, *and entry following*; residential schools

Inglis v. British Columbia (Minister of Public Safety) (2013), 212, 302

institutional violence, 3–20; care and loathing, as drivers of, 4–5, 13–15, 17–20; continuum of, from "cold" to "hot," 138; deinstitutionalization and, 5, 9, 15–16; disability studies scholarship on, 11; of Holocaust, 10; roots of, 5, 17–18; as structural violence, 10–11; total institutional model and, 4–5, 7–9, 13, 15–16, 17–18; in trans-institutional era, 5, 9, 13–14, 15, 18–19; unruliness/resistance and, 11–12

intellectually/developmentally disabled (I/DD) people, institutionalization of, 18, 115–29; in aggregate services settings, 122–6; carceral ableist logic of, 115; in criminal justice system, 125–6; in developmental services settings, 119–21; in dual diagnosis settings, 120–1; and indicators of institutions, as used to evaluate institutional systems/spaces, 117–18; and need for abolitionist movement, 129; and need for disability justice, 116–17; and need to recognize residents' positive rights, 212–13; and size of population, 118–19; and use of restraints, 117, 120, 122; and use of seclusion/solitary confinement, 117, 121, 125, 127; variables of violence in, as based on behavioural markers/capacity for confinement, 126–8. *See also entries below*

intellectually/developmentally disabled (I/DD) people, institutionalization of, aggregate services settings for, 122–6; carceral institutions, 125–6; custodial housing, 124–5; emergency shelters, 124; long-term care institutions, 123; psychiatric institutions, 122–3; retirement homes, 123–4; shelters/homelessness services, 124. *See also individual settings*

intellectually/developmentally disabled (I/DD) people, institutionalization of, developmental services settings for, 119–21; congregate settings, 119–20; dual diagnostic forensic psychiatric settings, 121; dual

diagnostic services, 120. *See also individual settings*
Ireland: Good Shepherd laundries/reformatories in, 47. *See also* Sullivan, Maureen

"John Be Gone" (Sydney, Nova Scotia prostitution sting operation), 240, 246–9; and earlier complaints about sex work, 246–7, 249–50; as following federal sex work legislation, 239–40, 241; media coverage of, 243, 244, 247, 248; neighbourhoods targeted in, 244; and police unit's recognition of sex workers' stigma/exposure to violence, 249–50; and portrayal of sex workers as victims of exploitation, 239–40, 250–3; and question of entrapment, 247, 256–7; source material on, as used ethically in study of, 243–6. *See also entry below*
"John Be Gone" list, of arrested men, 240, 246–9; and concept of list as instrument of discipline/delimitation, 238, 252, 259; and concept of "shameable lives," 250–1; as "deterrent for others," 247–8, 257; as leading to concealment of subsequent activity, 257–8; and listing in DNA registry, 247, 257, 261n10; and men's post-arrest experiences, 245, 247–9; shame/criminality brought on by, 250–1, 256–8
Joint Task Force on Deinstitutionalization, 202, 211
Juvenile Delinquents Acts (1908–84), 32–3, 36, 43nn5–6

Khan, Ummni, 246, 256, 258
Konstandinitis, Janice (former Good Shepherd inmate): on derogatory labelling of inmates, 55; on infantilization of inmates, 57; on inmates' embodied shame, 56; on inmates' loss of identity/self, 57; on post-release need to maintain perpetual cleanliness, 61; on "spectacles of humiliation" at Magdalene laundries, 50, 51, 64n7; on weekly "instruction" sessions, 52
Korchinski, Mo (former ACCW resident), 294, 296, 308; *Hope*, 304–5; *Jail*, 293–4; *Keys to the Gates*, 308–9; on prison as lifesaving community, 294; as survivor/community leader, 310; and *Unlocking the Gates* non-profit, 302; writings, poetry, and artwork of, in ACCW women's books, 305–6, 314n12

labour, institutional: Goffman on, 161, 164; at Good Shepherd laundries, 49, 52, 53, 58; at HRC/Mohawk Institute, 98–9; as indentured, on SAWP farms, 159–60, 161, 163–4, 165, 168–71; as "simulated," at sheltered workshops, 146, 148, 151–2; as slavery, 53, 159–60, 164, 170–1; in US, 144–5. *See also* Good Shepherd laundries and reformatories for girls/women; Seasonal Agricultural Worker Program (SAWP),

and entries following; sheltered workshops for I/DD people, *and entry following*; work, for I/DD people
Lady Williston Hospital (Ohsweken, Ontario), 106
Lafferty, R.N., 80–1
Lam, Elene, 243–4, 260n5
Leggo, Carl (professor/poet working with ACCW women), 293, 306–8, 309–10, 311; *Beset by Questions*, 307–8; found poems created by, 313n5: *Hope Abecedarian*, 298; *Hopes for Release*, 302, 306; *Mentors: A Love Note*, 303–4; *What Is Hope?*, 312
Leroux v. Ontario, 214
Link, Bev (HRC survivor), 84–5
list, as instrument of discipline/delimitation, 238, 252, 259; and DNA registry, 247, 257, 261n10. *See also* "John Be Gone," *and entry following*; sex workers' clients, public listing of
loathing, 13–15; as affective force, 13–15; and devaluation/degradation of institutionalized people, 5, 14–15; of I/DD children/adults, 82–4, 86–7, 92, 126–7, 138, 139–43, 149; of Indigenous people/culture, 92–3; of migrant agricultural workers, 162; in settings of ostensible care, 5, 19–20; in trans-institutional era, 5, 13–14, 18–19. *See also* care and loathing, as drivers of institutional violence; institutional violence
Logie, Brian (HRC survivor), 83, 85, 88n5, 101; psycho-emotional impact on, 74; sexual abuse of, 72, 73, 77–8; use of straitjacket on, 86
long-term care institutions, for I/DD people, 123; high injury/mortality rates in, 123; as often places of last resort, 123; in Ontario, 123; specialized wings for younger people in, 123

MacDonald, Ashley, 240
MacKay, Peter, 241, 252–3
MacMurchy, Helen, 82
Magdalene laundries, 48, 53, 56, 60–1, 63n1; exchange of holy cards at, 59–60; as run by several religious orders, 64n3; "spectacles of humiliation" at, 50, 51, 64n7. *See also* Good Shepherd laundries and reformatories for girls/women, *and entries following*
Malacrida, Claudia: on institutionalization/eugenics in Alberta, 76, 180. *See also entry below*
Malacrida, Claudia, autoethnographic account of adolescent trauma and survival by, 17, 27–44; on author's experience of sexual abuse/juvenile justice system, 28–33, 40; on author's family, 28–30, 31–2, 36–7, 38, 39–40, 43nn2–3; on author's pregnancy/denial of access to abortion, 28, 30, 32–3, 37–8, 43n4; on author's probation experiences, 33, 40; on author's university education/teaching methods, 41–2; on Child and Youth Services Remand Centre, 30–3, 38–40; on court-appointed

psychiatrists, 32, 33, 38, 40; on institutional networks of power, 35–7; on institutional violence, 37–40; on legacy/effects of institutional violence, 40–3; on total institutions, 33–5
Martin, Ruth Ellwood (ACCW doctor), 296; and participatory action research project on women's health, 300, 301, 313n4; and publication of prison/community narratives, 307, 308
McIsaac, Peter (Cape Breton police chief), 244, 246–8, 250; on "John Be Gone" list, as "deterrent for others," 247–8, 257; on Sydney business owners' complaints about sex work, 246–7
McKeough, T.J. (lawyer for several men arrested in Sydney sting operation), 243, 261n8; on DNA registry, 261n10; on "ridiculousness" of case, 259
media coverage: of conditions at HRC, 98, 100–1; of issues at SAWP farms, 159, 161, 166, 167, 168; of Sydney prostitution sting operation, 243, 244, 247, 248; of Windsor's unhoused population "crisis," 179, 185–7, 191–2
menstruation, methods of managing/suppressing, in I/DD people, 14, 20, 201, 203, 206–8; "Ashley Treatment," 218n1; forced sterilization, 42, 180, 203–4, 207–8; hysterectomy/surgical ablation, 207, 218n1; oral contraception, 207, 208. *See also* group homes, gendered disability violence in, *and entries following*; reproductive violence, against I/DD people; sterilization, forced, of I/DD people
Mental Health Acts, provincial, 120, 121, 122
Michener Centre (formerly Provincial Training School for Mental Defectives) (Red Deer, Alberta), 76, 204
Missing and Murdered Indigenous Women and Girls, National Inquiry into, 211
Mohawk Institute (Brantford, Ontario): founding/early history of, 94–5; government involvement at, 95, 98, 100, 101, 102, 104, 106–7; off-property work programs run by, 99, 105; poor hygiene/sanitary conditions at, 100–2; preventable deaths at, 103–4, 106–7; unqualified teachers at, 97; women's group's tour of, 97–8, 100, 101–2; Woodland Cultural Centre established on site of, 92, 93. *See also entry below*
Mohawk Institute, institutional violence against othered bodies at, as compared to Huronia Regional Centre, 17–18, 92–108; as capitalizing on forced labour, 98–9; and devaluation/degradation in death, 105–7; and forced conformity through education, 96–8; and institutional goals/funding/management, 94–6; and malnutrition, 102; and neglect/negligence, 100–2, 103–4; and poor quality

of education/educational facilities, 97–8; and presence of unmarked graves, 92, 107; and sexual abuse, 104–5; and social hierarchies of abuse, 103–4
Montaigne, Michel de, 82
Muir, Leilani, and court case of, 203–4, 217
Muñoz, Rogelio Santos, 159
mutual aid, among shelter residents, 287

naloxone kits: as unavailable, 277; Windsor Police Service's delayed use of, 189–90
National Inquiry into Missing and Murdered Indigenous Women and Girls, 211
New Brunswick, Good Shepherd laundries/reformatories in. *See* Bowman, Chaparral
New England Company (NEC), 94–5
New Zealand, Good Shepherd laundries/reformatories in, 47. *See also* Reid, Kate
Nova Scotia v. CKZ, 210

Oliver, Mary, 315n18
Ontario departments/ministries: Children, Community and Social Services, 203; Health, 95, 105; Provincial Secretary, 95; Public Works, 95
Ontario Disability Support Program (ODSP), 146
Ontario Human Rights Code, 150
Ontario Human Rights Commission, 150
Ontario Human Rights Tribunal, 150
Ontario Ombudsman, 125, 203
Operation Northern Spotlight, 254
Orillia Asylum, 93, 94; as teaching hospital, 97. *See also* Huronia Regional Centre (HRC), *and entries following*
"other(s)": institutional violence against, as permissible, 105; marginalized people as, 269; neighbourhood resistance to care/integration of, 182, 184; Said's concept of, 257; sex workers' clients as, 247–8, 257. *See also* Huronia Regional Centre (HRC), *and entries following*; Mohawk Institute, *and entry following*
Our Lady of Charity of the Good Shepherd of Angers. *See* Good Shepherd, Sisters of, *and entries following*; Magdalene laundries

Pacey, Katrina, 246, 261n9
parenting supports, barriers to, forOur Lady of Charity of the Good I/DD people, 14, 20, 201, 203, 209–10; and control/scrutiny of mothers, 209–10; andOur Lady of Charity of the Good *Re: Eve* case, 203–4, 207, 208; and removal of children, 209, 210. *See also* group homes, gendered disability violence in, *and entries following*; reproductive violence, against I/DD people
Pelletier, Mary Euphrasia (founder of Sisters of the Good Shepherd), 47, 63n2
People First of Canada, 152, 207
Plett, Donald Neil, 246, 261n9
Potter, Beryl, 151

pregnancies: complications of, for Black women, 217; of HRC and Mohawk Institute residents, 104–5; of I/DD girls and women, 104–5, 208, 209; and institutional denial of access to abortion, 28, 30, 32–3, 37–8, 43n4
prison and police abolitionist movement, 15–16; in context of anti-slavery movement, 15; and gendered disability violence, 217; and I/DD people, 115, 116–17, 129; as "project of building," 129; and shelters for unhoused, 270, 287, 288
prisons: group homes as, 216; as "heterotopias of deviation," 53, 64n10; I/DD people as overrepresented in, 125; SAWP farms as, 166–7; separation of mothers from children in, 212; sex workers in, 239, 241, 258; shelters as, 282–3, 285; solitary confinement in, 127; and Stanford Prison Experiment, 283. *See also* Alouette Correction Centre for Women (ACCW), *and entry following*; Malacrida, Claudia, autoethnographic account of adolescent trauma and survival by; total institutions
prostitution. *See entry below*; sex workers, institutional violence against, *and entries following*
Protection of Communities and Exploited Persons Act (PCEPA): as based on Swedish legislation, 255, 257–8; and criminalization of both clients and sex workers, 239–40, 241; and history of Canadian/US sex work legislation, 241–3; and listing/shaming of men caught in sting operation, 240, 246–9; parliamentary committee's report on, 259–60; and portrayal of sex workers as victims of exploitation, 239–40, 244, 246, 250–3, 260n1; and post-PCEPA experiences of sex workers, 243, 246, 249, 254; support for, 246, 248, 256
Provincial Assessment Centre (BC dual diagnostic services facility), 120
Provincial Training School for Mental Defectives (later Michener Centre) (Red Deer, Alberta), 76, 204
psychiatric institutions, I/DD people in, 122–3; challenges of discharge/community placement for, 120, 122; use of chemical restraints on, 122
"psy sector"/psy disciplines (system of professionals growing alongside total institutions), 36; discourse/power of, 191–2; interventions by, 179, 180, 182, 185, 190, 191–2

R. v. DAI, 206
R. v. Minassian, 121
R. v. Slatter, 206
RADAR (Montreal initiative against human trafficking/sexual exploitation), 252
Rawls, John, 139–40, 154
Re: Eve (court case on application for forced sterilization), 203–4, 207, 208, 217
Recounting Huronia Archive, 93

Regional Psychiatric Centre (RPC; Saskatoon), 125–6
Reid, Kate (former Good Shepherd inmate): on loss of ability to maintain eye contact, 55, 62; on nuns' surveillance, 56
Releasing Hope (ACCW women's book), 313, 314n7, 314n14; as containing women's community narratives, 305; Korchinski's contributions to, 293–4, 305–6, 308–9, 314n12; Leggo's poetry in, 302, 306, 307–8, 312, 314n12
reproductive violence, against I/DD people, 14, 201, 203–11; barriers to parenting supports, 14, 20, 201, 203, 209–10; barriers to socialization/forming relationships, 201, 203, 208–9; castration, 207–8; forced sterilization, 42, 180, 203–4, 207–8, 210, 217; lack of sexual health information/education, 208, 209; menstrual management/suppression, 14, 20, 201, 203, 206–8; UN on, 205, 208, 210. *See also* menstruation, methods of managing/suppressing, in I/DD people; sterilization, forced, of I/DD people
residential schools, 3, 34–5, 141, 145, 271; and institutionalization/assimilation of Indigenous children, 92–3, 96–7; student-to-student abuse/ peer punishment at, 103–4; unmarked graves at, 92, 107. *See also* Mohawk Institute, *and entry following*
retirement homes, I/DD people in, 123–4
Romero, Bonifacio Eugenio, 159
Romero, Rachael (former Good Shepherd inmate), 54
Royal Commission into Violence, Abuse, Neglect and Exploitation of People with Disability (Australia), 211

safe/supervised injection sites, 190, 277
Said, Edward, 257
Scott, Cindy (HRC survivor), 86, 88n5; forced enema administered to, 73, 78–9; on playroom, 84; psycho-emotional impact on, 74
Seasonal Agricultural Worker Program (SAWP) (Ontario), 19, 159–72; and affective economy, 160, 164–5, 172; and global capital-labour relations, 159–60; as managed by private company, 162, 171; obstacles to immigration opportunities under, 162–3, 171–2; and temporary foreign worker program, 161–2, 164. *See also entries below*
Seasonal Agricultural Worker Program (SAWP) farmsteads: care and loathing at, 160, 162, 164–5, 166, 170–1; closed contracts at, 163–4; exploitation of racialized migrants at, 159–60, 162, 164–5, 168, 171, 172; indentured work/unfree labour at, 159–60, 161, 163–4, 165, 168–71; master-slave relationships at, 164, 170–1; media coverage of issues at, 159,

161, 166, 167, 168; as small-scale versions of total institutions, 161–5; spread of COVID-19 at, 159, 161, 165, 166–7, 169–70; workers' descriptions of, as "prisons," 166–7
Seasonal Agricultural Worker Program (SAWP) farmsteads, examples of institutional violence on, 160–1, 165–8; constant risk of illness or injury, 168, 169; COVID-19/quarantine abuses, 159, 167, 169–70; dirty/overcrowded/unhygienic housing, 159, 161, 165, 166, 167–8; employers' grocery shopping abuses, 167, 168–9; financial abuse/wage theft, 168–9, 170; lack of healthcare access/employment protections, 163, 169; lack of privacy, 165, 167; long working hours, 159, 161, 168; restrictions on workers' movements/time off, 164, 166; threats of job loss/deportation, 166, 168, 169–70, 171; worker dependency on/"debt" to employers, 160, 162–3, 165, 166, 168
seclusion/solitary confinement, 4, 144, 180, 211; of entire institutional population, 39; of Good Shepherd inmates, 57; of I/DD people, 117, 121, 125, 127
Services and Supports to Promote the Social Inclusion of Persons with Developmental Disabilities Act (Ontario), 206, 212
Seth, Patricia (HRC survivor), 149
Sex Purchasers Act (Sweden), 249, 255, 257–8
sexual abuse, familial, 49, 78, 300; as recounted by Malacrida, 28–30, 40
sexual violence, against HRC residents, 69, 72–3, 77–9; in playroom, 85; and pregnancies of young women, 104–5. *See also entry below*
sexual violence, against I/DD women in group homes, 20, 201, 204–5, 217; as enabled by lack of sexual health information/education, 208, 209; legal redress for, 212–13; as under-reported/under-prosecuted, 205–6, 209, 212–13
sex workers, institutional violence against, 20, 238–62; as affecting almost all aspects of their lives, 238–9, 242–3; and Canada's prostitution "protection" law, 239–40, 241; in context of Canadian/US prostitution laws, 241–3; and Indigenous women, 249–50, 252–3, 255; by law enforcement, 238, 239, 242, 249, 252, 254–5; and movement to decriminalize sex work, 259; and public listing/shaming of clients, 240, 246–9, 256–7; as sites-specific, 20, 239; source material on, as used ethically in study of, 243–6; and surveillance by community members, 20, 239, 251–2. *See also entries below*; "John Be Gone," *and entry following*; *Protection of Communities and Exploited Persons Act* (PCEPA)
sex workers, portrayal of, as victims of exploitation: and

concept of grievable lives, 249–50; and concerns over human trafficking, 239, 250, 251–2, 254, 261n5; in federal legislation, 239–40, 244, 246, 250–3; as marginalization/silencing strategy, 255; as not preventing police raids/interventions, 239, 252, 254–5; as preventing them from working, 246, 253, 258; and surveillance by "caring" community members, 20, 239, 251–2

sex workers' clients, public listing of, 240, 246–9; and concept of list as instrument of discipline/delimitation, 238, 252, 259; and concept of "shameable lives," 250–1; as "deterrent for others," 247–8, 257; as leading to concealment of subsequent activity, 257–8; and listing in DNA registry, 247, 257, 261n10; and post-arrest experiences of listed men, 245, 247–9; shame/criminality brought on by, 250–1, 256–8

sex work legislation: as driving activity to other locations, 257–8; in Sweden/other countries, 249, 255, 257–8; in US, 242, 258. See also *Protection of Communities and Exploited Persons Act* (PCEPA)

sheltered workshops for I/DD people (Ontario), 18–19, 137–56; and background/history of sheltered workshops, 137–8; and capitalist state control/loathing of I/DD people, 139–43, 149; compared to rehabilitation programs in total institutions, 143–5; in context of citizenship, 139–41, 144, 147–9, 150–1, 153–4, 155; in deinstitutionalization era, 137, 138, 142, 144–9, 154; and disability activism, 150–3; and dispersal of disability institutionalization into community, 146–8; as justified by goal of vocational training/"rehabilitation," 146, 148–9; as operating outside employment standards regulation, 146; planned closures of, 150, 156n5; as quarantined environment, 147, 148; "simulated" work done at, 146, 148, 151–2. *See also entry below*; work, for I/DD people

sheltered workshops for I/DD people (Ontario), forms of institutional violence in, 145–53; controlled/regulated environment, 147; exemption from social benefits, 146; payment of sub-minimum wages, 146, 148, 150; poor transition to labour market/independence, 146; repetitive nature of workplace tasks, 147; segregation from community/labour market, 147–8

shelters and homelessness services, I/DD people in, 124; calls to police about, 127

Shelter Video Project Collective on Colonial/Capitalist Violence (Toronto): *We Want You To Listen*, 20, 268–90; on institutional violence, 271–3; on need for decision-makers to live the

shelter experience, 287–9; on political economy of shelters, 285–7; and reasons for people's living in shelters, 273; on shelter as final/permanent destination, 282; on shelter as prison, 282–3, 285; on shelter conditions, 274–8; on shelter culture, 273–4; on shelter discipline/ carceral continuum, 278–85; and society's denigration/ discrediting of marginalized people, 269–70; and staff power/ abuse of power, 275–6, 278, 279–81
Shingwauk School (Sault Ste Marie, Ontario), 102
Shunn, Richard, 79–80
Slark, Marie (HRC survivor), 85, 149
slavery, 15; of institutional labour, 53, 159–60, 164, 170–1
Smith, Dorothy E., 261n10
Smith, Effie ("accident" victim at Mohawk Institute), 104–5
socialization/forming of relationships, barriers to, for I/DD people, 201, 203, 208–9. *See also* group homes, gendered disability violence in, *and entries following*; reproductive violence, against I/DD people
solitary confinement. *See* seclusion/ solitary confinement
Spears, Britney, 218
Spivakovsky, Claire, Linda Steele, and Penelope Weller, eds., *The Legacies of Institutionalisation: Disability, Law and Policy in the "Deinstitutionalised" Community*, 11
Stanford Prison Experiment, 283
Stella, l'amie de Maimie (Montreal sex workers' organization), 252
sterilization, forced, of I/DD people, 42, 203–4, 207–8; feminism and, 217; landmark court cases involving, 203–4, 207, 208; as racist/colonialist strategy, 180, 204, 217; UN on, 208, 210. *See also entry below*; group homes, gendered disability violence in, *and entries following*; reproductive violence, against I/DD people
sterilization, forced, of sex workers, 238
stigma: of former prison inmates, 294; of Good Shepherd inmates/ survivors, 48, 54–7, 61–2; of men on list of sex workers' clients, 243, 256–8; of sex workers, 249–50; of teenage pregnancy, 38; of unhoused people, 272, 273, 288
Stone, Deborah A., 142, 152
Stop Enabling Sex Traffickers Act and Allow States and Victims to Fight Online Sex Trafficking Act (SESTA-FOSTA; US legislation), 242; crackdown on websites by, as endangering sex workers, 242, 258
Sullivan, Maureen (former Good Shepherd inmate), 55; on loss of identity/self, 56; on prohibitions on contact/ conversation, 59
Switter (Australian sex workers' social media platform), 258
SWOP behind Bars (Australian sex workers' advocacy group), 258

symbolic violence. *See* Bourdieu, Pierre, on symbolic/soft or "gentle" violence

Tanudjaja v. Canada, 214
Taylor, Sunny, 137, 153, 155
temporary foreign worker program (TFWP), 161–2, 164
Tole, Brenda (first ACCW warden), 295–7, 300, 308, 310; employees hired by, 295–6; inmate advisory committee created by, 299
total institutional model, 4–5, 7–9; affect in, 13; care in, 5; as dispersed into community through deinstitutionalization, 9, 115, 138, 146–7, 164, 180, 202; Foucault on, 35–6; Goffman on, 7–9, 33, 161, 164; roots of violence in, 5, 17–18; "psy sector" and, 36; and white supremacism/settler colonialism, 15–16. *See also entries below*
total institutions: group homes as, 20, 202; SAWP farms as, 161–5; sheltered workshops as, 137, 138, 142, 144–9, 154; as spaces of imprisonment, 156n4; variables of violence at, 126–7. *See also* prisons
total institutions, as studied by Goffman, 7–9; definition of, 7; four features of, 7; identity breakdown/rebuilding in, 8–9, 33; Malacrida on, 9, 33–5, 41, 42; "spoiled identities" in, 16; staff-inmate split in, 8; and trans-institutionalization, 9; unfree labour in, 161, 164
transinstitutional era, 9; carceral archipelago/matrix of, 9, 15; loathing in, 5, 13–14, 18–19
Truth and Reconciliation Commission (TRC), 211

"unhoused" (term), 269, 290n1
United Nations Convention on the Rights of People with Disabilities (UNCRPD): and definition of institution, 117; and gendered disability discrimination, 205; and incarceration of I/DD people, 125; "Right to Work" program of, 152
United States: forced sterilization of I/DD people in, 203–4, 207, 217; institutionalized I/DD labour in, 144–5; sex workers'/clients' ability to travel to, 261n8; sex work legislation in, 242, 258; slavery/racialized labour in, 15, 164
Unlocking the Gates (ACCW peer mentorship program), 301, 314n7; and mentors' meeting with released residents at prison gates, 302–4; as non-profit society, 302–3, 304

Victim Quick Response Program (VQRP+; Ontario), 213
Victims of Crime Assistance Program (Alberta), 213
Virginia State Colony for Epileptics and Feebleminded, 204

Werbin, Kenneth: on list as capture/punishment mechanism, 238, 243, 252

Wesley, Sandra, 252
West Coast LEAF Mothering Project, 211
Williston, Brian, 253, 254, 255
Williston, Walter, 101, 145
Windsor, Ontario, unhoused population of, 19, 179–92; and city's economic recovery/business improvement efforts, 179, 183, 186, 187, 188; as concentrated in downtown core, 183; in context of "urban crisis" discourse, 179–82; in context of violence in community care, 183–5; in context of white settler colonialism, 180–2; criminalization of, 188–9; and dehumanization/devaluation of street people, 181; and dispersal of disability institutionalization into community, 180; as filmed by onlookers, 186–7; and lack of harm reduction services, 189–90, 191; media coverage of, as contributing to sense of "urban crisis," 179, 185–7, 191–2; and neighbourhood resistance to community care, 182, 184; policing/security measures against, as institutional interventions in public space, 187–91; and public preference for closed/in-patient treatment facilities, 190–1; social service agencies for, as blamed for "urban crisis," 187
Windsor-Essex County Health Unit, 189, 190
Windsor Police Service, 188–9, 189–90
Wolfensberger, Wolf, 145
Women in2 Healing (ACCW support group), 301, 314nn7–8
Woodland Cultural Centre (Brantford, Ontario): as site of former Mohawk Institute, 92, 93
work, for I/DD people: and capitalist state control/loathing, 139–43, 149; in context of citizenship, 139–41, 144, 147–9, 150–1, 153–4, 155; in deinstitutionalization era, 137, 138, 142, 144–9, 154; and disability activism, 150–3; and "Employment First" policy, 152; and exploitation of unpaid labour, 144–5; and value of life without work, 137, 155. *See also* sheltered workshops for I/DD people, *and entry following*
Worth, Patrick, 115